Imagining Childhood, Improving Children

From as early as the 1920s, state policy towards children in south India was framed through the lens of a universal ideal of modern childhood. This reflected the participation of policymakers and civil society activists in global discourses of child saving and the new opportunities of governance under the constitutional reforms of 1919. Children became viewed as both objects to be saved and investments as future citizens. The book considers how adults used this concept of universal childhood to conceptualise themselves as both modern and avuncular, gaining authority through an appropriation of familial terms as well as the claim to modern, scientific expertise. Through a detailed study of education, health and juvenile justice, the book reveals that the implementation of policy was still informed by other markers of difference, and contrasts adult intentions with the autobiographical memories of school, family and peer relationships.

Catriona Ellis is a teaching associate at the Centre for the Social History of Health and Healthcare, University of Strathclyde. She graduated from the University of Edinburgh in 2017 and has published widely in the history of education and history of childhood in India.

Imagining Childhood, Improving Children

The Emergence of an 'Avuncular' State in Late Colonial South India

Catriona Ellis

CAMBRIDGE
UNIVERSITY PRESS

University Printing House, Cambridge CB2 8BS, United Kingdom

One Liberty Plaza, 20th Floor, New York, NY 10006, USA

477 Williamstown Road, Port Melbourne, vic 3207, Australia

314 to 321, 3rd Floor, Plot No.3, Splendor Forum, Jasola District Centre, New Delhi 110025, India

103 Penang Road, #05–06/07, Visioncrest Commercial, Singapore 238467

Cambridge University Press is part of the University of Cambridge.

It furthers the University's mission by disseminating knowledge in the pursuit of education, learning and research at the highest international levels of excellence.

www.cambridge.org
Information on this title: www.cambridge.org/9781009215206

© Catriona Ellis 2023

This publication is in copyright. Subject to statutory exception and to the provisions of relevant collective licensing agreements, no reproduction of any part may take place without the written permission of Cambridge University Press.

First published 2023

Printed in India by Avantika Printers Pvt. Ltd.

A catalogue record for this publication is available from the British Library

ISBN 978-1-009-21520-6 Hardback

Cambridge University Press has no responsibility for the persistence or accuracy of URLs for external or third-party internet websites referred to in this publication, and does not guarantee that any content on such websites is, or will remain, accurate or appropriate.

For Tim

Contents

Acknowledgements	ix
List of Abbreviations	xiii
Introduction	1
1. The Child at School: Compulsory Education in the Madras Presidency	24
2. Educating the Child: The Introduction of Compulsory Education in Madras City	47
3. Imagining the Child as Learner: Progressive Pedagogy in the Madras Presidency	72
4. Producing the Healthy Schoolchild	98
5. Saving the Child: The Madras Children Act, 1920, and the Beginnings of a Juvenile Justice System	125
6. Protecting the Poor Child: The Practical Expansion of Juvenile Justice	153
7. Defining Childhood: Sexual Parameters of Childhood	180
8. Remembering Childhoods: Childhood Memories in Autobiographies	205
Conclusion: Children, Childhood and the Growth of the Avuncular State in South India	230
Notes	243
Bibliography	310
Index	338

Acknowledgements

In my experience, the much-quoted proverb 'it takes a village to raise a child' applies as much to the writing of a book as it does to the parallel journey of my family. The intellectual and personal debts built up over this period have been extensive and changing.

    This book has benefited from the wise inputs and challenging questions formulated in two institutions. In their very different ways, my PhD supervisors Dr Crispin Bates and Dr Louise Jackson at the University of Edinburgh have provided invaluable intellectual contributions and practical advice. The various and changing personnel of the Asia, Africa—now Global and Transnational—group at Edinburgh University provided a supportive and intellectually engaging environment in which to pursue research. Particularly appreciated have been the conversations with Dr Christopher Harding, Dr Caroline Lewis, Dr Ashok Malhorta, Dr Gajendra Singh and Dr Talat Ahmed. More recently my colleagues at the Centre for the Social History of Health and Healthcare, University of Strathclyde, have provided a new and stimulating environment in which to research and teach. My thanks to Dr Jim Mills, Dr Patricia Barton and Dr Emma Newlands. The students in both institutions have been a constant source of inspiration and are too many to name, but they have all been a valuable part of this journey. In recent years, the conversations and insights of the (South Asian) Critical Childhood and Youth Studies Collective and the interactions with Dr Parimala Rao and the History of Education Research

Interest Group of the Comparative Education Society of India have been particularly generative.

The staff at the British Library and the National Library of Scotland have been unfailingly helpful and tolerant both of my continual requests for material and of my irregular working patterns. The staff and fellow postgraduates in the Tamil Nadu State Archives and Library, Chennai, provided rich material, helpful local knowledge and inspiring company. The administrative staff at the Archives Department of the Chennai Corporation are deserving of special mention for accommodating me in their working space, promptly actioning all my requests and allowing unrivalled access to the collections. The managers of the Children's Garden School, Chennai, provided access to their archives and a tour of the school, and were exceptionally helpful. I am grateful to the staff at Madras Institute of Development Studies, Chennai, for their help in facilitating my research visa.

A previous version of Chapter 3 appeared in *Writing Postcolonial Histories of Intercultural Education* (2011), and my thanks go to Dr Heike Niedrig and Dr Christian Ydesen for their editorial input at that early stage. An overview of Chapter 8 was published in *Social History* (2019), and a section of Chapter 4 was part of a chapter for a special issue on the politics of diet published in *South Asia: Journal of South Asian Studies* (2021). My thanks to the editors of both journals, in particular Dr Harald Fischer-Tiné, Dr Ashok Malhotra and Dr Julia Hauser, and the anonymous reviewers for their feedback.

Sohini Ghosh, Priya Das and the publishers at Cambridge University Press have been very helpful throughout, and I am deeply indebted to the anonymous reviewers for their insightful comments and helpful suggestions.

But the journey is personal too. There are too many individuals to name, but I am especially thankful to Dr Francesca Young Kaufman, Dr Hia Sen, Joanna Manners, Dawn Cuckney, Verity Scougal and the Bathgate and Friend families for their encouragement and wisdom over the course of many conversations. The support and encouragement of my Ferniehill church family has been a great blessing. Many members of the Brown family have provided invaluable practical support, and the continuing care of both the Brown and Ellis/Brien families is much appreciated. As a Christian I have experienced what it is to be loved and to love, and that has been the greatest gift of all.

Ingrid, Arwyn and Imogen have grown alongside this book, have been integral to it and have tolerated with amazing good humour the impact my unstructured working patterns and many ideas have had on family life. I am so grateful for my little women, so impressed with how they have coped with these years of pandemic and disappointment, so humbled by the wonderful, gracious, funny, loving people they have become. You three, together and individually, have taught me more than you will ever know. This book is for Tim, for a hundred thousand reasons and with my heartfelt thanks.

Abbreviations

CMRA	Child Marriage Restraint Act, 1929
CPM	chief presidency magistrate
DEC	District Educational Council
DPAS	Discharged Prisoners Aid Society
DPH	director of public health
DPI	director of public instruction
EEF	Elementary Education Fund
ICS	Indian Civil Service
IJC	Indian Jails Committee
IPC	Indian Penal Code
MCA	Madras Children Act, 1920
MCAS	Madras Children's Aid Society
MLC	Madras Legislative Council
MSPC	Madras Society for the Protection of Children
WIA	Women's Indian Association

Introduction

Geneva Declaration of the Rights of the Child, 1924[1]
According to the present Declaration of the Rights of the Child, commonly known as 'Declaration of Geneva', men and women of all nations, recognising that mankind owes to the Child the best that it has to give, declare and accept it as their duty that, beyond and above all considerations of race, nationality or creed:

1. the child must be given the means requisite for its normal development, both materially and spiritually;
2. the child that is hungry must be fed; the child that is sick must be nursed; the child that is backward must be helped; the delinquent child must be reclaimed; and the orphan and the waif must be sheltered and succoured;
3. the child must be the first to receive relief in times of distress;
4. the child must be put in a position to earn a livelihood, and must be protected against every form of exploitation;
5. the child must be brought up in the consciousness that its talents must be devoted to the service of fellow men.

The Geneva Declaration of 1924 was the first coherent definition of modern childhood, its rights and privileges, to be widely accepted among the international community. The declaration was based on the supposedly self-evident assumption that childhood was a natural stage of life, that all children were equal, that all followed a similar development pattern and that all were deserving of the same protections and assistance. Together they positioned the modern child as vulnerable, sexually innocent, playful, in Zelizer's well-used phrase 'economically worthless though emotionally priceless' and with a right to the resources of the state and even the international community.[2] This book considers the conceptual and practical implications of these ideas in the south Indian context by assessing how they came to be widely accepted as universal in state policy and among the professional and humanitarian elites.

The central contention of this book is that this construction of universal modern childhood became normative in state discourse and policy in south India during the 1920s and 1930s. Age was established as both a category of governance and a new form of collective identity in legislation and policies enacted as a result of the devolution of limited powers to politically moderate Indians under the constitutional changes of 1919. The moment that established a framework for understandings of childhood in India that would remain dominant throughout the twentieth century was therefore not the result of colonial rule or of new ideas emerging within the nationalist movement or its local manifestations or even the new constitution in 1950, as is usually assumed. Rather, the actions taken by a group of generally wealthy, well-educated, politically moderate Indians, operating within government not only as politicians and officials but also as scientific experts and within civil society organisations, to intervene in the lives of children fundamentally changed the interaction between the state and children, both in conceptual terms and in practice. This established a pattern of relationships between the state, the family and the child in which children were regulated and institutionalised into new forms of behaviour and were ascribed new forms of worth. Indeed, many of the unresolved tensions that emerged in the 1920s and 1930s between childhood as a modern universal category, the authority of Indian adults to implement child development policies specific to the Indian context and the child's experience grounded in time, space and community continue to characterise the discussions around children in India today.

Taking a detailed case study of the Madras Presidency, and looking at government and civil society interventions in health, education, sexual maturity and juvenile justice, this book sheds new light on the construction and political uses of childhood as a conceptual category, including the tensions between the child framed as an individual rights-bearer, the child as vulnerable and in need of protection and the child as a future citizen of an independent nation. In particular, the book traces the ways in which south Indian policymakers, experts, civil society activists and children themselves sought to reconcile the intellectual and practical contradictions inherent in their attempts to adhere to a universal ideal of childhood as set out in the Geneva Declaration while also claiming the cultural specificity of the Indian child. Yet, contrary to the perception in the existing literature, this was not an area of intense political dispute, but these conversations developed within the broadly consensual realm of the social. The new recognition that child welfare was the state's responsibility, the expansion of new forms of governmentality and the formation of new political subjectivities were supported across the political spectrum at different levels of government, even as the details were at times contested.

The new claim to act on behalf of children was crucial to the self-positioning of this newly influential elite, given increased responsibility through the constitutional changes. This book agrees that these individuals legitimated their intervention in terms of their modern expertise but argues that equally important was their claim to authority as avuncular, as if part of wider kinship and relational structures. As 'uncles' and 'aunts', they claimed a semi-familial legitimacy and a responsibility towards all children that was framed as more culturally sanctioned than that of the colonial state. Examining the interactions between adults in authority—parents, teachers, politicians or philanthropists—the book explores the extent to which the avowedly universal category of childhood was subsumed beneath other identities based on race, class, caste and gender, both in children's experience and in the ways in which policy was implemented to foreground the tensions within all these categories. This introduction explores the historiographical background to some of these ideas in more depth; for those unfamiliar with the south Indian context there is a detailed overview at the end of this introduction.

Modern Childhood as a Universal Category

This book considers how and why a particular construct of modern childhood came to be accepted as universal in South Asia even though it marginalises the representations and experiences of vast numbers of children on the subcontinent.[3] The 1989 United Nations Convention on the Rights of the Child expanded and built on the Geneva Declaration to provide the most commonly accepted global definition of modern childhood. It defines the universal needs and rights of children, and provides the conceptual and legal basis for state, provincial government and civil society intervention in contemporary children's lives across the world, an assumed standard for what constitutes 'the best interests of the child' (Article 3). The Convention promotes a hegemonic discourse about modern childhood whose continuing conceptual and practical power comes from its claim to be both 'universal' and 'truth', even though it is widely recognised that this perception of childhood emerged from the particular historical development of European modernity.[4] India is a signatory to the United Nations Convention on the Rights of the Child (UNCRC) and the normative power–knowledge constructions about modern childhood encapsulated in this convention continue to dominate popular consciousness, state policy and humanitarian representations of India and continue to inform the aspirations underpinning developmental interventions for children.[5]

Yet, in reality, the inability of many children within the subcontinent to reach this normative modern ideal of what a child should be and do means that South Asian childhoods remain characterised in terms of victimhood, lack and otherness.[6] Recent films such as *Slumdog Millionaire* (2008), *I Am Kalam* (2011) and *Lion* (2016) tell the stories of individual Indian children—Saroo Brierley, Jamal Malik or Chhotu—who have overcome poverty and adversity to forge new lives for themselves.[7] These popular contemporary representations continue to inform the predominant global image of the Indian child as characterised by material need; as an object to be pitied; as cute and lovable; as failed by family and as unable to attain the modern ideal of a rights-centred childhood encapsulated in the UNCRC. This book shows that the contradictions between the adherence to a universal ideal of modern childhood as a signifier of the modernity of the state or at least state actors; the reluctance to articulate alternative visions of modern Indian childhood through fear of appearing backward; and the failure to grasp the limitations of that ideal when faced with everyday social realities so that all children are implicitly imagined in policy as male, high caste and Hindu can be traced to the political and social context of the interwar years. The continued unwillingness of policymakers, experts and civil society activists to engage meaningfully with the tensions inherent in the idea of the global child suggests that this construction was more important as a political strategy to establish their own position as universal citizens and to reinforce their new authority as state actors than as a means to improve the lives of the poor, low caste or marginalised children they claimed to protect.

Even within this broad global framework of shared assumptions, the idea of what constituted modern childhood was neither coherent nor self-evident, particularly when these vague principles were applied in state action. That the boundaries and definitions of childhood remained contested reveals a wider conceptual problem, although rarely articulated in the 1920s and 1930s, that the concept of childhood is not a self-evident category, it is socially constructed and therefore varies across time and space, even though one particular construction in the UNCRC remains hegemonic.[8] Historians and social scientists have long acknowledged the existence of 'multiple childhoods' constructed by and for children.[9] It is now widely accepted that the ways in which childhood is imagined are culturally, geographically and historically determined, reflecting societal boundaries, representations and typical forms of conduct in areas as diverse as politics, labour, consumption, education, sexual consent, affective behaviour and criminal responsibility. In the last twenty years, historians, social scientists and practitioners in South Asia have interrogated hierarchies of caste, class, region and gender as well as normative concepts such as childcare, child labour and education, situated in particular times and spaces, to demonstrate a wide variety of changing and often coexisting childhood forms and understandings.[10] The emphasis on multiple childhoods has helped to decentre the idea of a universal modern childhood, which Indian children fail to obtain, even as this idea remains a politically important category in humanitarian and international discourse. This research has also revealed the problems inherent with the notion of a culturally specific Indian or South Asian childhood that, for example in the work of Sudhir Kakir, has often regarded male Brahminical assumptions about childhood as normative.[11] Moreover, the failure to historicise South Asian childhoods, to see multiple childhoods changing over time, as well as space, has often essentialised cultural difference as unchanging, in unthinkingly orientalist ways.[12] In viewing both historical and contemporary childhoods, it is important therefore to hold in balance both the significant differences in identity, hierarchy, opportunity, conceptual framing and experience of children in south India, juxtaposed with a recognition of the 'subaltern status of *all* children' as the object of the state's disciplinary power—in the clinic, the school, the playground, the reformatory—and as subordinated to differing forms of adult power and subject to changing adult discourses.[13] While this research does not attempt to interrogate the multitude of ways in which childhood was constructed in South Asia during the 1920s and 1930s, the wide range of assumptions about children, childhood and the role of the state that participants brought to the negotiations were evident in the constant petty conflict when policy was developed and implemented.

Research on South Asian childhoods has generally focused on the politically contested arenas of education and sexual consent or on the childhoods of the marginalised, characterised by Hia Sen as 'fundable childhoods', the objects of humanitarian and governmental discourse.[14] This has both reinforced the perception of lack and Otherness, obfuscating the lives of the majority, and has meant that research fields tend to be siloed, rarely speaking to each other within the broader framing of childhood. The fracturing of the field has been a particular problem for historical understandings of childhood, creating obvious blind spots through the claim to exceptionalism and the discovery of a 'moment' when modern childhood was accepted as relevant. Ishita Pande's work on the Child Marriage Restraint Act, 1929, is the most obvious example, but this claim to the discovery or introduction of modern childhood is also found in texts on the history of education.[15] This book takes a very different approach by integrating these different strands into the same conceptual framing of childhood within the 1920s and 1930s, highlighting the ways in which discussions in a number of diverse policy areas, often influenced by the same small network of interconnected individuals, informed and reinforced each other. By looking at educational policy (Chapters 1 and 2), pedagogical literature (Chapter 3), health (Chapter 4), juvenile justice (Chapters 5 and 6) and sexual consent (Chapter 7), this book will show the cross references within the geographical and cultural limitations of south India.

Analytical Approaches

These chapters are based on a wide variety of source material, primarily documents that are intrinsically linked to the institutional and cultural practices of late colonial rule, such as the Verbatim Proceedings of the Madras Legislative Council. These documents largely reflect the speech, anxieties and actions of the English-educated middle-class Tamil elite. These institutional records are set alongside the records of non-governmental expert organisations, such as professional journals like *Educational India* (Chapter 3), the reports and correspondence of civil society organisations, such as the Madras Children's Aid Society (Chapter 5), St Christopher's teacher training college (Chapter 3) and the submissions by individuals to the Joshi Committee (Chapter 7). Only the records of the Children's Garden School, maintained by the school itself and used for publicity purposes (see Chapter 3) were not found within the colonial archives.

It is particularly significant here to recognise that institutional and adult-authored sources can obscure children as distinct historical actors, making them merely the object of adult actions and childhood merely a discussion of the imposition of adult power.[16] This book frames children as subalterns, as subject to the changing decisions and actions of adults and as symbolically important, but *also* as themselves agents of change, contributing on a very small scale to significant historical and societal processes and relationships of power, such as constitutional change, imperial power, the transmission of knowledge and the reformulation of boundaries of gender, race, caste and class, attributing different meanings and bringing alternative and constantly changing world views.[17] Wagner and Roque, and their contributors, have convincingly shown that the colonial archives should be read as sites of interaction and encounter, where imprints have been left by other actions, world views and perspectives rather than merely in terms of colonial epistemic violence.[18] As with other subordinated groups, it is impossible, and perhaps even undesirable, to evidence their 'voice' or agency as individual, autonomous actors, and in these terms, their perspectives are 'unknowable'.[19] But, as Chakrabarty argues, 'the very act of listening', the attempt to trace imprints, is a political gesture of recognition that children were historical actors whose actions mattered and who were not merely objects of compassion.[20] Wherever possible, in Chapters 1–7, evidence is highlighted that indicates the reactions of adults to children's agentive actions, either as individuals or as a group, even if the children's voices themselves are absent. Teasing out the ways in which children performed and embodied roles prescribed for them by adults provides a means of considering history 'through children', even as this can overly emphasise children as individual, rational actors, and can underestimate the complicated nature of reaction to adult authority by prioritising actions and speech recorded in resistance rather than in support or accommodation, or can misread the variety of intersectional power relationships that make some children's voices more important or louder or some actions more visible than others.[21]

The final chapter (Chapter 8) takes a different approach and considers autobiographical memories of childhood, foregrounding the varied life experiences of individual children, allowing them to 'inhabit their own histories'.[22] It considers how discourses of childhood were constructed through the memories of adults, recognising that the ways in which autobiographical memories are organised, chosen and represented are often more reflective of the contemporary political and social concerns of the authors than of the experiences of childhood itself.[23] At the same time autobiographical memory provides fragmentary, though adult-mediated, evidence of toys and play, of school and learning, of how authority and emotion worked within the extended family, all firmly situated in the everyday. These contribute to an understanding of how childhood was experienced and imagined by children themselves, a balance to the earlier chapters when adult voices are so clearly dominant. In addition, the chapter considers the ways in which adults remembered identity and difference in childhood, recognising the intersectionality of children's experiences and their self and contextual positioning through a wide variety of changing power relations, reflecting biological growth, position in the family and changing social spaces, as well as gendered, racialised and communal differences.[24] That is not to underestimate or romanticise their actions or to undervalue the ways in which children themselves used power over their peers or subordinated adults but to recognise the ways in which children's agency was both constrained and enabled by political structures, cultural representations and economic trends, remembering that childhood is both a changing and a permanent structural form.

Tracing the Emergence of a Consensual Sphere

If a particular form of modern childhood continues to provide the conceptual framework impacting both intervention in children's lives and how childhood should be represented, then one aim of this book is to investigate how and when such a view of modern childhood came to be widely assumed as normative at the level of the state, the expert and civil society, despite widespread recognition of its limitations when policies were implemented. Olga Nieuwenhuys has traced this to the colonial encounter, in which a wider infantilisation of all Indians informed British paternalistic approaches to social policy.²⁵ The perception that childhood was just another area of political contention, in Satadru Sen's words a 'juvenile periphery', continues to characterise much of the historiography.²⁶ Children were viewed as both symbolic and material sites of conflict between competing groups of adults, both British and Indian. This was distinctly racialised, and while white children embodied anxieties about racial purity and innocence, Indian children were framed as the recipients of imperial benevolence, ultimately justifying the colonial project.²⁷ In Karen Vallgårda's paraphrase of Spivak, colonialism became a 'project of white adults saving brown children from brown adults'.²⁸ The institutionalisation of children and the production of new forms of childhoods therefore became a new site for the exercise of imperial power.

The dominance of British power was contested from the late nineteenth century when Indian experts, trained in Western ideas and methodologies, began to use their involvement in children's lives to demonstrate their own modernity and expertise, and thereby undermine the colonial rule.²⁹ These debates were not merely ideological contests for power and authority but worked out in practice in children's bodies in enclaves of modern disciplinary power such as the school or the reformatory.³⁰ Most historians of South Asia have read the social policy initiatives of the interwar years through the same lens of the political turmoil of imperial politics and the increasingly fractured nationalist politics, or the expansion of 'authoritarian' governmentality, encapsulated most dramatically in response to Katherine Mayo's polemic *Mother India* and the all-India Age of Consent debates of 1929.³¹ Often these debates have been framed in terms of the nature of authority and claims of competing patriarchies, frequently within the conceptual division between the private and the public sphere, even if this was more porous in practice.³² This seriously underestimates the impact of the new constitutional settlement on the formation of social policy and overplays the formation of policy at an all-India level.

The participation of Indians in government as a result of the 1919 reforms frayed even the imagined margins between these two bounded areas of private and public, home and world, colonial and Indian. Using the new, albeit very limited, powers under dyarchy, Indians self-consciously acted as the state. Very few of the policies directed at children were politically contentious. This book suggests that rather, by decentring political conflict, social policy was formed within a broadly consensual sphere, a set of mutual understandings that children had rights, particularly to protection, and that they were valuable assets for an emerging nation. The evidence here centres on the complexities of exchanges between the provincial government, the central government, municipal corporations and a variety of social actors, including urban professionals, political, religious and caste representatives, and civil society organisations, as well as parents, family members and, rarely, the children themselves. These individuals, the vast majority of whom were Indian, operated within broadly agreed boundaries of what constituted childhood and comprised legitimate state action. This reflects what historians of late nineteenth-century Europe have identified as 'the social', a new depoliticised arena of expert intervention. The social reflected the wider expansion of the welfare state, in which power functioned through discourse and networks within a shared consensus and set of frameworks and understandings outside the sphere of direct politics or ideological conflict.[33]

This book reveals a similar process that was happening within south India by the 1920s, though the parameters of what constituted the social were set by a wealthy, upper-caste elite. Rather than fault lines of competition, the interwar years were characterised by dialogue, negotiation and compromise across political parties and interest groups, which contributed to a consensus on the nature of modern childhood and informed the ways that legislation was formulated and implemented to protect, control and coexist with children. Chapters 5 and 6, for example, detail the relationship between the provincial government, the administrators of the Education and Home Departments, the judiciary, the police and experts and activists working within the Madras Children's Aid Society and Madras Society for the Protection of Children. While debates over the age of consent remained a noticeable exception at all-India and international levels, perhaps reflecting the continued political symbolism of control over female sexuality, the submissions to the Joshi Committee (Chapter 7) reveal a much more nuanced and complicated picture at the provincial level, demonstrating an underlying consensus on the nature of childhood, anxieties about adolescence and the role and duties of the state.

Even if we trace a modern universal childhood to an intellectual framework that emerged in the modern West, to see it merely as a further example of the continuing 'colonisation of the mind' or a slavish adherence of the political and social elites to Western modernity is to fail to understand the specific circumstances of the 1920s and 1930s.[34] Three intertwined themes were particularly important: the relationship between scientific authority and practices of governmentality, the global intellectual networks of the elite and the impact of constitutional change in 1919. Control over the child's mind and body through education, medicine and the criminal justice system established the authority of modern scientific methodologies and their practitioners, and facilitated the statistical surveillance of new populations as Indian elites established their own practices of governmentality. These approaches professed to be modern, based on reason and the apolitical application of universal principles established through scientific methodologies of observation, experimentation and quantification, often modified to integrate indigenous concepts and contexts.[35] This was seen in scientific approaches to normal child development and to play as a medium of education as the child learned to conquer his environment, in the writings of pedagogues in the journal *Educational India* (Chapter 3), or in the medical inspection of school children for 'defects' (Chapter 4). The collection of statistics on school attendance compiled in terms of communities (Chapter 1), the detailed regulation of the daily lives of children incarcerated in the certified schools (Chapter 5) and the application of biological science to definitions of puberty (Chapter 7) or paediatrics (Chapter 4) meant that science both shaped governance and informed the methodologies and regulatory practices through which governance was carried out.[36] The authoritative status of new disciplines such as nutrition, paediatrics, psychology and pedagogy boosted the prestige of the experts—almost exclusively Indian—who carried out the research, and of the politicians who claimed the educational training to understand it and believed in its transformative potential.[37] While specific expertise differed, the mutual respect grounded in a shared perception of modernity encouraged collaboration that could contest the scientific modernity of British rule on its own terms and could be used by the governing elite to distinguish themselves from the 'non-modernity' of the ordinary citizen. The workings of power in the modern Indian state were based on the methodologies of modern science.

This urban, highly educated elite gained authority not only from their intellectual heritage and modern education but from their interpersonal and professional links with a variety of global organisations. An important element of this was the development in the 1920s of a global humanitarian child-saving movement, which built on previous philanthropic efforts but was more explicitly global in scope. This can be traced in organisations such as Save the Children, set up in 1919 in response to the distress in post-war Europe, and the interest of the League of Nations in juvenile justice and anti-trafficking. This reflected the shift in international power from the colonial strongholds to the centres of international diplomacy such as New York and Geneva, as well as Washington.[38] Prior to 1914, there had been a number of philanthropic bodies, both Indian and colonial, interested in specific humanitarian relief such as famine relief, education, penal reform or women's rights.[39] However, it was in the 1920s that children became sentimentalised as a particular target of global humanitarian and feminist concern.[40] As noted earlier, the 1924 Geneva Declaration issued by the League of Nations listed the basic rights of the child and expanded the aspiration that 'mankind owes the child the best it has to give' into global discourse. This perhaps articulated an emerging normative assumption but certainly radically expanded its discursive power and established children as what Marshall calls 'an official object of international relations'.[41] Exploitative social practices, especially those which entailed moving across borders, such as *mui tsai* (an East Asian practice of selling girls as domestic labour) and the trafficking of women and children, became the object of international concern and subject of considerable debate.[42] The global focus on 'the best interests of the child' also gave moral authority to the elites wanting to intervene in the lives of poor children.[43]

The relationship between universalising constructions of modern childhood and the participation of Indian adults in these globally entangled projects can be evidenced in a wide variety of organisations. As well as participating in broad activist movements as diverse as international communist, missionary and anti-colonial networks, the Theosophical Society, the Boy Scouts and birth control leagues, elite Indians engaged with specialist networks of information exchange.[44] These included international pedagogical networks such as the New Education Fellowship (Chapter 3), a wide variety of international feminist campaigners interested in the age of marriage and reproductive health (Chapter 7) and campaigning bodies such as the League of Nations' Advisory Commission for the Protection and Welfare of Children and Young People (Chapter 5). These 'webs of empires' were also personal; individuals such as Dr R. Muthalakshmi Reddi, Mrs Hume Stanford and C. Swamikannu Paul travelled and corresponded with a wide variety of contacts across imperial and non-imperial spaces. Indian legislators, pedagogues and social reformers used their participation as equals and as experts in these global discourses as a political strategy to resist and counter the claims of backwardness made by the colonial state. The child as an object of reform thus became crucial to the positioning of an elite as self-avowedly modern and provided a conceptual space where the adult as a colonised subject could participate as a universal citizen. This was particularly the case for middle-class women, and participation in feminist and child-saving networks became an important aspect of respectable participation outside the home in a sphere that was not directly political and provided an opportunity to demonstrate their competence. It was this claim to modernity, this assertion of a universal childhood for all children, without recognising its gendered, classed, communal and cultural limitations, which helped to establish a particular understanding of childhood as normative in south Indian policymaking. A commitment to the idea of the global child as a political strategy as well as an ideological conviction meant that policymakers and civil society activists were unable or unwilling to grapple with the tensions inherent within this universalising idea when policies were implemented. The failure to confront the theoretical and practical limitations of the global child in the south Indian social context left uneasy assumptions in place that would continue to influence policy for decades to come and result in the further marginalisation of disadvantaged children.

Changing Government Structures and the Impact of Constitutional Change

These new claims to modernity and consensus were crucially linked to the devolution of political power in the interwar years. Central to this research is a new understanding of the state, and the impact of constitutional reform on children. Following the 1919 Government of India Act, the powers of politically unimportant departments—education, justice, local government, public health—were devolved to the provincial assemblies, which were now majority Indian and had some limited tax-raising powers. A further, much more significant devolution of political power, including an extension of the franchise, happened in 1935 with the implementation of a bicameral legislature and further representation for Indians who could now propose, debate and implement legislation, whether in the Madras Legislative Council, as part of voluntary associations, or as government officials. Judith Brown characterised these new relationships between Indians and the colonial state as a 'ritual dance'; it forced Indians to both collaborate as government in some institutions and policy areas thereby demonstrating themselves 'fit' for governance, while opposing the British Raj in others.[45] The focus on ultimate independence, the clear democratic limitations of the acts, the refusal of many anti-colonial campaigners to participate and the more dramatic events of the nationalist movement have meant that few contemporaries or historians have provided thoughtful, political theorisation about the nature of dyarchy as anything more than a state of transition, reducing attention, in Brown's words, to the more oppositional aspect of the dance. Only recently have historians highlighted that the 1919 reforms profoundly changed the relationship between Indian society and state power, impacting approaches to citizenship, individual rights, religious beliefs and the economy.[46] Most significantly, it was these new ideas, established in the constitutional legislation and honed in the practical politics and negotiations of the 1920s and 1930s, which informed many of the assumptions on which the Indian Constitution of 1950 was based and impacted child welfare policies in the years following independence.[47]

Dyarchy represented a 'decisive shift' in power to Indians, who could now conceptualise themselves as fulfilling the functions of the state.[48] This was more than a 'negotiated space of power' allowed by the British (like the princely states).[49] Instead, this book continues the shift from a focus on the political constraints of dyarchy to consider how the small number of politically moderate Indians who chose to participate used the limited opportunities available to carry out a variety of innovative social justice reforms and institute a new welfare state, and in doing so reformulated the relationship between state, family and the future citizen. Hence the book reframes the question of constitutional change by looking at the 1920s and 1930s in their own terms rather than as merely precursors to an independent nation. Crucially, it situates this change in the provinces, rather than in Delhi, as the centre of political power. While there were limitations to the powers devolved to the provincial assemblies and municipal corporations, it is clear that in the realm of the social, the state was Indian in character and in personnel. Legislation regarding children was discussed by Indians, enforced in departments led and staffed by Indians and the authority figures—teachers, administrators, jailors—were also Indians.

Dyarchy thus provided the conditions that encouraged consensus among the elite within the realm of the social. The close personal networks and easy access of civil society activists to the source of political power and to the financial levers over change undoubtedly contributed to this, even if tax-raising powers were limited. These networks were based around campaign groups such as the Theosophical Society and Women's India Association, as well as within and between the Justice and Congress parties and, later, the Self-Respect movement. As both Sarah Hodges and Samiksha Sehrawat have highlighted in the context of public health, the exchanges, which were often robust, about the details of compulsory education (Chapter 2), care of offenders before trial (Chapter 5) or food suitable for a child's diet (Chapter 4) occurred within an underlying consensus about the state's relationship with the child and a broadly scientific, or modern, approach to the solution.[50] British interference was limited, and political acrimony was much more likely in the area of caste politics or opposition to British rule.

Constructing the Child as a Focus for State Action

Dyarchy fundamentally changed how Indians, acting as part of the state, both conceived of childhood and their responsibility towards the child, and then intervened in the bodies and minds of individual children. The first legislative interventions were initiated after the dyarchy had been announced but before it was implemented, and in 1920, the Madras Presidency underwent a decisive shift in relation to children with the introduction of the Madras Children Act and the Madras Elementary Education Act (see Chapters 1 and 5). These acts, which were largely based on earlier British legislation, profoundly altered the way in which the state's relationship with children was imagined in education, juvenile justice and child health policy. The new legislation was based on the twofold claim that the Indian child should have similar rights and protections as the British child and that the state had the right and authority to intervene in children's lives and within the family. Underpinning this was a political claim to universalism, the assertion that the Indian child should have the same rights as children in New York, London and Paris, that the Declaration of the Rights of the Child, 1924, or British legislation such as the Children Act, 1908, could be directly applied in India. All children were constructed as vulnerable and irrational, in need of competent adult guidance, care and protection. Inherent within this was a claim to equality for all children that radically challenged the racial hierarchies of late colonial rule. Yet, at the same time, the Indian political elite claimed to be the only ones who as a result of their education and their own national identity could fully understand these rights to protection and education in the Indian context. In other words, it was only culturally specific adults who could meaningfully interpret and understand universal childhood experiences in a particular spatial and temporal setting. It is my contention that this paradoxical juxtaposition, which sometimes imagined the child as universal and sometimes as Indian, laid the foundation for the insufficient theorisation of childhood in south India, with long-term consequences for social policy. That these assumptions were so rarely contested was a tribute to their normative power.

Within a wider consensual discourse about the state's need to protect children, children came to be viewed discursively and actually as future citizens. This made them objects of the state's benevolence and concern, not only as vulnerable but also as a future investment, entitled to the state's time and resources. Children were not merely socialised into a relationship with the British Crown as imperial subjects, but were imagined as future citizens of an Indian welfare state.[51] Regulating children's bodies and moulding their pliable minds gave Indian civil society activists and legislators an opportunity to carve out a new space in which to imagine the future nation state's relationship with its future citizens who, they hoped, would attain adulthood and freedom concurrent with a newly independent state. The child became the centre of new articulations of citizenship, a conceptual space to work out the wider unease about whether citizenship should be seen in terms of the rights and responsibilities of the individual or as evidence of loyalty and belonging.[52] Additionally this established a direct relationship between the state and child, which bypassed the authority of the family.

Yet this is to simplify a changing and contested relationship and ignore the wider context of the interactions between family and state authority. While social policy was now located in the hands of the Western-educated urban elite, the practical manifestations were not dissimilar to modes of colonial governmentality. This new elite, operating at a local level, may have been motivated by their desire to 'save' and improve the lives of 'poor' children but this revealed anxieties about the 'non-modernity' of the non-elite Indian home and family with its traditional beliefs and practices.[53] Of particular concern were religious and superstitious habits, the reluctance to provide formal education to children, illiteracy, early marriage, and the perpetuation of unskilled labour and unscientific methods of small-scale industry. Policymakers and activists expressed concern about the threat to the body of the child and his or her future health as a result of unsanitary living conditions, poor diet and insufficient protection from harm, particularly prostitution, smoking and travel accidents. This often reflected gendered anxieties about the influence of illiterate grandmothers and mothers over their sons and grandsons, and detaching children from these traditional influences became a recurring theme in policy formation. These tensions were reflected in autobiographical memories, with grandmothers remembered as bastions of conservative values but also the main source of emotional stability for many children. Jessica Hinchy's work on north India highlights the longer context of intervention in perceived non-normative families, particularly non-kinship households such as *hijra*s or those associated with hereditary criminality.[54]

There was, however, continued reluctance to contest the patriarchal authority of the poor family. Mytheli Sreenivas argues that the family as both an idea and an institution was central to understanding Tamil social relations, a key site where modernity was shaped and reformed.[55] Studies on the role of women and servants, and the economic and reproductive role of the family, have shown that the home and the family were imagined as a patriarchal power structure, albeit impacted by hierarchies of gender, class and caste.[56] The family assumed new ideological weight, and even though the regulation of private spaces, domesticity and conjugal relations were discussed within the public sphere, there was a marked reluctance by colonial or Indian officials to intervene in family practices or to contest patriarchal authority.[57] The deference to paternal authority was most noticeable in the age of consent debates but was also clear in the unquestioned assumptions of policymakers and politicians surrounding everyday practices of familial care and responsibility for education and behaviour. No child was to be placed in school if this posed a financial threat to the family (Chapter 2), school meals were intended to supplement, not replace, family meals (Chapter 4) and every effort was made to return convicted juvenile delinquents to their families, who had to demonstrate their responsibility for the child by paying fines (Chapter 5). Whatever the crime, it was only children with no known relatives who were incarcerated in the certified schools (Chapter 5), and there was almost no political will to intervene in the private marriage arrangements of families, even after the legislation of 1929 (Chapter 7). The state thus sought to reinforce the authority of the family through reforming some of its more obviously problematic practices, and the consensus was to work *with* rather than against the family, emphasising the patriarchal authority situated in the normative family. However, this cannot be adequately explained by either the reluctance to antagonise powerful male figures or the ideological commitment to the family as a modern institution or the practicalities of tight budgets and limited enforcement mechanisms.

Instead, south Indian policymakers, civil society activists and experts sought to negotiate the tension between patriarchal authority and scientific modernity by framing themselves as uncles and aunts, as members of the extended or joint family.[58] In framing state intervention as 'avuncular', they claimed *both* traditional forms of legitimacy as familial with a cultural claim to responsibility for the child population while also basing their authority on their modern expertise. This mirrored the practical and emotional support provided by biological uncles and aunts, as remembered in the autobiographies in Chapter 8, who were uniquely able to assume responsibility for children in ways that reinforced rather than challenged familial authority. While this claim was sometimes explicit, more often state intervention was framed in implicitly familial or kinship terms, which gained discursive power in contrast to the outsider, the colonial state. This assertion of a more culturally sanctioned avuncular authority that purported to work within the existing kinship structure without contesting paternal authority was less contentious, less dismissive of traditional practices and more familiar to the cultural understandings of the poor while being less aggressive in its interventionist claims. The terms uncle and aunt are not used—and the councillors refer to themselves in Chapter 2 as 'godfathers'—but I argue that framing authority as avuncular allows us to move away from terms such as 'surrogate parents', which implies a much stronger denigration of parental power than was evidenced either in the political debates or implementation of governmental or civil society schemes.[59]

The symbolic power of the term avuncular was evidenced in the immediate post-independence period by Nehru himself. Vijayalakshmi Balakrishnan has demonstrated that Nehru conceptualised his own relationship with the nation's children as that of *chacha*, or uncle, and sought to frame the state's paternalistic claims to care and authority in terms of familial and kinship relationships.[60] Operating within the boundaries of familial trust, Nehru avoided challenging the rule of the family patriarch and only proposed action in a crisis, operating effectively as a guardian of last resort.[61] Balakrishnan argues that this gave legitimacy to intervention, but it also honoured the cultural allegiances of both nuclear and extended or joint families. A detailed study of the 1920s reveals that Nehru was building on patterns of relationship and governance already established when Indians assumed more significant power under dyarchy. This approach to state power was manifested at the level of legislators or activists framing the discourse, but also those who had direct contact with families and children—school teachers, prison wardens, education officers and probation officers. And while the term avuncular is gendered, in social practice, women were involved as 'aunts', for example, the lady honorary magistrates in the juvenile court (Chapter 6), the school nurses (Chapter 4), nursery teachers (Chapter 3) and the female philanthropists involved in organisations such as the Madras Children's Aid Society. Using a variety of examples across the chapters, this book argues that we can better understand the claims to authority of Indians operating as state actors under dyarchy if we frame them both as interventionist adults—as professional, modern experts and civic activists—but *also* as claiming authority through the relational metaphors of the extended family.

Implementing Social Policy

Ideas about childhood were not merely decided in the corridors of power but were constantly reformulated in the tensions of everyday rule, the harsh realities of implementation and budgetary constraints and in conversations with both childhood practitioners and even children themselves. Each section of this book considers how the child was imagined in legislation, such as the Education Act, 1920 (Chapter 1) or the Children Act, 1920 (Chapter 5). It then looks at how these ideas about childhood and children were implemented at the level of social policy, with the formulation of schemes to provide midday meals (Chapter 4), enforce compulsory education (Chapter 2) or establish a juvenile court (Chapter 6). The correspondence between a variety of levels of government decision-making, the budgets, the minutes of civil society organisations, the teachers' professional journals, the curriculum of the teacher training colleges and the submissions to the Joshi Committee reveal the deep-rooted tension between the universalising discourse of the global child and understandings of childhood articulated and experienced by those in daily contact with Indian children. Tracing the relationships between state and non-state actors, parents, teachers and sometimes children reveals a stark contrast between the value placed on children at a policy level and the lack of political will to divert the limited state resources to improve the living conditions and life chances of poor children. In particular, it highlights the persistent disjunction between rhetorical promises to the child as vulnerable and as an investment and the lack of political commitment to fund intervention, whether in the provision of food (Chapter 4), adequate buildings for schooling (Chapter 2) or of personnel to facilitate the rehabilitation of youthful offenders (Chapter 5).

In practice, the child who was imagined as 'universal' was in practice assumed to be male, upper-caste, Tamil-speaking, physically able, Hindu and urban. The failure to adequately deal with child poverty, illiteracy, discrimination and abuse was thus based on a conceptual gap about the nature of childhood. Social and educational policies were structured to mean that any child who failed to meet these assumed criteria failed to reach a normative standard of 'modern' and 'universal' childhood and was constructed as the 'Other'. Indeed, the ways that implementation was structured for the majority both highlighted social difference and even strengthened social boundaries. This was seen most clearly in the formation of educational communities based on caste, religion, gender and language, and in intersectional hierarchies of exclusion, which meant that education was not even offered, even denied, to groups such as poor Muslim girls (Chapters 1 and 2). The majority of children, subject to at least one though more often many, of these perceived social disadvantages thus failed to reach a normative standard of 'modern childhood'. And to be Other was to be insufficiently childlike, and so the failure to be fully 'a child' and thus entitled to the nation's resources could therefore be located not only in colonial strategies of rule as shown by Satadru Sen but also embedded in the workings of power by Indian lawmakers and officials.[62] The fitful and uneven ways in which ideas and practice changed reveal a consistent lack of political will, the limited financial power available to state and civil society actors, combined with an unproblematised theorisation of modern childhood, which set a pattern in policy failure that continued in state policy long past independence.[63]

Understanding the Context of the Madras Presidency

The analysis is embedded in the broader cultural, societal and intellectual trends of the Madras Presidency, reflecting the need to decentre or 'provincialise Bengal' and later Delhi within the history of Indian modernity and social policy.[64] The emergence of the middle classes in Madras reflected its distinctive history, its unique Dravidian literary and linguistic heritage, local cultural concepts of religiosity and education and the presence of both transnational economic links such as trade across the Indian Ocean and transnational intellectual movements such as the Theosophy movement.[65] The presidency was also distinct in its experience of colonial social, economic and administrative structures, such as the *ryotwari* land revenue system. The Madras Presidency was divided into three areas, whose economic character was reflected by the 1920s in their political systems. The dry areas with limited irrigation (North Arcot, South Arcot, Salem, Coimbatore, Madura, Trichinopoly, Tinnevelly) and the Ceded Districts (Anantapur, Bellary, Kurnool, Cudapah) had large peasant populations living at subsistence level that contributed to a political system based on patronage, reflecting the economic wealth and political power of local headmen. By contrast, the wet areas of the Cauveri and Kistna–Godaveri Deltas were characterised by intensive rice cultivation, a larger class of wealthy, educated peasants and a much more vibrant engagement with new administrative structures and political movements. Madras City, and to a lesser extent the urban centres of Madura and Coimbatore, were thriving centres of commerce and cultural exchange and home to a significant Western-educated elite.

While the presidency was seen as a provincial backwater, the 'gentlemanly façade' of Madras politics changed significantly between 1920 and 1940.[66] It was also a period of significant socio-economic change reflecting the impact of the Great Depression, the collapse of rural landholding systems, urbanisation, the rise of political caste associations and the growth of labour unrest. Formal politics was dominated until 1935 by the Justice or Non-Brahmin Party, a loose coalition of interests that emerged in 1916 to contest the domination of the Indian National Congress by the Mylapore Brahmin elite. The Justice Party prioritised stable governance and pragmatic cooperation with the British to increase non-Brahmin access to state power rather than a radical ideology of egalitarianism and worked within, rather than radically reforming, existing state structures of governance. The local Indian National Congress Party was bitterly divided. The moderate Swarajists led by Satyamurthi participated in government at both the provincial and municipal levels, but it was the more radically Gandhian wing led by Rajajopalachariar which took power in the new Legislative Assembly in 1937. New forms of access to state power, underpinned by the decisions of the Swarajists, Justice Party and nominated representatives to work within the new dyarchical provisions, promoted moderate change on the basis of shared assumptions about the nature of childhood and the imperatives of state welfare.

The distinctive nature of south Indian politics and social activism reflected the identity divisions of the area.[67] Dravidian language politics became increasingly important, linked to the Tamil (41 per cent of the population), and later Telegu (38 per cent), languages and the development of a cultural nationalism based on a distinctive literary, caste and religious (Shaivite) heritage. This built on earlier work within the Justice Party as a way to contest the dominance of North India and to articulate the fear of domination by the Brahmin minority (3 per cent), seen most clearly in the increasingly vocal, radically egalitarian Self-Respect movement.[68] Caste difference remained a significant political marker of party affiliation, labour and industrial action, and the 1920s saw the growth of increasingly influential caste associations, often encouraged by dyarchical electoral politics. Caste continued to inform bureaucratic decision-making and modes of governmentality, seen most clearly in the appointment of a British commissioner of labour specifically charged with improving the material situation and educational opportunities of the Dalit community. The implementation of policy, as well as the autobiographical memories of childhood (Chapter 8), serve as a reminder that caste remained a 'meaningful social institution' in daily life.[69]

The religious communities of the presidency remained no less distinctive and complex; in 1921, the presidency had a population of 41 million, of which 3 per cent were Christian, 7 per cent Muslim and the rest Hindu.[70] Yet religious identity was entangled with other social markers, and while Muslims were viewed as a distinct religious community, their changing relationship with the main political parties often reflected the socio-economic and linguistic divisions within the community rather than communal voting.[71] The formulation and enactment of policies for children, often targeted according to class, caste, religion, language and poverty, played into these wider identity politics. Understanding these specifics is important in considering the detail of the legislation and its implementation.

1

The Child at School

Compulsory Education in the Madras Presidency

The Madras Elementary Education Act, passed in 1920, was intended to facilitate the reorganisation of educational provision and encourage the introduction of compulsory education in local authority areas throughout the Madras Presidency. This was innovative on its own terms and stands in stark contrast to the complex and multifaceted opposition to compulsory education at an all-Indian level.[1] Although still an optional, rather than required, function for local councils, it was part of a raft of measures that contributed to a wider re-conceptualisation of both Indian childhood and the relationship between the state, the family and the child in the interwar years. Compulsory education was a significant symbol of the progressive modernity of the Indian legislators and social activists, seen to be an essential component of the modern industrialising state and modern forms of governmentality to which these elites aspired. Underpinning this was a new normative characterisation of the child as a learner and in school, a sharp contrast to the manual and household labour that had previously been the experience of most children.[2] The institutionalisation of children within the spatial, temporal and authoritative boundaries of government-approved learning demonstrated a commitment to a universal idea of children as malleable and vulnerable and as the responsibility of the modern state. Central to this conception of a normative childhood was the increasingly widespread belief that education should be free and accessible to all. The inherent contradiction that this would only be applied in areas with sufficient political will and sufficient funding and infrastructure was largely disregarded.[3]

The first part of this chapter considers the figure of the normative modern child in school and the ways in which Indian politicians and officials increasingly conceived childhood as defined by chronological age boundaries. Yet, in practice, when the Education Act was implemented, children were more often imagined within the identity politics of the presidency, and compulsory education actually strengthened the production of educational communities based on social categories of caste, class, religion or gender. Historians such as Barnita Bagchi, Joseph Bara and Latika Chaudhary have already demonstrated how social hierarchies informed children's access to education and were used to maintain an elite's access to power, revealing how the diversity of communities in south India impeded the expansion of education.[4] The focus here is to explore the tensions between the emerging discursive category of universal childhood and the ways in which other social identities informed children's discursive and practical interactions with the state. In practice, the structures that promoted equality of access based on an idea of normal childhood learning perpetuated and reinforced existing social hierarchies, contributing to the formation of distinctive educational communities.

If modern education was to be universal and compulsory, then there was consensus across parties within the Madras Legislative Council that the only way to enforce this fairly was to make education free. Free education for the undifferentiated child became an ideological commitment intended to display the modernity of Indian legislators and signal a redefined relationship between the child, the family and the state. The second half of the chapter considers the act's governance structures and financing to unpack these new claims to responsibility for children as part of a wider understanding of the institutionalisation of children as a key function of the modern state, bringing the child into direct contact with new authority structures, not just in the schools itself but also civic activists within the District Educational Council. This was a significant challenge to the authority of the patriarchal family. By considering the enforcement of compulsion, the controversy over religious education and the fraught compromise over the payment of school fees, it becomes clear that this was much more complicated than a mere rejection of traditional authority. Either for practical, or I would suggest, ideological reasons, Indian legislators, teachers and social activists were limited in their claims to intervention and reluctant to challenge or undermine the authority of the family, even as they saw it as backwards and unmodern. Instead, a close reading of the sources would suggest that they claimed an authority based on a wider notion of kinship, a claim that relied on the presence of the colonial state as an alternative, foreign source of power and on fundamentally anti-modern concepts of authority, legitimacy and familial responsibility rather than modern expertise.

Madras Elementary Education Act, 1920

A bill for the expansion of elementary education was introduced in 1918 'as an essential accompaniment of all large measures of social, political or economic reform', a critical aspect of the functioning of a modern state.[5] The bill was recognised as a 'working compromise', reflecting the input of a number of educational interests. It was modelled on the English Education Act, 1902—quite different from the education bills of other presidencies, which were more explicitly based on Gokhale's defeated all-India Elementary Act of 1911.[6] An earlier bill, much closer in tone to Gokhale's, had been defeated in 1915 but began the process of establishing that it 'shall be the duty of the parent of every child' between five and ten years to send their child to school as 'adequate fulfilment of parental responsibility', with penalties for non-compliance.[7] In 1918 the Education Department claimed that the colonial government in Madras had made 'sustained efforts' to 'stimulate and assist' elementary education but, for progress to continue, education had to be placed on a statutory level as the direct responsibility of the state, not just reliant on parental enthusiasm. Of the approximately 2.7 million boys in the presidency on 31 March 1918, around 1.2 million studied in recognised elementary schools for non-Europeans.[8] This included 11,358 (1 per cent) in government institutions, 47,822 (4 per cent) in schools run by municipal boards, 363,490 (29 per cent) in local board institutions, 735,608 (58 per cent) in private aided schools, 100,763 (8 per cent) in unaided schools, with a further 167,143 girls studying in designated boys' schools. The vast majority of schools were run by private agencies but received financial support from the government as a result of a Grant-in-Aid Scheme introduced in 1906. This scheme provided financial assistance to institutions based on the standard and number of teachers, average attendance and the general efficiency of the school.[9] After 1911 the provincial government also subsidised the opening of elementary schools in villages with more than 500 inhabitants. While a further resolution in 1913 by the Government of India encouraged district boards to spend 'not less than 15% of their income from taxation' on schools, this rarely happened in practice.[10]

The primary aim of the new legislation in Madras was to introduce a 'central co-ordinating authority' in the form of the District Educational Council (DEC). This would serve as a regulatory body, facilitating the expansion of elementary education in each local area. The DECs were charged with doubling provision in ten years, having the power to decide local education grants and raise additional local taxation, a similar model to the English Education Act, 1902. Taluk boards and municipalities were to manage both the schools and new tax, supervised by the DEC but funded by an additional 2 lakhs a year from the provincial government budget.[11] After detailed negotiations, the act received assent from the viceroy in November 1920, being explicitly formulated not to embarrass or curb the future Indian minister of education after constitutional reforms were enacted.[12] By the time the act came into force on 1 April 1921, the Montague–Chelmsford Reforms had significantly altered the Madras Legislative Council (MLC), which became predominantly Indian, elected on a small franchise with responsibility for transferred areas such as education and health.

One of the most important innovations of the Education Act was the possibility of compulsory education, dealt with in Chapter 5, Clauses 44–52. Under Clause 44, compulsion could be introduced at a meeting of the local authority expressly convened for the purpose, for the whole or just part of the local area, and specified according to specific categories of religion and sex. In order to gain government consent (Clause 45), the local board had to submit, to the DEC and governor in council, a declaration of 'its readiness to levy tax' at 'such rates as may be necessary to meet the expenditure involved'. They also had to provide 'sufficient' school places. The aim was explicitly 'to banish illiteracy from the land' through a basic education and, when this was achieved, to further expand the curriculum.[13] The resolution received widespread support across the Advisory Council—from the Dalit representative M. C. Rajah to the Brahmin lawyer T. R. Ramachandra Iyer—amid fears of the social consequences of illiteracy for stable government.[14] Compulsion was perceived to be necessary for the expansion of mass education both to attract children to school and to ensure their attendance for longer than the current average duration of just over two years.[15] The decision to leave the initiative with local bodies but the ultimate financial control to the provincial government was undisputed. This broad consensus on the desirability of compulsory education is significant, particularly given the significant opposition within the Congress party at the all-India level.[16]

The act allowed for exemptions to compulsion under Clause 50 for children with no school within 1 mile of their residence, children suffering from infirmity, children receiving instruction at home 'declared to be satisfactory to the prescribed officer' and children contributing to the household income. This was to be monitored by Attendance Committees (Clause 51) and ultimately magistrates were expected to enforce school attendance. Parents were liable for a 5-rupee fine rising to 50 rupees after more than two offences, although revised from the original figure of 100 rupees.[17] There was a consensus that 'a good deal of coaxing should proceed' any penal action and a manifest reluctance to intervene in opposition to parental authority.[18] Consistently, legislators recognised that they were introducing only a 'modified form of compulsion calculated not so much to ensure that every child entered a school as to prevent the child who had entered a school from being removed from it within the period of school-age'.[19] Two points are significant. First, this emphasised that the state did not intend to force parents to send their children to school (and the final exemption clearly excused working children), but once that relationship had been established, they intended to maintain and pursue it. Second, the rhetoric of compulsion indicated a new departure, emphasising that the normative place for childhood learning was within the school, and the school was under the control of the state, either directly or financially. As the school became institutionalised as the site of modern childhood, this de-legitimised other sites of learning and the acquisition of other knowledges and skills within the family or workplace as traditional or backward, particularly those associated with artisanal work, the lower classes and girls.[20] By 1925 eighteen *mufassal* municipalities had introduced some form of compulsion, including Chingleput, Conjeeveram and Vellore.[21] In 1926 the Education Department even initiated a compulsory education scheme in Saidapet as an 'experimental measure', which ran from 1928 to 1931 to examine the functioning of compulsory schooling in rural areas.[22] As Hendrick argues in the British context, the regulatory impact of this was that children could now be 'monitored, surveyed, calculated'; regulated into the correct forms of belief and behaviour and brought into a direct, and potentially long-term, relationship with the state outside the mediation of the family.[23]

The normative image of the child learner was predicated on an understanding of the term 'school-age' children. However, there were extensive debates in the Legislative Council over the numerical boundaries of 'school-age', the debates becoming so fractious that ultimate authority was given to the British as the arbitrator. Under these rules, the schoolchild was defined by 'such age as the Governor in Council may prescribe in respect of children of either sex in any local area of any particular community' although within the broad parameters of 'not less than five and not more than twelve years'.[24] This reflected the wide variety of practices across the subcontinent, although there was no consideration of the widely recognised inability of many children to self-define their ages due to a lack of birth registration.[25]

The lack of clear numerical boundaries meant it was very difficult to enforce compulsion. In Erode, for example, the 1921 census suggested that there were 1,366 boys between the ages of five and ten years, of which 152 were Muslim. When Muslim boys were counted in 1922 in preparation for compulsion, the enumerators found only 61 between the ages of eight and thirteen years.[26] In Negapatam, the estimated pupil numbers and then later surveys differed radically.[27] In Madras City compulsion was enforced for boys aged between six and eleven years, Muslim boys aged between eight and thirteen years and girls aged between five and ten years.[28] This variation was even more significant in rural areas, and the intensive survey of Saidapet in 1924 included a variety of contradictory estimates on school population and attendance but no clear specification of the age boundaries.[29] This made it almost impossible to accurately assess numbers, which had a significant impact on the provision of adequate accommodation and teachers. The definition of the child by age remained fluid and contested, hampering the expansion of educational provision. It also contributed to the formation of 'educational communities' defined by a variety of other social identities.

The Development of Educational Communities: Female Education

The widespread support for compulsory education suggested that most politicians accepted the normative idea of the child identified primarily as a learner and as in school. However, when the Education Act was implemented in the different municipal areas, it became clear that children were categorised in different ways, not merely by a numerical boundary of age. The clearest distinction was sex and the act explicitly allowed differentiation in the schooling of girls and boys. In the extensive discussions about the introduction of compulsion in Conjeeveram or Saidapet, there was only passing recognition that frequently mentioned that 'child' was, in fact, a male child, and that female children were outwith the scope of the compulsory education scheme altogether.[30] This encouraged the perception that girls were a separate educational community, othered from this normative male ideal. Few councils followed the example of Erode, where the municipal council introduced compulsory education in 1922 and requested additional government funding, matched at 125 per cent of the education tax because they were the first area in the presidency to advocate compulsion for both sexes, although the proposals still contained a specific exemption for Muslim girls.[31] The chairman of the Erode Municipal Council claimed this demonstrated that Erode was 'educationally already much advanced than the great majority of municipalities' and that the proposed financial burden was 'light compared with the great step forward that the municipality will be taking'.[32] This reflected the wider politics in the presidency: the Erode Municipal Council was dominated by the Swaraj wing of the Congress party, increasingly keen to highlight their own progressive credentials and to oppose the Justice Party in the MLC, but also to contest the dominance of Madras City within the Congress party itself.[33] The Education Department cautiously supported the move as 'highly praiseworthy' and 'heartily approved' compulsion for girls in principle, but in practice, all the educational officials—the Education Department, director of public instruction (DPI) and inspector of municipal councils—urged caution and suggested the financial burden of including girls was unsustainable and the plan was too ambitious to be workable.[34]

Single-sex schools had long been a part of the educational landscape of the presidency and in 1921–22, for example, there were 2,631 registered elementary girls' schools.[35] Of these 64 per cent were in public management, 21 per cent were run by missions and only 15 per cent were aided non-mission, in contrast to co-educational schools, which were much more likely to be privately run with grants-in-aid. This was particularly stark in the rural areas, and the *Elementary Educational Survey Report* (1924) revealed broad correspondence between the presence of mission schools and girls' education. Ramnad, for example, was 'backwards' in respect of both boys' (30 per cent) and girls' (7 per cent) education, while Tinnevelly and South Kanara were known both for 'well conducted Mission schools' and the particularly high rate of education for girls (still only 13 per cent).[36] Popular support for girls' education increased during the 1920s, as evidenced by the Madras witnesses to the Hartog Commission on Education in 1929.[37] This changing attitude can be linked to the social activism of women in organisations such as the Madras-based Women's Indian Association (WIA), who both used their voices in the public sphere to make the argument for women's education and worked for the establishment of more girls' schools.[38]

However, the Public Instruction figures show that within the Madras Presidency, there were consistently more girls in mainstream co-educational schools than in single-sex schools, a statistic often obscured by the campaigning priorities of middle-class social reformers and the focus in the historiographical literature on the specifics of girls' schooling and curriculum.[39] By 1926–27, for example, there was a 28 per cent increase in the number of schools, with a 38 per cent increase in the number of girls attending, but a 54 per cent increase in the number of girls in co-educational schools.[40] The emphasis on extending compulsory education to all children, when this term effectively meant boys, contributed significantly to the de-legitimising of the educational experiences of lower class and caste girls, particularly in rural areas, and to the increased rigidity of the female-only educational communities preferred by the urban elite for their own daughters. This Othered the female students in school while also de-legitimising the childhoods of those whose learning happened in the community and not formal educational institutions. The assumption that the normative site of childhood learning was within a formal institution included a gendered preconception concerning what constituted both legitimate knowledge and a legitimate childhood experience.[41] Despite slowly changing attitudes, poor girls were discursively and practically

Othered from the normative experience of schooling and childhood, and this was accentuated when girls faced the 'double discrimination' of caste or religion, as well as sex.[42]

Religion and the Development of Educational Communities

By the 1920s religion and communal identity had become key signifiers of the child. The DPI reports consistently categorised children by sex and by community as non-Brahmin, depressed classes (Dalit), Christian, Muhammadan and Brahmin in order to trace the educational progress of each community, the categories of governance further rigidifying the boundaries between communities. Alongside this, the reports referred to particular 'exceptional' groups such as Europeans, Indian princes and criminal tribes, reflecting the categorisation and reification of social groups within the census.[43] Education became a way of 'perceiving difference' and facilitating comparison. Sanjay Seth argues that the 'educational backwardness' of the Muslim community was 'discovered' as figures for educational achievement provided a way to compare populations and compete over resources.[44]

By the twentieth century, Muslims were established as a distinct educational community within the presidency, although their position as a minority varied considerably between the Mapillas in Malabar, where they formed 35 per cent of the population, to Ramnad (7 per cent) or Trichinopoly (3 per cent).[45] The focus on religious education in the early years and training in the Qur'an before entering secular education in madrassas or at home meant that the numerical definition of school age was often different for Muslim boys, which again set them apart as having distinctive educational needs as a result of religious difference. This was recognised in the debates over a 'conscience clause' (Clause 53) added in the later stages of the Education Act in an attempt to counter the perceived threat of proselytisation by Christian missionaries. The clause included a provision to cut grant-aided funding for all schools that refused to offer exemptions to religious instruction. This was resisted by the Christian missionary E. M. Macphail who highlighted the number of aided schools, most famously Pachaiyappa's College Madras, which refused access to 'non-Caste Hindus, Muslims and Christians'.[46] Rather than debating the pedagogical impact of religious education or the susceptibility of children to conversion, the discussions surrounding the conscience clause were used to strengthen the claims of the Muslim community and British officials for the 'peculiar position' and educational requirements of the Muslim child.[47] This mirrors the Bengali situation, where Parna Sengupta argues that the expansion of modern education by Christian missionary organisations provided new educational spaces and conditions of access that encouraged the reformulation of a modern and distinctive Muslim identity.[48]

These new claims, which framed educational communities in exclusively religious terms, did not go uncontested. Lone voices, such as B. V. Narasimha Iyer, a Salem-based pro–Home Rule lawyer, rejected this, stating that the government should enforce 'equal access to all buildings and institutions' because a 'water-tight community' did not exist.[49] Likewise, twenty years later, a suggestion by the Congress mayor of Madras City that elementary schools should be linguistically rather than communally divided was strongly rejected as politically motivated.[50] However, recent research has queried the homogeneity of Muslims in the presidency, highlighting the linguistic divisions within the Muslim community and the high levels of integration of Muslim Tamil and Telegu speakers within wider rural communities.[51] While the Muslim Educational Association was the spokesperson of the Muslim community, it appears more representative of a particularly vocal Urdu-speaking urban-educated Muslim elite than the rest of the Muslim population. This group's claims to represent the Muslim community seem to have contributed to the over-simplification of religious and linguistic identities within the presidency and sidelined more nuanced voices.[52] This doubtless contributed to communal differences within the presidency, but possibly also prevented non-Urdu-speaking Muslims from accessing local elementary education. Similarly, access to formal schooling for Muslim girls was particularly limited and of peripheral concern to most in the MLC or the Muslim Educational Association, although it was a key area of concern for the Madras Municipal Corporation (see Chapter 2). While the commitment to education remained, the practical implementation was left in the hands of philanthropic lady experts, such as advisory boards of local Muslim ladies or the Madras Muslim Ladies Association.[53] In practice this meant that while Muslim girls emerged as a clearly defined educational grouping in the 1920s whose 'honour' was perceived to be the responsibility of Muslim pressure groups, the girls themselves were the responsibility of no one and received little attention, and certainly no funding, at the provincial level. Increased access to elementary education appears to have significantly contributed to a situation where children from minority groups were increasingly seen as members of a distinct educational community.

Caste as an Educational Identity

The claim of the Christian community to a separate educational identity on the basis of religion was complicated by their small numbers and by the lower-caste position of many Christians in the social hierarchies of the presidency. It was 'the declared policy of Government that no boy should be refused admission to a Government education institution merely on the ground of caste'.[54] Nonetheless, a debate in 1921 on government funding for mission schools highlighted the concern, particularly proffered by the Dalit representative M. C. Rajah, that publicly funded institutions 'still shut their doors against particular classes and communities of the land'.[55] The division of education by caste was opposed in principle by the educated middle-class politicians of the MLC, most of whom saw Dalits within the context of the wider Hindu community. Congress party members cautiously supported integration and viewed caste and communalism as 'obstacles to a healthy nationalism', which 'could only be annihilated only through the recognition of common ideals and interests, through common faith, through the development of a cooperative spirit among our younger generation'.[56] The suggestion that children were uniquely able to transcend social boundaries stood in stark contrast to the practical realities of schooling, detailed most painfully in the experiences recounted in Chapter 8. The Justice Party, on the other hand, used the democratisation of educational provision as an important tactic in their opposition to Brahmin domination. The Buckingham and Carnatic Mills strikes, however, had emphasised the difference between Dalits and the caste working classes within the non-Brahmin movement and the relationship was characterised by what Rupa Viswanath calls 'serious political animosity'.[57] Despite some interest from the Self-Respect fringes, neither the Justice Party in the 1920s nor later the Congress party were interested in Untouchability as an educational problem and evidenced very little interest in the systematic discrimination against Dalits.[58]

In direct contrast to the political discourse, the administration of the Education Department was premised on identification by caste.

Caste statistics featured heavily in administration reports, perpetuating a colonial rule of difference through strategies that facilitated the division of the population alongside the claim of benevolence towards disadvantaged groups such as Dalits.[59] Grant-in-Aid funding was predicated on the implementation of the Madras Educational Rules, guidelines initiated in 1892 and frequently revised thereafter, which specified castes eligible for preferential treatment, including Christian converts, but this was rarely enforced.[60] The 1920s saw a rapid increase in the number of Dalits enrolling in school: in 1922, 12 per cent of the 1.4 million pupils in schools were designated 'Adi-Dravida' or Dalit, rising to 13 per cent of the 2.5 million school population in 1935–36.[61] Retaining Dalit pupils proved particularly difficult, and a quantitative analysis provides little reflection of the qualitative consequences of systematic marginalisation reflected in teacher attitudes, access to learning materials and the Brahminical teaching content.[62] Access continued to be contested at a popular level, and while by 1937 there were over 400,000 Dalit pupils attending school, 81 per cent were schooled in government-run institutions.[63] Given the strength of the private aided schools as a proportion of educational provision, the preponderance of Dalits in government institutions reflects the reluctance of many aided institutions to accept Dalit pupils and the continued opposition to Dalit education. Compulsory education was abandoned in 1931 in Saidapet, largely as a result of the 'complete and successful economic boycott of the Adi-Dravida population' by their caste neighbours, and in 1933–34 twenty *panchayat* schools were closed because they refused to admit Dalit pupils.[64] There are two further points to note. First, by the 1930s schools run by mission societies or philanthropists, such as the Poor Schools Society or the Social Service League, continued to educate Dalits, but their numerical contribution was much smaller than usually reflected in the historiographical literature.[65] Second, most of the 'government institutions' that provided education for Dalits were under minimal control from the Education Department.[66] Instead, the Educational Survey of 1924 revealed the regional disparities in education provision, and by 1926–27 the Labour, Jail, Fisheries, Police, Salt and Forest Departments and the registrar-general of *panchayat*s were also running schools for Dalits designated as 'government'.[67]

The Labour Department was a particularly significant provider of education for Dalits. In response to the Gray Commission on Panchamas, a commissioner of labour was appointed in 1919 as 'protector' of the depressed classes. His duties included the provision of education in Tanjore, Godavari, Chingleput and Chindambaram taluk of South Arcot, which extended to cover the whole presidency by 1923.[68] The commissioner had the authority to provide additional resources to facilitate school attendance, such as books, scholarships, clothing and even midday meals.[69] Yet as early as 1922, the Labour Department was opposed by both the Justice and Congress parties, and its funding was severely curtailed.[70] The department was commended by the 1928 Hartog Commission on Education for its work to 'establish and maintain free elementary education' despite the lack of support from 'the usual agencies' for public education, yet even the Commissioner of Labour S. H. Slater accepted that his position was 'an anomaly'.[71] Slater regarded himself as 'largely responsible' for Dalit education, providing around 1,200 schools at the elementary level, with occasional supervision from the Education Department. The focus within these schools was on vocational training, either agricultural or industrial, according to the area, in addition to teaching basic literacy and personal hygiene. Slater also suggested schemes to 'subsidize school attendance' through financial incentives to the parents.[72] This contributed significantly to the formation of a distinct educational community for Dalits, in which caste status determined educational access, curriculum and success. Despite the emergence of a discourse in which the normative site of childhood was the school, for children from marginalised groups, other identities based on religion, gender and caste remained a more significant determinant of their educational opportunities. Within educational circles, it was becoming increasingly clear that to be a true child was to be male, of caste background and part of the Hindu majority community.

State Responsibility for Education

The rest of the chapter moves away from the child as an object of education to consider the governance and funding structures set up to facilitate educational expansion and what this reveals about the relationship between the modern state and the family and the child. The Madras Elementary Education Act of 1920 posited that the state had 'ultimate responsibility' for education and it was 'the primary duty' of government to 'devote all their energies towards the expansion of elementary education'.[73]

The act facilitated the creation of DECs as independent bodies that were to have 'the principal responsibility for ascertaining the educational needs of an area' and for 'stimulating such expansion as may be necessary'.[74] Decentralised from direct government control and situated in each local area, the councils were to be a body of 'broad-minded men who have really the interests of the young people at heart', avuncular figures from the local community rather than ambitious politicians who would work with the family for the sake of the children.[75] The DECs could recognise new elementary schools and supervise the distribution of Grant-in-Aid funding. Headed by the district collector, they comprised local experts, including heads of private institutions, members of the municipal authority and local social reformers.[76] Similar to the structures of the 1902 English Balfour Act, the DECs were to include 'self-respecting' or 'high-souled men' who had shunned overt political office but as 'persons of local knowledge and experience' would contribute to 'a healthy civic life' in the local areas.[77] In addition, the council provided an opportunity for groups usually marginalised in the political process to participate in government, including both representatives of the Dalit community and educated women.[78] The DEC became one aspect of the avuncular state characterised by civic activism in which local activists and local Indian officials could be responsible for the education and social uplift of the children in their area and hold significant influence over local educational organisations.[79] But the authority of these individuals was not uncontested: the positions were unelected, were vulnerable to political patronage and the lines of financial responsibility were blurred so that ultimately the DECs were abolished with little opposition in 1939.[80] This reveals an example of the tensions inherent in this emergent avuncular state, between local and traditional authority structures that had resonance in the local community, but which meant that more modern forms of political accountability were lost.

The new DECs were only one level of the variety of educational institutions facilitating the expansion of elementary education. Conjeeveram claimed the 'privilege' of being the first municipality to introduce compulsion from 1 September 1922, and the development of the scheme demonstrates the variety of organisations involved.[81] According to the 1921 Census, 1,800 (39 per cent) of Conjeeveram's 4,600 boys received no elementary education. In April 1922, the municipal council voted to introduce an education tax raised from 2 per cent property tax and 12.5

per cent professional tax in the budget of 1922–23, along with an equivalent contribution from the government under section 37 of the Education Act, with the hope of making education compulsory for 'all boys of school-going age'.[82] The details were worked out after extensive correspondence between the chairman of the Conjeeveram Municipal Council, the president of the Saidapet DEC, the DPI and the Education Department regarding pupil numbers, school facilities and tax changes.[83] Interventions were received from the Chingleput DEC, local sub-assistant inspectors of schools, officials from the Education Department, the inspector of municipal councils and even a visit from the Minister for Education A. P. Patro himself.[84] A similar resolution in the Madras Municipal Corporation in March 1924 included a comparable set of negotiations involving municipal and provincial political representatives, the DEC and officials from the Education Department, inspectors and the corporation commissioner.[85] The details of both schemes are themselves unimportant but demonstrate the webs of communication between political and administrative organisations at the municipal, district and provincial levels. These meant that lines of financial or political accountability were almost impossible to trace. Within these networks of correspondence, there was a shared assumption that the state was responsible for the educational progress of children, but what precisely constituted 'the state' and the division of responsibility between local agencies and provincial government departments was changing, contested and difficult to ascertain. In the morass of bureaucracy and competing agendas of adult activists, the small illiterate child was easily forgotten.

Financial Implications of Compulsory Education: Free Education for All

A central goal of the Education Act was to alleviate the widely acknowledged funding crisis in elementary education and provide additional educational facilities.[86] Under Chapter 3 of the act, local areas could levy a tax that would contribute to an Elementary Education Fund (EEF) solely for the purpose of primary level education. This tax was to be no more than 25 per cent of local tax revenues (Section 34), match-funded by the government. The provincial government argued that until 1920 funds had been 'spasmodic and precarious' but that the new system was to be uniquely progressive in India.[87] The act was intended to demonstrate the government's commitment to decentralisation 'giving to the local residents the principal voice in determining to what extent and in what direction they wish their elementary education to be extended' although with the corresponding pledge that the provincial government 'had no desire to divest themselves of their financial and general responsibility'. In practice, municipalities such as Negapatam were pressurised to introduce an education tax and the commitment to match local funding meant that while educational spending increased, the provincial government retained control over local budgets.[88] The local DEC became liable for a failure to expand educational provision, but subsequent protests that it was 'the essential duty of the State to provide adequate funds' were ignored.[89] The decentralisation of education control and finance not only blurred accountability for educational provision, but enabled provincial and district bodies to espouse compulsion as a demonstration of their own modernity and concern for the child but to avoid the duty of paying for it.[90]

These tensions were exacerbated when compulsory education was introduced. It was strongly felt within the Madras Legislative Council that compulsion was necessary but that 'generally in all countries wherever you compel a man to send his boy to school then you cannot ask him to pay school fees'—compulsory education was to be free and equally accessible to all.[91] As a result, Clause 47 established the 'abolition of all fees in elementary schools' within the compulsory area, partly because other schemes such as fee reductions for poor students were deemed to be too difficult to administer.[92] This made the state directly responsible for financing education, without parental contribution, even if what constituted 'the state' was disputed. Elementary education in the presidency was dominated by private aided institutions, mission (15 per cent) and non-mission (44 per cent) schools comprising 59 per cent of educational provision in 1932.[93] These institutions demanded fees from students in addition to their government grant, and accordingly a commitment was given that if compulsion was introduced and fees were abolished, 'the loss sustained by institutions under private management must be made good by the DEC'.[94] If fees were abolished so that there was equality of access, these institutions faced a considerable shortfall and so the Madras Educational Rules established a basic rate of compensation for the lack of fees, to be applied at the discretion of local authorities.[95]

While free education appeared to be a reasonable suggestion on paper, there was limited discussion about the practical implications. This became very clear when Madras City began to implement compulsory education in 1925.[96] Initially compulsory education was to be introduced gradually over seven years, starting with three divisions in 1925–26 and gradually extending by about three divisions per year until 1932 because of these financial constraints.[97] It was financed through a separate EEF financed by an Education Tax of 0.25 per cent on the annual value of the property, introduced from April 1925 and applied across the municipality.[98] The corporation would then contribute a sum of 2.4 million rupees from the general revenues, with the MLC funding an equivalent amount under the Education Act, 1920, Section 48. In exchange, property tax was to be reduced by 1.5 per cent, meaning that funding for slum improvement and other social investments was to be sacrificed for the sake of education.[99] While there were a few dissenting voices, the vast majority of councillors agreed that 'the Corporation should be prepared to spend any amount on education'.[100]

However, the Municipal Corporation of Madras depended on the aided schools to provide accommodation for the staged introduction of compulsory education, and so it became liable to compensate these schools for the income they had previously received from fees. It was agreed that assuming direct management over these aided schools was 'prohibitively high', although the schools were widely perceived to be 'less costly but equally efficient' to those under public management.[101] It was therefore decided by local councillors and the Education Department that these aided schools should receive full compensation in line with the existing rates of school fees, around four or five times the so-called 'ridiculously low' rate set out under the Educational Rules.[102] This very quickly caused a funding crisis, with almost all the money raised in taxes and set aside for compulsory education being used to compensate the aided schools for their lack of fees.[103] This had a devastating impact. The 1931 Census recorded up to 15,000 children without access to schooling in the compulsory area, and there were insufficient buildings to house all eligible children if they had wanted to attend.[104] The new building programmes were woefully underfunded while existing buildings were in terrible condition—indeed, the corporation cattle yards were alleged to 'be in a better sanitary condition' and the chairman of the Education

Committee suggested that some schools were 'fit objects to be investigated by the Society for the Protection of Children'.[105] Limited investment in buildings or teachers could be made while the funding situation remained so precarious.

What followed was extensive debate between departments and levels of governance over how this should be resolved. There was no political appetite for the direct management or the municipalisation of aided schools and this was widely recognised to be financially impossible anyway.[106] Instead, the funding crisis was used by another group of councillors who lobbied for the rights of parental choice, that the rich should be allowed to spend their money providing better quality education for their own children. Councillors, such as the Labour leader and Justicite V. Chakkarai Chettiar, argued, 'Our business is only to see that the children of the city are educated' and if 'parents are prepared to pay for their children's education' then 'what do we care if they do that so long as their children do not go without education?'[107] As the extent of the financial burden became clear, both the Justice Party and Congress Swaraj Party in the corporation agreed to defy the MLC, break the terms of the Education Act and refuse to pay compensation to private aided schools but allow private school managers to charge fees within the compulsory area ultimately forcing the MLC to amend the law.[108] The Education Amendment re-centred the role of parental choice in education, allowing parents to decide between aided schools that could levy fees and the free corporation schools, despite the recognition that this would cause variations in educational standards and exacerbate existing educational divisions, again highlighting the centrality of wealth and family in educational opportunity.[109] The opposition of those who represented the poor, either Dalit leaders or the Provincial Labour Party, was drowned out by the practicalities of finance and the increasingly expressed commitment to parental choice and responsibility.[110] Reducing the financial dependence of the aided schools also reduced the influence of the local authority over the education provided by them.

The debates in the MLC and in municipal bodies reveal the widespread commitment by members of the political and administrative classes to the education of all children within the presidency, with little consideration of party political boundaries. However, the continuing reluctance to provide sufficient funding, either through new tax revenues or a bigger proportion of provincial resources, demonstrates the extent to which children were forgotten when the state decided how to use its resources.[111] As the trade union leader E. L. Iyer pointed out, getting the child into the school building was more important than the quality of education they received.[112] Idealistic support for compulsory education was more important as a claim to modernity for the elite, a symbolic gesture of benevolence, than as implemented reality, meaning that children—albeit the future assets of the state—were not important when hard decisions had to be taken about the division of limited financial resources.

Parental Authority

The recognition that richer parents desired to contribute financially to ensure their child received a better quality of education was symptomatic of a wider trend in which the state deferred to familial authority and choice. Parents were recognised in the Educational Rules as a key site of authority in the child's life, and from the earliest debates, it was agreed that compulsion should be introduced very gradually for 'if there is any social custom that will create resentment it will be the punishing of parents for not sending their boys to school'.[113] The approach was to be non-punitive, with a strategy based around 'persuasion in the first instance and compulsion by slow degrees' using local agencies such as the DEC and village *panchayat*.[114] The aim was to provide 'inducements' to parents while educating them to 'understand the value of education' so that they came to 'look upon the education of their children as a paramount duty cast upon them'.[115] The terminology was consensual and persuasive, reflective of a widely held belief that non-attendance reflected a failure among the lower classes to understand the value of formal education in the context of their lives, particularly in rural communities.[116]

The rhetoric of persuasion and the deference to familial authority was reflected in the reluctance to legislate against the employment of children.[117] While the penalty for neglecting to send a child to school was harsher than in other presidencies, there was no corresponding penalty for 'unlawful employment of child during prescribed school hours'.[118] Likewise, the commitment to free education recognised the impact on family finances of losing the child's income. On the rare occasions that child labour was discussed, it was in terms of ignorance and want, not the morality of employing children. Parental decisions were framed in terms of poverty and ignorance, and the parent was still regarded as the ultimate authority in the child's life, despite potentially damaging their life chances.[119] This reflects Sarada Balagopalan's argument that earlier colonial schemes for education used a discourse of 'liberal benevolence' in respecting parental choice for their child's continued participation in child labour. She posits that this is not evidence of actual parental preference; instead, it reflects paternalistic perceptions of lower-class parenting among legislators.[120] Given the commitment of the Dalit and labour representatives to compulsory education and the lack of other non-elite voices within these debates, it seems likely that this was also the case in interwar Madras.

Parental views were also paramount in the issue of religious education when the legislators attempted to change the 'conscience clause' because of concerns that anxieties about religious freedom and the possibility of conversion would prevent parents from sending their children to school. While most presidencies were content to leave untouched the religious neutrality of Wood's Educational Dispatch, 1854, the legislators in Madras felt that this was sufficiently significant to address explicitly.[121] Two measures were brought in to appease these concerns. Clause 49 ensured that if and when compulsion was introduced, the government would have 'some means of safeguarding the religious sentiments of parents' and parents were protected from prosecution for not sending their child to a school of a different faith when there was no alternative in the area.[122] For those who chose to attend a government grant-aided school because of the lack of alternative educational provisions in the local area, Clause 53 provided exemptions from religious instruction lessons, provided no less than ten parents complained.[123] This was largely based on the assumption that an increase in school provision would negate 'the necessity for such exemptions' and that as school provision increased, it would mirror educational communities of religion and caste.[124] The Indian members, led by N. Subba Rao, a Brahmin Congress lawyer, preferred a more radical approach, arguing that the guardian should be required to formally opt-in to religious instruction and schools that contravened this should have their government grants halved, but this was defeated by the British majority in the pre-dyarchical Advisory Council.[125]

A further two days were spent discussing the conscience clause when the Education Act reached the MLC in September 1920. These debates provided a space to articulate new concerns that children could become 'Europeanised' through secular education, which would encourage critical thinking about all religious traditions.[126] The primary focus, however, was to establish that 'religious and moral education must be in the hands of parents themselves' and that teachers could model moral behaviour but not push a religious agenda.[127] With the mission schools often known for their high-quality education and the clear social opportunities gained through learning English, this protected higher-caste families in the urban areas who wanted to send their kids there but feared religious conversion. Concluding the debate, the president reiterated that religious instruction was the responsibility and duty of the parents, and that 'the basis of religious instruction which is given to any child must be given by the parent in his own home'.[128] The home was therefore an authoritative site of knowledge transmission, regardless of community. This reflected a well-established colonial division between public and private spheres, and the reluctance of the colonial government to interfere in matters of religion and personal law, but also the limits to the authority of the school and the state as education provider. As suggested earlier, the conscience clause facilitated the growth of emerging educational communities so that children became increasingly defined and divided by their religious identity, which was deemed to be more important than anything else.[129] While the state, often acting through civic agencies such as the DEC, had begun to claim a relationship directly with the child through the educational system, its influence was circumscribed by the continuing dominance of the family as the key site of authority in the child's life.

Conclusion

The Madras Elementary Education Act, 1920, had widespread support from differing layers of political institutions across the presidency. While change was often discursive rather than actual, the promotion of compulsory education by the political classes and state agencies meant that the school was increasingly regarded as the normative space of childhood. In the context of India in the 1920s, this was in itself a radical demand, designed to produce social change and to demonstrate the progressive modernity of the legislators. The numbers not in school remained significant, but children were imagined as learners institutionalised within the school and this provided a more formal boundary between childhood and adulthood. This further de-legitimised other experiences of education within the home or workplace, meaning that non-schooled children were seen as transgressing increasingly popular universal or self-evident norms of childhood needs and rights, guaranteed by the state. Imagining the child in school thus contributed to a dominant construction of 'the child' as male, Hindu and of caste background. This was not merely reflective of the 'unevenness' of educational provision.[130] Rather, children outside this implicit normative definition were categorised into distinct educational communities, which reflected other social identities such as gender, caste and religion and, while sometimes increasing their access to schools, further emphasised their difference from a universal norm. Belonging to one of these marginalised educational communities often became a more significant indicator of childhood experience, opportunities and boundaries, rather than age or immaturity.

The assertion of state responsibility for the child contained within the Elementary Education Act was a claim to modernity; a claim by Indian legislators to participation in global forms of modern governmentality, often explicitly based on the English and Welsh model. Whilst the perceived 'duty' of the state to provide education was acknowledged, discharging this responsibility involved a variety of actors. This included a wide variety of government agencies, including the newly formed DECs, local and municipal councils, private aided schools, the DPI, the Education Department and the Labour Department. Each of these bodies claimed to uphold the best interests of the child by providing education but lacked the political will to take financial responsibility and risk the consequent unpopularity of increasing taxation. This meant that despite the grand promises, elementary education remained in the same 'miserable chaotic condition' and the decentralisation of provision gave more control to local elites but also increased regional disparities and blurred the lines of political accountability.[131] While local philanthropists and civic activists involved in increasing educational provision could claim legitimacy as modern, they also conceived of their role in avuncular terms, as a result of being Indian and local, almost framed within the scope of the extended family. Although the dyarchal state claimed a new relationship with the child through these local actors, its interventionist potential was limited by the continuing recognition of the authority of the family and its right to make decisions on behalf of the child, particularly in matters of religious conscience, school attendance and school fees.

2

Educating the Child
The Introduction of Compulsory Education in Madras City

The introduction of compulsory education by the Madras Municipal Corporation signified a new departure in the history of children in the city. It meant that children became identified first and foremost as learners to be found within the institution of the school, even if this reflected a change in discursive emphasis rather than in lived reality. Chapter 1 has shown how the Madras Elementary Education Act, 1920, encouraged the introduction of compulsory elementary education throughout the presidency and the discursive, administrative and financial implications of this. Focusing on the specific local example of Madras City, this chapter starts by considering how compulsory schooling impacted the ways in which children were imagined by the modern Indian state. The child at school was not only a learner in the present but also a future citizen and adult-in-the-making. Education was linked to future democratic participation and to civic responsibilities within Madras City, and the child was brought into a direct relationship with the state as a valuable asset for the nation's future. This rhetoric surrounding the child as potential and as an investment was counterbalanced by an increasing sense of duty, couched in terms of a child's right to education, an idea that reflected south Indian participation in global humanitarian networks focused on children's rights. Moreover, by the 1930s there was a growing awareness of the child's capacity as a contributor, not merely disciplined into forms of being predetermined by adults but an active participant in their own educational process. All three of these aspects of childhood—as becoming, as being, as contributor—can be seen to some limited degree within the corporation debates.

The practical operation of the compulsory education scheme reveals the strategic priorities of the Madras political elite and the civil society activists who aided their endeavours. The tensions in the way that children were imagined were as much revealed in, and formed by, the small-scale interactions between children, their parents, teachers and the local councillors in the Standing Committee (Education) as in the grander discursive claims of the provincial assembly or main corporation proceedings. These exchanges reveal a widespread commitment to modern ideas of the child as intellectually malleable and physically vulnerable and as a learner identified according to a universalised category that prioritised biological age and drew a sharp distinction between the adult and the child. However, the discussions around how compulsion should be enforced, what children should be taught and how difference between children was constructed, challenged and enforced reveals a more complicated picture. While the image of the universal child was important to the role and self-identity of modern state actors, in practice children shared a variety of social identities with adults in educational communities defined by sex, religion and language. Focusing on two exceptional categories—the Muslim girl and the 'poor child'—this chapter will consider the limitations of this model of universal childhood and argue that in the minds of the councillors the child was assumed to be male, middle class, upper caste, Hindu and Tamil-speaking. All other children were thereby characterised by 'lack' for failing to reach this normative standard, and yet it was these other children who became targets of the state's pity and liberal benevolence.

Compulsory schooling was introduced in 1925 within Madras City and continued until 1943 with the administrative chaos after the evacuation of the city under threat of Japanese invasion.[1] In 1924 approximately 35 per cent of the schools in the city were directly managed by the Madras Municipal Corporation. The rest were administered by aided agencies, both mission and non-mission, and by the provincial government under the broad oversight of the corporation-led District Educational Council

(DEC).² By 1941, 46,000 or 53 per cent of children were educated in the corporation's 140 elementary schools.³ While the thriving aided schools were a testament to middle-class anxieties about new social opportunities for their own children, the corporation schools witnessed the greatest expansion by targeting the provision of basic literacy and numeracy to socially and economically deprived areas that had previously been ignored. The corporation itself was a civic body responsible for the administration of amenities and services within Madras City. From 1892, the majority of the elected representatives were Indian, representing a variety of political parties, such as the Justice Party, the Indian National Congress or the Muslim League and constituencies or interest groups, such as the trade unions, Dalits, women or merchants. The corporation debates were chaired by an annually elected president, or mayor after 1933, who was assisted by the commissioner, the most senior administrator responsible for providing information and implementing decisions. More mundane administrative matters, such as decisions on where to build schools, were dealt with at the level of the standing committees. The deliberations at both these levels were recorded in the Proceedings, and these form the evidence base for this chapter.

Introduction of Compulsory Education

The Draft Scheme of Free and Compulsory Education for Boys and Girls in the City of Madras was introduced on 28 March 1924 at a special meeting of the corporation by T. Varadarajulu Naidu (1887–1957), the Justice Party chairman of the Education Committee, often known as 'the Gokhale of this presidency'.⁴ The scheme was initiated in response to the newly recognised 'duty' of the corporation to impart elementary education to its citizens following the 1920 Education Act and the 1921 census, which revealed that 'half the males and nearly five-sixths of the females' failed to reach even basic literacy levels.⁵ It was designed to expand educational access to a further 20,810 children, including 8,560 boys and 12,250 non-Muslim girls.⁶ In his opening remarks, Varadarajulu Naidu introduced a number of themes that would characterise the discourse around children for the next twenty years. He argued that the scheme was founded on 'the now well-accepted principle of the civilised world, that no child should be allowed to grow in ignorance', which, he suggested, was fully in tune with the principles of 'our ancient law-givers' such as the

Hindu Dharma Shastra. The aim was to ensure children gained a 'workable knowledge of the three Rs'—reading, writing and arithmetic—in the vernacular and a civic education, which would allow them to work more effectively and participate intelligently in civic and political life as adults.[7] Varadarajulu Naidu 'vigorously pleaded' that 'throughout the civilised world the education of children is a primary duty of the State and the local bodies'. He ended with an appeal that compulsory schooling was not 'an ideal' but 'a necessity' that would affect 'the whole of our future *as a nation*' (italics mine).[8] The measure was seconded by the lawyer Dr S. Swaminathan who argued that the 'opportunity' to gain literacy and numeracy was a 'birth-right' or 'elementary right' because 'the boys and girls of today are the citizens of tomorrow'.[9]

Underpinning the introduction of compulsory education was a discourse of universal rights, of the duty of the modern state to care for and protect the child and of the child as a future citizen, which would set the tone for future debates. There was almost unanimous support for these measures across the corporation, which, combined with widespread public support, meant that even when faced with severe financial difficulties in 1930, councillors had to constantly reaffirm their commitment to the principle of universal education, free and available to all.[10] Importantly, these ideas did not emerge in the post-independence Nehruvian world but were directly related to the participation of Indians in municipal and provincial government during the 1920s. Despite the limitations of political devolution, Indians were prepared to use the opportunities available to them to change the nature of the relationship between the state and the child, and in doing so, prove their own modernity as legislators.

The 1924 discussions around compulsory education, and then subsequent debates, were predicated on a notion of 'natural justice', which suggested that education was a self-evident right because childhood was the stage in life when a person had the most capacity to learn. The Justice Party member Dr C. Natesan explicitly used the terminology of rights, highlighting the 'birth right of every civilised child' and suggesting that the corporation had a role in 'fighting for rights'.[11] These rights had global resonance, and Natesan was keen to emphasise that these developments would be noticed in the 'eye of the civilised world and in the eye of the brother Corporations'.[12] The comparative context was important to many of the councillors, who did not merely want to give rights to children but wanted to be seen to be doing so, both in comparison to other presidencies in British India and other nations across the world, including Great Britain, Japan and the Philippines.[13] The desire to be viewed by their contemporaries as progressive and 'pioneering' was evidence of the extent to which local pride and the distinctiveness of Madras was a motivating factor even before the formal inception of Dravidian nationalism.[14] The claim that Indian children had the same right to education as other children also allowed the councillors to contest the racial hierarchies of late colonial rule. The frequent use of these concepts shows the extent to which these middle-class, well-educated councillors were familiar with the terminology of children's rights centred in Geneva and the League of Nations with the 1924 Declaration of the Rights of the Child. The councillors were sufficiently engaged in transnational networks of intellectual exchange that they were able and prepared to deploy the concept of children's rights as part of pushing through reform. Underpinning the support for universal education was a claim to participate as equals in a modern, global public sphere in which children's rights were emerging as a particular focus of humanitarian concern and as proof of enlightened modernity.[15] Furthermore, this fledgling discourse of rights was becoming normalised within local civil society long before independence or the right to education was established at a national level or within the nationalist movement.

Investing in children's education was also a practical means of investing in modern urban governance. Education might contribute to the 'future strength of the nation', but it was also argued that 'primary education is essential for carrying on our civic life'.[16] Good quality education was recognised as important for 'the advancement of the city'.[17] This investment was explicitly intended by the councillors to reduce the budget requirements in other areas and increase the efficiency of both public health and sanitation measures by disciplining the future citizens into the normative practices of civil society and a better understanding of, and compliance with, municipal regulations.[18] This was a more pragmatic approach to children as a resource which reflected the specific concerns of the councillors administering the city, particularly the need for urban planning, easier administration and more effective communication with a largely illiterate population. While perhaps more often assumed than discussed, the focus on basic literacy, time discipline and vocational training which came to underpin the curriculum can be traced to this approach, in which children's key value was their potential as responsible adults.

Support for compulsory education was also given by councillors such as Dr S. Swaminathan on the basis that 'the boys and girls of today are the citizens of tomorrow' who are 'entrusted to our care'.[19] The suggestion that children were future citizens was introduced in the debates in 1924 but gained particular resonance after 1935, probably reflecting the expansion of the franchise with the Government of India Act that year and the need to prepare for a wider electorate. Councillors within the corporation were very aware that they were responsible for 'educating the mind of the child of today and making him the citizen of tomorrow' and producing 'self-respecting citizens' who would 'build the future nation'.[20] This was directly linked to rational democratic participation, as N. Rajagopalan explained: 'They are the future voters of the city. We must literate them in order that they may exercise the franchise properly when they grow up.'[21] This brought children into a direct relationship with the state, mediated by the teacher rather than the parents, and sought to instil new values and priorities as well as new responsibilities. It was explicitly recognised that the child in school could be taught a shared sense of community and commitment to the wider goals of the emergent nation state, and the investment in education did not merely benefit the child themselves but was intended to 'develop in growing children patriotism and other moral virtues. They will thereby become valuable citizens and enhance the country's position and prestige.'[22] The benefit of compulsory education was that this project was now available across social boundaries to the poorest, expanding beyond the confines of the middle-class Bengali, and now Tamil, elite.[23] Importantly, this citizenship was linked to a shared sense of national identity rather than citizenship as rights and was intimately tied to the devolution of political power to Indians.

The desire to instil a commitment to the Indian nation was demonstrated in the space and content of education. In 1936, for example, the Congress party introduced a proposal that a portrait of Gandhi should be hung in all educational institutions as a symbolic gesture of nationhood and to contribute to the 'moral elevation and mental enlargement' of 'our future citizens'.[24] The corporation textbooks were also designed to 'imbibe' in children the ideals that would enable them to become 'proper, honest and good citizens' and instil the correct social positioning of 'nationalism, patriotism, manhood and womanhood'.[25] These discourses emphasised the intellectual plasticity of the child and the influence of teachers in determining the loyalties and values of their pupils. In this context, the opposition of Mrs Ammu Swaminathan, chair of the Education Committee, to the production of standardised textbooks across corporation schools is interesting.[26] She emphasised a threefold approach to textbooks: 'From the point of view of the children being poor, the point of view that the children are going to be our future citizens and the point of view of making education interesting for children.'[27] This conception of children was critical and encapsulated the changed views of children by the late 1930s, held not just by experts but across the political classes. It acknowledged that the children's socio-economic circumstances affected educational opportunity and capacity to learn and it reflected the need to teach in ways that regulated the poor into middle-class perceptions of their correct place within the nation. It engaged with the idea of the child as an adult-in-the-making and a future resource for the nation, but it also considered the child in the present actively engaging with the content of education and being legitimately bored when it was repetitive.

Children as the Recipients of Education

The awareness that children were not merely moulded into the correct forms of being but that textbooks were read by children who could critically engage with the content was evidence of a wider shift in understanding from the mid-1930s.[28] There was more overt awareness that educational theory was insufficient, and that children were the recipients of education and were active agents in the educational process, not merely subjects to be acted on by adults in authority.[29] There was concern, for example, that staff poverty was not only impeding the teacher's ability to teach but also impacting the children's ability to learn.[30] Those supporting the teachers also recognised the limitations of their transformative power, emphasising that teachers 'take the material that is submitted to them. They cannot perform magic. They cannot transform individuals who have not had any intellectual training into first-rate personages.'[31] While the tone itself might betray a hierarchical dismissal of the intellectual abilities of poor children, the debate revealed a new awareness of the limitations of education as a form of regulating children into the correct behaviours, with an implicit recognition that some might be unwilling or unable to comply. During a debate on the periodical transfer of staff between schools, which was opposed by the Parents Association and the Corporation Teachers Association, the Labour leader C. Basudev sarcastically commented that 'our Congress colleagues are the custodians of everything and represent everybody—the expert, the parent, the child and the teacher'.[32] He then went on to argue:

> Mr Satyamurti [Congress mayor] may say that if the children come and say that they do not want the transfer of teachers he will drop it. The Premier said that if the pupils come and say that they are not going to study Hindi he would drop it. Mr Satyamurti will not accept expert advice, but may hear the child; let them wait on him in a deputation.

Another councillor claimed support by suggesting that 'if probably the children are asked, they will also say so'.[33] In a later discussion regarding school attendance, Basudev contended that policy could be changed if the Justice Party led 'a deputation of children'.[34] These comments, which contain a hint of adult alarm, suggested that the politically active child could claim attention and precedence over the expertise of politicians, parents and professionals because of their juvenile status. While the practical impact of this should not be overstated, the frequency of these comments and the recognition that successful education was 'a good and abiding contract ... between the teacher, the pupil and the parent' was indicative of a change in tone regarding children, and a recognition of their growing significance as a political community.[35]

The child was now counted as one of the interested parties in education. When a new school was debated in November 1939, Councillor N. Rajagopalan proffered that 'every child who wants to learn in the Corporation school must be admitted'.[36] This was supported by G. Rajamannar Chetty when he suggested including 2,000 rupees in the budget for prizes as 'an incentive to poor pupils to attend school regularly'.[37] While it is unlikely that it was children rather than parents who made the decision to attend school, the terminology used by the councillors to discuss children again shows the beginnings of a recognition that children could be active contributors and were not merely subject to the demands of their fathers. This had policy implications, so that in November 1939 the reforms to school buildings were explicitly designed to reflect 'the best interests of the children and the best interests of the city'.[38]

The interrelationship between different views of the child and the strategic use of childhood as a rhetorical device was demonstrated in the debates over the Tamil language in which children were used as proxies for a much wider political debate about the nature of Tamil identity. Education in the vernacular was guaranteed in the 1920 Education Act, and this had long been the policy of the Provincial Education Department. In 1931, Congress leader Satyamurti suggested that Hindi should be introduced as an optional subject in the higher standards (V–VIII) of elementary school because it would soon become the national language of India and was an essential preparation for independence, although Muslim children who learned Urdu were exempt because of the similarities in the script.[39] When Congress gained power in the Legislative Assembly in 1937, they attempted to make Hindi compulsory in secondary schools across the presidency. This was consistently opposed by the Self-Respect movement and the Justice Party, both in the corporation and in the assembly.[40] This was a key moment in the formation of the Dravidian nationalist movement, and the protection of the Tamil language became central to cultural nationalism in the presidency while Hindi came to symbolise the political dominance of the North.[41]

Both sides couched their arguments not only in terms of identity and language politics but also within a discourse of the child. A frustrated Satyamurti claimed, 'We know what is good for our children', and many of the debates featured similar claims to understand the child as a learner, and thereby represent them.[42] Often this was linked to new scientific understandings that the more malleable mind of the child had a unique advantage in language learning.[43] Opposition was framed in similar terms and linked to both the primacy of the vernacular as the medium of instruction for young children and to concerns that children were being 'overburdened' by excessive academic teaching.[44] Tamil language campaigner T. S. Nataraja Pillai, for example, argued that it was 'positively sinful' to introduce Hindi because it had no connections to the home setting and therefore no emotional attachment for children, and would involve 'burdening the young minds unnecessarily'.[45] Protecting the 'burdened' child, and the identity of the child as representative of an oppressed minority, were powerfully emotive political tools that highlighted the universal vulnerability and plasticity of children as much as their potential as national investment. At the same time, there was a distinct lack of interest in supporting vernacular schools for the sizeable Urdu- and Telegu-speaking populations.[46] Concerns about the minds and bodies of children could be deployed in politically significant ways, which ignored the practical and funding implications of these arguments for marginalised communities but were used to give resonance to wider political arguments.

Within the corporation, the ways in which the child was constructed changed over time. In the 1920s, the child was imagined as a future citizen with civic responsibilities; by the 1930s there was an increased awareness of the child participating in the democratic process as a future adult and as a future member of a national community. While there was some recognition of children's individual rights, this globalised language of rights appears to have been used primarily as evidence of the modernity of the councillors. And by the end of the period, there was a much greater acknowledgement that children were themselves active contributors to the educational process and were valuable in the present, not just for their future potential. These ideas were held in tension, each used strategically when the political situation demanded. While it is important not to overstate the practical impact of these discursive trends in elite discourse, it was also significant that these competing ideas were well established in policy discourse long before the advent of political independence.

The Implementation of Compulsory Education

The implementation of the compulsory education scheme revealed a noticeable disjunction between the rhetorical commitment and the reality, not dissimilar to the juvenile justice reforms considered in Chapters 5 and 6. Despite widespread support for the suggestion that 'the Corporation should be prepared to spend any amount on education', most councillors recognised that the scheme was 'a pious resolution' rather than a well-considered financial proposal.[47] Compulsory education was introduced first in 1925 to three divisions within the city, then extended in 1926 to a further three, specifically because they were among the poorest and most educationally deprived areas.[48] Following the perceived success of this, the initial seven-year plan was abandoned and compulsion was immediately extended across the city.[49] The scheme was funded through an Elementary Education Fund (EEF) financed by an education tax of 0.25 per cent on the annual value of property, introduced in April 1925 and applied across the municipality.[50] The corporation then contributed a sum of 2,40,000 rupees from the General Revenues, with the Government of Madras funding an equivalent amount under the Education Act, 1920, Section 48. In exchange, property tax was to be reduced by 1.5 per cent, meaning that funding for slum improvement and other social investments was to be sacrificed for the sake of the long-term investment in the civic life of the future through education.[51] However, by 1930 the fund was running into real financial difficulties. This reflected the decision to pay fee level compensation to aided schools (as discussed in the previous chapter) and the rapid rate of expansion, so that while in September 1927 there were 632 teachers and 20,129 pupils, by May 1930 the figures were 724 and 21,972 respectively, with the number of teachers increasing disproportionately.[52] While around 12,000 children were still to be provided for, the shortage of funds caused serious concern, with spending forecasted to rise to 9.65 lakh rupees in 1930–31.[53] The 1930s debates were dominated by discussions over the budgetary shortfall.[54]

These debates were characterised by serious concerns (from all political parties) about the extent of the financial burden, a desire for efficient spending, and a deep and often repeated commitment to literacy for all children. There were attempts to reallocate budgets, but there was a consistent refusal by the Congress and the Justice Party to raise taxes, despite repeated urgings by the Labour and Dalit representatives.[55] By 1939, long-standing justicite T. R. Kothandarama Mudaliar acknowledged that compulsion was 'a fiction' and that councillors 'delude ourselves' into thinking that they were 'doing our duty by the children of the City'.[56] This attitude underlined the entire history of compulsion until it was suspended in 1943. Despite multiple commitments and extended speeches by councillors, compulsory education was consistently underfunded and many budget decisions were never actioned or even seriously considered for implementation.[57] As with many initiatives for children, the desire to be perceived to be as modern in legislation was not underpinned by a commitment strong enough to incur the political hazards of raising taxation.[58]

The councillors were not the only adults involved in the education system; parents had to be persuaded and schoolteachers recruited to provide the teaching and to act as intermediaries. Insufficient accommodation and teachers proved a continuing concern for the councillors.[59] Parents were persuaded rather than compelled to send their children to school, and the DEC prioritised the need to 'educate public opinion' about the value of formal schooling and to persuade children to attend school with 'the minimum of inconvenience to their parents'.[60] Corporation schoolteachers played a crucial role as state functionaries. They were required to compose registers of children, which were moderated by the local medical registrars and superintendent of schools.[61] They were also encouraged to use every Saturday morning visiting the local area to provide progress reports to parents and 'to persuade other parents to send their children to school'.[62] The schoolteacher was thus used as the local embodiment of the interventionist state and as a symbol of a new Indian modernity able to penetrate within the family setting but not threaten familial authority.

When persuasion by teachers failed, civil society bodies had a role to play and voluntary attendance committees were set up to enforce the attendance of those already enrolled in schools. These had a secondary aim of expanding the educational provision to those who had no previous contact with the school system.[63] Each municipal division had an attendance committee of fifteen 'local men and women of light and leading … public-spirited persons to shoulder the responsibility' who had the power to prosecute 'defaulting parents' whose children were enrolled but consistently failed to attend.[64] This delegated power to civil society bodies to intervene in the family, although there were firm regulations for the conduct of meetings and 75 per cent of members had to be present before a decision for prosecution.[65] Three attendance officers were also employed by the corporation in 1929.[66] This was contested by Congressman Satyamurthi, who argued that compulsion should be enforced 'gently', through 'talking' and only 'through an honorary agency' in contrast to 'officers who will drive in motors or cycles [who] will frighten the people out of their wits'.[67] The role of the unpaid voluntary agencies, who occupied a liminal position as not-quite state and not-quite family, seems to have been encouraged as a way of making state intervention appear more acceptable to the family. It mirrored the role of honorary agencies implementing juvenile justice provisions, as seen in Chapter 6. As noted in other chapters, these were avuncular citizens who positioned themselves as both modern and as familial and who claimed an authority to act based on both aspects of their position. It also evidenced the underlying reluctance of the state to contest parental authority.

A number of interventionist schemes were initiated to encourage parents to send their children to school. This included the Midday Meals Scheme discussed at length in Chapter 4. V. G. Vasudeva Pillai, the so-called 'champion of the Depressed Classes', also moved the radical solution that compensation should be awarded to parents who had lost income from their children attending school.[68] This suggestion, that compulsory education should not be enforced 'at the expense' of the poor, was also supported by the Muslim representative Abdul Hameed Khan, and it was noticeable that the most radical solutions consistently came from the representatives of the most deprived communities.[69] The legislation itself provided exemptions, allowing attendance at a part-time school if the child's earnings were 'absolutely necessary for the maintenance of the family'.[70] While there was no legislation explicitly banning child labour in the Madras Presidency, it was recognised that work by children as young as eleven years in *beedi* factories, coffee hotels and theatres was 'against all canons of humanity' and that this was a very short-term strategy on the part of the parents.[71] At the same time there was widespread support for the authority of the poor family, a focus on persuasion and a sympathetic recognition of the impact of poverty on parental choices.[72]

The physical body of the child became a particular target of the state's care and protection.[73] The child had to be physically present in the school to be able to learn, but the journey there, the liminal space between the school and the home, was the source of considerable anxiety and the focus of more corporation debates than the content of the curriculum. Compulsion was introduced on the understanding that a school would be provided within half a mile of every home, though in the 1920 Education Act itself 1 mile was thought to be reasonable.[74] The school commute was discussed in terms of 'cruelty', 'trouble' and 'hardship', revealing a real concern about the danger posed by the increasing amount of traffic in the city.[75] When further proposals were introduced in 1931 to amalgamate schools at the higher standards (V–VII) to improve educational efficiency by sharing teachers and resources, the plans were again fiercely criticised, not because of the diverse educational needs of the different linguistic and religious communities but rather because a longer journey to school would compromise the physical safety of the children.[76] The proposal to extend the number of schools eligible for conductors, servants who transported boys safely from home to school, received widespread support based on the perceived vulnerability, and possible stupidity, of children in congested streets.[77]

The anxieties over the physical vulnerability of children reflected wider questions surrounding parental and state responsibility. While Justicite M. Sundaram Naidu opined that 'it is the duty of the parents' to send their children to school and ensure their safe arrival, fellow justicite K. Sreeramulu Naidu wondered, 'Have they not any Godfathers in this Council' to care for them?[78] This was a significant allusion to the semi-familial way in which councillors perceived their own relationship with the city's children. The term avuncular alludes to this; the councillors sought to justify their policies and desire to control and protect children's bodies on the basis of a semi-familial concern—as godfather or uncles— which coexisted with familial authority, but also on the basis of their understandings of the modern state's duty to protect the vulnerable. This was reflected in the role of the attendance committee and the schoolteachers too. Yet despite this combined rhetorical concern for the children's welfare, no one was prepared to pay for it.[79]

Schools for the Poor

When the child was mentioned in the corporation debates as a future citizen or with the right to education, they were discussed in universal terms, undifferentiated by race, sex, religion, caste or class and defined by physical vulnerability and intellectual immaturity as well as biological age. Yet, as Chapter 1 has indicated, childhood was not the only signifier of identity or even the most important for many children and, in reality, children were organised into educational communities, which impacted their educational access and opportunities. In practice, 'the universal child' was Hindu, Tamil speaking, middle class, upper caste, male and able-bodied, and any children who failed to reach this normative standard was Othered when educational policies were implemented. To unpick further the tensions within these new universalising discourses of childhood, the rest of the chapter will consider two particular groups: the Muslim girl and the 'poor child'.

The councillors within the Madras Corporation specifically targeted 'poor children' in their educational provision. Under the 1920 Education

Act, it was mandatory that all schooling in compulsory areas was free to ensure absolute equality of access and quality, and the Madras councillors were quick to affirm their commitment that all children would be 'placed on a footing of equality as regards facilities and opportunities for education'.[80] This was repealed in 1932 (see Chapter 1), and it was clear that in practice those labelled 'the rich man's children' could afford a better quality of education in less crowded conditions in the aided schools and were eager to maintain their privileged status by paying fees.[81] The poor were perceived to be the particular responsibility of the corporation, and there was a broad agreement that municipal schools should be only 'for the sake of the poor and the Depressed Classes', positioning the corporation as having unique responsibility for the poor child.[82] As Balagopalan has argued, this assumption that the poor are 'uneducated' and require additional support reflects particularly modern constructions of both poverty and education and assumptions about the poor as the target of the state's educational benevolence.[83] It suggested that the only legitimate transmission of knowledge could happen within the state-managed classroom, ignoring the passing of artisan skills and world views across the generations.[84] Free education for the poor should also be seen in the context of wider paternalistic improvement schemes for slum areas, including housing improvements and bathing fountains.[85]

The councillors were interested in raising the educational level of poor children and encouraging their development as future citizens and civic participants but were not concerned about engaging with the structural causes of poverty as a barrier to educational opportunity. There was, for example, very limited scrutiny of caste as impacting a child's ability to access education or gain from it. This was in direct contrast to the presidency-wide Education Department, the Public Instruction reports and the Madras Labour Department, established specifically to encourage Dalit education. These institutions, much closer in their organisational structure to the colonial state, used caste difference as a basic element of both policy and statistical analysis (see Chapter 1).[86] By contrast, the councillors in Madras were much more likely to highlight poverty, undifferentiated by caste. In 1928, during a discussion about Muslim education, Justice Party founder Dr C. Natesan argued that separate schools were necessary for the elevation of the Dalit community in recognition of the structural disadvantages they faced.[87] This was fiercely opposed, with councillors of all political parties arguing that 'Adi-Dravida boys are allowed admission into any schools' and would not benefit from separate caste institutions, in stark contrast to the decision to promote separate educational provisions for Muslims. This decision was ideological as well as financial. The Congress party was committed to including Dalits within the Hindu community, opposing attempts at self-representation as at the Round Table Conferences, 1930–32, while the Justice Party claimed to represent all non-Brahmins, and by the 1930s was influenced by the radically egalitarian ideals of Periyar and the Self-Respect movement.[88] This meant that neither wanted to situate Dalits outside their own electoral community. While there was no recorded political opposition to the Dalit community receiving schooling in the corporation schools, this merely reflected the choice of the upper castes to send their children to government-aided private schools, thereby maintaining caste purity.[89] By 1939, Dalit children were 'coming in larger numbers than ever before', and there was a growing realisation that the lack of qualified teachers from the community was impacting their educational experience.[90]

The responsibility to provide free education for 'poor children' was strictly defined. This included the provision of teaching staff and buildings without the payment of fees. However, additional resolutions to provide free books or clothes for those designated 'poor' were not successful, even when some teachers refused to accept pupils without equipment.[91] In 1937, Labour leader C. Basudev argued that 90 per cent of the 35,000 corporation school pupils were 'children of the poorest of the poor in the city' and that an estimated 95 per cent of parents could not 'afford to give them good clothing and the necessary books and slates'.[92] These 'little urchins' had 'poverty ... written on their faces' and struggled to find even 'the barest minimum of clothing', causing disquiet to their wealthier peers.[93] Lack of adequate resources, particularly textbooks, increased inequality within the classroom and had a disastrous impact on homework which in turn was 'the most fruitful cause of irregular attendance'.[94] These observations were ignored, although Madras City was a frontrunner in the provision of free school meals to poor children as an attempt to facilitate 'regularity and continuity' of school attendance (discussed at length in Chapter 4).[95] There were also opportunities for particularly bright children to gain additional scholarships on the basis of exam grades, although to gain the scholarship, the child had to be certified poor by the divisional councillor or honorary magistrate, a humiliating but also logistically difficult task.[96] Councillors signalled their own modernity in their commitment to educating poor children, but this was narrowly conceived and they were content with the basics of educational provision.

The nature of the education provided was also intended to be suited to the needs of the poor child, to be useful and relevant to the lives of children to justify the loss of income. In 1924, the councillors set out their objective that basic literacy was necessary 'for all children' specifically so that 'labouring classes and the menial workers may do this work whatever be their own sphere of life with more intelligence [and] with more enthusiasm', effectively training future workers into a more disciplined and pliant workforce.[97] These sentiments were mirrored in the 1925 resolution that 'besides the three Rs the further curriculum of studies ought not to be maintained in all schools in the City *but the same vary according to the class of children attending the school*' (italics mine).[98] Basic literacy was supplemented by vocational education, which was perceived to be an antidote to the oft-mentioned fear that children were 'overburdened' or 'over-worked and over-taught', although this was specifically a middle-class problem.[99] Vocational education received extensive attention within educational circles during the 1930s as more sympathetic to the learning needs of the child, reflecting the new global interest in progressive pedagogy (see Chapter 3).[100] In 1927, vocational courses were established in a number of corporation schools, usually focused on weaving or net weaving, but also lace-making, brickmaking, carpentry and embroidery.[101] According to N. Sankaran, who claimed authority as a 'humble pedagogue', this would give the children 'a chance to improve their thinking power' and would 'help to form the habit of hard work which is good for our children'.[102] While the ideas surrounding vocational education were justified in terms of India's heritage of 'craftsmen' and modern pedagogical theories, this was also a functional approach to education driven by social class.[103] The Swaraj politician Bakthavathsulu Naidu maintained that 'vocational training is absolutely necessary for the children of the labouring classes' who were affirmed as the key focus of corporation schools.[104] Children were to be given training in their parents' occupation, which was seen to give them the chance to 'eke out a livelihood' and 'cultivate their aptitudes' but not to expand their intellect or educational opportunities.[105] As a minimum, the skills learned might provide a 'supplementary vocation' specifically for poor boys.[106]

There was some opposition to this educational strategy, primarily because it was considered a waste of limited resources better spent on improving literacy. The real expertise in teaching many of these crafts lay with the artisan communities the children came from, not with the classically trained teacher, and even if they acquired basic skills, the chances of moving between caste occupations were small.[107] This suggests that the compulsory teaching of a skill in schools was intended to reinforce the primacy of institutional learning and to discipline future adult citizens to maintain their place in the social hierarchy. As Sarada Balagopalan has argued, vocational education for the poor was used as a means of limiting the aspiration of the lower classes, whilst disciplining them into a new relationship with the state as citizens, and encouraging them into a disciplined and pliant workforce who would contribute to a modern industrial economy.[108] The content of education seemed designed to strengthen rather than contest the social hierarchies of class and caste.

The complicated relationship between what constituted 'elementary education' and the opportunities available to poor children was confirmed in 1936. There was a move to provide financial incentives for 'the children of the labourers' to remain in school for V and VI standards.[109] These plans were defeated due to shortages in funding, as were further attempts in 1937 and 1938.[110] While supported by the Labour leader C. Basudev as a 'bare necessity', the proposal was rejected by the commissioner as a wasted resource, given that 15,000 children continued to receive no schooling at all.[111] In 1939, the Education Committee proposed to extend the length of education at the cost of minimal fees in standards VI (12 *annas* per month[112]), VII (14 *annas*) and VIII (1 rupee). Concessions were to be made 'to all the Muhammadan boys, scheduled caste boys, backward class children, to poorer children of other classes and to girls'.[113] This tacitly acknowledged the assumption of the Education Committee that five years was sufficient to teach children basic numeracy and literacy, therefore any further education could not be counted as either 'compulsory' or 'free'. The proposal was passionately opposed as 'an act of criminal folly' because funding constraints meant that certain children from these communities would progress and that their success would 'deprive others from having even elementary education'.[114] These limitations only applied to children of poor communities; other parents were able to fund a longer and more academic education in government-aided schools. Access to education therefore reinforced, rather than contested, existing inequalities of wealth and extended government control over the lives of future citizens without the prospect that they would benefit personally.[115] Poverty, caste and social class remained key deciding factors in the quality and length of educational provision. Also implicit within these discourses was an assumption that the poor child was male.

In a further debate in 1939, the Labour representative C. Basudev argued that all elementary education should be free and should continue for eight years, emphasising:

> [The] hunger for education among the working classes. They refuse to stay where they are. They refuse to allow their children to stagnate in the same wretched condition of life into which their birth has confined them. They want their children at least to become clerks, not remain manual workers. It is our duty, if we really are here to work for the uplift of the working-class, to see that birth is not an obstruction to the achievement of human ambitions.[116]

This remained a minority view that education could lead to a radical change in life opportunities rather than a slightly more comfortable existence. What these discussions did reaffirm was the commitment that 'we, representatives of the poor, have certain duties and responsibilities' and that those attending corporation schools were 'children mostly drawn from the slum areas'.[117] This series of debates revealed the continued commitment within the corporation, fifteen years after the institution of compulsory education, to the ideal that free education should be available to all children and that it was the responsibility of the corporation to provide for the poor. However, for most councillors, education was concentrated on basic literacy and numeracy to enable the production of more disciplined citizens—there was no corresponding commitment to a sufficient standard of education to provide the skills or opportunities for social progression. This fits into a longer trajectory of educational reforms, including those instituted by Gandhi, which Parimala Rao argues were consistently designed to strengthen rather than contest class hierarchies.[118] It also was premised on the councillors deciding what was best for lower caste and class communities, despite a lengthy history that demonstrated that these groups were eager to expand their intellect as well as their employment prospects through modern education.[119] Acting on behalf of, rather than listening to, poor communities became established as a pattern of behaviour by Indian policymakers that continued to characterise state actions well into the post-independence period. The revolutionary commitment to universal education promoted by Madras politicians thus quickly degenerated into the advocacy of segregated and dual-track education under the combined pressures of financial constraints and caste and class prejudice.

Educating Muslim Girls

While children from a wide variety of castes and backgrounds were brought together under the heading of the 'poor child', there was one particularly distinctive group that caught the attention of the corporation councillors—Muslim girls. When compulsory education was introduced in 1925, a special meeting of the corporation agreed that Muslim girls would be exempted. This was a response to widespread protests by the Muslim community that the secular education of girls was against ecclesiastical law (Sharia).[120] The debate mirrored wider concerns about Muslim education, reflecting the different definitions of what constituted a child (see Chapter 1). A separate provision was underpinned by two parallel arguments, that the Muslim child has distinct pedagogical needs and that separate schooling was required as a form of positive discrimination towards a particularly disadvantaged community.[121] The exemption was temporary while the Muslim councillors sought to reassure Muslim opinion, and it was agreed that they were the only ones who could negotiate a compromise, a contrast to the limitations put on low-caste decision-making.[122] This assumption that separate schools were necessary for Muslims was opposed in 1928 by the Communist Party leader M. Singaravelu Chettiar:

> We do not know what will become of India if we introduce communalism in our schools by establishing separate schools for Anglo-Indians, for Mohammadans, for Sikhs … the sympathy of our comrade Mrs Angelo will be better shown in asking for more schools for all children in the city of Madras, irrespective of religion, caste or creed. After all, who are these so

called Anglo-Indians, Hindus and Muslims? They do not belong to different races. They are all born in India and have to die in India.[123]

This was ignored across the chamber, with the explicit recognition that one of the 'stern realities of Indian life' was that Muslims were 'still lagging behind' in education and wanted to 'preserve a civilisation and culture of their own'.[124] This was a policy promoted by a majority Indian government, not colonial divide-and-rule tactics, but intimately tied to the structures, communal electorates and administration of both the provincial and municipal governments. During the 1930s, there were attempts to integrate schooling as a means of 'removing communal misunderstandings' and to recognise that the decision to 'perpetually isolate children of the community' and divide the country into various groups had 'serious consequences' for communal relations and undermined the production of the new Indian nation.[125] Nonetheless, in practice, education remained segregated on communal lines and the continued underfunding of Muslim schools confirmed the suspicions of the Muslim community that neither the Congress nor the Justice Party were committed to more than hollow words.[126] The complicated realities of the paternalistic state's claim that it was responsible for all children meant that, in practice, 'Muslim boys' were increasingly set against the definition of a 'normal boy', highlighting exclusionary patterns of behaviour and attitudes of mind which were difficult to change.

If Muslim boys were Othered in educational provision, this was even more the case for girls. Non-elite Muslim girls and their experiences of elementary schooling rarely feature in the extensive and rich historiography of institutional education for girls in colonial India.[127] Similarly, within the corporation there was very little engagement with female schooling by the councillors, other than a concern that male teachers did not have sufficient technical skills in music, *kolattam* dance and needlework and a fear of the social consequences of co-education.[128] However, the area that did command significant political attention was the provision of transport for the small minority of Muslim girls attending school, again highlighting this emphasis on the fragility of children's bodies. Both this controversy and the initial reluctance of Muslim leaders to sanction education for girls should be read within the terms of Urvashi Butalia's analysis of partition, encompassing the ways in which women embodied the honour and purity of the community and the link between gender, physical vulnerability and honour.¹²⁹ The most frequent and voluble controversy centred on the corporation's agreement to pay for bullock carts and conductresses in order to maintain purdah restrictions for Muslim girls while travelling to school.¹³⁰ The 1931–32 budget, for example, provided 5,000 rupees for conveyance charges for Muslim girls, although the schools themselves were agreed to be 'simply hopeless' in academic learning.¹³¹ The carts regularly contained ten–fifteen girls, and there were frequent accounts of injury because of overcrowding.¹³² The limited number of carts meant that

> after school is closed, girls have to remain until 7 in the evening before the late batch can leave and reach their homes at 8pm. On account of this, little children are subjected not only to great inconvenience but to a risk to their lives also sometimes, and this meant that children went without proper meal times.¹³³

Similarly, in 1937 there were reports of girls spending twelve hours a day at school and travelling, and of the occasional girl falling from overcrowded carts.¹³⁴

The councillors were sympathetic to tales of danger and inconvenience and suggested a number of solutions, including purchasing Ford Pleasure cars and buses, though these ideas were always defeated through a lack of funds.¹³⁵ In response, the Education Committee appealed for private donations by 'people who are interested in educating the Muslim girls'.¹³⁶ This was firmly resisted by the trade unionist Albert Jesudasan who argued that 'Muslims are also citizens of Madras; they are also paying taxes' and as such had equal 'rights' to an appropriate education. This was agreed by K. Muhammed Ibrahim, who feared the 'invidious distinction between the education that is imparted to Muslim children and that of the children belonging to other communities'.¹³⁷ These councillors were eager to emphasise the idea of equal rights for all citizens, highlighting how the acceptance of communal difference and disparities in funding played into well-established discourses of political inclusion and exclusion, reinforcing the marginalisation of the Muslim community and particularly Muslim girls. It questioned the commitment of the corporation to see Muslim children as within their commitments to 'all children' rather than an inconvenience that failed to fit a normative pattern. Strikingly, the forgotten story was the growing number of Muslim girls who engaged in significant personal sacrifice, braving dangerous travelling conditions and often missing meals to attain a poor quality education, showing a desire for educational opportunities not commented on by the councillors or many subsequent commentators.[138]

Conclusion

There was broad consensus by 1924 among the political classes in Madras that compulsory elementary education was necessary for the future of India as a modern nation. Compulsion institutionalised children, particularly poor children, into a new relationship with the modern state, and meant that in both elite discourse and popular consciousness, the school became the normal site of childhood. The emergence of the school as the legitimate and primary space for children reinforced the separation between schooling and work as a defining boundary of childhood, while the focus on institutional education downgraded knowledge learned in the home, community or workplace. However, the failure to adequately finance the education scheme meant that 17,000 children were still not in school even in 1939.[139] These children missed out on the practical benefits of literacy and numeracy, thereby constraining their future life chances as adults, but this failure to reach an emerging normative ideal of the schoolchild meant that their childhoods were also characterised in terms of lack and were perceived to be quintessentially unmodern. A disproportionately large number came from structurally disadvantaged communities, and even for those who attended school the educational opportunities were varied, and children faced daily discrimination and opposition as a result of their caste, language, religion and sex. While all children had free access to education in principle, in practice, to be fully counted as a child with all the rights and possibilities that this entailed was to be an able-bodied, wealthy, upper-caste, Tamil-speaking boy. This schoolchild merited municipal investment as a future citizen. Education was intended to make populations easier to manage and to regulate individuals into a relationship with the state, manifested both as the provider of local services in the municipal council and as the emergent nation, facilitating new forms of democratic participation but requiring new patterns of loyalty. By the end of the 1930s, there was also an emergent discourse on children's rights and signs of recognition that the child possessed the capacity to make decisions and hold opinions, that they were contributors to the educational process rather than passive recipients and that they should be counted as political agents who claimed political attention specifically as children, even if their voice was muted and their opinions often ignored.

The increased desire and capacity of teachers, councillors and educational committees to intervene in children's lives threatened the authority of the natal family. Schooling impacted the everyday routines of children's lives, bringing new opportunities and engendering new forms of loyalty, often threatening the livelihood of the poor family. The schoolteacher assumed a new, modern role as the local manifestation of state power, although the autobiographical memories recounted in Chapter 8 suggest that this was more ambiguous and contested than the official documents would suggest. The claim to pursue a globally recognised modernising agenda was central to the decision to introduce compulsion but had the potential to undermine the dominance of the traditional family. In practice, however, compulsion was only enforced for children who had been already enrolled by their family, and the attendance committees and teachers were characterised by the overarching desire to work with, rather than against, the family. Numerous mitigations, such as free school meals, were introduced, and there was widespread unease about causing 'inconvenience' to local households. Indeed, the schoolteachers, honorary attendance committees and councillors saw themselves as 'godfathers' to the local children and framed their interventions as within the accepted boundaries of avuncular authority.

The corporation schools were specifically designed to provide education for 'the poor' of the city. Although the child was imagined as being in school with the capacity to learn, the emphasis was on achieving basic literacy and numeracy, vocational skills and disciplining children into the routines and authority of the classroom. This was not education designed to enhance opportunity or develop skills, and any education beyond standard V involved prohibitive fees. Instead, it was intended to maintain and regulate the behaviour of the labouring classes, socialising children into new understandings of work and time discipline, but not to provide any challenge to the social order. Within these discourses, the idea of 'the poor' became an important identity, highlighting the often ignored class-based nature of politics in Madras, and the instincts of a reforming, philanthropic middle class, couched in terms of liberal benevolence. Focusing on 'the poor' also allowed the councillors to imply that poverty and inequality were socio-economic problems, implicitly linked to imperialism rather than a result of more complicated structures of religion, caste and gender. How these ideas were theorised and negotiated by the pedagogues themselves, rather than by politicians and policymakers, is the focus of the next chapter.

3

Imagining the Child as Learner
Progressive Pedagogy in the Madras Presidency

Pedagogues and teachers working at a local level made significant contributions to the discursive construction of childhood in south India. Their work ran parallel to the expansion of elementary education within the Madras Presidency as a result of state action, as considered in earlier chapters. The introduction of compulsory education had encouraged the institutionalisation of childhood and meant that, in popular and state discourse, children were now assumed to be in school and were perceived primarily as learners. Beginning from this assumption, south Indian educators were interested in what happened within the classroom and the detail of how knowledge was transmitted to children. The writings of these pedagogues reflected the new global interest in 'progressive education', which emphasised the central role of the child as a recipient of elementary education and focused on pedagogy and educational methods rather than the content of the curriculum or the structures of the educational administration. The tension between these universalising ideas and the local context is the central concern of this chapter.

The writings of Indian pedagogues in the *Educational India*, an English-language pedagogical journal printed in south India during the 1930s, reveal contemporary theory about what was to happen within the classroom. These pedagogues sought to distance themselves from traditional education and emphasised learning through activity, an approach based on a very different understanding of the innate characteristics of children and their capabilities as learners which sought to put the child at the centre of the educational process. Pedagogues claimed a role for themselves as scientific experts and constructed pedagogy as a science. Significantly, this established the children as the objects of scientific endeavour, knowable through the methodologies of modern pedagogy. Moreover, as experts, these pedagogues claimed the authority to negotiate the relationship between new innovative Western pedagogies and their application in the Indian context. This was part of a longer trajectory where pedagogical strategies were formulated and reformulated in different local contexts, an example being the introduction of the Madras Method of monitorial teaching into early Victorian Britain.[1] The period after the First World War saw a particular interest in these exchanges, based on a new scientific emphasis that all children matured along a broadly universal developmental sequence, regardless of background, race or community. This both challenged prevailing beliefs in racial hierarchy and reinforced a particular construction of healthy, male, educated children as normative, delegitimising childhoods that failed to reach this standard. The local pedagogical elites writing in the *Educational India* sought to negotiate not only the tensions between this universalising idea of childhood and its practical implications for the Indian classroom, but also in relation to the authority structures within the Indian home.

The new pedagogical ideas that appeared relatively coherent in theory were challenged and reformulated when implemented in schools. The commitment of pedagogues to reform meant that progressive education was advocated and taught in a number of progressive female teacher training colleges. This chapter investigates the curriculum and teaching at Lady Willingdon College and St Christopher's Training College to analyse how trainee teachers were taught to apply these ideas about modern Indian childhoods in the classroom. The chapter ends with a detailed consideration of how the Children's Garden School, one of the few local schools whose records have survived since the 1930s, attempted to implement progressive methods. An examination of the ways in which these organisations negotiated the gap between theory and practice, the individuals involved and the practicalities of implementing new ideas in material culture, in ethos and in practical activity, contributes to a wider understanding of the ways in which ideas about childhood, and particularly the Indian child as a learner, were constructed.

Traditional Education and 'New Education'

Progressive education, termed 'New Education' in India, was fashioned as a modern methodology inherently opposed to traditional education, both in content and transmission. This involved an unequivocal condemnation of the 'old' or 'traditional', encompassing both colonial and pre-colonial educational approaches. As frequently noted in the historiographical literature, the curriculum of colonial education was intended to support British rule by inculcating British values and priorities as normative, thereby encouraging support for the Raj and ensuring a steady stream of educated employees to fill low-grade posts.[2] Although very varied in expression, in general terms colonial education was associated with poor pedagogical methods, including an overemphasis on literary education, examinations and rote learning under the guidance of all-powerful but low-status and badly paid teachers.[3] While a modern education was highly prized both by the Indian middle classes and aspirational lower-class groups, the low quality of education in many of the government-linked schools meant that even the auxiliary committee to the Indian Statutory Commission doubted whether those who did attend learned anything of practical, intellectual or moral worth.[4] Pre-colonial education was symbolised in the *pial*, or veranda school, which was directed by one teacher who emphasised oral traditions, commanded absolute obedience and often used excessive discipline.[5] While Gandhi lamented the demise of the 'beautiful tree' of Indian education, there was no real commitment among Indian pedagogues to revive it and references by nationalist leaders were largely nostalgic.[6] Those who did attempt to restore the learning of Indian culture and religion, such as the Central Hindu School established in Varanasi in 1898 by Annie Besant or the Sikh Kanya Mahvidyalaya, Ferozepur, often used the technologies of Western education such as uniforms, curriculum structure and timetabling, thereby, perhaps inadvertently, reinforcing Western categories and knowledge hierarchies.[7] In practice, many of the pre-colonial *pial* schools had merged into the new colonial system, and Kumar argues that the practical differences for children were probably less significant than previously thought.[8]

The growing rejection of 'traditional' education led a number of Indian, colonial and missionary pedagogues to focus on educational methodologies rather than the content of the curriculum. New Education stressed the central role of the child and encouraged learning through experience at a pace that suited the individual, with less emphasis on both curriculum and teacher.[9] This was influenced by a number of Western pedagogues such as Dewey and Montessori; theories such as Group Method and Project Method, Dalton Plan and earlier ideas such as Froebel's Kindergarten movement and Pestalozzi's Object Lessons.[10] Parna Sengupta details early experimentation with object lessons in Bengali mission schools where they were used to encourage Indian children to progress from describing objects to categorising them to then expressing abstract ideas, reflecting the intangible truths and ideas associated with Protestant Christianity.[11] The global circulation of these ideas and the emergence of Indians as 'co-producers' of educational knowledge has been the subject of considerable recent historiographical attention and was indicated in affiliations and contacts between educational experts internationally.[12] For example, the International Movement in Progressive Education and New Education Fellowship gained particular prominence in the 1920s, a specifically Indian section being started in 1933 under the presidency of Dr Rabindranath Tagore.[13] This reflected wider global networks of exchange, often centred around new hubs of international cooperation and knowledge exchange, such as the League of Nations.[14]

The pedagogical journal the *Educational India* was established in 1934 as a forum for Indian educational theorists and practitioners to engage with these new pedagogical ideas at a local level. The journal was billed as 'a high class monthly'. It was edited by a number of prominent pedagogues, including M. Venkatarangaiya of Andhra University, along with C. Swamikannu Paul, M. Seshachalam, C. B. Krishnasastri and later D. Nityananda Sastry.[15] Based in Masulipatam, it received disproportionate interest and contributions from south India. While earlier pedagogical journals, such as the *Schoolmaster* from the 1880s and 1890s, were dominated by reprinted articles from journals abroad, the *Educational India* contained original articles generally authored by Indians. Most contributors had prominent jobs within the teaching profession—as principals of high schools or university professors—although some, such as the Dewan of Mysore, had been bureaucrats in the Madras Education

Department.[16] Despite a majority of male authors, a few women submitted articles; for example, Mrs Chenciah wrote extensively on infant education and Mrs K. Satthianadhan on education and parenting.[17] It is noteworthy too that while the contributors were highly engaged in global pedagogical theories and active followers of global trends, they were also definitely provincial and few had the personal networks or travel experience that defined the cosmopolitan elites of the all-India nationalist movement. The journal claimed to be 'devoted to the investigation … of the current problems of Indian education, from the theoretical as well as the practical standpoint' and to 'carry out such an analysis and suggest improvements based on the actual experience of the people at large'. It saw education as the 'primary responsibility' of the government as an 'organised representative of the nation', but suggested that the government needed to be 'guided by those who are in touch with public opinion'. The journal thereby claimed to be both expert and representative. It was explicitly designed for members of the teaching profession, managers of institutions and the general public, although the size of the print run and circulation is unclear.[18] The *Educational India* primarily reflected the sharing of ideas among a small professional local elite, with more evidence of entanglement in global theoretical debate than serious attempts to cause practical change in the lives of Indian children.

Learning through Activity

The fundamental premise of New Education was the engagement of the child-learner in structured activities rather than rote learning, and this was discussed at length in the *Educational India*. Children were expected to learn through self-experimentation and a 'scientific attitude of testing results and forming conclusions [which] is fatal to a blind belief in outworn tradition'.[19] The Moga teacher training school in Punjab was consistently cited as a model for progressive schools, and their teacher training course emphasised the importance of 'activity and experience rather than of knowledge to be accrued and facts to be stored'.[20] A further article on Moga emphasised that education should be 'student-centred' so that 'the student be made to think'.[21] While literacy and numeracy were vital outcomes of education, the implicit aim was to mould children into rationally thinking adults within their social context. Through attempting activities themselves, pupils were intended to understand the scientific foundations underlying the information they were acquiring, making it easier to remember and apply. For example, a craft such as weaving could be studied practically with each pupil participating. This, in turn, would lead to an explanation of its history, geography, and scientific and mathematical techniques, which could then be followed up by more extensive research in the school library. Learning would thus imitate at a very basic level the methodologies—hypothesis, experiment and conclusions—of experimental science.[22]

Literacy was to be taught through the active engagement of the pupils. For example, at Moga basic literacy was taught through 'a scientifically constructed method', which included material relating to the children's home experiences, story-telling, phonetics and silent reading.[23] Writing too was not to 'degenerate into a copying of set types' but rather become 'a satisfying creative effort' as the pupils were 'encouraged to express their real joys through the pen'.[24] Illustrations and excursions were to be utilised. Education was to be scientific, not literary, and was to cover not 'only the dreams of the power and transcripts of the novelists, but also the more concrete achievements of the scientist and social reformer'.[25] The sciences of biology, geography and economics thus took precedence over literature when it came to providing the emergent citizen with the skills and understanding to negotiate the modern world.[26] Geography, for example, was intended to provide the child with analytical and information gathering skills, to make the child aware of themselves and their distinctive place in the world and to foster an acceptance of cultural difference, which would contribute to 'universal peace'.[27]

While New Education was based on active learning and teaching scientific methodologies that exercised 'the elements of thought embedded in the juvenile mind', it was explicitly differentiated from the vocational education so favoured by the Education Department.[28] Moral values were intended to underpin the entire curriculum. Competitive recreation and team sports were intended to 'teach the boys to respect the rights of others and to trust those who play with or against them', while at Moga children learned prudence and budgeting through receiving monetary rewards for their work.[29] Living together in cottages gave children the opportunity to build strong interpersonal relationships within families and communities.[30] There was limited empirical evidence of the impact of these ideas, but the educational objectives were clear: the formation of children into trustworthy, self-aware adult citizens, trained through active cooperation and responsibility. In the end, these teachers believed 'the pen may be mightier than the sword; but the spade and the needle are better than either'.[31]

Pedagogy as Science

Rather than placing the curriculum at the centre of education, the educators at the Imperial Education Conference in London in 1923 reiterated that the child as a learner was to be the focal point.[32] Not content with teaching children scientific methods for acquiring learning, each child was to become a special object of scientific study, with pedagogy as a scientific discipline.[33] This was linked to an interest in the natural development of the normal child and pedagogical uses of psychology, as seen particularly in the works of developmental psychologist Jean Piaget.[34] G. S. Krishnayya, of Teachers College, Kolhapur, maintained that 'matters of the mind might be investigated with scientific precision and mathematical accuracy'.[35] This made possible a scientific approach within the classroom, and an understanding of child psychology and 'normal' child development was regarded as more important for trainee teachers than an understanding of the curriculum.[36] Numerous articles in the *Educational India* described the mind in great detail.[37] Purported scientific intelligence tests assessed a child's ability to acquire and process information. These were used to calculate the mental age of the child, in comparison with his/her chronological age, as set against the 'normal' average of 100 per cent.[38] The emphasis within the classroom was to categorise children by intelligence, thereby identifying 'laggards' who inhibited other students and were excluded to prevent their own supposed 'incurable inferiority complex'.[39] This involved the differentiation between those with 'remediable educational backwardness' and those with 'innate dullness'.[40] The 'feeble-minded' were not only presumed to be incapable of learning but were assumed to be more susceptible to social deviance. More explicit than the majority of educators, M. S. Srinivasa Sarma of National College, Trichinopoly, engaged directly with contemporary eugenics debates and highlighted 'imbeciles, idiots and morons' as a 'positive menace to society'.[41] This problematic entanglement of progressive pedagogy, scientific measurement of intelligence and eugenics was not uncommon in the British context, and clearly also impacted conversations on the subcontinent.[42] Equally significant, the child's mind was undifferentiated by race or caste in any of the discourses, a significant assumption of universality and a rejection of colonial racial hierarchy.

By establishing education as a scientific discipline that informed and legitimised 'progressive' pedagogical methods, the pedagogues claimed to be objective and rational experts who operated under 'the liberating force of the scientific spirit'.[43] By self-definition, their expertise was therefore in no need of regulation by either politicians or the public.[44] The Indian experts were keen to establish themselves as partakers in a Western intellectual heritage of specialist pedagogues, intimately engaged in a global project.[45] Indian educators tried to situate themselves as unequivocally equal participants in a global discourse and pointed to experiments, such as those at the Lady Willingdon College, as more progressive than the education system in both the United States and Great Britain.[46] This is perhaps reflected in their desire to publish so voluminously in English. Indian experts were claiming control not only over education policy but also over the understanding of children's minds in the name of their own scientific expertise.

The privileged place of the expert can be seen in the extended reaction to Gandhi's educational plans, which became the subject of many articles, including a critical editorial, in 1937 and 1938.[47] Gandhi argued that Indian handicrafts such as spinning should be taught 'scientifically' so that children understood the mechanical aspects and this would lead to a further investigation of literacy, history and arithmetic necessary for the successful completion of the process.[48] Gandhi's central argument—strikingly linked to progressive pedagogy in both methodology and terminology—was that learning should happen through scientific methods of observation and experimentation. This would help students develop their physical, rational and spiritual faculties and reinforce the dignity of rural labour without challenging the social hierarchy.[49] While there was broad support for the political goals of the Mahatma among the pedagogues, there was also an underlying frustration that his ideas were a less sophisticated model of their own ideas developed over the last twenty years.[50] In addition, his one clear innovation, that schools should be self-supporting by selling the children's craftwork, was bitterly opposed by pedagogues and politicians as effectively legalising child labour.[51] The fear that children were to be made financially responsible for their own education through a discourse of self-sufficiency illustrated a firm commitment to the vulnerable child and the responsibility of the state to provide for the child as a learner. It also demonstrated the concern of the pedagogues that a politician was threatening their claims of scientific expertise.[52] This may also explain why there was only one article on Tagore's educational experiment at Shantiniketan, and it is noticeable that while Tagore receives much contemporary attention for his progressive strategies, he received much less attention from contemporary pedagogues.[53]

Specialist pedagogues, headmasters and psychologists bolstered their own position as equals in an international discourse by embracing universality and scientific expertise over cultural specificity. This provided another space in which to defy British cultural imperialism.[54] The first edition of the *Educational India* reprinted both the 1924 Geneva Declaration and 'International Goodwill: League's Appeal to Children', emphasising that a rationalist education was essential to world peace.[55] Later, an article on the 'State and Education' emphasised that education was not 'a matter of charity and philanthropy; but today it is a matter of right'.[56] However, while the activities of the provincial governments were summarised in each issue of the *Educational India*, neither the idea of education as a 'right' nor the state's role in enforcing the child's right to education through compulsion received any further attention.[57] A terminology of children's rights was slowly beginning to be introduced in the state-level discourses of juvenile delinquency and compulsory education, demonstrating the global networks of the social reformers and political elites. The lack of attention paid by pedagogues to this parallel discourse perhaps reflects the particularly academic nature of their concerns about the child and the reluctance to engage with the messy business of interacting with real children and real parents.

Constructing the 'Normal' Child

Underlying the global theories of child-centred education emerging in the 1920s and 1930s were certain normative assumptions relating to what it meant to be a child whose claims were based on the scientific ability to know and analyse the child. At its most basic, childhood development was seen in terms of the psychological IQ tests in which children were categorised in relation to the 'average child' (mental age = chronological age).[58] There was frequent mention in the journals of the 'natural development' of the child and 'the law of the child'.[59] The primary feature of the normal child was their desire to learn through activity and active engagement with their environment.[60] 'Adventurous self-learning' was perceived to contribute to the child's gradual development in the rational understanding of the world.[61] The child was described as characterised by curiosity, creativity and the constant active search for new experiences through which to develop.[62] For Venkateswaran, this was not only a scientific observation but also a more sentimental Romantic celebration of childhood emotion:

> Self-activity is the picture of child-life. We cannot overturn children in their natural impulses for their benefit. Their fancies and moods, their picturesque yearnings and adventurous imagination, their make-believe raptures, their dream-glories, are the immortal traditions of their nature.[63]

The natural activity of the young child was to play this also received a great deal of attention in the pedagogical literature. M. S. Srinivasa Sarma of National College, Trichinopoly, argued that play was 'most valuable' because 'it gives not only strength but courage and confidence, and contributes energy, decision and promptness to the will'.[64] Cooperative play was seen as practice for cooperating with peers in later life while satisfying an inherent love for experimentation and liberty.[65] This was linked to a desire for spontaneity and freedom, as well as action and even referenced in the *Taittiriya Upanishad*.[66] Srinivasa Sarma again reiterated:

> Play is the making of the moral man. It is the nursery of virtue, and generates a sense of fellowship and exerts a tremendous influence in moulding individuals and preparing them for social life, for co-operation, for submission and for leadership. It encourages friendly intercourse and a healthy rivalry between the members, and thus tends to the increase of mutual understanding and sympathy.[67]

Elevating the normal child as learning through play and self-discovery was the basis of New Education. This prioritised a particular form of learning as universal and established a broad pattern of growth for every child based on their natural cognitive and behavioural development, regardless of context. This pathologised any deviance from this pattern and universalised an overtly masculine and Western experience of childhood behaviour as normative or universal.[68] Education became 'the problem of directing the *normal growth* of the desirable type of character'.[69]

Facilitating normal growth and natural progression still required 'enlightened discipline' by adults.[70] Corporal punishment was rejected and the primary methods of discipline were to be covert surveillance and the inculcation of self-regulation, and this surveillance was intimately linked to the idea of 'love', in which teachers constantly watched, monitored and classified children as if in a laboratory.[71] Freedom to act or to play was to be undertaken within strictly defined parameters, although children were given the 'illusion of choice'. Education was intended

> to habituate the child in consecutive acts of right choosing and well doing, to develop in him healthful and sustained activities, to generate in him a sense of enlightened freedom and individual responsibility, and to inspire in him noble and expansive interests.[72]

Srinivasa Sarma argued that this had to be carried out 'without doing violence to the originality and the creative spirit of the pupils' but instead by bringing children 'into personal and intimate contact with all that is good, beautiful, and desirable' and giving them 'ample opportunities to regulate and discipline themselves in the light of these high and sublime ideals'.[73] The individual was to become 'a responsible moral agent' through 'the internalising of the ruling sanctions and values of the community in such a manner that they become the individuals' own and receive his voluntary assent and support'.[74] As individual children developed self-control and an understanding of normative behaviours, this in turn facilitated new forms of social discipline aimed at controlling whole populations.[75] The school became central to the regulatory apparatus of the modern state, not only in the overt disciplining of the timetable, building and uniform but also in the ways that children were monitored and moulded into the correct forms of being, thinking and learning and where any evidence of deviance from this normal pattern was pathologised.[76] The theories of progressive pedagogy were thus central to the disciplinary practices of modernity.

The Gendered Child

Gender difference was not given overt prominence in Indian pedagogical journals of the 1930s. Every issue had a 'Women's Page' written by Mrs K. Satthianadhan, founder of the *Indian Ladies Review*, but there was little reference to the elementary education of girls.[77] In secondary school, girls were expected to learn domestic work, reflecting the concerns of the journal's middle-class audience.[78] Articles on girls' schooling focused on the scientific training of girls in housework, human biology and botany.[79] The training intended that the girl child become a better mother and housewife, fitting in with the domestic and spiritual ideals of both the nationalist movement and conservative feminist ideals of middle-class domesticity and femininity.[80] Despite the interest in the political sphere, there was no overt interest in the expansion of female education, with more interest in a modernist perspective of the child as ungendered, but in effect male.

Despite the lack of overt gendering, the New Education models were closely linked to colonial and nationalist ideals of masculinity. The pedagogues resisted Western depictions of deficient Indian masculinity, arguing that the purpose of education was to teach children to gain 'mastery' over their circumstances by acting, not accepting.[81] Learning was discussed in terms of aggressive masculinity, in normative features of activity and experimentation that denoted both strength and courage and led to the development of rational self-control. The child was expected to practice 'self-mastery', and education was perceived in terms of 'exploration and conquest'.[82] The particular focus on masculine power as normative reflected the assumption that reason and science were located in the normal development of the male body and its ability to control both itself and nature, which facilitated its grasp of knowledge and truth.[83] The Indian pedagogues claimed this for the Indian child, contesting the racial implications of contemporary colonial discourse, and imagining the Indian child as equal to and sharing in a universal pattern of development, discussed in terms of 'the healthy, happy growth and fullest development of each individual child'.[84] Rather than claiming the 'native genius' of the Indian child, the pedagogues were claiming participation in a normative and universal, although originally Western, ideal of the child as an individual separate from the community.[85] Any suggestion that this might 'overemphasise the individual' and fail to recognise the child in the community was rejected as insufficiently modern.[86]

Indian Educators and the Indian Home

The almost exclusively Indian experts writing in the *Educational India* claimed their authority on the basis of their modern scientific training in pedagogy and their participation in global networks such as the New Education Fellowship, which meant that they were aware of new developments in the field. This was evidenced in their understanding of the universal child, and this claim that the Indian child also shared the characteristics of universal patterns of behaviour both challenged the racial hierarchies of the West and simultaneously reinforced the dominance of colonial views of childhood in which the aim of the child's development was to dominate his environment. The pedagogues also claimed authority through their claim to represent the 'particular native genius' of the Indian people.[87] This understanding was based on the contention that the Indian context was distinctive while universalising the individual Indian child. There was no attempt, for example, to replicate the international study of the 'African child's psychology' for the Indian subcontinent.[88] There was also no reference to the distinct educational challenges of differing communities, such as Muslim girls, or even the specific educational requirements of the poor, which claimed considerable political attention (see Chapter 2). The occasional reference to a collective identity in the journals was only in the context of the *national* community and the rights and responsibilities of citizenship in relation to the nation state.[89] What is unclear is whether the pedagogues were so focused on a particular construction of the universal child's needs and wants that they viewed the specific context of community and identity as unimportant, or whether this absence was a more consciously political decision to reject traditional identities as uneducated bigotry in view of a more modern, secular approach to both education and the future Indian state.[90]

When the pedagogues in the *Educational India* discussed the Indian context, they prioritised themes of 'culture' and 'home' over racial and religious identity. In nationalist rhetoric, the home was constructed as the repository of the spiritual and cultural views of the nation, but this was in practice the home of the educated middle classes, reflecting the domestic situation of the Indian pedagogues themselves.[91] By contrast, the poor Indian home depicted in the journals was perceived to be the key site of threat to the child and was denigrated as the centre of traditional values and as a site of moral and intellectual corruption.[92] In particular, it subsumed the individual identity of the child within a collective identity of family and community. The poor home with its 'cribbed and confined domestic atmosphere' made it 'impossible' for children 'to feel youth's sense of adventure', endangering the child's ability to be a child and subordinating their desires to domestic and social pressures.[93] The child was in danger at home, but the threat came from moral corruption and lack of ambition rather than financial insecurity. Any differences in religion, class or caste were regarded as learned prejudice that developed within children as a result of a bad environment.[94] This was framed as the effect of uneducated parenting coupled with a flawed cultural understanding of the vulnerability of childhood and the need for education, de-legitimising other forms of identity as unmodern.[95] Sons were threatened by a lack of discipline and overindulgence by their mothers, while all children were perceived to be at threat from despotic fathers who were disinterested in parenting but violently enforcing their authority, often while intoxicated, and 'unfit to be the moral guardian of his children'.[96] The inability, or unwillingness, of poor parents to acknowledge and protect the perceived innocence of the child meant that children were exposed to moral danger, whether in the form of *nautch* (dance) parties, indecent language or corrupting outdoor spaces.[97] This reflects the concerns about prostitution in Chapters 5 and 7. The idea that most social problems could be traced to an 'unbalanced home life' reflected long-term anxieties by the colonial state and Indian middle classes about the unregulated space of the poor Indian home.[98]

If learning in the early years was primarily based on observation and imitation, Srinivasa Sarma maintained that the 'chief incubator of nervous disorders and misanthropic tendencies is the home'.[99] This suggests a class-based modernising agenda that gave the experts the power to represent, analyse and control lower-class children whose parents endangered the normal development of their children through traditional beliefs and disciplinary practices. The pedagogues provided the solution in the person of the modern teacher, who could both teach new values and model new ways of being modern.¹⁰⁰ The modern knowledge and discipline of the school were also to be brought into the home through the promotion of middle-class hobbies such as stamp collecting or uniformed organisations such as scouting.¹⁰¹ Nandini Chandra has shown how comics such as *Amar Chitra Katha* were used to promote national values and new loyalties and ways of seeing the self, family and nation, bringing modern values into the home.¹⁰² Pedagogues, such as Dr G. S. Krishnayya of Teachers College, Kolhapur, provided extensive advice to parents on discipline, leisure and play, while others wrote explicitly in terms of the 'regulation of home life'.¹⁰³ Expertise gave authority to intervene in the family and proved that education could only be conveyed properly by those trained to provide it.¹⁰⁴

While introducing Indian content into the curriculum, the pedagogues writing in the *Educational India* constructed the home environment of the child in terms of lack. The study of pedagogy and child development claimed to be both universal and politically neutral but was founded upon hegemonic cultural and epistemological assumptions that emphasised a particular understanding of individuality, rationality and masculinity.¹⁰⁵ These were not borne of foreign cultural assumptions but resulted from the maintenance of a particular view of childhood as universally applicable, modern and scientifically proven, de-legitimising the multiple other experiences and understandings of childhood as incomplete and inferior.¹⁰⁶ The child was designated as a learner at a particular stage in a universal understanding of childhood development. This defined the child's identity as based on age rather than engaging with the multiple identities of caste, class and religion, which were part of the daily life of children in south India, and which directly affected their educational opportunities. Indian pedagogues sought to encourage a relationship between the individual child and the modern state, justifying their intervention in children's lives as experts, which in turn proved their own claim to intellectual equality with the West. In doing so, they were much more unequivocal in their condemnation of the poor Indian home than their political colleagues and allies.

Training Teachers in Progressive Pedagogy

The introduction of progressive educational methods into the classroom proved difficult. There was some attempt by the educational authorities to introduce vocational education in schools, but funding constraints meant that the primary mode of teaching remained rote learning.[107] Progressive pedagogy was taught to new teachers at a couple of the male teaching colleges, namely the London Mission Society Rural Community Training School, Erode, and the National Theosophical High School, Rishi Valley, Madanapalle. By comparison, a number of female-only teaching colleges prioritised training teachers in new ways of teaching and learning, perhaps sensing a new opportunity to develop a further area of specialisation for women.[108] The director of public instruction's (DPI's) *Quinquennial Reports* (1927–28 to 1931–32, 1932–33 to 1936–37) devoted an entire chapter of what was a largely statistical report to the pedagogical experiments of the Lady Willingdon Training College, Madras. This demonstrated support at the highest levels of the government for new educational techniques. The college, and the associated practice school, were established in 1922 by R. S. Subbalakshmi, the first woman graduate from the Madras Presidency and a renowned educationist.[109] Prominent in social reform networks, Sister Subbalakshmi had previously established a hostel for child widows and used the college as a means of educational and employment opportunities for them.[110] Leadership was later continued by two British women, Miss Gerrard and Miss R. Barrie, gaining sufficient recognition that they were interviewed by the Education Commission in 1928.[111] New pedagogical techniques were also used at the Teachers College, Saidapet, and the National Girls Schools, Mylapore, but archival evidence for all these institutions is very limited.[112]

Similarly, progressive techniques were used at the St Christopher's Training College, a missionary-led training college for women started by an Englishwoman, Miss Brockway, in 1923 in Madras.[113] In 1936, St Christopher's merged with the neighbouring Bentinck Girls High School in Vepery and was supported after 1942 by government grants.[114] St Christopher's was based explicitly on a tradition of educated Indian women, such as Nur Jahan or Mumtaz Mahal, as well as the example of St Christopher himself, who in the Christian tradition was recognised as 'the seeker who found God through helping a child'.[115] The institutions catered only for young women and were led by reforming headmistresses such as Miss Marjorie Sykes (Bentinck High School, Vepery), Miss Helen Veale (National Girls School, Mylapore) or Miss Carrie Gordon (Teacher's College, Saidapet), providing leadership opportunities for British women not possible in the metropole.[116] The young women who attended were a tiny minority, but teaching was becoming a socially acceptable opportunity for public service and a career for Indian women, particularly for child widows, while tertiary education significantly improved marriage prospects for middle-class girls.[117] Using progressive methods in female teacher training confronted the symbolism of the all-powerful male teacher and challenged earlier educational strategies of excessive discipline and rote learning. This trend towards training women teachers was not reflected in the *Educational India*, which remained predominantly male in authorship and focus, further reiterating the disjunction between theory and practice and the gender hierarchies of the presidency.

The teacher training schools explicitly rejected traditional pedagogies as producing 'parrot-like glibness' in which the majority of children 'remained apathetic, dull and uninterested'.[118] The teacher training involved a complete rejection of an 'unpractical and bookish mentality', replacing it with 'awakening intelligence' and, at Saidapet, 'cultivat[ing] individual freedom and self-control'.[119] The experiments at Lady Willingdon College had three explicit aims:

1. to fit pedagogical methods more soundly to the psychological needs and the laws of child development;
2. to make teaching and curricula progressively more scientific and more socially and culturally effective;
3. to discover how to utilise the natural self-activity of the child for its own 'self-education'.[120]

The first aim emphasised the child as the site of scientific experimentation and entailed teaching physiology, psychology and pedagogy so as to equip teachers to understand the child. Similarly, the training at St Christopher's was explicitly based on the theories of recognised progressive pedagogues and psychologists such as Dewey, Thorndike, Kilpatrick and Bagley.[121] The nursery teacher, Mrs Suganthy Charles, visited Westhill College, Birmingham, to be trained in Froebel's Kindergarten ideas, and Maria Montessori herself visited the campus in 1939.[122] The students in all institutions were encouraged to recreate the scientific laboratory in the classroom through observation of the subject-child and applying a terminology of scientific principles. By 1936–37, students investigated 'the working and development of the human mind by observation, psychological experiment, intelligence testing and test analysis'.[123] This involved the complete study of the child, including anthropometric measurements and reports on social and family environment, school attainment, personality and health. All this work was undertaken on the assumption that individual children could be categorised according to their position on a normative developmental pattern and mirrored the scientific casework model used widely used in British social work from around the beginning of the twentieth century.[124]

At Lady Willingdon College, the students were taught to categorise the children to ensure their engagement in the correct stage of the 'great game of learning'.[125] As in the *Educational India*, the manuals described learning in masculine metaphors of mastery and control over activity, and the trainees were taught how to modify their lessons according to the intellectual development of each child. Children were categorised as 'the clever, the average, the dull' with a view to producing teaching strategies that meant that each child had a 'chance to work at his own pace'.[126] While the content was important, teachers were advised that keeping children interested and active meant that they were easier to control.[127]

The child at school was to understand, and thereby conquer, his environment. However, despite a brief mention of 'the demands of general culture' and the interest in learning Tamil, there was no engagement with education as specific to the Tamil or Indian context at Lady Willingdon College. By contrast, at St Christopher's, the young women had to engage more directly with the local environment. South Indian music, art, folk dance and handicrafts were taught with the intention that the children would be 'engaged in handwork of some delightful sort, not very easy to distinguish from playing with toys'.[128] A Girl Guide company was set up in 1926–27 with two teachers as captains, reflecting an increasingly popular way for Indian girls to engage with concepts of international sisterhood and to participate in international organisations and knowledge networks.[129] Through this the trainee teachers were taught 'Guiding as an Educational Method' and 'made experiments in Indianising the Guide ceremonies', for example, by saluting the Guide World Flag instead of the Union Jack.[130] Teaching was carried out in Tamil, although Telegu was later introduced, and there was a particular focus on training the teachers in Indian culture and history through a focus on natural history and on excursions to significant historical sites, originally Mahabalipuram and Vellore, but venturing to the cities of north India and the Deccan in subsequent years.[131] St Christopher's also engaged more self-consciously in reformulating ideas of the Indian home. The headmistress argued that parents and the Education Department inspectors were 'bewildered by the freedom allowed to the children', and that it took some time to persuade children to play with the toys 'creatively and imaginatively' in contravention of parental demands 'to be sure to be good and sit still!'[132] The Indian home was recognised as an 'affectionate hospitable place' but lacking in regularity and discipline in sleeping and eating habits.[133] At Saidapet, the course was explicitly geared to 'establish connections' or 'bridge the gulf' between schoolwork, the 'natural activities of children' and the home, which was described very consciously as an 'ally' in the educational endeavour.[134] Using the model of learning through activity, teachers taught children to 'acquire habits of healthy living' by practising good hygiene, although there was no evidence of attempts to teach a gendered curriculum of domestic work so often evidenced in secondary education of girls.[135] This focus on the 'cleanliness of person, surroundings, cleanliness in thought, word and deed' evidences a subtler attempt to regulate the children's home; to use children as a force for modernising change within the household and to educate subsequent generations in modern ideas of hygiene and cleanliness.[136]

In the 1920s and 1930s, there was a clear acceptance in the female training colleges that school should be characterised by a 'happy atmosphere of interested activity'.[137] A new generation of female teachers was taught to implement new scientific theories of child psychology and pedagogy in their everyday practice, and to categorise children according to their abilities. Trainee teachers used local material culture and traditions as teaching resources, and the children's homes and families were regarded as both allies and as the targets for improvement through the medium of increasing the hygiene and time discipline of the children. At the same time, there is no evidence in the surviving archives that teachers were taught how to negotiate the consequences of local identities based on caste, religion and gender identities on children's educational opportunities and experiences. The failure to train new teachers to reconcile the local and universal in social practice was perhaps another indication of why the changes in pedagogical thinking had so little practical impact and of the continued disjunction between 'espoused theory' and 'theory-in-use' in the classroom.[138]

Working Out Progressive Pedagogy in the Local School
The Children's Garden School was set up in Madras in 1937 with the specific intention of implementing progressive education in an Indian environment.[139] The founders were a husband and wife team, Mrs Ellen Sharma and Dr V. N. Sharma; Dr Sharma was a Telegu Theosophist and Mrs Ellen a German educated in history, art and psychology.[140] They met at the pioneering Odenwald Schule in Germany before moving to Madras, starting a school with seven children in September 1937. The school grew steadily, introducing free midday meals in 1938, and it was recognised by the government as a special school in 1939.[141] By 1942, 132 pupils attended and the school moved to its current location, adding a middle school in June 1945, followed by a training school for Kindergarten teachers, a women's hostel and a crèche.[142] By the 1970s it had become an important teacher training institution and in the last five years has received considerable international attention.[143] The school provided education in the mornings from 8 to 11 a.m. for children aged three–eight years, with instruction in English, Tamil and Telegu. There was an admission fee of 1 rupee with a continuing monthly fee of 3 rupees.[144] In 1941 the school was divided into eight educational stages by intelligence rather than age.[145] The following discussion offers a qualitative assessment of the school's values and practices as the founders sought to create 'a new system of education, uniting the best of what they had learnt in Europe, with the ancient traditions and culture of India'.[146] This was an explicit attempt to situate these new ideas about the child and education in the local Indian context, although they recognised that this view of a child had a distinctively European heritage.

The Children's Garden School clearly paralleled the scientific pedagogical rhetoric of contemporary educational journals, claiming authority through scientific understanding based on detailed information gathering. The annual inspection of 1944 reported that the kindergarten section was 'pre-eminently a pedagogic laboratory'.[147] Teachers compiled a 'detailed personal history of each child', and watched 'the activities and interests of the child, keeping careful records of its psychological and mental reactions'.[148] The overt philosophical influence was German; the founding quotation 'Let each be perfect in himself' came from Goethe, while the school's name was inspired by Froebel as a 'garden of learning, where children could learn through play, without fear, and with freedom to express themselves and to awaken their innate talents'.[149] According to the former headteacher of the kindergarten, and confidante of Ellen Sharma, M. S. Rajalakshmi, '... the works of these German intellectuals helped Indians to know India.'[150] At the same time, she condemned colonial and missionary education, which turned children into 'imitative parrots' through rote learning and produced a system in which Indians 'blindly aped Western ways ... totally unaware of art, culture and greatness' of India and alien to Indian 'ways and values'.[151] The Sharmas were also critical of the focus on religious texts within Indian pedagogy, unequivocally rejecting both 'religious dogmatism and cultural and economic imperialism'.[152] By contrast, Rajalakshmi claimed Ellen Sharma personified 'the spiritual wisdom of India and the scientific outlook of the West', an explicit recognition that the school was attempting to combine principles espoused as universal with local traditions and understandings.[153]

While Goethe provided the foundational quotation, the school emblem was the banyan tree as an 'ancient symbol for wisdom and shelter', with children swinging from the roots. The Garden School was designed to reflect the *gurukala* system, based on a 'feeling of familial closeness' centred around Dr Sharma as the *guru*.[154] The school was imagined in terms of an extended family and community, with the Sharmas assuming the role of 'surrogate parents' and fulfilling positions in the school that mirrored the gender relations of Victorian domestic life.[155] The education received was to 'train the child as a member of the community sharing its life with others and helping comrades as a preparation for wider and fuller services in the world'.[156] This involved removing the child from the influence of servants and ayahs and placing him under the 'careful guidance of trained teachers' who would encourage the child to become 'independent, courageous, spontaneous, active and social'.[157] When inspected by the DPI, the Sharmas argued that it was one of the few 'child centred' schools where teachers 'play the part of guides', a mentoring rather than overtly corrective role.[158] A retired teacher insisted that 'discipline begins outside the self with submission to authority, but true discipline ultimately comes largely from within'.[159] Using love to encourage self-regulation was key to the disciplinary strategy of the school.

The material culture of the school was to be both Indian and progressive. The initial exhibitions for parents and supporters included dolls and cars for the younger children, a handiwork table, an individual occupations table, a group work table and a school material table.[160] The curriculum involved traditional Indian *kummi* (folk) exercises, and the equipment was made of Mysore wooden beads, tamarind and eucalyptus seeds, coconut shells, pine cones, waste paper, colourful threads and palm leaves.[161] Ellen Sharma also began working with toy manufacturers to produce specifically Indian toys as a way to persuade parents that toys were a necessary investment in children's development and play was a natural part of childhood.[162] Songs and play materials were all sourced locally. Local dances were a particularly important aspect of school life used to teach 'undisciplined wild little fellows' self-control and 'obedience to an idea, not to a person'.[163] Lessons were taught through play; for example, the children set up a small bazaar in class and bought and sold goods, while grammar was learned through language games and flash cards and maths through indoor and outdoor games and drawings in the sand.[164] The outside too was refitted with a playing field, skipping ropes, a sandpit, a climbing ladder and see-saws, and the school had two groups of cubs and bulbuls, as well as scouts.[165] Yet, while the teacher had a role as a facilitator, it was recognised that 'you cannot teach a child any more than you can grow a plant ... the child also teaches itself'.[166] The child here was primarily seen as a learner engaging actively with their surroundings and seeing inspiration and opportunity in their community and cultural traditions.

The Sharmas aimed to institute policies that would explicitly contribute to a 'more all-India and International (Universal) atmosphere in all spheres of our educational work'.[167] This meant that all pedagogy should be 'what distinctly suits the Indian child'.[168] With this focus on the formation of 'a real India school', the Sharmas emphasised that 'there is no differentiation in the school between castes and creeds, poor or rich'.[169] Equality was absolutely fundamental to the ethos of the school, and rich, middle-class and poor children were all explicitly welcomed and treated equally 'so that no distinction or bar may be felt in the plastic minds of the little ones themselves'. Teaching was carried out in a multiplicity of Indian languages—Marathi, Malayalam, Bengali, Canarese and Tamil—although with an overarching focus on English as a common language. There was an explicit recognition of all religions so that 'no child is compelled to do anything against his or her creed', but respect for all was cultivated, alongside a teaching of morality and ethics.[170] Within this school, both universal norms and communal identity were explicitly recognised as necessary for the development of the child.

Undoubtedly the school progressed because it was supported by prominent members of the community. The school was opened by Sri Sami Saswatanandaji, president of Ramakrishna Mission.[171] An advisory committee was started in 1938, and a parents' committee in 1940, and parents were encouraged to get involved in the school. The advisory committee comprised of prominent social reformers, such as Sister R. S. Subbalakshmi, former headmistress of Lady Willingdon College, D. T. Chiranjivi, principal of Wesley Training College Dr Sharifa Hamid Ali, a leading Muslim campaigner for women's rights within the All India Women's Conference (AIWC) and Mrs A. C. Krishna Rao, a founder (along with the Sharmas) of the Stree Seva Mandir to provide for poor women and children. It was presided over by S. N. Panchanadeswar, a prominent educator.[172] They were visited by a number of illustrious people, including the minister of education and the chief minister, and received donations from individuals such as the last British governor of Madras, Sir Archibald, and Lady Nye.[173] When the new building opened in November 1941, it was blessed by his holiness Sri Swami Sasvatananda Maharaja with public support from the advocate general and the Madras Children's Aid Society (MCAS) member T. R. Venkataram Sastri, the district education officer and the assistant commissioner of police.[174] These, predominantly Indian, individuals were involved in social reform movements and philanthropic work but had very close ties as officials and professionals to the political and bureaucratic establishment.[175] The mention of so many prominent names highlights not only the degree of commitment to children's education but also a general agreement with the Sharmas' interpretation of progressive pedagogy. This can be extended to suppose a broad agreement, among this elite, with their perception of what constituted the child learner.

When New Education was implemented, the practitioners had to engage with the context of India in a much more profound way than the pedagogues who merely engaged with ideas in the *Educational India*. While the Sharmas accepted these new pedagogical theories, and applied them scientifically, they had to use the limited materials available imaginatively and also to engage with the everyday reality of the child. This meant that there was much more focus on the daily concerns of teaching in multiple languages, of providing breakfast to poor children and developing strategies to deal with a number of conflicting religious beliefs. In addition, the Sharmas had to demonstrate to the surrounding community the validity of these ideas to maintain funding for the school. While the impact of the school might have been more limited than the journals, the Sharmas suggested a more nuanced appreciation of the combination of Western and Indian ideas regarding both pedagogy and children. This was revealed in the gentler pedagogical focus on activity rather than mastery; the more thoughtful interaction with the context and the frequent use of horticultural examples, which indicated more awareness of the limitations of training a living being.

Conclusion

A study of the introduction of New Education adds a further layer to our understanding of the discursive constructions of Indian childhood by a small professional elite in Madras in the 1920s and 1930s. By specifically distancing themselves from 'traditional' India seen in both colonial and pre-colonial pedagogies, and by dismissing the more overtly political educational ideas of leaders such as Gandhi and ignoring political debates over the expansion and funding of compulsory education, the pedagogues writing in the *Educational India* proved their own credentials as modern scientific experts. As Indians, the pedagogues claimed a unique role in understanding and representing the child in the Indian context. However, their power to define and explain was legitimised by their role as experts in a universal science of pedagogy and the use of scientific testing and categorisation. The emphasis on science reflected the self-positioning of a locally based elite eager to resist British colonialism through a demonstration of intellectual and moral equality and keen to contribute to what they perceived to be a global circulation of modern ideas. This scientific authority also justified the disregard for the Indian home, which was framed as a threat to the child and to the modern project. This contrasted with the more overtly political educational actors seen in earlier chapters.

Underpinning the new pedagogical ideas was a particular construction of the child as a learner, to be found within the institution of the school.

This child was playful and malleable and acquired knowledge through engaging actively in the learning process. Through activity the child could gain mastery over the curriculum but also over themselves, internalising the values of rationality and self-discipline. This positioned Indian children as equal to those in the West, including both in a universal developmental sequence. This normative construction contributed to the emerging global idea that biological immaturity—recognised variously as innocence, physical vulnerability or intellectual plasticity—was the most important social identity in the life of the child and informed all their social relationships. There was no perceived need to theorise the 'Indian child', despite the multiplicity of ways in which childhoods were experienced on the subcontinent. Rather, in their writings about children, the pedagogues placed age, or childhood, as the primary identifier above national, communal or gender identities, which were associated with non-modernity or assumed to be important in adulthood.

The claim that the modern view of scientifically measured childhood was universally applicable de-legitimised the multiple other experiences and understandings of childhood as incomplete and inferior. This de-legitimised the childhood experience of the majority of children within the presidency who failed to attend even elementary schooling.[176] The individuals working with children on a daily basis, at the teacher training colleges and the Children's Garden School, evidence a much more nuanced understanding of this relationship between universal childhood and the Indian context. While Lady Willingdon College implemented the more theoretical aspects of pedagogy and science, both St Christopher's College and the Children's Garden School used Indian materials and local dance traditions within their teaching. Not merely focusing on the child as an individual, the Sharmas and other trainee teachers directly sought to acknowledge and accommodate the multiplicity of the cultural, religious and socio-economic backgrounds of the children in their classroom. While the teachers remained committed to the progressive theory, and were concerned about the home situation of many children, the daily engagement with poverty, with parents and with the children themselves, seems to have made the teachers more understanding of the role of the individual within the wider community. They were noticeably less critical of the Indian home, or of the parents.

The interest in the Children's Garden School demonstrated the close links between the pedagogues and the reforming networks involved in other aspects of the child-saving project. As with the networks of juvenile justice reformers discussed in Chapter 6, the teachers were much more aware of their avuncular role within, rather than external to, the home community. The teachers legitimised their authority to intervene not only from being experts but also as semi-familial, as understanding the Indian home and context. Furthermore, the difference between the pedagogical journals and the practicalities of working with children evidences another form of the disjunction between theory and practice so often noticed by contemporaries and in the historiographical literature. This may also have a gendered dimension, with teachers at the training colleges and the Children's Garden School being almost exclusively female. Ultimately, constructing modern binaries of 'adulthood and childhood', of playful versus responsible, or of learning versus working, was not appropriate in the lives of most children in the Madras Presidency and certainly did not reflect their experience or opportunities.

4

Producing the Healthy Schoolchild

The intimate link between the body of the child and its intellectual development became a key aspect of the expanding educational concerns within the Madras Presidency in the 1920s and 1930s. The agreement within the Corporation of Madras that 'if you cannot feed the body of a child you cannot feed the brain' reflected a radical redefinition of the role of education authorities and a significant change in state welfare provision.[1] This chapter explores the links between health, nutrition and education and the expansion of the authority of the state over the body of the schoolchild, and the implications for the child's position as a future citizen. The introduction of the medical inspection of children allowed policymakers to 'know' the child statistically and to chart the health of the school population. This increased knowledge provided the statistical backing for a number of practical interventions, the most notable being the attempt to establish a paediatric hospital and the introduction of a scheme to provide free midday meals for impoverished schoolchildren funded by the Madras City Corporation.

The new interventions in children's health reflect the self-positioning of a modern elite who demonstrated their right and ability to rule through the introduction of progressive and science-based welfare reforms.[2] Attempts to define the child statistically, departmental differences over funding and organisation and political discussions over intervention, all reveal that south Indian policymakers and politicians saw themselves as the state, were prepared to use the new powers granted in the Government of India 1919 Act and actively claimed the authority and responsibility to intervene in the intimate sphere of the family.[3] This was not an overt rejection of colonial practices of governmentality but rather their reformulation within a local context by Indians as they established themselves as modern state actors, often through similar strategies of population control and development that built on earlier colonial practices.[4] The details of the health schemes reveal how this functioned in the local context, in the relationships between provincial and municipal governments, and as the definitions of education and public health were reformulated at discursive and practical levels. While the nationalist elite was beginning to articulate new visions of the post-colonial state, the *practice* of self-government at the level of province and municipality changed how Indians perceived the role and function of the state in society, encouraging a commitment to a socially interventionist state that would continue to inform the welfare and planning policies of a newly independent India.

The elite policymakers and civil society actors combined a commitment to modern science with a new claim to authority to intervene in the basic functions of the Indian family. This authority was firmly based on the emerging discipline of nutritional science and wider assumptions about biomedicine and its legitimacy to inform modern state practice.[5] It mirrored a wider internationalist humanitarian agenda that promoted famine relief and health provision for the vulnerable by the state and civil society organisations, but contained its own implicit epistemological violence by prioritising Western scientific practices. Modern science de-legitimised traditional healing and feeding practices, or indeed other ways of considering medicine, the body and health, including traditional Ayurvedic and Unani medical traditions.[6] This was closely linked to the claim to intervene in the family as Indian, a contention based not so much on racial or national differences as not-British, but on a semi-familial understanding of local, cultural and household practices and hierarchies in which the middle classes seem to have seen their role almost as part of the extended family. The ways in which these new forms of authority changed relationships between experts, parents and local councillors formed an important backdrop to new ideas about the child and child health.

Interventions in children's health offer another perspective on the way childhood itself was imagined and the link between the physical and intellectual development of the child, reflecting the earlier chapters on compulsory education. Increasingly, this reflected a wider conceptualisation that the health of the child's body represented the health of the nation itself, and building up a strong and virile nation was an important aspect of countering racialised colonial claims about Indian ability to govern.[7] Interventions to improve children's health were strategic investments in the nation's future, paralleled by investment in other sectors such as workers and pregnant coolies.[8] Children as 'becoming' were therefore increasingly recognised as valuable to the state as future citizens. This dovetailed with the growing interest in universalising narratives of the child's right to health and education. Children had a dual role as the vulnerable targets of welfare provision and as embodying the modernity of the state and the modern practices of its governing elites. There was also a hint of recognition of the child as 'being', with an independent opinion that adults should consider before making decisions, even if this was largely performative. This tension between the discursive construction of childhood as either universal or as specifically Indian was challenged as new health schemes were debated, implemented and the supposedly 'poor child' emerged as the particular target of modern state action.

Medical Inspection of Schoolchildren

The idea of the medical inspection of schoolchildren in the Madras Presidency appears to have been introduced first by the health officer for Bangalore at the 1912 Madras Sanitary Conference.[9] Although the idea was dismissed, a further two articles appeared in the *Lancet* in 1913, demonstrating the growing interest in the impact that school sanitation had on the health and productivity of students.[10] The idea was seized upon with alacrity following the First World War. A number of expert bodies were formed to provide advice, such as the Advisory Committee on Public Health Administration (1922), comprised of both medical practitioners and local councillors.[11] This reflected a growing, particularly gendered, interest in maternal and infant health interventions both within Madras and across British India.[12] It also reflected the priorities of the Indians now participating in governance. In 1926 the provincial government introduced a scheme of school medical inspection for all students in secondary education under the direct control of the director of public instruction (DPI).[13] The scheme was extended in 1928 to include colleges and all elementary schools in areas where elementary education was compulsory and became a condition for government funding for all schools under private management.[14] In 1932 the scheme was abandoned due to budgetary restraints, with the exception of schools within the Poonamalle Health Unit, a rural area to the west of Madras City that acted as an experimental site for provincial and international health programmes.[15] This paralleled developments in other provinces. Eventually, in 1941 the all-India Central Advisory Board of Education and Central Advisory Board of Health formed a joint committee to provide 'systematic attention to the health of children'.[16] This aimed to encourage educational success through cooperation between departments and between regions of India.

Running parallel to the presidency-based initiatives, in 1922 it was decided by the Health Committee of the Municipal Corporation of Madras that the medical officers in charge of corporation dispensaries should carry out a medical inspection of all children in elementary schools under direct corporation management.[17] The scheme was quickly deemed impracticable and a special officer was appointed as an 'experimental measure'. This second proposal was initiated by the Education Committee and received support from across the chamber—particularly from the Justice Party—although the cost of implementation was disputed.[18] By the end of 1923, 5,670 boys from thirty-eight corporation schools had been inspected, allowing the public health commissioner to declare 'school medical inspection, though in its infancy, has taken root'.[19] The corporation continued to expand medical inspection throughout the city for elementary schools, particularly in areas under compulsory education. In 1939 four medical inspectors and two female inspectors carried out the inspection of 17,258 boys and 11,884 girls (about 87 per cent and 83 per cent, respectively, of those on the school rolls).[20]

Driven by modern scientific ideas of governmentality and progress, the statistical surveillance of the population facilitated public health interventions and new modes of governance and assisted in the creation of new forms of political subjectivity, not 'colonial' given the influence and strategic direction provided by Indians, but certainly not distinctively Indian either.[21] The medical inspection of children enabled policymakers to evidence their own modernity and the modernity of the state while increasing the regulation of children's bodies, which began to take on a role as almost embodying the modernity of the state. This mirrored earlier developments in Britain in which a statistical 'knowing' of the child helped to radically redefine the state's role in relation to children.[22] Within the corporation, each inspection was carried out by a doctor of the grade of sub-assistant surgeon and included a full body examination 'from top to toe', which lasted about fifteen minutes.[23] In 1939, for example, the statistics detailed 9,357 boys (54 per cent) and 5,235 girls (44 per cent) as 'defective' and requiring treatment. Around 9 per cent boys and 3 per cent girls were listed for poor cleanliness and 13 per cent boys and 2 per cent girls for malnutrition.[24] This not only brought children under the intimate scrutiny of the expert but also brought them into personal contact with a representative of the state other than the teacher, still within the classroom but outside the control of parents and in very intimate ways. The production of statistics also contributed to the scientific evidence required within the emerging discourse of the body of the normal child and new assumptions about a normative development sequence.

Taking Responsibility for Children's Health

In his report of 1919, the health officer for the Madras Municipal Corporation made an impassioned plea for medical inspection. He argued that while provisions had been made for infant welfare and improvements to public health and sanitation, the corporation also had a responsibility for schoolchildren. This was not legally binding but rather 'a moral code, a code of conduct' that would facilitate the entry and retention of poor children in school and thereby 'be of the greatest advantage to the health of the whole Presidency'.[25] The health officer argued that 'any scheme for national well-being and prosperity' needed to start with children for 'the child of today is the citizen of tomorrow, and would be a useful asset or a drag on the nation according to its health'.[26] The idea of the child as a future citizen—and consequently as both an investment in the future nation and a responsibility of the modern state—was seen in the director of public health's argument that 'civilised humanity has come to realise, more particularly during the last 25 to 30 years, that the child problem is the greatest social question of the day'.[27] An interest in child health was not merely for the benefit of the child itself, but 'the welfare of the child is the welfare of the nation'. As Sudipa Topdar argues, the bodies of children became 'metaphors of citizenship and nation'.[28] This mirrored wider nationalist discourses that sought to build a healthy nation and to foreground the 'harmony between body, mind and spirit' as central to the cause of regenerating an independent Indian nation.[29] It reflected both international concerns about eugenics and national health and provided a space in which Indians were allowed, under the terms of devolved government, to imagine a future nation state.[30] In particular, modern science now highlighted the impact of 'minor disabilities appearing in childhood or early youth' and the possibility of 'far-reaching effects on health in later years if they are not properly treated in their early stages'.[31] In this discourse, children were portrayed as future adults, worthy of investment for their potential.

The child was imagined not only in terms of future value as an adult-in-the-making but also as a current rights holder who as a child, both innocent and vulnerable, had a claim to the protection of the state. The director of public health argued:

> Every child has the right to a fair chance of enjoying its heritage of life, and if the individuals primarily responsible for his birth are lacking in the knowledge essential for the fulfilment of their obligations to the child, it becomes the duty of the state and of society at large to interfere on behalf of those.[32]

This echoed British discourses, often linked to the British Chief Medical Officer Dr George Newman, who emphasised the need to 'arouse in the parents an interest in and a sense of responsibility for the care of their children'.[33] The corporation health officer agreed that compulsory education

> carried with it the further obligation on the parent or guardian to keep the children in a fit state of health for school attendance. The parent's duty is to see that the body of the child is maintained in a cleanly state; the master's to attend to the moral and mental equipment of the child.[34]

Later, in 1941, the all-India Jolly Report on medical inspection highlighted 'the essential unity of the child's life in his home and in the school'. However, when the parents failed to adequately care for their children, the report advocated that governmental agencies should step in, and the teacher was 'called in to use his influence and persuasive powers over the parents'.[35] In 1934 a list of the defective pupils was maintained by each teacher, whose duty was to 'sermonise as much and as often as possible to the parent on the adage—a clean mind in a clean body'.[36] In a rarely used phrase, the teacher was required to act in loco parentis, taking 'charge of sick children, as if they were their own parents'.[37] As the personification of the modern developmental state within the community, the health of the schoolchild also became the responsibility of the modern teacher.

The assumption that parents required external help to take an interest in the health of their children situated threat within the family and home, but recovery within the school.[38] This was seen when the corporation health officer stressed the 'extraordinary perfection commonly found in the newly-born' only to emphasise the corresponding problem that many children were 'doomed in advance to ill health and early death' largely as a result of the 'social customs, traditions and habits' which he perceived to be 'in many cases eminently hostile to his healthy development'.[39] While in the discourses of education and juvenile justice the parents and home were accepted as legitimate authorities, for example, in matters of religious affiliation, within public health discourses they were viewed as a particular danger and site of threat to the physical body of the child. In 1926, 27 per cent boys and 40 per cent girls were 'found to be dirty in their person and clothing, about 40% of them being verminous'.[40] The corporation health officer was clear that 'uncleanliness constitutes a sign of parental irresponsibility', an argument revisited in a number of debates over parental failure to supply adequate, or at least clean, clothing for their children.[41] The failure of parents to look after their children's health was linked to both ignorance and neglect. The corporation health officer assumed that disease was the result of 'insanitary conditions of the home' but that treatment was problematic because 'parents are very loathe to follow up the latter [hospital's] advice'.[42] Few of the boys prescribed treatment actually attended the hospital. This was probably a result of poverty but was attributed to the 'conservatism and mostly superstitious ignorance' of the parents.[43] In 1937, 4,860 parents were present during the medical examination of their children, although this initial attribution of care was undermined by the claim that parents were using the inspection as an opportunity to receive treatment for their own ill health.[44] While there was continued anxiety that poverty prevented treatment, the 1941 Jolly Report made it clear that the home (and particularly the mother) was a site of threat to colonial—and dyarchical—modernity and a source of opposition to modern hygiene and biomedicine, and that Indian experts viewed this as predominantly a cultural, not socio-economic, issue.[45]

Within the overarching claims of state interest, it was harder to define which elements of the government apparatus had responsibility for children's health. There remained continued confusion as to whether the gathering of statistics relating to schoolchildren should be a public health or educational concern, and whether this was the responsibility of the provincial government or the local authority. At the provincial level, inspection was carried out by medical practitioners but the results were organised and collated by the Education Department, which had oversight over the sanitation in schools using guidelines issued by the director of public health.[46] Within the corporation inspections were carried out under the oversight of the health officer, who issued a detailed annual report of statistics with funding provided at the local level.[47] Health Department officials worked closely with the Education Department and often reiterated that the importance of 'the education of the masses' was to combat 'ignorance and superstition', which continued to 'circumvent the best efforts of the sanitarian'.[48] More than that, officials argued that health improvements required an intentional collective societal effort, the health of the nation being 'a big and complicated question that can be satisfactorily solved only when all of us—the rich, middle classes and the poor—are all educated enough for citizenship and for properly discharging our duties by one another'.[49] Ultimately, citizens were intended to fit within the self-regulatory apparatus of the modern state.

Within the corporation scheme, medical inspectors were paid at the level of sub-assistant doctors. The 1938 budget introduced a scheme that used honorary medical inspectors to enlist public-spirited practitioners, paying them a small honorarium, strikingly similar to the honorary judges discussed in Chapter 6.[50] This fitted the principle of minimum expenditure, espoused by the Congress party councillor and former mayor S. Venkatachalam Chetty, who argued:

> It is our duty so far as the children in our schools are concerned to study finances and their health, and if possible, to help them to develop their

bodies. So it is not with a view to shirking our responsibility that I am making this proposal but I do want that the expenditure should be curtailed as far as possible.[51]

Despite initial support, the scheme was condemned in 1939 as an 'utter failure' apparently due to doctors being more interested in their own more lucrative private practices, and many councillors disowned the policy.[52] Equally significant was the growing disquiet felt over medical inspection itself and the feeling that the scheme produced 'no tangible good' and was an 'enormous waste of money' within a particularly stretched budget.[53] As with the question of education, there was a difference between a theoretical acceptance of the need for medical inspection and a political commitment to pay for it. The corporation health officer's frustrated comment in 1921, describing politicians as 'talking platitudes but achieving little', seems characteristic of the next twenty years, the ambition of the state rarely realised in practice.[54]

The quantitative collection of statistics and their reproduction in tables and graphs facilitated the monitoring of mortality rates and diseases of children in school, allowing a better understanding of children's bodies.[55] In 1936–37, for example, 17,761 boys and 11,615 girls were inspected, out of which 51 per cent boys and 36 per cent girls were recorded as 'defective' (14 per cent and 2 per cent respectively suffering from malnutrition).[56] Many were undernourished 'mainly due to lack of balanced diet and vitamins necessary for proper growth and development'.[57] The better result for girls appears to reflect the smaller numbers and higher socio-economic status of the girls attending school. The statistics contributed to the formation of a normative modern discourse surrounding the child as healthy, male and in school. Furthermore, it reflected Indian participation in wider global discourses that emphasised the universality of childhood development patterns, highlighted the normal body of the child as physically and statistically distinct from the adult body and provided the state with the tools with which to manage children's bodies. The director of public health stressed that 'it is not enough to point out defects without indicating how they can be rectified'.[58] Likewise, in Madras City there was a call for the chief medical officer not only to oversee the medical inspection but to 'find remedies', reflecting changing notions about governmentality and the interventionist potential of the modern state.[59] There was also significant support for early intervention and a recognition that medical inspection 'was more as a prevention than as a cure'.[60] This move from curative and reactive medicine—focused on epidemics and starvation through famine—to preventative medicine was part of a wider change in public health under dyarchy.[61] Medical inspection signified a distinctive change in the way the modern state's relationship was conceived, balancing both a modern responsibility to care for the vulnerable and a new governmental imperative to invest in future citizens.

Formulating a Response: Paediatric Medicine

One of the political responses to the health statistics at a provincial level was Dr Muthulakshmi Reddi's attempt to establish a hospital for children in Madras City in 1927.[62] This was intended to encourage the introduction of paediatrics as a medical specialism based around children, but not maternity, and the development of specific spaces to treat them.[63] The proposal in the Madras Legislative Council (MLC) was seconded by another medical practitioner, Dr B. S. Mallayya, who noted that children comprised about one-fifth of the population of Madras, and that of the 22,000 children born every year about 8,000 died from disease, with a mortality rate of ten times the adult population but with only one-tenth of the facilities.[64] Dr Mallayya alleged that this 'criminal waste of life among children' was because government funding was directed towards adult health, for example, the building of a new consumptive hospital rather than investment in the treatment of sick children. He also suggested that the overcrowded and unsanitary living conditions of the poorer classes which were so often the cause of illness were the result of long-term government neglect.

Reddi's own arguments were based on the notion of universalism, encapsulating both a universal childhood development sequence and the universal rights of the child. She argued that the lack of adequate healthcare was 'in direct contravention of the recognised principle observed in other civilised countries: "Mankind owes to the child the best it has to give"'. This quotation from the 1924 League of Nations Declaration on the Rights of the Child demonstrated Reddi's familiarity with the international feminist and child rights movements based around Geneva (see also Chapter 7 on the age of consent). The participation of Indian feminists in a 'transnational movement of ideas, personnel and technologies' and their membership of a global community of 'like-minded progressive thinkers' around issues such as child marriage and the trafficking of girls has been well established.[65] The claim to universalism was important. Reddi was constructing the child as a rights holder in the present and claiming that Indian children were equal to Western children and equally deserving of attention and resources. This directly contested both the racial hierarchies of imperial rule and the authority of the imperial power to decide the solution.[66] Likewise, Reddi demonstrated her engagement with childhood specialists such as Dr George Newman but also claimed authority as an Indian doctor and a woman to provide solutions specifically for the problems of the subcontinent, focusing on malaria or tropical jaundice rather than diseases peculiar to cold countries.[67] Indian specialists demonstrated their capabilities in contemporary research methodologies that reflected their training in biomedicine, which conceived of children as the object of experimentation and which focused on the production of quantitative evidence to define the healthy child as seen in the health officer's statistics. This was reinforced in the MLC by Reddi's more emotive appeal when she contrasted 'the anaemic, pale, sallow cheeks', 'thin wasted limbs' and 'melancholy and dejected looks' of Indian children with 'the rosy, fleshy, cheeks', 'muscular, round limbs' and 'cheerful happy expressions' of the Western children.[68] This was a radical argument built on a foundation of racial equality and health as a universal right and possibility, but complicated because universal development was to be measured against a European norm.

Allied to this was a desire to place the proper treatment of children within the confines of the hospital building and as subject to the treatments and methodologies of modern medicine, which Dr Mallaya argued would save about 80 per cent of the children. Crucially the children had to be 'properly treated in hospital', 'saved by proper medicines' and supported by adequate 'amenities'. The alternative was to leave the child 'at the mercy of the grandmother and the barber women, and their patent medicines' and extensive detail was given in the debate to local remedies administered by the family such as Kodambakam oil or Chingleput oil, to the role of local ayurvedic practitioners with their *gorochana* and musk pills or neem oil. Paediatrics as a discipline was based on an overt claim to a superior understanding of the child's body and behaviours through scientific study and observation, a superiority based on a modern, European understanding of biomedicine and in explicit opposition to traditional knowledge and remedies.[69] Importantly, this was situated in the hospital as a medical therapeutic space away from the family which could be used to inculcate new morals and habits and thereby impact the behaviours of the whole family.[70] In the Indian case, this was aspirational rather than actual but provided an insight into the growing dominance of allopathic medicine and the ways in which the Indian middle classes used this rejection of traditional practices as part of their own claim to modernity and a means to contest colonial assumptions regarding Indian backwardness.[71]

Reddi argued that a hospital was needed 'to give relief to our innocent young, the speechless and helpless millions of India who are to be the future bulwarks of the State'.[72] Other contributors agreed; Congressman A. B. Shetty argued that nation-building used to be seen in regiments, dreadnoughts and tariffs, 'but today they are thinking in terms of babies and motherhood' and 'if we neglect children, we deprive ourselves of the very first element of racial success and national greatness'. Likewise, Syed Pajudin Sahib noted that 'the first requisite for national prosperity is the physical wellbeing of the children of that country'.[73] This reflected the growing familiarity in the political discourse with what would become a Nehruvian idea of the child as a future citizen. Yet neither the twin strands of the child as an investment nor the child as immediately vulnerable and as a rights bearer in the present proved sufficiently compelling to induce legislators to include the proposals in the budget. Funds were given to rent temporary accommodation to establish the Children's Hospital, but the idea was quickly forgotten.[74]

More successful were focused health campaigns that involved international partners. As part of direct medical intervention to eradicate hookworm, the Madras Medical Association initiated a campaign to eradicate the parasite in 1922.[75] The initiative bore similarities to earlier vaccination campaigns and received funding from a number of international bodies, such as the Health Section of the League of Nations, the International Health Board of New York and the Rockefeller Foundation.[76] Beginning with a pilot project in Munnar, Western Ghats, the campaign expanded from the Telegu- to Tamil-speaking areas. The focus was the 'mass treatment of school children' with Western drugs and an educational campaign, with some resources also spent on sanitation.[77] The whole project was estimated to have reached 345 schools and around 30,450 children.⁷⁸ This campaign and the subsequent interest in infant health for five years at the Poonamallee Health Unit reflected both the strategic priorities of international organisations and a focus on Western drugs as the solution, and Indians themselves were very much the junior partners.⁷⁹

Formulating a Response: Malnutrition

In the interwar years global attention shifted from an interest in curative medicine to a focus on prevention, a concern with the long-term impact of a limited food supply rather than the immediate threat of extreme hunger or famine.⁸⁰ Malnutrition was recognised as not only an immediate cause of hunger and discomfort but also as having a longer-term impact on the child's health and resistance to disease.⁸¹ Some experts continued to see malnutrition as a social malady, directly linked to poverty that could ultimately be traced as the consequence of British misgovernance in India.⁸² However, there was a significant shift in the way that malnutrition was conceptualised, and the attention focused not on the quantity but on the *type* of food consumed. David Arnold has highlighted that this contributed to a wider medicalisation of poverty, which ignored wider issues of socio-economic exploitation and made malnutrition the result of parental or societal ignorance and cultural misunderstandings of the scientific value of foodstuff.⁸³ Three groups became particularly responsible for solving the problem. Nutritionists, such as Walter Aykroyd at the Coonoor Research Laboratories, were expected to produce scientifically based guidelines to encourage nutritious food choices so that the solutions were modern and science-based.⁸⁴ Rich donors or 'philanthropical gentlemen' gave 'magnificent donations' of educational resources and food.⁸⁵ This reflected 'an intelligent interest on the part of the educated classes' and 'a willingness on their part to devote thought and leisure to the improvement of the unhealthy conditions under which their less fortunate countrymen live'.⁸⁶ However, private philanthropists merely supplemented more state-driven efforts.⁸⁷ The state assumed new responsibilities to feed children and used collective feeding both as a way of claiming a new and modern relationship with the family and the child and as a disciplinary means of inculcating in children a new set of normative behaviours and social responsibilities.⁸⁸ As the dyarchy became embedded as a mode of governance, the Indian middle classes came to see themselves as state actors and this recognition that it was the state's responsibility to provide food 'not as charity, but as a valuable means to control malnutrition' among schoolchildren led to the formation of a Midday Meals Scheme in Madras City.[89]

Midday Meals Scheme

The Madras Corporation's free Midday Meals Scheme heralded a radical change in state intervention in the family.[90] The scheme grew out of earlier initiatives designed to improve infant health, such as Rao Bahadur Cunnan Chettiar's feeding home for infants, the Corporation's child welfare schemes and the Triplicane Milk Depot which provided milk for undernourished babies.[91] The scheme was initially an 'experimental measure' in the Cochrane Basin School and drastically improved school attendance in what was characterised as a very poor area.[92] The same year, the Madras District Educational Council appears to have set up a month-long experiment designed to support headmasters to 'appease the unbearable hunger of these children'. The plan included 'funding hungry children' to 'experiment and ascertain what would be the average cost of a midday meal' at St Ann's Convent Girls School and a secular school run by the Social Service League headed by T. Varadarajulu Naidu, the chair of the Education Committee.[93] The idea of providing free school meals on a wider basis was raised formally in 1924 at the special meeting of the council for the introduction of compulsory education. T. Varadarajulu Naidu argued that free midday meals were necessary, along with night and part-time schools, to help 'remove all possible hardships in the case of such poor children', increasing equality of access. Designed as an education rather than a public health initiative, the scheme was intended to discourage child labour and promote 'the higher interests of moral and mental development' of the children.[94]

The Education Committee initiated a further experimental scheme in 1925, which provided free school dinners to children in two divisions of the council.[95] The provision was gradually expanded and in 1930 two centres, at Chintradripet and Peters Road, were established as a temporary measure to coordinate the preparation and distribution of food during term time, with Chintradripet becoming the permanent centre in May 1935.[96] Eight cooks worked from 3 a.m. to 1.30 p.m. to prepare food, which was then circulated to all relevant schools. Distribution was supervised by the head teacher, with occasional surprise inspections by supervisors, medical inspectors and educational officers. In 1937, 4,500 children from eighty-four schools received midday meals provided by the corporation.[97] This was expanded in 1939 to include ninety-six schools comprising 6,000 children, and buttermilk was added as a supplement.[98] In 1943, 5,750 pupils received free school meals, with continuing 'clamour for food for more deserving poor children' to be included.[99]

The Midday Meals Scheme profoundly redefined the role of the state in relation to the child.[100] The councillors may have drawn inspiration from the 1906 Education (Provision of Meals) Act in Britain or the School Lunch Committee in New York City from 1909, although, in contrast to educational and juvenile justice provisions, these global connections were not explicitly mentioned. This was not merely the collection of statistics to regulate a population but active intervention in an area of life—the feeding of children—which was usually assumed to be the responsibility of the family.[101] The scheme eroded the boundaries between the public and private worlds of children, enabling what Ruis calls in the New York context a redefinition of 'the boundaries between home and state, private rights, and public welfare'.[102] This became a new way to influence private behaviours and to discipline families into a new, more reciprocal relationship with the state as citizens with rights.[103] At the same time, as diet became a shared responsibility, Barona argues that it took on a moral dimension, becoming evidence of the state's own modernity and potential to regulate the population through science.[104] The move was also indicative of a 'radical redefinition of the role of preventive medicine'.[105] Vaccination programmes had been an early indication of the modern state's role in preventing disease and in claiming the right to intervene in children's bodies on behalf of the health of the nation, but were linked more closely to the medical aspects.[106] Intervening to provide nutrition, in what was an everyday rather than exceptional occurrence, was therefore something entirely new both in practical application and in claim. While this prerogative was perhaps more important in rhetoric than in practice given the relatively low number of children involved, it revealed a significant shift in the role and claims of public health, despite being driven at the policy level by the Education Department. Food was only to be provided within the context of the school, administered by teaching staff, for children of school age. This again reinforced the emerging assumption that the defining place of childhood was the school.[107]

The decision that the provision of food for schoolchildren was an educational concern highlights the tensions between a number of state agencies at different levels of the government. Significantly, the Midday Meals Scheme was run by the local council's Education Department. A similar scheme was rejected by the provincial government in 1924 because it was assumed that truly deprived children would be in the labour force, not in school. Furthermore, the cost, estimated at 43.20 lakh rupees on the basis of the current school-going population, was considered 'prohibitive'.[108] While it was recognised that the provision of midday meals would be 'administratively difficult and financially costly', there was also significant concern about the caste and purity implications of inter-dining in schools, the satisfactory cooking arrangements and the presence of Dalits spread across the presidency rather than clustered in one area.[109] Even a small experimental scheme, backed by the DPI and the commissioner of labour, was blocked by the Finance Committee as being outside the jurisdiction of the provincial Education Department.[110]

By contrast, the Corporation of Madras decided to take responsibility for undernourished children and provided around 5,000 rupees for midday meals as part of the Elementary Education Fund (EEF). This was intended to encourage poor children to continue attending school rather than to attract new pupils. However, the corporation's education budget of 1926, submitted for approval in exchange for funding, was rejected by the provincial Education Department. As noted in Chapter 1, under Section 37 of the Madras Elementary Education Act, 1920, the provincial government was liable to match the money provided by the local authority for elementary education. Including the Midday Meals Scheme in the education budget meant that it could potentially have extensive financial repercussions for the provincial government, which would have been required to fund similar schemes across the presidency. While both Minister for Education Dr P. Subbarayan and the Education Department supported the provision of food, they were adamant that it was a public health initiative, not an investment in education.[111] They argued that it was illegal under the Education Act to pay for food from the EEF but were very happy for it to be funded through the corporation's general revenues budget, raised through municipal taxation.[112] This caused great consternation in the corporation, the provision of school lunches having been financed from the education budget since the initial experiments in

1919.[113] The dispute demonstrated the close control attempted by the provincial government over local authority budgets despite the lip service paid to the devolution of power to local areas. Ultimately the extensive discussions, and sustained defiance by the corporation, led to an amendment in the Education Act in 1931.[114] By contrast, there was little reference to the provision of food when the Madras Public Health Act was passed in 1938 as an attempt to bring public health interventions together on a legislative basis.[115]

Imagining the Poor and Hungry Child

The dispute over funding emphasised the growing symbolic value of the vulnerable child. Refusing to accept the government's position, M. Singaravelu Chetty, the new Education Committee chair and a prominent social reformer in the Self-Respect movement, argued: 'There is no use of crying over what has been done already. You cannot starve the children, simply because you are fighting a battle against the Act....'[116] A later proposal to increase the budget for midday meals from 20,000 rupees to 50,000 rupees was rejected on the grounds of cost but only after a debate that emphasised the threat of leaving the defenceless child hungry.[117] Councillors from both the Justice Party and the Congress claimed 'responsibility for the welfare of the children', although both accused the other of 'crocodile tears' for 'the unfortunate children'.[118] The debates sentimentalised the poor child who was 'to be pitied', like the juvenile delinquent an object of care, subject to the reforming schemes of more knowing and powerful adults (Chapter 5).[119] During further discussions in 1937, the Congress chair of the Education Committee Mrs Ammu Swaminathan argued:

> The children of the city should be the first care of the Corporation. We cannot afford to neglect their welfare. They are the future citizens, and it is up to us to see that they grow up in healthy surroundings. How can we expect them to grow into healthy men and women, how can we expect them to have any kind of proper education if they continue to remain under these circumstances?[120]

The consistent, and often emotional, appeal for better resources for 'poor children' received widespread support.[121] This reflected the claim by all parties to a new responsibility to protect the hungry child, which in turn strengthened the claims of the Indian state to a global modernity based on care for the vulnerable. It also represented an investment in the nation's future. As with the 1906 act in Britain, these claims represented both a political investment in national regeneration and a more nuanced contribution to, and participation in, wider socio-economic and cultural change, including ideas about bio-medicine, state intervention and the normal child.[122]

Midday meals were provided for 'poor children' in response to 'the duty of the Government to encourage the backward, the helpless and the forlorn', a particularly emotive representation of children, which again reinforced their dependence.[123] The recipients were predominantly from the Dalit community, but the scheme was not administered on caste lines. Instead, while the Justice Party Education Minister Patro claimed to 'understand and sympathise with Adi-Dravidas [Dalits]', he framed the provision of food as a response to 'the poverty of the students' and should include 'deserving boys of all classes'.[124] This meant that there should not be 'any unjust execution of the rules' that would exclude Other Backward Castes, Muslims and Christians. In a debate in the corporation in 1930, the trade unionist and independence activist V. Chakkarai Chettiar spoke in terms of 'responsibility' and 'duty' and 'justice' to provide food for 'all the children' in the compulsory education areas, regardless of caste.[125] This was agreed by politicians of all parties and mirrored the approach taken for compulsory education (Chapter 2).[126] This reveals a number of issues. The frequent use of the term 'deserving', which was used again in 1941 with the suggestion that the scheme should be extended to 'children active in scouts and guides', hints that the Victorian notion of the 'deserving poor' continued to inform interventions in subtle ways, highlighting a continued engagement with the poor as victims rather than poverty as a cause.[127] At the same time, N. Rajagopalan argued that 'every poor child in a school is entitled to have this food', hinting at a new discourse surrounding the right to food, foreshadowing claims not made more widely until 2001, and revealing a very different liberal view of the child as rights-holder.[128]

The decision to administer food 'irrespective of caste or creed' reveals the tensions between those who regarded all children as equally deserving and those who were aware of the inequalities caused by caste and community. For some, the definition 'poor' was a further opportunity to claim a share of the state's resources for their own, often very impoverished, community. Abdul Hameed Khan, a prominent campaigner for the Muslim community, argued:

> There are very many poor people in other communities also who deserve such kind of help and support. The facilities that are afforded to the Depressed Classes and other backward communities should be extended to the poorest people who cannot afford food to their children.[129]

His fellow Congressman Satyamurti recognised that most poor children came from the Dalit community, but this was rarely openly acknowledged.[130] There was some awareness that the 'scale of poverty is different' among the Dalit community and that they lacked 'the wherewithal to organise their own *sangams* and funds to educate the poor', requiring more directed state attention, and this was particularly supported by Dalit representatives such as Vasudeva Pillai.[131] However, there was limited recognition that the structural inequalities of caste and community were such that positive action was required to provide a level playing field. This may have reflected anxieties about inter-caste dining and the concerns about integrating Dalits into mainstream education. The claim to scientific modernity, which was so central to the modern self-identity of those in power, meant that older, traditional, often religious, identities were hard to negotiate and understand, which in turn reflected the privilege of their own position.

The reluctance to define modern intervention through caste (although in practice it was often the determining factor) reveals the limitations to the radicalism of both the non-Brahmin Justice Party and the Self-Respect movement over caste and reflected the ongoing conversation between Dalit leaders and the Congress party over reservation, and the relationship between Dalits and the majority caste Hindu community within the wider independence movement. The striking reluctance of state actors to engage with the inequalities of caste was also intimately tied to the nature of dyarchy itself and the need to appeal to particular voting constituencies. This mirrors Viswanath's argument that the major parties were unwilling to categorise 'labour' in Madras as anything more than a socio-economic definition, thereby exacerbating tensions between communities and further compounding—perhaps deliberately—the discrimination against

Dalits in the labour movement.[132] This tension between the equality of access and the lived experience of structural inequality set a pattern for state behaviour that continued into the post-independence period. Importantly, only the Labour leader C. Basudev explicitly recognised 'poor children' as 'the children who are *unable* to find a school, unable to clothe themselves and unable to get one meal per day'.[133] This appears to be the only engagement with the poor child who failed to attend school, demonstrating the increasing hegemony of the equation of the child with the scholar.

Feeding Children

Childhood poverty does not in itself explain why the Education Department of the municipal corporation found it necessary to supplement the responsibility of the family in providing food for children. At a time when food interventions were primarily designed to prevent starvation, intervening proactively to prevent malnutrition was a far-reaching move.[134] Free school meals were initially introduced as a way to boost attendance, based on the initial results of the Cochrane Basin School.[135] The provision of food compensated families for a potential loss of earnings for previously employed children, reflecting the decision to attract pupils to education rather than prosecute non-attendance (see Chapter 2).[136] Attendance figures were closely monitored, and the cost of corporation schools—28 rupees per pupil in comparison to government (18 rupees) and private schools (10 rupees)—was justified on the basis of the provision of food as well as the quality of the education provided.[137] When compulsory education was extended in 1926 to a further three of the poorest divisions in the city, Chair of the Education Committee M. Singaravelu Chetty argued for a parallel extension of the Midday Meals Scheme. Chetty cited a 90 per cent attendance rate in areas 'where food is given', insisting that without it attendance was 'a mere farce and the compulsion is merely illusive'.[138] It became the received, even frequently cited, wisdom that school attendance fell by 50 per cent while the scheme was briefly discontinued in 1927.[139] Even when budget restrictions meant that teacher salaries were reduced, there was little appetite to take 'the retrograde step' to 'deprive these poor children', which was 'an incentive for them to go to school' and part of 'advancing education which is the primary duty of the Corporation'.[140] Again, in 1938 it was argued that the provision not only improved health but also facilitated 'regular attendance in the schools'.[141] To have this level of consensus for a scheme not widely recognised as an educational tool in the rest of India was remarkable.

The provision of food was intended to retain pupils and improve the quality of learning based on the 'elementary fact that hungry children are not able to absorb teaching as readily as children whose stomachs have been attended to by the midday meal'.[142] The provision of food at school was part of a wider nutritional discourse that linked the strength of the child's physical body to its intellectual capacity. The health officer argued that 'ill-fed' children 'are listless and pine away in some corner of the classroom, taking little or no interest in what is going on in the School'.[143] Likewise, Slater, the commissioner for labour in Madras, insisted that children attending schools missed their midday meal and 'are thus half starved and unable to apply themselves to anything'.[144] This link between nourishment and education was widely accepted across departments.[145] The relationship between mind and body has usually been stressed by historians in the context of physical education, and the production of an adequately disciplined, usually male, body was seen as a contribution to empire or nation-building.[146] The investment in children's health and educational attainment through the provision of food reflected a further extension of this project that politicised children's bodies, regulating them into correct forms of knowledge and loyalty, so that food became a strategy to improve intellectual capacity and school results.[147] This was intended to improve the life chances of the children, but also as an investment in the 'moral, mental and physical training' of the 'citizens of the future' and which would thereby contribute to nation-building. As in wartime Europe, children and workers also became the focus of collective feeding programmes as a means of increasing their productivity.[148] More than that, there was some emerging realisation that adequate nourishment would 'contribute to a child's readiness to learn and ability to participate in his or her own educational process' in addition to increasing the child's quality of life and 'joie de vivre' in the present, and that this was a legitimate use of the state's resources.[149]

Nutrition for Children

The type and quality of food were the subjects of more debate than any other aspect of the Midday Meals Scheme. In 1930, Councillor

G. Narayanaswamy Chetty wrote to the commissioner 'complaining bitterly' that 'the food given to these children' was 'making them sick instead of making them healthy' and calling for provision to be stopped until an adequate system of funding and inspection had been established.[150] Inspection of the quality remained a challenge, variously described as food 'which even the crows will not touch', 'not even suitable for beggars' and 'injurious to health'.[151] Alleged corruption and adulteration were persistent problems.[152] This fitted again into the rhetoric of the vulnerable child, exploited by adults even in the provision of basic nourishment, and reflected the logistical difficulties in administering such an innovative scheme.

The language of nutritional science informed the debates regarding the type of food to be made available in schools. Chairman of the Health Committee Dr Syed Niamatullah, a practitioner of Unani medicine, was concerned that the rice and *sambhar* provided by the corporation had 'little nutritional value' and was often 'thick and coarse', meaning that children refused to eat it 'with the result that they are unhealthy and rickety in their constitution'.[153] He proposed that the Health Committee should investigate alternative options 'as we thought best in the interest of the child'. In 1939 it was suggested that a series of experiments should be undertaken by Justicite Dr U. Krishna Rao to prescribe food that was appropriate for different communities, cost effective and scientifically proven to be 'wholesome and nutritive'.[154] These discussions re-emphasised the scientific authority of the medical practitioners on the Health Committee, highlighting science as the basis for decision-making. This paralleled the extensive research into the diets of south Indian schoolchildren carried out by W. R. Aykroyd and his Indian colleagues at the Coonoor Research Laboratories, which used modern scientific methodologies to demonstrate the long-term impact of malnutrition on the physical and mental development of the child.[155] This research was used by nutritionists and dieticians to carve out a new space for intervention based on their authority as scientific experts and who through experimentation could define both the optimum and minimum diets for health.[156]

The investigations were opposed across the chamber. This reflected concern by the councillors that the experiments would provide opportunities for the funding to be reduced. There was also overt concern over the ethical context of bio-medicine, which included an explicit rejection of conducting an 'experiment upon the stomachs of these unfortunate children'.[157] Congress leaders such as Satyamurthi emphasised that children should not be experimented on 'simply because they come under your guardianship', while Gopala Menon argued that throughout history, exploitative experiments had been conducted on those who were already marginalised, such as enslaved women in the USA.[158] There does seem to have been considerable political concern that modern science required an ethical political context so that vulnerable minorities would not be targeted without consent, a standard rarely reflected in the global context until at least the 1950s.[159] The debate ended with widespread agreement that more research was needed to increase the nutritional value of food provided, although the move to increase funding from 25,000 rupees to 75,000 rupees was soundly defeated seventeen to eight.[160] Once more, the concern for children did not reach as far as the provision of adequate finance.

The opposition to nutritional experiments reflected an earlier discussion in 1930 when the commissioner of the corporation proposed a scheme to feed children bread and milk despite the added cost. 'Nutritional experts' recommended this diet as more effective in reducing deficiency diseases than the typical diet of rice and curds.[161] This again reflected the concerns surrounding the nutritional value of 'the ordinary diet of Madras Presidency'.[162] It also reflected international experiments, both the provision of midday meals in London schools and an experiment in Edinburgh, which had demonstrated the particular nutritional value of bread and milk for growing children.[163] These ideas dovetailed with the Coonoor experiments by Aykroyd's team, which specifically investigated the nutritional needs of schoolchildren using hostels as a controlled environment.[164] The suggestion that the child's body required different nutrition than the adult body, and that Tamil children had an equal need of and right to this food as British children, also reflected the changing perceptions of the body of all children as distinct from fully grown adults. This mirrored earlier scientific discourses surrounding paediatrics as a distinct discipline.[165]

Although nutrition was important, there was a strong body of opinion that favoured the use of local foodstuffs to feed children. Mrs Hannen Angelo, an Anglo-Indian who founded the Madras Nurses Association and stood as a candidate for the Women's Indian Association (WIA), was particularly concerned that the food choices reflected 'the habits of people of this country' while others feared the introduction of nutritious foodstuffs which would offend religious sensibilities and be 'revolting to the sentiments of the people'.[166] A number of councillors also argued that the food provided had to be 'liked by all the children in our schools'.[167] *Sambhar* was a popular choice, both for its nutritive value and because many children were too poor to be given it at home.[168] In addition, *sambhar* was cited as 'more palatable to these children', meaning that it would encourage attendance.[169] Ragi, a particularly nutritious form of millet from Kerala, was rejected even though it could be mixed with other foodstuffs such as jaggery, sugar or *badam* to suit 'the different temperaments of the children' because it was not considered of sufficient nutritional value to be worth causing opposition by parents and children.[170] Attempts were made to introduce variety, and there was concern that the diet should include rice, curds and *sambhar*, varied either according to season, on alternate days or even with the occasional addition of wheat cakes, bread, *halwa* or ragi flour chapatis.[171] Even in certified schools, students were given a roll and two bananas 'now and again for a change'.[172] This was not formulated on the basis of nutritional variety but because 'poor children will not like a monotonous diet' and 'prefer a variety'.[173] The suggestion that the type of food should reflect the opinions of local children rather than the absolutes of nutritional science recognised some awareness on the part of adults that children had valid opinions and indicated the limits of the imposition of adult will upon children's bodies.[174] It revealed the pragmatic realities of intervention, and while there remains no direct evidence from the children themselves, it demonstrated an awareness that even hungry children had legitimate concerns and preferences, perhaps reflecting the British experience where oral histories reveal that the school meal provision in the 1940s was so unpalatable that it was often seen by the children as 'social punishment' rather than 'entitlement'.[175] In practice, the cost seems to have been the deciding factor, and there seems only to be records for tenders for the provision of rice.[176]

Nutritional supplements were also provided for children who were diagnosed as 'undernourished' during the medical inspection.[177] This involved a course of cod liver oil and tonics geared towards 'proper growth and development' of the child's body.[178] Milk was made widely available, reflecting the earlier focus on the provision of milk in the child welfare centres as a means of advancing infant and maternal health.[179] Buttermilk was advocated in 1930 as a 'very nutritious' foodstuff, particularly important in building physical strength.[180] It was cost effective, being produced by diluting thick curds with water, although the climatic conditions made storage difficult, and the temptation to over-dilute meant that practical nourishment was often minimal.[181] It is difficult to assess whether the fetishisation of milk as a supplement, both in the corporation discussions and Aykroyd reports, reflected the British experience or a universal idea that milk was particularly suited to children as well as infants. Scientific experts such as the Coonoor Nutrition Research Laboratories supported milk as producing 'excellent results on the health and physique of children', but this may partially have been driven by the need of the Australian and New Zealand butter industries to export milk as part of the wider colonial economy.[182] The debates around appropriate food and supplements evince a wider engagement with the culturally specific preferences of the Indian child. They reflect the tastes and habits of a particular region of India, but also the growing acceptance that the child's body was physically, as well as intellectually, distinct from that of the adult body.

Conclusion

By the end of the 1920s, there was an emerging consensus that the state had both the right and the duty to intervene in the health of the schoolchild, without reference to parents. This reflected wider universalising narratives that characterised the normal child as a pupil. The school became the legitimate place for intervention, whether through inspection or the provision of supplementary food. This allowed state agencies to ignore the position of the child not at school, although these children remained the majority. South Indian politicians contributed to an emerging understanding of the child's body as distinct from the adult body, evidenced through the collection of normative statistics, the beginnings of paediatric medicine and the research into the specific nutritional requirements of children. This discourse focused on a universalising conception of childhood in which the child was undifferentiated by gender, race or class. The idea of universal childhood was based on two entangled discourses: one grounded in the scientific measurement of the child's body and the other linked to a new claim to the universal rights of the child. Both these avowedly modern discourses reinforced the authority of adult experts, the first by establishing the primacy of both nutritional science and Western medicine to improve and understand the body of the child, therefore strengthening the position of the medical profession. The second revealed Indian legislators asserting their own modernity by constructing the Indian child as having the same access to rights as the British child and by emphasising their participation as equals in global child-saving and child-rights networks. The poor child in school thus came to both embody the modernity of the state and was a particular target of the modern state's regulatory actions. In practice, this made it difficult for policymakers to engage meaningfully with the realities of children's lives and the inequalities they negotiated on a daily basis.

While the legislators in the MLC attempted to take political credit for reforms in child welfare provisions, most significant interventions happened at the level of the municipality within the Corporation of Madras. By facilitating the feeding of children, an activity particularly associated with the home, local councillors began to radically reformulate the relationship between state and family. In this the state sought to supplement the authority and responsibility of the family in a way that was much more aggressive than in the discourse of juvenile justice or education: the home and family were much more directly constructed as a site of threat to the physical body of the child. The family was regarded as having neither the capacity to provide a sufficient quantity of food on account of poverty nor the knowledge to provide adequate nutrition or see the long-term benefits of schooling rather than work for children. The provision of food at school was conceptualised therefore as an educational rather than public health initiative. The mediating voice of authority between child and state in terms of health was not the parent but the local schoolteacher. The teacher became the local proxy for the legislators themselves, a figure whose authority derived from their modern education but who claimed to be uniquely suited, as Indian, to understand the home context and could conceptualise themselves as 'avuncular' or framed within the context of the extended family. While less threatening than earlier colonial measures, the state became recognised as a benevolent avuncular provider of welfare in everyday life. The child might be framed as a rights bearer, but this rarely meant that it had a claim on the state's resources. These schemes may have changed civil society attitudes towards state involvement in the family and the necessity of welfare planning, but these health interventions were the budget areas that suffered the earliest and most severely from financial retrenchments.

Childhood was not merely an idea based on concepts of rights, intellectual malleability and innocence, but the child's body became a site for exercising power. As a result, personal hygiene, physical vulnerability and educational achievement became linked to the production of a healthy body. In turn, the child was to become a virile and strong citizen contributing to the future health of the nation, and as such the cost of intervention and growth of preventative medicine was justified as an investment in the nation's future. Yet within this overarching discourse, there was growing acceptance that children not only deserved both investment and protection as a result of their age and vulnerability, but a pragmatic recognition that they had opinions on the forms of intervention, and particularly food, which they considered acceptable. These changing ideas about childhood affected all children but were particularly apparent in the lives of children in conflict with the law, as seen in the next chapter.

5

Saving the Child

The Madras Children Act, 1920, and the Beginnings of a Juvenile Justice System

The children considered in the preceding chapters were part of what could be categorised as an expected interaction with the modern state. The next two chapters consider a much smaller group of marginalised children whose interactions with state institutions were based on their perceived criminality or extreme poverty, who were subjected to the penal gaze of the state, who were not merely to be moulded into future citizens but who needed to be saved much more directly from their current circumstances.

Though there had been previous attempts to engage with juvenile justice, the Madras Children Act, 1920 (MCA) marked a new beginning in both thinking and practice surrounding children in contact with the law and the perceived responsibilities of the state towards such children. The act was the first to afford a distinct legal status to children; it legally defined the child as different from adults and initiated the expansion of a justice system centred on the specific needs of the child. These changes will be analysed by considering the discourses surrounding juvenile justice and the construction of the child as a 'delinquent' or 'destitute', as an object of reform, an object of welfare or a future citizen with rights. The chapter interrogates the aspirations of both colonial and Indian penal reformers and legislators, seen in documents such as the 1919–20 Indian Jails

Committee (IJC), academic writings on juvenile justice and then in the content and significance of the 1920 act itself. Mirroring the methodology of the education chapters, these notions are set alongside a profiling of juvenile crime in court and administration records and then a detailed study of the act's practical consequences for the bodies and minds of children through the expansion of government-funded certified school provision. The role of civil society groups will be analysed in more detail in Chapter 6.

The 1920 act reflected a decisive shift as the state decided it had a duty to intervene in the lives of children because they were in particular need of 'care' or 'control'. This was not a moment when the 'juvenile delinquent' was discovered as a social menace with the recognition of urban youth crime as a particular social problem as in some other British colonies such as Nigeria.[1] Nor does it reflect the complex anxieties about the moral reformation of middle-class youth increasingly drawn to political nationalism.[2] Rather, subjecting marginalised children to the penal gaze of the state appears to have been a means to control the current bodies of children, to shape their future relationship with the state but primarily as a way to signal the modernity of state actors, both colonial and Indian, through their claim to progressive penal policies as well as engagement with modern universalising ideas about childhood.

The colonial concern for children in need of protection or correction was evidenced first in Mary Carpenter's work in the 1860s in Bombay.[3] Although a reformatory school had been established in Chingleput, near Madras City, in 1887, the first legislative response was the all-India Reformatory Schools Act, 1897, which made the juvenile delinquent an important focus for the colonial penal project.[4] The aim was to provide children with moral structure and disciplined habits, enabling them to 'become useful members of society' and prevent 'relapse into crime', thereby encouraging the productivity of the colony.[5] However, these institutions were widely regarded by British experts as a 'productive failure', and the failure to reform the delinquent child was taken as evidence of the innate racial inferiority of Indians, and specifically their supposed biological propensity to lie and murder rather than a failed, and inadequately funded, scheme of reformation.[6] These overtly racialised ideas were increasingly contested by Indian reformers and experts such as Cornelia Sorabji, and Satadru Sen has demonstrated how the body of the incarcerated child, or the child criminal, became the site of intense contestation by competing adult voices, each determined to show their own modernity and authority.[7]

The reforms of 1920 drew from this long heritage of contestation and racial competition but also from a number of new sources, most notably the radical changes in British and American views on juvenile justice. This was evidenced in the introduction of the juvenile court in Birmingham in 1900 and the passing of the Children Act in Britain in 1908. These legislative actions were the result of, and spawned, a growing normative global discourse of reformative juvenile penology, which emphasised the uniqueness of the individual child as a future citizen and encouraged the psychological categorisation of children.[8] By 1920 the juvenile court, embodying the modern state, was envisaged as the successor to the feudal government of kings as *parens patriae*, as 'an embodiment' of both 'an ancient doctrine and of modern methods in the exercise of power of the state as the ultimate parent of the child'.[9] This effectively bypassed the family, situating the child in direct relationship with the state or state practitioners, the object of official love and direct object of state power.[10]

The following chapters reveal how both British legislators and the cosmopolitan Madras elite negotiated these differing tensions, and the need for a culturally specific form of juvenile justice appropriate to the Indian context while also holding on to an idea of childhood as universal. A key element of this was the role of the family, variously characterised as morally threatening to the child or unable to provide basic socio-economic security. Conversely, it was the family that continued to hold primary authority over the child, and which was to be the primary site for reformation and control. These relationships reflect the ways in which children in contact with the law were conceptualised and the tension between the child imagined as 'dangerous' or delinquent, and the child as 'in danger' or destitute. This goes to the heart of whether the juvenile justice system was intended to be preventative or rehabilitative or whether these terms were mutually reinforcing in practice. The disjunction between the rhetorical constructions of the child and the practical implementation of the act in the courts and certified schools are central to this.

Discourses of Delinquency

The most obvious colonial manifestation of changing approaches to penology was the IJC, which gathered evidence in 1919–20, publishing its report in 1921. Alongside the wider post-war political reforms, the IJC was a British attempt to modernise the justice system and encourage 'elements of decency and humane administration', including more limited use of corporal punishment and concern for the moral reformation of the criminal into a 'useful citizen'.[11] Chapter 15 of the IJC's report focused exclusively on the child criminal and was explicitly influenced by changing theory and practice in Britain and America.[12] The report contested racialised juvenile penology on a number of levels. It argued that successful reformation was more likely to happen in childhood, reflecting wider discourses about the malleability of the child.[13] It questioned the suggestion that Indian children rarely committed serious crimes, dismissing this as 'merely due to ignorance of the facts'.[14] Significantly, the report claimed that the Indian child should have the same access to a specialist juvenile court as the British child and should be tried as a 'child' rather than as an 'Indian child'.[15] In this, and in comparing an Indian child with a street Arab of London, a Paris *gamin* or a New York gutter-child, there was the evidence of a discourse of equality in the conceptualisation of childhood that would become increasingly important in the following twenty years, even if it continued to reflect the racialised labelling of children in the West.[16] The exceptions to this were the children of the so-called criminal tribes, who continued to be held in 'preventative detention' alongside other members of this 'incorrigible class', often segregated from their parents.[17] There was some concern about separating families within the settlements but no debate over the racialised or biological categorisation of criminality.

The IJC also interrogated the role of the family. There remained a fear of the failed family; if the home circumstances were regarded as unfavourable, it felt necessary to remove children and place them with adoptive parents, or in a rescue home run on cottage system lines.[18] This meant that the solution was familial, and children failed by their birth families were to find replacement families within the criminal justice system. However, in contrast to earlier approaches, while some respondents saw the juvenile court as 'quasi-parental', their claims to authority were grounded in their expertise and understanding of modern and scientific approaches to criminology rather than the assumption that they should themselves assume a surrogate parental role.[19] In the majority of cases, returning the child to the natal family was seen to be a more effective restorative strategy than institutionalisation, and the IJC advocated the implementation of a probation system that acted 'in the interests both of the child and of the community'.[20] E. A. Davis, of the Indian Civil Service (ICS), argued, 'As a rule, however, I am very strongly of the opinion that any child under 12 should invariably be handed over to the parents to be dealt with unless there is proof of parental neglect or training in crime, or unless the crime committed shows abnormal precocity.'[21] Similarly, the final report argued that the 'most satisfactory solution of the problem will be to entrust the child to his relatives, if there is any reasonable prospect of their exercising better care of him in the future than in the past and if the home is at all a decent one'.[22] If this failed, then the attitude of the judge was to be 'parental', and he was to develop specialist knowledge of children.[23] This demonstrated both the fear of the 'failed' family and its influence on the malleable child, and the perception that the family, or at least familial structures, was also the solution and a potential focus for social action.

The IJC provided the impetus for a number of penal justice reforms and revealed changes in contemporary thinking on juvenile penology. However, the inadequate theorisation of juvenile justice among both colonial writers and Indians themselves was striking. In Madras a number of child protection agencies were established by elite Indians, mirroring earlier interventions in Bombay, most significantly the Society for the Protection of Children in Western India established in 1917. Parallel practical efforts in 'child-saving' in the Madras Presidency will be discussed in detail in Chapter 6. Despite the extensive literature produced by Indians on social issues such as education, poverty or the age of consent for marriage, there was no equivalent discursive engagement with specifically Indian forms of juvenile penology.[24] This pattern was established by the journalist Saint Nihal Singh in his *Plea for an Indian Juvenile Court*, published just four years after the British Children's Act of 1908. Singh suggested reforming the approach to juvenile justice for the 'manufacture of good citizens out of misguided youth' but saw the English model as a frontrunner in the field.[25] Later writers such as Lt-Col Barman also detailed the English Borstal System, although the introduction suggested these methods 'might be adopted—not necessarily copied—in the East'.²⁶ The lack of detailed engagement with developing a culturally specific model of juvenile justice mirrored the attempts by pedagogues in Chapter 3 to introduce an educational system based on universal ideas about childhood that failed to engage with the practicalities of the Indian setting. At the centre of this approach was the child as a future national asset, but the child was not constructed according to a language of cultural or racial difference, as is usually argued.²⁷ Rather, this new system claimed discursive power from what the Ishita Pande calls 'a globalised paradigm of child-protection'.²⁸ This language of universalism became the most effective way to critique colonial racial hierarchies, revealed the transnational interactions of those legislating for children and was used by them to signal their own modernity as equal participants in a global system of child-saving.²⁹

Global interest in child-saving and the developing influence of changing international views on children's rights became particularly strong following the adoption of the Geneva Declaration in 1924.³⁰ The child rights movement was largely aspirational, but in 1934 the League's Advisory Commission for the Protection and Welfare of Children and Young People carried out a global investigation into the functioning of juvenile courts, as note 2 of the Geneva Declaration urged that 'the delinquent child must be reclaimed'. In the Indian context, the gathered evidence demonstrated the provincial nature of children's courts but showed Madras as among the frontrunners in Indian juvenile justice.³¹ Although the scope and remit of the league's activities were limited, the discursive influence of growing international networks of child-savers in spreading normative assumptions about delinquency should not be underestimated.

The only person who really grappled at a theoretical level with juvenile justice in the Indian context was Clifford Manshardt, an American sociologist who established the first Child Guidance Clinic in Bombay in 1937 and became the first director of the Tata Institute of Social Sciences in Bombay. It was only after Manshardt published his book *Delinquent Child in India* in 1939 and then the establishment of the *Indian Journal of Social Work* that these issues received serious academic attention. The first issue in June 1940 covered topics such as 'child welfare', looking at 'children in industry' and 'juvenile delinquency'.³² Again Manshardt contested the twin racialised notions of an innate Indian propensity to crime and the inheritability of criminality. Although he recognised the impact of family circumstances, he refused to solely blame the child's environment, arguing that even with a background of immorality, neglect and poverty, only a small percentage of children became criminals.[33] Comparing India with the Western experience, Manshardt argued that while 95 per cent of children arrested in England were charged with housebreaking and theft, in Bombay, 1927–37, 43 per cent were arrested for destitution, and emphasised that 61 per cent of children came from outside the city, urban centres proving a magnet for those seeking to escape rural poverty. While these figures were unverified, Manshardt's argument was that the child offender was 'generally a victim rather than a conscious offender' and that most crimes were caused by socio-economic deprivation.[34]

To Manshardt the child was uniquely vulnerable, and any legislation—like the earlier Bombay Children Act, 1922—should be protective and preventative rather than penal, and he frequently emphasised the 'paramount need of the unprotected child'.[35] The child was also 'a valuable asset' and the future of both child and state were bound together through the development of good, pliable and productive citizens: 'good workmen, leading honest, clean and healthy lives'.[36] Although Manshardt recognised the value of juvenile institutions and was a pioneer of the child guidance clinic, he regarded the parents as central to the child's education and rehabilitation, seeing the family as 'central to our social organisation' and the protection of 'the stability of family life' as necessary for 'the proper functioning of the social whole'.[37] Intervention was described in familial terms, and the new juvenile court was to have 'special jurisdiction of a parental nature'.[38] This reflected a greater emphasis on the family in Western child-saving discourses in the interwar years but also an increased focus on the family in India as the centre of social action.[39] Manshardt was committed to the study of 'the Indian child in his Indian environment', recognising the unique position of the Indian child but also the similarities with its American counterparts, and he ended with a call for an Indian children's charter based on the universal rights of children as established in the American 'Children Charter' of 1931.[40] He argued that 'certainly an Indian child is of no less value than an American child' and required 'the highest possible standards' of care and protection from the state.[41] This attempt to reconcile the Indian context with increasingly hegemonic global discourses of the individual rights-bearing child predated later attempts to grapple with the question of whether child rights was a Western construct or a helpful tool in improving the lives of at-risk children.[42]

Legislative Changes

The Madras Legislative Council (MLC) passed the Madras Children's Act into law in 1920, following three years of discussions and re-drafts. It was the first of its kind in India and was first introduced in 1917, predating both the IJC and the constitutional change, which meant that a majority Indian government was ultimately responsible for its implementation. The act was intended to replace the existing 'defective and inadequate' Reformatory Act, 1897, and ultimately contained six sections dealing with (1) definitions of childhood; (2 and 5) certified schools; (3) responsibility of parents and guardians; (4) children at risk because of poverty or at threat because of their home surroundings; and (6) the juvenile court. The act established the boundaries of childhood in legal terms so that the designation 'child' could be used for a person less than fourteen years old, continuing longer if already under certified school discipline.[43] The young person (sometimes 'juvenile adult') between fourteen and sixteen years also had limited criminal responsibility, while a later Madras Borstal Schools Act, 1926, provided for young adults between sixteen and twenty-one.[44] The MCA was closely modelled on the British Children Act passed twelve years earlier in 1908, and was followed by Children Acts in other provinces.[45]

In the early discussions in the Legislative Council, most members—both Indian and British—expressed themselves to be in favour of humanitarian legislation, explicitly in line with legislation in the West.[46] Indeed, criticism was centred on the terms in which the MCA differed from the British iteration, and there was concern that the MCA should be extended to provide further 'special protection' for infants of less than seven years and further protection against cruelty to children as was contained in the British equivalent.[47] The bill went through several stages of reading and a select committee before passing into law. The recurring and primary source of controversy was the relationship between state institutions and civil society or philanthropic organisations, both in control over institutions and in responsibility for funding.[48] Rangachariar, speaking for the Congress party, favoured strengthening civic activism by extending the role of local committees and voluntary agencies and was keen to avoid any involvement of the police.[49] Already involved in the Madras Society for the Protection of Children, he was particularly concerned with facilitating the expansion of specialist knowledge within the voluntary sector. Supporting this, M. Ramachandra Rao, a Mylapore Brahmin, argued that while the skills and personnel should come from both civil society organisations and salaried professionals, funding should be guaranteed by the government.[50] This was supported in a later debate in March 1920 by Congress member Venkatappayya who maintained that it was 'the duty and the function of the Government to maintain such children', although this funding could be administered at a local level.[51] The Indian advocate-general, on the other hand, argued that the government could not assume statutory financial responsibility but would be liberal in the provision of Grant-in-Aid funding to individual schools. He also argued that private and philanthropic endeavours were preferable to local government involvement.[52] The position of the government was therefore deeply ambiguous. Although unwilling to accept financial responsibility, the government wanted the power to regulate certified schools and was unwilling to countenance competition for this responsibility from other levels of government or civil society organisations. Chapter 6 reveals how this changed after Indians took control over the government under dyarchy.

Further controversy surrounded the nomenclature, 'Reformatory' or 'Certified School' revealing an underlying confusion as to the purpose of the legislation and the role of the state.[53] The debate centred around whether the incarceration of children was based on sentiment or justice and whether the intended purpose was protective rather than penal, rehabilitative rather than punitive. This suggests that the rhetorical impact was as important as its physical manifestations, and being seen to protect childhood was perhaps more important than the protection of real children, which in turn accounted for the lack of financial support. The insertion of an additional clause that gave the government power 'to exclude any class of children, young persons or youthful offenders from the operation of all or any of the provisions' was passed without significant comment, on the understanding that there was a lack of facilities for female children and it would be inappropriate to include them in a certified school.[54] This mirrored the exemptions for girls under the compulsory education schemes (Chapters 1 and 2). However, as with the IJC, children from groups designated criminal tribes were also assumed to be outside the scope of the act. Similar to its British predecessor, the Children Act began on the premise that children have a special right to protection, but in the Madras context this could be withdrawn from those who did not fulfil a normative idea of childhood, explicitly excluding children from legal status as individuals on the basis of gender and community.

Clause 29: The Child in Danger

Clause 29 proved to be the most consistently controversial aspect of the act. This clause facilitated sending children to a junior certified school or placing them in the control of a designated guardian if they were 'found wandering and not having any home or settled place of abode, or visible means of subsistence'; had 'no parent or guardian'; were 'destitute'; were 'under the care of a parent or guardian who, by reason of criminal or drunken habits, is unfit to have the care of the child'; or kept the company of thieves or prostitutes. The child 'in danger', the marginal child threatened by either moral corruption or poverty, appeared to have a special claim to the protection of the state while still coming under the penal gaze of the state under the same terms as children who had broken the law in the expectation that without state action they would, almost inevitably, find themselves in a life of crime. This was made explicit by the British acting inspector-general of police, H. F. W. Gilman, when he reintroduced the bill in March 1918. He claimed that the government was motivated by 'the utter inadequacy of the power to protect young children who were, so to speak, potential criminals but had not committed any crime'.[55] The anxieties over 'potential criminals' were widespread and can be seen in a context of increasing support for state welfarism and state responsibility for the destitute, evidenced in the provision of food (see Chapter 4) and ultimately given legislative form in the Vagrancy Act of 1943.[56] The terms of the debate around Clause 29 demonstrated this support and enabled the state to 'look after people who would otherwise not be looked after'.[57] At the same time, there was concern that begging should not be outlawed, as it contributed to the subsistence and cultural practices of Brahmin students, and the legislation was explicitly designed to target 'persons belonging to the lower classes'.[58] The law therefore had the dual function of providing for the poor but was also a means of signalling class difference and privilege, as poor children became objects to be saved. Significantly, the structural causes of poverty, particularly the role of caste, were never mentioned.

Clause 29 clearly indicated a concern among legislators regarding the impact of poverty but contained within it an underlying assumption that the state should only intervene if parents were absent or demonstrably harmful to their children. The chief inspector of certified schools emphasised 'the special responsibility of the Government to these children who in such cases have no home to go to and no one to take care of them'.[59] However, proposals by the Madras Corporation, Public (Police) Department and the Madras Children's Aid Society (MCAS) for the 'establishment of a Children's Home in the city to which children begging in the streets should be compulsorily sent by law' were rejected in both 1925 and 1935 due to lack of finances.[60] This was seen in the statistics of certified schools, so that in 1936 while 623 children were admitted to certified schools, only 44 (7 per cent) were detained directly under the destitution clauses of the MCA.[61] This can be understood in terms of a reluctance to finance intervention but also because of an underlying unease around criminalising children on account of poverty. Although Clause 29 was intended to protect the vulnerable child, it was also perceived as a means to 'enforce the responsibility of the parents for the good conduct of their children'.[62] This was a significant shift from nineteenth-century schemes to remove authority from Indian parents and was part of wider attempts to control or modernise the poor family by teaching the poor to parent properly and to control their habits, economic choices and hygiene. The act was intended to modernise familial forms of authority, emphasising the nuclear family and reinforcing that the father was responsible for the behaviour of the children. This removed other generations, particularly grandmothers, from the authority structure and reinforced the cultural and social significance of the family unit.[63] Families thus became both a source of threat to the moral and physical well-being of children and a key ally in the production of modern citizens.

Under Clause 29 the state had the power to intervene if the family was deemed a source of threat to the morality of the child. A number of amendments were suggested 'for the protection of poor innocents who are taken into houses of fame in order to be brought up as prostitutes' or who were dedicated as *devadasis*.⁶⁴ This was supported on the basis that 'girls need this protection much more than boys'; and it was emphasised that a 'person who brings up girls for the sake of prostitution does not deserve any consideration', having effectively forfeited their right to parental authority (see Chapter 7).⁶⁵ In a national public sphere where the division between public and private space was increasingly significant to both colonial and nationalist claims to authority and regulation, and the nuclear family was becoming increasingly important as a signifier of modernity, the sexual innocence of children was particularly threatened by the behaviours and practices of non-traditional family structures, particularly those without a strong male head.⁶⁶ Very quickly, the terms of the debate moved from 'the good of the child' to the 'good of the country', intersecting with wider anxieties surrounding the female body, normative sexual practices, family honour and the social body of the nation.⁶⁷ Ultimately, these amendments were withdrawn on the promise of a more wide-ranging bill to deal with prostitution from the Imperial Council in Delhi. Yet despite the numerical definition of childhood within the MCA, children who were sexually active were legally defined in terms of gender rather than age, and for girls, sexual innocence appears to be the key boundary of childhood (see Chapter 7).⁶⁸ The state therefore had to negotiate between the twin duties of care for 'children who may soon become offenders unless they are protected' and guarding the innocence of those already incarcerated to ensure 'proper control is exercised that they are free from contamination'.⁶⁹

Sexual activity was not the only moral threat to the child. The judge M. D. Devadoss introduced a further section, Part VII, Offences Relating to Children, which covered wilful assault, neglect or ill-treatment by those with custody or care of the child that would endanger the child's physical or mental well-being, including the sale of cigarettes, beedis or intoxicating liquor to those under fifteen years.⁷⁰ This challenged the behaviours and responsibilities of the father much more directly, but despite receiving support from the Madras Municipal Corporation, the amendment was withdrawn due to a lack of evidence. The issue of child exploitation was revisited with a proposed amendment in 1932 to bring the MCA into line with subsequent acts from other provinces and align it more closely with its British antecedent.⁷¹ A. B. Shetty, a Theosophist, independent member of parliament and former minister for public health, joined with the chief inspector of schools in his 1931 report to argue that 'the exploitation of children' should become 'a punishable offence' and required early intervention so that 'these unfortunate children can be saved from a life of crime' enabling them 'to grow up as good citizens'.[72] This reflected widespread concern about the seduction of minor children for 'immoral purposes', but also a change towards active protection, not only removal 'from an immoral atmosphere' but also the prevention of smoking, gambling and 'neglect of and cruelty to children'.[73] Although the motion was carried, there was serious concern that this would compromise the ordinary corporal discipline of the family as well as prove financially and logistically impossible.[74] A further amendment in 1936 sought to replace institutional care with the extension of probation by relatives or 'suitable gentlemen'.[75] Within the discourses surrounding the MCA, there emerged a commitment to the protection of children as future citizens or national investments, a recognition of the duty of the state to intervene if the family posed a threat to child's moral well-being, but also a continuing reluctance to actively intervene in the family and undermine the power structures there.

The suggestion that the government spent 'more on the young criminal than on the honest youth' and saw this as a 'sort of insurance provision against crime' was controversial.[76] The practical outworkings of this complex relationship between the state, the parents and the destitute child were highlighted in a legal case in 1942.[77] In July 1942, the sub-divisional magistrate of Bezwada tried a group of five children (aged eleven–thirteen years) who had been arrested by the Railway Police. He ruled that the children were particularly lacking in familial control:

> ... forsaken destitutes with no means of subsistence except begging ... causing a lot of inconvenience and annoyance to the travelling public, and they were also committing petty offences such as pilfering away the food bundles of the passengers.... These children have no control exercised over them, they have no means of livelihood. It is therefore obvious that the respondents are fit subjects for the exercise by the state of guardianship over them.[78]

The five were committed to the junior certified school at Bellary, where they lived until December 1942, when eleven-year-old Gullipalli Yerrayya took the opportunity to protest to the Committee of Visitors that the Railway Police had assumed that he was abandoned but that he wanted to return home to his elder brother.[79] After extensive correspondence between the Committee of Visitors, G. Narayanaswami Chetty, inspector of certified schools, and Chief Inspector G. S. Gill, it was agreed that incarceration was not appropriate if their parents were alive, but that the decision was taken after extensive investigation into the personal circumstances of the boys and scientific verification of their age by the assistant surgeon.[80] The district superintendent of Railway Police defended the decision to use Clause 29 (1) because 'the respondents have no visible means of subsistence and that they [the family] have not exercised *proper guardianship*'.[81] Ultimately, the boys remained at Bellary, but the case indicated that the boundaries of incarceration were clearly grounded in parental control, or at least familial assumption of responsibility for moral and physical well-being.[82] There was underlying concern that it was easier for magistrates to send destitute children to certified schools than carry out the necessary investigations to trace parents, but the Bezwada case demonstrated the ambivalence of the state towards destitute children and the continuing assumption by all adults involved that the primary responsibility for the child lay with the family.[83] Most remarkable of all, this case came to government attention when a child queried the terms of his own imprisonment. The key determinant of state intervention was, therefore, not poverty or criminality so much as the absence of parental, or familial, authority and care.

Profiling Juvenile Crime

There are very few court records documenting the treatment of children in the 1920s. A small sample based on the records of the presidency magistrate courts in Georgetown and Egmore detail the juvenile cases dealt with between 1922 and 1924, in a document produced for the Education Department to assess juvenile crime rates and provide a statistical basis for future action.[84] These records are among the few that include information about individuals. For example, Case 18334 refers to a boy of fourteen years called Munisami who was convicted of stealing (Article 379 of the Indian Penal Code) in the Georgetown Presidency Magistrates Court on 16 October 1922 and who received six lashes in punishment. The records detailed 240 cases for the Georgetown Court and

103 for Egmore. This did not include night cases from Egmore under the City Police Act, which merely gave the number of cases brought by the police, with no specific crime mentioned. The child was defined by age, although with the lack of birth registration there was no proof that children knew their own ages accurately and no mention was made of the criteria used by magistrates to define age, a perennial problem.[85] Home district was not recorded, despite the position of the Egmore Court beside the city's main railway station and evidence that migrant children were more likely to be in need of both protection and care from state agencies.[86] Despite the political focus on gendered crime and prostitution during the 1920s and the increasing importance of educational communities defined by caste and religion, none of these categories were recorded. As well as demonstrating again the arbitrary nature of colonial categorisation, the fact that age was the primary mode of identification reveals the beginnings of a numerical obsession as defining the boundaries of childhood by biological age despite obvious concerns about accuracy. This was a significant new development for the presidency, which reflected international trends in child-saving rather than colonial trends in statistics and governance.

The children were charged with a number of crimes, mostly related to theft or house-breaking or nuisance crime under the City Police Act.[87] Only six were held under the MCA and none were arrested for begging, despite the emphasis in the act. Between both courts, there was only one acquittal, suggesting a presumption of guilt rather than a process of criminal justice, emphasising that the child was in need of protection rather than of lesser criminal responsibility. In Egmore, 18 per cent were discharged 'after due admonition' compared to 7 per cent in Georgetown, although more often in Egmore with a surety of 50 rupees (occasionally 100 rupees) paid by the father on condition of good behaviour. The preferred Georgetown method was to use minor fines, ranging from 2 *annas* to 5 rupees, which made up nearly 50 per cent of all punishments, again reflecting the financial responsibility of the father. Corporal punishment was the most common penalty, always for theft, and six lashes were administered 'in the manner of school discipline' in 49 per cent of the Egmore cases. By contrast, the Georgetown magistrates were significantly less likely to sentence corporal punishment (36 per cent), but it was usually much harsher: of the 85 individuals thus sentenced, 21 per cent received ten lashes and 19 per cent received twelve. The courts appear to have used punishment as a deterrent while attempting to enforce the responsibility of the parents by giving them a small financial burden. The disparity in practice shows the local and somewhat arbitrary nature of criminal justice and the need to look beyond justice theory to its implementation, which varied even between two adjoining areas in Madras City. The Egmore magistrates seemed more progressive, being more likely to recommend probation (10 per cent) and certified schools (16 per cent) and using less severe corporal punishment. Of those sent to certified schools, whether senior or junior, six were sentenced under Clause 29 of the MCA, and whether the rest were repeat offenders or lacked parents is unclear; there is nothing to suggest that the crimes for which they were accused were any different in type, though perhaps in scale, from their peers. In a climate of financial constraint when adult justice was still considered the priority, the state was reluctant to assume a parental role, either in responsibility or financially, and the overriding impetus appears to be enforcement of parental responsibility rather than the establishment of legal innocence.

The children sent to certified schools lived under the gaze of the state to a far greater extent than the majority and are more visible, albeit as statistics rather than personalities, in the surviving records. In 1919 the government managed one reformatory with 252 inmates.[88] By 1940, there were five institutions with 1,426 inmates, of which 10 per cent were female, 9 per cent were Dalits and 45 per cent were from rural communities, reflecting the general demographic profiling of the presidency.[89] A comparison of the literacy rates on admission for 1931, 1935 and 1942 (22 per cent, 33 per cent and 41 per cent, respectively) demonstrated that the expansion of education provision to lower-class boys was bearing fruit, although the percentage who self-described their occupation on admission as 'school pupils' remained low (in 1942, only 3 per cent). By 1942 the vast majority (73 per cent) were 'not in employment', whereas in previous years the variety of employment was much greater, whether in professional handicrafts, agriculture or as labourers. There was also a decline in those categorised as 'beggars and wanderers' (1931: 11 per cent; 1935: 15 per cent; 1942: 3 per cent), although the total number of children admitted in 1942 (960) was much greater than in previous years (172 and 334 in 1931 and 1935, respectively).[90] It is unclear whether this indicates a rise in child poverty, a reluctance to employ children or a greater desire on the part of the state to provide for children with no means of subsistence. Of course, these figures were unverified and were reliant on the children's testimony.

While most children were incarcerated for two–three years (31 per cent), the administration report of 1935 indicated 32 (10 per cent) were sentenced for between five and ten years, and 19 (6 per cent) for more than ten years. From the age profiles, 35 per cent of those under twelve years would spend over five years in the certified school, implying extensive disruption to family life or, more likely, incarceration because no family could be traced. In 1931, 31 per cent of those sentenced for over five years were committed under Clauses 29 and 30. For example, in one 1925 case, five children were sent by the Georgetown Magistrate Court to the Madras Society for the Protection of Children (MSPC) Junior Certified School for between six and two years until they reached the age of sixteen 'or until such time they are claimed in the meanwhile by their relatives', 'as evidently there is no one to take care of them, and as they are destitutes'.[91] This was reinforced by the figures on sentencing from the remand home run by the MCAS, where the vast majority were returned to their parents or released with warnings and a very small proportion were sent to certified schools, probably because their parents could not be traced.[92] This contradicts the arguments of Sen and Balagopalan that state actors were interested in becoming 'surrogate parents' and that the removal of the child from the irretrievably flawed poor family was a key aspect of the legislation.[93] The MCA might have been rhetorically about the reclamation of the delinquent child, but in practice it provided care for those without family support networks and reinforced the authority of the family.

Implementation through Certified Schools

It proved easier to produce a broad consensus among legislators that the child be saved from a life of crime than to agree on how this would be funded and which department was responsible. Current writings on the Indian juvenile justice system demonstrate the fundamental disconnect between the espoused rights of children in law and the 'rightlessness' of practice, children remaining an especially disempowered and marginalised group.[94] The seeds of this were obvious in the Madras Presidency, and five years after the legislation was passed, the MCA applied only to Madras City, Chingleput and North Arcot and only to male children.[95] Other limited sections applied to Cuddalore, Salem, Trichinopoly, Coimbatore and Madura and within the jurisdiction of the Railway Police. In September 1925, only Sections 25 and 26 were in force for all children of both sexes throughout the presidency, highlighting exclusions based on age, gender and provinciality but due largely to the lack of political will to fund the other functions of the act.[96] It is significant too that the only operative sections were those that related to parental responsibility for the conduct of their children or the need to appoint alternative guardians to fulfil that role.

The MCA was implemented through civic activism but also through institutions directly funded and managed by the state: the certified schools. The Chingleput Reformatory, renamed as a senior certified school, was established under the Reformatory Schools Act, 1897, and had a record of functioning effectively, and a junior certified school was established at Ranipet, the first boys arriving there in April 1923.[97] A further school was temporarily established in Rajahmundry, but transferred to Bellary in November 1931. By 1937, there was also a senior certified school for girls in Madras City run by the MCAS, a junior certified school run by the MSPC and St Mary's Adi-Dravida Girls School in Vellore, the only explicitly caste-based institution.[98] A remand home run by the MCAS was recognised in 1926 as an institution to offer temporary accommodation to children awaiting trial or found in the city without parents.[99] There was also a government-managed borstal (or boy's penitentiary) at Palayamkottai for adolescents between sixteen and twenty-one years.[100]

The certified schools were managed by a number of government departments. The act was initiated by the Law (Education) Department after the passing of the Government of India Act, 1919, but before it came into operation. Until 1939 the statistics for the certified schools were discussed in the Annual and Quinquennial Reports of the director of public instruction (DPI), and the schools continued to be funded through the budgets of the Law (Education), then Law and Education and then Education Department, making it a firmly educational endeavour. In 1919, there was a brief attempt to bring in a member of the medical service as superintendent of Chingleput tasked with improving the physical health of the boys there.[101] When the MCA came into force, he was replaced by a member of the Madras Educational Service under the supervision of the inspector of European schools, now redesignated chief inspector of certified schools.¹⁰² In 1923–24, another officer from the Madras Education Service was appointed but was regarded as 'not really of the proper type'.¹⁰³ He was replaced by an officer of the Jail Department on an enhanced salary, in line with other penal institutions. This issue was used by V. T. Krishnamachariar of the Education Department to move the certified schools to the administrative jurisdiction of the Jail Department, despite the 'sentimental objection to associating them with Prisons' because of the lack of interest shown by the Education Department and despite the opposition of the DPI.¹⁰⁴ The decision was based on the 'special science of juvenile penology and prevention of crime', which required that staff 'apply to their treatment of the subject the modern methods which we are already trying to apply into the Prisons Department'.¹⁰⁵

In 1925 A. P. Patro, as Justice Party minister for education, highlighted the complicated nature of the management of the certified schools, with the MCA funded from the education budget but the home minister being the responsible member in the MLC. He emphasised that while the certified schools were not penal institutions, the specialisms for dealing with rehabilitation lay with the Jail Department, and the educational officers lacked both 'experience and training' in modern penology. He also pressed, without avail, for the use of 'highly trained specialists' involving 'the application to each case of medical science in the form of psychiatry'.¹⁰⁶ The Justice Party was interested in portraying juvenile justice as rehabilitative, not penal, based on the idea of the child as an individual and emphasising the production of law-abiding citizens rather than the criminalising of a community—by caste or socio-economic background. Both Chingleput and Ranipet were transferred to the control of the Inspector-General of Prisons Lt-Col Cameron, although Cameron continued to use the inspectors from the Education Department.¹⁰⁷ The slow expansion of other provisions of the act, including the juvenile courts, was carried out meanwhile under the control of the Home Department. While children were the emotive centre, they were used in power struggles between ICS departments and budgets and indicated the increasing power of professionals, themselves in conflict about the differing priorities of modern educational and criminological practices, although the discussions reveal a wide consensus regarding the need for rehabilitation. A symbolic and discursive concern did not mean funding, however, and the money spent per head decreased significantly between

1919 and 1939.[108] This focus on rehabilitating child criminals who in practice were incarcerated primarily because they had lost contact with their parents reveals a conceptual flaw at the heart of the juvenile justice project.

The Content of Schooling: From Orphans to Rehabilitated Citizens

The different ways in which the MCA was interpreted by the judiciary, legislators and officials reveal discursive confusion over the balance between care, protection, punishment and rehabilitation in the certified schools. The causes of incarceration appear to have had little impact on educational practice and all children were viewed as flawed, malleable and vulnerable objects to be reformed in the service of the nation. The rules governing the certified schools were agreed upon by politicians in the MLC and mirrored the rules for accommodation, sanitation and curriculum established by the DPI for other educational establishments. The schools were controlled by a superintendent, and assisted by a medical officer. The aims were summarised by the chief inspector of certified schools in the annual report for 1931:

> We try to broaden the mental outlook, teach the responsibilities of citizenship and equip each lad with a sound practical grounding in some useful industry. Great stress is laid upon the importance of character building during the years of school life. School discipline doubtless has a very definite effect upon the training of pupils for after-life and the development of worthy ideals of conduct and given the opportunity of clean and healthy physical exercise and recreation in the jolly atmosphere of comrade-like emulation, good results must naturally follow. The basic idea is that a lad brimming over with the vital energy of youth will develop a sound moral sense if he gets the right outlets for exercising that energy healthily and the right atmosphere in which his own innate instincts of fair play, good sportsmanship and observance of the square deal in his association with his fellows, can expand and flourish. The gymnasium gives him a paradise for play; these strenuous games challenge physical strength and health and such play becomes the compelling force, calling a boy of his own volition to a standard of clean living. As the long school day passes every detail of it is meticulously regulated thus helped the lad to

make the most of himself and enable him to bear his own burden on discharge.[109]

The focus on the 'mental outlook' meant that children received basic literacy and general education, as well as a vocational training which would provide practical skills. Ranipet developed into a higher elementary school with six standards, while Bellary gave pupils a general education and a choice of weaving, carpentry, tailoring and gardening. The curriculum at Chingleput was divided into two three-hour sections. The general education course endeavoured to educate the children as 'citizens-in-waiting' into a relationship with the nation state through a study of English, geography, Indian history, civics and hygiene.[110] In the industrial section, specialist instructors taught trades such as carpentry, blacksmithy and weaving. In the girls' schools, the children learned 'feminine handicrafts' of tailoring, lace-making, weaving and rattan work. The emphasis on vocational work was also intended to provide children with an honest trade to use on release, a strategy intended to prevent long-term poverty as the primary cause of crime. While three years at school was regarded as the minimum time needed to reform the character and instil a disciplined attitude to labour, it was also the minimum required to adequately teach a boy a trade.[111]

The reformative results of this education were monitored and a detailed statistical account kept of discharged children, although the figures were necessarily limited given the large numbers who did not report back. To some extent the education was successful, and when in 1927, 74 pupils were discharged from Chingleput, only 3 were reconvicted. Although rarely mentioned in the official documents, it was not insignificant that the schools claimed full literacy on release, a considerable advantage for the children when general literacy rates remained low in the wider population. Some children profited more directly from their association with the penal system, gaining social capital through literacy and becoming teachers, jail instructors or railway workers, career options not available to most impoverished children and ones which ensured continued contact with the state.[112] This was encouraged by the superintendent at Chingleput, who encouraged boys to be licensed out for a year prior to their release, particularly to the army or other forms of government employment, as a form of gradual reintroduction to society and because public departments were more likely to provide 'the moral ballast which they need'.[113]

A career in the brass band was considered one of the optimum choices for a boy from a certified school, providing 'the morality of an honest livelihood' and a continuing ethic of military discipline.[114] Nicola Sheldon has argued that music was an important pedagogical technique in British reformatories, encouraging moral values such as self-discipline but also providing a creative release for the boys and the opportunity for talent to emerge.[115] By the twentieth century, brass bands had become an embodiment of the imperial experience, linked to the military, Empire Day and missionary uplift projects.[116] In 1927–32 the junior school at Rajahmundry (then Bellary) provided instruction in bugle and band skills while Ranipet included bugle, flute and bagpipe.[117] Chingleput had a strong music curriculum: for example, in 1934 ten of the fourteen who studied band left to join regimental bands, either in the military, police or the Jail Department.[118] The school had invested in music and in the relationship with the regiments since the late nineteenth century, and its reputation was well established, although there is no evidence of them having their own band.[119] Again, for a minority of children, music provided the social capital needed for an independent career, yet one still closely tied to the structures of the colonial state.[120]

For the majority, the vocational instruction had little long-term impact and most returned to a life of agricultural labour. In 1931 none of the children from Bellary followed the vocations taught in school, and in Ranipet less than 40 per cent did so.[121] This would suggest that the skills gained were insufficient to sustain a livelihood. While some items produced by the children were sold and there was a drive for self-sufficiency and some limited remuneration for the children, it appears that the products produced were of limited interest or quality. There is no evidence of investment in tools upon release, but also no reference was made to the wider societal beliefs surrounding caste and occupation and whether the children would be able to integrate into a skilled community. It is more likely that practical instruction was used as a tool in the moral reformation of character. Balagopalan and Sen have previously highlighted the disciplinary impact of vocational crafts and strict school timetabling, with the institutionalised child regulated through time discipline, the meticulous regulation of the day mentioned earlier, into a life of honest and productive labour and approach to employers and authority characterised by 'docility and subordination'.[122] It is also likely that practical subjects were the easiest way to keep the boys occupied and out of mischief.

School and the Body

Particular attention was paid to the reformation of character through the regulation of 'the vital energy of youth' to produce the 'manly body'.[123] More important than intellectual achievement, self-discipline, fair play, comradeship and clean living were to be embodied by the children and games were intended to promote 'healthy thought and conversation'.[124] Chingleput was particularly noted for its excellence in athletics and the school won a number of local athletic competitions.[125] This was hardly surprising, given an hour every morning and afternoon was devoted to team games, boxing and athletics in the belief that 'in the playing field and the gymnasium self-control and good sportsmanship are more or less self-taught'.[126] Madras Presidency was a frontrunner in encouraging scouting in the certified schools, and as a result the Third All-Indian Conference of Inspectors-General of Prisons resolved unanimously to introduce scouting in all institutions for young offenders across India as 'it was felt that the basic principles of the Scout Movement and the Borstal System have much in common'.[127] Scouting reinforced the idea of self-disciplined and militarised masculinity but also helped encourage contact with those outside the penal regime, particularly in inter-school competitions, important events for children who could spend up to ten years in a certified school.[128] The Ranipet troops, for example, were represented at the District Scout Rally at Vellore in August 1924, where the scout troop came sixth, and the cub pack won the cub flag.[129] The 1936 report praised the Chingleput scout crafts exhibition, and the Girl Guides of the MCAS school gained prizes in the National Health Association essay competition, the music concert and the arts and crafts exhibition.[130] The competitive pride in an institutional identity, expressed through scouting, was also an important disciplinary tool in engendering state loyalty and raising the profile of these institutions in the population more generally.

Ideas about colonial masculinity were closely linked to the production of a healthy body in the barracks as well as on the playing field.[131] In 1919 and 1936, Chingleput went through extensive changes in sanitary provision, medical care and a dietary review, as did Ranipet in 1925. This was supported by the collection of health statistics, for example, the monthly registers of weight and prescription of the specific, size-related amounts of food due to each child bringing each child under the governmental gaze of state actors.[132] Sen has argued that a fear of juvenile homosexuality helped to produce the normative discourses on gender, generation, race and sexual preference used to justify the colonial and incarceration projects.[133] These anxieties were seen in the evidence to the Jails Committee; for example, Mr A. J. Nicholas, superintendent of Tanjore Borstal, wanted the removal of sexually active boys to an adult jail, drawing the boundaries of childhood in sexual innocence rather than numerical age, as was often the case for girls.[134] However, none of the administration reports from the 1920s or 1930s mention sexual activity, possibly through lack of evidence or effective surveillance, or perhaps because this might suggest that the state was a failed parent unable to protect the vulnerable.

Children with the certified schools were subjected to corporeal control and moral rehabilitation through work discipline, an incentive regime, surveillance and control over bodily practices and, more directly, coercive disciplinary practices. School discipline was recorded in detail, with detailed discussion of good conduct badges as a financial incentive and of remuneration for industrial work, children receiving a small percentage, half for saving, half for sweetmeats or toys—an interesting concession to childish desire. Boys were disciplined according to a monitor system, with punishment by loss of marks or good conduct badges, deprivation of play hour, temporary cessation of family visits, corporal punishment and deduction of earnings. Boys were also allowed a monthly visit from parents and no more than six leaves of absence annually to visit relatives if behaviour 'justified such a privilege'.[135] Vast numbers of administrative statistics were produced, including library catalogues, clothing receipts, pupil savings bank accounts and histories of discharged pupils, reflecting a colonial desire for control through classification and surveillance over the minutiae of daily life.[136] The school superintendents also continually stressed the lack of physical enclosures as a pedagogical technique: 'there were certainly a good many escapes' but if 'our object is to awaken a sense of personal responsibility and teach boys to be confident, straightforward and self-reliant, it is necessary to trust them and give them some measure of freedom'.[137] In 1930, for instance, there were twenty-two escapes, and of these seventeen were recaptured. The chief inspector maintained the escapee tended to be a recent offender, not yet institutionalised, who was still 'developing his power of choice between right and wrong' but 'may fail and take a false step towards liberty especially during the early period of training when he is homesick'.[138] Encouraging the boys to internalise values of self-discipline was central to the moral disciplinary regime and the long-term production of docile subjects.

While the normal workings of the school were centred on the production of disciplined future citizens, punishment for misdemeanours was still necessary, reinforcing the coercive physical power of wardens and teachers. The report of 1930 detailed 84 offences, most related to breaking school rules, although 7 were issued because children were found with prohibited articles and 10 were assaults. The punishments involved: two confined to barracks, four warnings, one whipping, eight had their status as monitors reduced and sixty-nine received 'cuts' on the palm.[139] In the 1934 report, there were 178 offences, 5 being assaults and escapes, 25 relating to prohibited articles and the rest relating to the school rules. There were 613 inmates so this could have involved nearly one-third of the children, although it is not clear whether any were repeat offenders. The punishments included nine being deprived of marks and leisure hours, one warning, nine status reductions, 147 received 'cuts' on the palm and thirteen other punishments, but there was no case of whipping.[140] The pattern of limited punishments reflected a global trend towards progressive penology, with the use of controlled physical pain against the body of the child remaining the most common. The details of children's actions or motivations are limited; there was sufficient evidence in the many minor offences committed (which might be called 'weapons of the weak') to cause upset to the colonial 'parental state' or at least minor disruption to the life of the reformatory.[141] This provides some indication not only of how the children managed the disciplinary boundaries set by adult authority but also how their own actions contributed to discourses of control and power within the certified schools.[142]

Given the sanitising effect of colonial reports, it is difficult to ascertain how daily life was experienced by the children themselves within the certified schools. The only clear division that emerges is between sexes, although female children seem to have been segregated on the basis of sexual innocence. Although the difference between destitute and delinquent children remained a point of contention and children from criminal tribes were not under the jurisdiction of the Children Act, within the certified schools themselves there seems to have been little differentiation in status or treatment. Statistics were kept for religion, occupation and age, but there was no interest shown in caste. The ethos was one of care and the production of future citizens through education and internalising values of hard work and self-discipline, although with limited corporal punishment to reinforce authority. The success of these measures in the lives of the children is very difficult to assess, as is the impact of institutionalisation on the emotional well-being of the child. While the certified school may have been seen as an oppressive centre of adult authority, it may also have been a rational short-term survival strategy, which provided shelter and food and relief from adult responsibilities, or even long-term advantage in training and employment opportunities to those without family support.

Conclusion

The 1920s and 1930s were crucial decades for the foundation of child welfare in the Madras Presidency. This reflected a growing discursive consensus shared by legislators, practitioners and theorists and was based on a claim that an Indian child should be equally entitled to the same protection and treatment as a British child. This meant that the legislative provisions of the 1908 British Children Act and 1920 MCA should be equivalent, and there was increasing reference to global discourses surrounding the universal rights of the child based on a numerical definition of age. This actively contested long-held colonial arguments of Indian racial and cultural inferiority, and the claim to equality and the universality of children's rights provided another means by which Indian elites could undermine the political hegemony and claimed cultural superiority of the British. However, using the discourse of universality as a political strategy to prove their own modernity meant that both politicians and practitioners were reluctant to engage with culturally specific ideas about criminology and juvenile penology. At the same time, the failure to consider what juvenile justice could or should look like in the south Indian context, in turn, reinforced the hegemony of an idea of modern childhood that traced its intellectual heritage to the emergence of modernity in Europe.

The MCA and the juvenile justice system in the Madras Presidency were based on two broad principles. The first was that criminal justice was intended to fulfil a rehabilitative rather than penal function. The agreed responsibility of the modern welfare state was to protect and care for vulnerable children using recognisably modern disciplinary methods, rooted in the belief that all children, except those of the criminal tribes, had the capacity to become productive citizens. Any conflict that emerged reflected minor disagreements about the authority and financial resources of the differing government departments. The second principle was that the family remained the key focus for state intervention and was much more important than the individual child. The irregular family was a potential threat to the child, either through poverty or moral failing, yet the patriarchal nuclear family was also the most effective tool of restoration. The judiciary and policymakers sought to teach poor fathers to take more active responsibility to provide for and to educate their children, and at times the enforcement of parental responsibility physically and financially (Clauses 25 and 26) was the only juvenile justice provision in place for most of the presidency. Despite the emphasis on the need to care for the destitute child, the defining reason for a child's institutionalisation was the absence of parents rather than criminal responsibility or socio-economic distress. In practice, and perhaps implicit in theory, juvenile justice was concerned primarily with the regulation of the poor family into a new relationship with the modern state.

The certified schools focused on the reformation of the child's character through corporeal control and education in order to produce future citizens of the nation who had been educated into a disciplined and productive labour force. To some extent they succeeded, and with full literacy on release, the employment and future opportunities of individual children were significantly enhanced. The volume of statistics produced was impressive, and reveals a state motivated by a desire to be perceived as modern, competent to govern and in tune with emerging global discourses of juvenile delinquency. The radicalism of the MCA should not be overlooked, given that it was the first of its kind on the subcontinent. It claimed equality for Indian children with children across the globe, and it defined the child both as a future citizen and as the responsibility of the state in ways previously unknown in British India. The MCA was one of the first pieces of legislation that defined the child in terms of age, introducing a new category of governance where numerical age was consistently more important than race or caste. Yet, in practice, the legislation impacted very few of the many vulnerable children in the presidency, largely due to a lack of capacity. It appears that the provincial governments of Madras were more interested in being seen to protect childhood than in protecting significant numbers of real children.

6

Protecting the Poor Child

The Practical Expansion of Juvenile Justice

The passing of the Madras Children Act, 1920 (MCA) demonstrated a new concern for children among legislators, and the development of a consensus regarding children as uniquely vulnerable because of their age, as worthy of investment as future citizens and therefore as the responsibility of the state. Although the act attempted to signal the modernity of the state, the responsibility for the implementation of the act was unclear, with the exception of the government-run certified schools discussed in Chapter 5. This chapter explores the ways in which civil society assumed the responsibility to extend juvenile justice provisions, albeit still in conjunction with state actors such as politicians, officials and salaried magistrates, and how these societies and their members became important contributors to the discourses surrounding childhood and the child in need of care or control. During the 1920s the Madras Children's Aid Society (MCAS) emerged as the most significant child-saving organisation, and this chapter interrogates its position in the public sphere of the Madras Presidency as well as its aims and methods. The second half of the chapter considers the implementation of the MCA in the juvenile court, with an analysis of the space and personnel of the juvenile court system, the probation service and the boys club.

Within the context of juvenile justice, between 1925 and 1940 there was a marked expansion of 'the social' as a depoliticised area at the intersection between the state, the family, civil society and expert professionals.¹ This was in contrast to the political sphere, which was characterised by increasingly assertive nationalist attempts to contest both the exercise of power by, and the moral foundations of, the racialised colonial state, often through social questions such as the age of consent (see Chapter 7).² While many of the individuals were actively engaged in the anti-colonial movement, the Indianisation of state structures through dyarchy and newly reformulated ideas about philanthropy and civil society encouraged highly educated middle-class Indians to participate in public life based on new notions of social service and civic activism as a form of patriotism, even as these ideas were to some extent a reformulation of previous ideas about religious duty and social reform.³ In the European context, Garland argues that this new sphere of the social was 'an *alliance* between the private and the public, the state and the volunteer' in which the state 'empowered' the implementation of policy by middle-class experts and volunteers.⁴ However, to analyse this only through the lens of class is insufficient and underplays the specific historical moment, although the regulation of lower-class families, their norms and behaviours remained important.⁵ Anne Logan has highlighted how policy in Britain was formulated through a small group of interconnected individuals and activists in the labour, feminist and penal reform movements, often with personal links to the civil service.⁶ This chapter considers the complex and gendered networks involved in child welfare and juvenile justice in the Madras context, the nature of their relationship with the state and the ways in which an emphasis on humanitarian care for the child and the implementation of progressive policy cemented their position as a globally networked modern elite and helped to promote, and indeed justify, their participation in the public sphere. Unpicking the details of these ideas, individuals and interactions further helps to uncover the way in which children were constructed as objects of social action.

Examining the ways in which civil society organisations implemented policy around juvenile justice refines our understanding of how childhood was imagined by the educated middle classes. In particular, it demonstrates the vibrant ways in which individual Indians were part of global networks of information exchange regarding children's rights to protection and care as universal expectations, and the creativity and anxieties with which they engaged with questions surrounding the cultural specificity of childhood when faced with real children. Furthermore, the ways in which the MCAS organised and funded the juvenile courts and probation system reveal how destitute children in contact with the law—whether they were beggars, were found wandering or had committed petty crime—were envisaged as victims and as objects of protection and of care rather than as rights-bearing future citizens who deserved legal protection, or even as immature subjects with less responsibility because of their youth. This entrenched a welfare model of juvenile justice that was to last well into the twentieth century.[7]

An important aspect was the role of the poor Indian family and the extent to which these new ideas interacted with changing perceptions of the Indian family structure.[8] If the parents were to be responsible for the child under the terms of the MCA, how this was to be implemented in practice is important. One of the ways in which outsiders justified intervention was by using the metaphors of the family, particularly as maternal. The civil society activists, the men granted probation rights and the employees such as the probation officers saw themselves in terms of wider familial relations, as closer to the child than the colonial state and as therefore within the extended family as avuncular. This gave legitimacy to intervention and contributed to the changing interpretations of the family, but it also honoured the cultural norms of both nuclear and extended families.[9]

Child-Saving Organisations

The MCA confirmed a new consensus among policymakers that a child was a distinct legal entity and was entitled to state action to defend their rights to protection and care. However, the implementation of many of the provisions was left to civil society. This fell initially to the Madras Society for the Protection of Children (MSPC), a non-governmental organisation established in 1908 for the protection and maintenance of orphan and destitute children under fourteen years of age, although with a particular focus on those under the age of eight.[10] The managing committee in 1922 was male and highly educated. It included C. Cunnan Chetti, a noted educational philanthropist; Sir C. Sankaran Nair, former judge and member for education in the Viceroy's Council; and Sir John Wallis, an Anglo-Indian advocate-general and former chief justice. With the governor-general as president, the management of the society had close personal links with the governing establishment.[11] The MSPC ran a home in Madras City, which its managing committee hoped could be certified as an industrial school under the MCA.[12] The home provided shelter and tuition in gender-based skills: the boys in carpentry and gardening, and girls in sewing, knitting, basket-making and cookery.[13] This work was funded by public subscriptions and a government grant which was to be two-thirds of the public subscriptions collected in the preceding year. Public contributions were not inconsiderable; in 1920 these were received from prominent philanthropists, such as the donation of 20,000 rupees from the Dr Varadappa Naidu Fund, as well as small-scale contributions of 2,415 rupees.[14] By contrast, repeated grant applications to the government for additional facilities were refused because there was no provision in the budget. By 1923 both the MSPC and director of public instruction (DPI) were claiming that the home was one of the few that could carry out the provisions of the MCA and therefore required a 'liberal grant' in 1924–25.[15]

The MCA was expanded under the authority of the Education Department, and after 1935 by the Home Department. No evidence has emerged that it was ever costed by the government but was merely implemented as a principle. In 1925 the Education Department wrote to the MSPC expressing concern that the society's work was concentrated on the children's home and 'the large problem of rescuing and reforming the incipient criminal is not prominently kept in view'.[16] This was a deliberate strategy on the part of the MSPC, which carved out a role as a Clause 29 organisation, interested primarily in rescuing orphaned children from destitution rather than reforming those already in contact with the justice system.[17] Indeed, 'the classification of both children not at fault and at fault' was central to their practical governance.[18] Provision for the destitute child in need of care remained central to their purpose, although they became briefly involved in negotiations in 1925 for the establishment of the State Children's Council to assist in the functioning of the MCA. The two organisations continued to work closely together and the MSPC continued to receive financial support from the state. This funding was strictly controlled, so that while a project in 1930 to construct a weaving shed to provide clothes and employable skills for the children received strong endorsement from the three inspectors of jails, schools and industries, it was paid for by private donation from a retired education officer.[19] The annual subsidy from the Madras government remained equal to subscriptions and donations, subject to a maximum of 3,000 rupees.[20] This was strongly enforced when the donations fell below 3,000 rupees, but when in 1930 the society raised 5,000 rupees, the request to match this figure was refused.[21] In 1935 the government only matched the 1,830 rupees that the society managed to raise, despite reserving 3,000 rupees in the budget and despite the attempts to argue that they were hampered by the global economic situation. They also claimed they particularly deserved financial support because 'the institution is the only one in South India which admits all castes', a very rare reference to caste.[22] Instead, the Managing Committee had to cover the shortfall from their personal wealth.[23] The Madras government was therefore reliant on private philanthropy to fund the basic provision of food and shelter, which they had themselves established in law as universal rights. Undoubtedly, government budgets were limited, particularly in the early 1930s, and many services were underfunded, but despite the rhetoric of protection and the assumption of responsibility, it was clear that destitute children were not a funding priority and it was instead the responsibility of wider civil society and upper-class philanthropy to invest in poor children as the future resource of the nation.

While the MSPC cared for the destitute, the other terms of the MCA existed only in the statute book. Accordingly, in December 1924 Mrs Hume Stanford wrote on behalf of the Women's India Association (WIA) to the government regarding the 'poor and uncared for children' of Madras.[24] Three months later, the WIA offered to establish and administer a children's court, providing honorary magistrates and supervising a 'place of safety' for the children under the terms of the act.[25] This was part of a wider set of correspondence which emphasised that among the primary concerns of the WIA, the foremost women's association in the presidency, was 'securing the welfare of children through health, legal and social agencies' to make the MCA 'a practical working protection for the children of Madras'.[26]

In response to the WIA agitation, the Education Department decided to create 'an experienced and energetic sub-committee of the MSPC'. Mrs Stanford was appointed the secretary, although controls were established to 'ensure that she has no right to supersede the officers and members of the society', a reflection on the restrictions placed on the philanthropic activities of white women.[27] Invitations to serve on the committee were sent to ICS education official V. T. Krishnamachari, a number of prominent Indian and British barristers and Mrs Vira Sing Chinnappa, superintendent of the Madras Corporation Child Welfare Scheme.[28] The discussions resulted in the establishment of a 'State Children's Council' specifically responsible for 'rescuing' children 'not acceptable to the [MPSC] Society' and to 'advise Government as to the measures to be taken in *the best interests of the children of the Madras city*'.[29] This concept of 'best interests' was to emerge as one of the most powerful phrases in later international child rights legislation, but the concept of 'best' was already enshrined in the Geneva Declaration of 1924. That the interest in children started just months after the declaration was signed and used similar terminology perhaps reflected the participation of the WIA in global networks of information exchange. The stated need was

> a powerful non-official society which will act as an agent and representative of the Government in handling generally the problems connected with the rescue and reformation of children in Madras city who are either reconvicted of crime or need to be taken out of surroundings and locations which threaten to undermine and pervert their moral character and make them easy victims to the temptations to commit crime.[30]

The new organisation was thus to control and care for both convicted and potential criminals, and to do so as a non-state actor.[31] Yet while the personnel and management were 'non-official', it was to be largely state-funded through the Jail Department budget, although the certified schools came from the education budget.[32] In addition to an annual grant, further financial assistance could be obtained 'on the basis of guaranteeing two Rupees for every one Rupee collected by subscription', again placing the onus on charity and voluntary giving.[33]

Madras Children's Aid Society (MCAS)

The State Children's Council became permanent in March 1926 as the MCAS.[34] It was established as a non-official body with strong support from the judiciary, particularly the chief presidency magistrate (CPM) Dr Pandali.[35] The president was the Justice Party politician Muhammad Usman and the vice-president was the Anglican Lord Bishop of Madras.

The executive committee was formed of seven annually elected members, and three government nominees who were specifically charged with monitoring spending.[36] The initial committee included officials such as V. T. Krishnamachari, philanthropists such as S. V. Ramaswamy Mudaliar and politicians such as Justicite G. Narayanaswamy Chetty and lawyer M. A. Tirunarayanachariar. It also included the WIA and Theosophist leader Dr Annie Besant, Mrs Venkatasubba Rao (who established the Madras Seva Sedan as part of her social service to destitute girls) and Mrs Stanford as the secretary.[37] Under this leadership the MCAS began by establishing a remand 'home of shelter' for children 'pending their trial', 'committed to its custody by the court' or 'destitute and uncared for' and found wandering the streets. In 1927 this was used by sixty-two boys and four girls, in 1928 by fifty-four boys and fifteen girls, although the length of stay was not mentioned.[38] The MCAS then established a junior certified school and employed a probation officer.[39] By 1929 the society also ran a senior certified school for girls, which housed and educated twenty-two girls and was connected to other schemes for rescuing girls under the Suppression of Immoral Traffic Act, 1928.

Funding for all these endeavours remained precarious. In 1920 the government had assured legislators that it would provide 'liberal grants' to a committee that 'offered good guarantees of permanence and satisfactory working', including inspection of the accounts under the Education Department's Grant-in-Aid Scheme rules.[40] The government provided funding to feed the children in the remand home and half of the other remand expenditure, with the daily maintenance costs estimated at 7 rupees for a boy (remand home) and 12 rupees for a girl (certified school).[41] This was supplemented by a separate grant covering three-quarters of the maintenance of the senior certified school to an annual maximum of 5,000 rupees.[42] The shortfall, primarily staff salaries and administrative functions, was paid by voluntary subscriptions and 'private benevolence' was central to the funding model.[43] The precarious nature of the finance caused such concern that in 1927 the MCAS sent a deputation directly to the governor.[44] In the private brief notes, the Education Department acknowledged the potential cost required for the functioning of the Children Act, adding that the 'Government knew full well that they should bear its financial responsibility'.[45] The official position remained that the cost of carrying out the specified provisions of the act should be met by the government while additional costs, including schooling for inmates, 'should be provided for by private effort'.[46] The dialogue resulted in an increased grant of 7,200 rupees to cover the normal cost of maintenance for the remand and senior certified schools.[47] This was raised annually with an additional grant sanctioned by the governor in 1929–30.[48] This provided the society with a budget of 10,250 rupees a year, which increased to 15,250 rupees in 1930 after the establishment of a working boys' hostel.[49] Funding remained precarious and was largely dependent on voluntary subscriptions, based on an appeal to the 'humanitarian duty' of the wealthy.[50]

The aim of the MCAS was to care for the 'poor young delinquent and destitute boys and girls of Southern India'. These children were 'at a turning point in their lives' with the potential to 'become criminals' or 'become good citizens, living straight, self-supporting lives' and the 'work of the society is to set the feet of each child in the latter path'.[51] The child, as both currently malleable and as a future resource for the nation, was to be engaged in a relationship with the modern state which encouraged him or her to contribute to society as a future citizen, disciplined into a productive labour force. Whether the children had been convicted of a crime or were merely poor appears to have been of little consequence; more significant were their future prospects.[52] The CPM was particularly supportive, seeing the work of the MCAS as a means of preventing 'the large number of poor and uncared for children' 'from entering the avenues to crime'.[53] Likewise, Mrs Stanford argued that the principal object of a children's court was 'to create an agency for the prevention of begging by juveniles'.[54] This involved returning 'juvenile beggars' 'to their parents or guardian with a warning against repetition' or sending them to a home 'in case of persistent repetition or where there is no parent or guardian forthcoming'. This suggests that both the juvenile court and residential care were conceived of as preventative strategies, suggesting a close conflation of the destitute as a potential criminal and the delinquent as a destitute child who had been apprehended. This mirrors the experience of other practitioners, for example, the London Metropolitan Police, for whom 'care' and 'control' were 'mutually reinforcing rather than conflicting concepts'.[55]

The probation system instituted by the MCAS in the 1930s differentiated between three types of deserving children. The first were orphans released from certified schools and the second were impoverished youngsters who had never been incarcerated but attended night schools to gain basic literacy. A third category was children 'lost in the city' who were sent by the police to the girls remand home until 'claimed by their parents', with those unclaimed dispatched to the MSPC home.[56] The 1931 report for the MCAS specified four categories of children whom they considered their particular concern: 'delinquent or youthful offenders, the majority of whom have parents or guardians', 'destitute innocent orphans who are homeless and parentless', 'diseased children' rescued from brothels being brought up as prostitutes and 'the mentally defective'.[57] The binaries used in this categorisation between orphans and those with parents, the delinquent and the destitute, the diseased and the healthy body, the mentally defective and the healthy mind, included serious, and perhaps deliberate, oversimplification of the experiences of these children. Each of these categories also linked their situation directly to the role of parents, whether as irresponsible, absent, morally questionable or unable to provide adequate care. The different circumstances of the children might have been acknowledged, but it appears the crucial distinction in deciding whether they became the responsibility of the MCAS was the existence of parents. There is no evidence to suggest this decision was based on parental care as either cost effective or important to the emotional needs of the child, but seems rather to reflect a wider anxiety around usurping parental authority and establishing paramountcy of the (nuclear) family. In an article in *Stri Dharma*, the WIA underlined the belief that 'kith and kin however poor they may be' should be required to take responsibility for basic maintenance costs, the child being entitled to state or civil society intervention only when the family had failed completely.[58] The clearest exception to this were children from the criminal tribes who were assumed to be biologically predisposed to crime. These children were explicitly excluded from the MCA but were tried directly by the presidency magistrates under the Criminal Tribes Act, 1924.[59] This caused concern to the CPM and the MCAS, although in practice children from the criminal tribes were detained with other children in the certified schools.[60]

Girls were also classified according to presumed sexual activity, particularly within the girls certified schools. While sleeping arrangements for girls aged ten–sixteen years were made on the basis of the cottage system ostensibly to learn household management and other gendered vocational skills, it also allowed subtle segregation of those who had previously been sexually active.⁶¹ Childhood was numerically defined in 1920 but in practice for girls sexual innocence was a more important marker:

> It is wrong in principle, because children's outlook is different from that of the adult's—the child is innocent, guileless, trustful while the majority of the adults in our institution being widows have tasted the bitterness of life and can never make suitable classmates and companions to these young innocent children.⁶²

Often these 'adults' were the same age as the 'innocent children' but were widows. There was also segregation based on whether previous sexual experience was deemed to be legitimate (marriage, widowhood) or illegitimate (prostitution). Girls 'rescued' in the WIA-led campaigns against prostitution, trafficking and *devadasi*s were more likely to be cared for by the Madras Vigilance Association, whatever their age. This involved a subtle gendering, and childhood bounded by age was in practice imagined as male, while the childhood defined by sexual innocence was constructed as female.⁶³

The Sixth Annual Report ended in an emotional appeal for funding:

> We appeal to the public, particularly to every parent, to think of the needs of these neglected, unwanted, destitute, helpless children who are here not because of their own faults but because their own parents, relations and community have failed properly to discharge their duties by them. We appeal to them all to devote a small percentage of their income for sheltering, educating and training these children to a useful and happy life.⁶⁴

The MCAS saw the delinquent child as 'sinned against rather than being themselves sinners and criminals', as in need of care and education, as rightfully happy and the result of recognised familial failure, which is interesting as it is one of the few references to the extended family and local or caste community as well as parents.⁶⁵ Equally, the appeal was not for the state to accept parental responsibility and intervene in families, and the duty of families to their offspring was implied. Rather, it was an emotional plea for middle-class social service as part of a joint or extended family system and a perception of national responsibilities in familial terms. In supporting the MCAS in 1936, the advocate-general, Sir Alladi Krishnaswami Ayyar, claimed he found 'a growing belief in the dignity of human brotherhood and the duty placed on the people' and growing recognition 'on the part of more fortunate countrymen that they owed a duty to their less fortunate brethren'.[66] These views are significant because they reveal an emotive representation of the child as part of a wider community of the nation, imply a changed relationship between the giver and object as reflected through a semi-familial community and suggest a right to intervene but with very limited personal sacrifice or interaction. Again, it is possible to characterise this relationship as avuncular, as having the right to intervene but not the responsibility of parenthood.

Associates in the Voluntary Sector

The MCAS was part of a wider philanthropic community of middle-class individuals interested in the nation's future. First among these was the WIA. The MCAS was located within the WIA headquarters on Poonamallee Road and a number of individuals were prominent in both organisations. The annual reports of the MCAS were published in the WIA's monthly journal *Stri Dharma*, an English-language journal based around the parallel, but ultimately conflicting, ideals of liberal feminist internationalism and anti-colonial nationalism and edited by Margaret Cousins and then Muthulakshmi Reddi, both also active in the MCAS.[67] *Stri Dharma*'s ethos of a gendered division of public work and the promotion of respectable activism for women was demonstrated during the civil disobedience campaign 1930–34 when it used the terms of the Geneva Declaration to claim that although 'the noblest man [Gandhi] living among us is in prison … the child in distress must be relieved, the hungry child must be fed, the delinquent must be reclaimed and the sick child must be nursed'.[68] Accordingly, the WIA promoted its members to a unique role as women on all children-related voluntary committees.[69] This claim that the 'mothers'—or perhaps 'aunties'—of the nation contributed to the nationalist movement by caring for the future citizens of the nation facilitated the activity of middle-class women outside the home, but ultimately limited the role of women by contributing to a gendered belief that women had a distinctively maternal role to play in understanding children.[70]

It furthermore helped to move childhood firmly into the social, rather than political, sphere.

Later histories of the WIA characterised 1924–26 as 'the child welfare period', with the 'criminals of the future' as a central concern.[71] The WIA annual reports of the early 1930s detailed the specific interventions of its members as lady honorary magistrates and within the MCAS.[72] However, juvenile justice was consistently overshadowed by the focus on the position of *devadasi*s, and the Age of Consent and the Suppression of Immoral Traffic legislation, perhaps because it was on these issues that elite Indian women most distinctively found a political voice separate from male nationalist or white imperial feminists.[73] By 1934 the WIA's Five-Year Action Plan and the Women's Manifesto focused on preventative action in maternal and child health, compulsory education and prevention of child labour, making only limited mention of 'neglected and destitute orphans [who] turn delinquent for want of protection and care'.[74]

The formal ties between the WIA and MCAS might have weakened during the 1930s, but many activists remained prominent in both organisations and were often also associated with both the Theosophical Society and the independence movement. This included Dorothy Jinarajadasa and Mrs Stanford, but also the juvenile court honorary magistrates, such as Lady T. Sadasiva Iyer who was also married to a judge and Justice Party politician; Mrs Margaret Cousins, editor of *Stri Dharma*; and Mrs Malati Patwardhan.[75] Mrs Clubwalla Jadhav, lady magistrate and honorary secretary of the MCAS from 1938 for twenty-five years, also worked in the Seva Samajam Children's Home, was vice-president of the Madras Discharged Prisoner Aid Society (DPAS) and later vice-president of the Indian Council of Child Welfare.[76] The MCAS Girls Club was formed by the Congress social worker and child welfare activist Durgabi Deshmukh. Another noteworthy representative of this group of philanthropic professional women, mentioned in previous chapters, was Dr Muthulakshmi Reddi. A medical doctor and the first woman voted to the Madras Legislative Assembly in 1926, Reddi established a children's ward at the Madras Hospital, championed the implementation of the Suppression of Immoral Traffic Act, 1928, and was active on the committees of the MSPC and MCAS.[77] Reflecting her connections with international child-saving movements centred around Geneva and the League of Nations, Reddi argued: '… it is recognised by all civilised nations that the first and primary duty of the State is to secure for every child the right to be bodily, mentally and socially fit.'[78] Furthermore, 'it is the State and the Society that has to bear the whole burden and the responsibility' for the protection of the child.[79] Reddi established the Avvai Home, Mylapore, in 1930 for 'neglected vagrant and destitute children' because they are 'one human family and that all children are entitled to our protection and care'.[80] The home moved to Adyar in 1936, added a primary school in 1939, and by 1949 provided for about 100 children.[81] Like the MCAS, the Avvai Home was not the direct responsibility of the WIA, although the WIA offered scholarships.[82] Compared to her peers, Reddi was much bolder in her claims that the state was responsible for the normal development of the child as a rights holder and potential national resource, was much more prepared to engage in a language of universal rights and entitlements, and was much more likely to claim a parental role for state actors. Yet she also included the 'wives and mothers' of civil society movements within this definition of state activity and responsibility, revealing the extent to which the lines between state, public and voluntary activity were blurred by the 1930s.[83]

Further evidence that child welfare was driven by a small network of individuals was demonstrated in the 1932 MCAS report. The tone is self-congratulatory, reflecting the contributions of the managing committee, such as the president, Sir M. Krishnan Nair (Justice Party), and other professionals such as the chief inspector of prisons, Dr Muthulakshmi Reddi, and the presidency magistrates.[84] The listed individuals ranged from Mrs Candeth, wife of the deputy DPI, for providing magazines to A. Appadurai Pillai, retired director of industries and Justice Party leader, for help with the boys club workshop. The donors followed a similar pattern and only eight donors did not have an official position or a spouse connected to the MCAS.[85] Prominent couples donated individually; Dr and Mrs H. S. Hensman were both committee members, he as a jail reformer and professor of mental health, and she as a politician and lady honorary magistrate.

The minutes of the 1940 Executive Committee show a similar profile and many of the same individuals, such as Mrs Clubwalla.[86] The committee remained largely male, although the secretary was now an experienced Anglo-Indian lady honorary magistrate, Mrs Hilde Theodore. Sir Mohammed Usman, for example, was the first president of the MCAS in 1926 and was still active in 1940.[87] As a Muslim member of the Justice Party, he had a distinguished political career: president of Madras Corporation, 1924–925; home minister, 1934; and governor of Madras, 1934. Other reformers, such as B. Moppurappa, served on the committees of both the MSPC and MCAS as the government nominees, maintaining government participation in both societies, while Chief Probation Officer Sri K. Palani continued to attend.[88] Other groups also operated 'for the rescue and protection of the child life of the city', including the Madras Child Life Protection Society and Child Welfare Association, but have left no archival trace.[89] The MCAS expanded in parallel with other penal reform movements such as the DPAS and Borstal Association, both specialising in probation and functioning as non-official bodies funded by the government and often sharing personnel with the MCAS.[90] Committee members had individual links to both the Congress and the Justice Party, but party allegiances were rarely in evidence and there was little reflection of the wider disagreements that characterised more overtly political debates. Rather, there appears to be a growing consensus among a small number of interconnected and highly educated Indians who forbore from the increasingly bitter tribalism of political parties for the sake of children's welfare. The extensive and cordial alliances between legislators, the judiciary, government officials, individual activists and members of philanthropic societies reveal the extensive networks of communication across Madras City; the development of a new consensus on child welfare and the role of the state; the influence of the local connections and global interactions of individuals and the beginnings of a new discourse on children's rights. This reveals how Indians used the increased constitutional powers granted in 1919 and 1935 to carve out new spaces for state action and a new role for the state in relation to its future citizens against a backdrop characterised by coercive colonial policies from Delhi and London and an empowered, popular but increasing fractious nationalist movement. 'The child' was placed resolutely in the social, not political, arena.

Space of the Juvenile Court

The juvenile court was to be a central institution for any modern scheme of juvenile penology, centred on the idea of rehabilitation rather than punishment.[91] The aim was a court intended solely for children, where cases were decided by a panel of magistrates but without the presence of other adults, whether jury, police or legal support, with extensive input from child welfare agencies and sentences that reflected the age and vulnerability of the child and their supposed capacity for reformation. This was legally established in Part VI of the MCA and attempts were made to avoid the appearance of uniformed policemen and of a criminal court, although the same building was still used and there was no place of detention for children awaiting trial.[92] Under pressure from the WIA as part of their wider push for the implementation of the act in 1924, the CPM strongly supported the idea of a juvenile court, but emphasised the lack of suitable personnel and the financial constraints.[93] After discussion, it was agreed by the DPI, CPM and chief inspector of certified schools that there was an 'immediate need for the establishment of a juvenile court' with a presiding stipendiary magistrate and honorary magistrates 'including women', which would meet two or three times a week.[94] The CPM also advocated the establishment of a remand home and there was general agreement that this should be run by a non-official but government-funded 'philanthropic body'.[95] The alternative option, just to ignore juvenile nuisance cases, was opposed by the police as it 'would greatly aggravate the insanitary condition of Madras streets' and provide an additional incentive for adult criminals to exploit children.[96] In contrast to the more consensual rhetoric of the politicians, the implementation of the MCA was left to negotiations between different government departments, who wanted to protect their budgets and were often more concerned with the deterrence of petty crime rather than the future of the poor or criminal child.[97]

The attention secured some change and by 1925 juvenile cases were being tried 'outside the ordinary court hours and in a private room and every effort is made to see that the procedure followed is as informal and elastic as possible'.[98] Likewise, the second and third presidency magistrates tried the children's cases during the court's lunch break.[99] Children were usually dealt with on the same day or 'released on bail to their parents'.[100] However, the CPM remained concerned that a specialist juvenile court should be established, and in May 1925 temporary provisions were issued to recruit two benches of honorary magistrates and facilitate speedy sentencing under the Police Act for 'nuisance cases' of minor vandalism and petty crime.[101] Progress was slow and the records are sketchy, but the rules governing the proper functioning of the Madras juvenile court were agreed in 1930.[102] Dr Pandalai, the CPM, drew on the already functioning rules of the Calcutta Juvenile Court where, under the Bengal Rules for the Conduct of the House of Detention, children could be tried from the age of ten years, were separated by sex and could only be visited by parents and guardians or a legal practitioner accompanied by parents.[103] He also relied extensively on international sources, particularly the Australian State Children Act.[104] This supplemented Mrs Stanford's experience in the South African juvenile courts demonstrating the influence of personal networks in circulating information and the growing transnational discourse on children.[105]

The growing interest at the national and international levels was demonstrated in the resolution at the all-India Inspectors-General Conference of 1927 that a juvenile court was of 'paramount importance' and the 1929 League of Nations Questionnaire.[106] The answers suggested that in Madras City, the chief and other presidency magistrates heard cases against juveniles in a separate room 'out of the regular court hours'.[107] A similar pattern was followed by the district magistrates who responded; for example, in Tinnevelly the magistrates used 'their Bungalows or the private room attached to their courts'.[108] The district magistrate in Chingleput claimed children were dealt with 'during morning hours when no other case should be posted and the general public were excluded'.[109] The space of the court as distinct from the adult court, and as private, had thus become an acknowledged standard. However, the inspector of junior certified schools discovered that the general public was ignorant of the existence of the Children Act and recommended public education through social workers or the DPAS.[110] The chief inspector of certified schools criticised the lack of a formal juvenile court and argued that 'no real headway has been made'.[111] This was despite the MCAS offer that the court could be held in their remand home.[112] It appears from the MCAS report of 1931 that a separate juvenile court came into operation at some point in later 1929.[113] The evidence of the functioning and personnel of this court is very difficult to trace, and only fragmentary accounts can be found in the archives.

By 1935 there were two juvenile courts functioning, one in Madras City and the other in Vellore.[114] According to the commissioner of police, these were 'a parental enquiry into the shortcomings of children' in which an experienced magistrate was 'given the charge-sheet, the summary of the evidence of each witness, and if necessary the case diary' that being sufficient to 'elicit the facts and administer justice' in order that 'the youthful offender should not be frightened by the full paraphernalia of the law'.[115] This re-established the principles that the 'normal atmosphere of court was entirely undesirable' for children, and consequently, the police should be in mufti and lawyers, with their competing claims to truth, should be forbidden. These provisions were supported by the recognised experts: Mrs Jinarajadasa of the MCAS, the CPM, District Magistrate S. Ranganathan and the acting inspector-general of prisons who worried that the adult court would 'weigh on the mind of the child'.[116] However, the inherent assumption that the juvenile court was used to adjudicate on suitable welfare provisions for destitute children was contested by the second presidency magistrate who presided over the juvenile court in Madras. He argued that if children plead not guilty, they should be entitled to an adequate trial with prosecution, defence and evidence tested by cross-examination. This would inevitably involve the presence of adults but would also provide the child with better legal representation as well as an acknowledgement of individual rights and legal subjecthood. The compromise suggested was an amendment to Section 44 (3) of the Juvenile Court Rules, which allowed the defendant to engage legal support if they so wished.[117] Fifteen years after the MCA was passed, the judiciary directly involved was still ambivalent as to whether the court was judging guilt or evaluating the child and his environment, an uneasy compromise between justice and welfare, which continued well into the post-colonial state.[118]

Personnel of the Juvenile Court

According to the MCA and Juvenile Court Rules of 1930, the personnel within the court were to be as important as its designation as a distinct space, and 'public-spirited ladies and gentlemen' working as unpaid magistrates were essential to the functioning of the Madras courts.[119] As part of the initial discussions, in late 1924 the CPM agreed that the juvenile court should be presided over by a salaried male magistrate with the assistance of two honorary magistrates, one of whom should be a woman.[120] Of the thirteen honorary magistrates for Madras City suggested by the Education Department and the CPM in 1925, six were female.[121] Mrs Stanford of the MCAS consistently advocated the use of lady honorary magistrates, using her experience in South Africa to suggest that women's maternal instincts gave them a unique place in the functioning of the juvenile justice system because 'the children like their presence very much and speak out their mind freely'.[122] District Magistrate Tinnevelly likewise agreed that the presence of women 'helps considerably to reassure the child and give him or her confidence' and helped in understanding the children's replies.[123] This was widely supported, both by officials and the MCAS, who were keen to incorporate women on the Committee of Visitors and Mrs Dorothy Jinjaradasa became chief inspectress of schools.[124] This idea of a male, salaried presiding magistrate being assisted by an unsalaried, maternal lady honorary magistrate remained central to the way the juvenile court was imagined.[125] While providing additional opportunities for women's participation in public life and outside the home, this claim to a maternal role was ultimately self-limiting and meant that the courts effectively replicated the structure of the nuclear family, with caring feminine values constructed as additional to the authority of the salaried male.[126] Throughout the 1930s, the juvenile court was a sphere in which the presence of women was desired rather than feared, although this reliance on well-educated, wealthy women meant that it was also a cost-effective means of expanding state power.

The gradual expansion of the juvenile court meant that in 1940 the court in Madras held thirty-seven sessions dealing with 913 cases, and the court in Madura had thirty-five sessions dealing with 368 cases, giving an average per session of twenty-five cases in Madras and eleven in Madura.[127] There was concern at the haste with which these cases were conducted because it suggested a lack of specialised attention to which the juvenile accused was entitled.[128] The Home Department was reluctant to put more pressure on the existing specialist magistrates and had insufficient resources to employ a full-time salaried magistrate for children.[129] This meant that the chief inspector felt he had 'no alternative' but to recruit unpaid individuals who 'have special aptitude and knowledge required for the conduct of juvenile court', although he remained sceptical about their commitment, experience and desire to follow government guidelines. Equally important, he may have doubted the capacity of the educated middle classes to empathise with the condition of the poor, and stressed that any voluntary magistrates should 'have a personal knowledge of working class conditions and homes'.[130] The CPM, on the other hand, felt that honorary magistrates 'of competence' could invest more time, thereby improving the quality of the decision-making.[131] The CPM was particularly impressed with the work of Mrs Clubwalla, the lady honorary magistrate who sat on Wednesday mornings in the Madras City Court, but her interest was unusual, and of the fourteen currently functioning honorary magistrates empowered to sit singly, only three were willing to sit on the juvenile court, and of these two were required for adult work.[132] The third candidate—a retired deputy accountant-general with no previous judicial experience—was ultimately chosen on the basis that once familiar with the procedures, the key requirements for the juvenile court were 'nothing more than a reasonable amount of sympathy and worldly-wisdom' and 'sufficient leisure' to be able to undertake the work effectively.[133] In Madura the city magistrate struggled to secure competent honorary magistrates, while in Coimbatore the district magistrate relied on a retired deputy collector.[134] Ultimately, honorary magistrates were often retired bureaucrats, were required to own extensive property and were prepared to affirm the authority of the salaried magistrate, who was always male.[135] An understanding of children, or sympathy for their personal circumstances, was of less significance in this elitist and paternalist approach to justice.[136]

By 1942 there were juvenile courts functioning in the major cities in the presidency—Vellore, Salem, Madura, Coimbatore and Madras City. These varied in scope and organisation: in Salem, the court was presided over by two honorary magistrates, one a retired sub-magistrate and one a lady honorary magistrate who together dealt with 228 cases.[137] In Coimbatore the presiding honorary magistrate dealt with sixty-eight cases in 1942 and there was no remand home so children awaiting trial remained in police custody.[138] Meanwhile, in Madras City S. Muthuswami Iyer tried nearly 60 per cent of the cases himself.[139] Whether tried under the Indian Penal Code or the MCA, around 27 per cent of the cases were sent to certified schools, 50 per cent returned to the parents, while the remainder were admonished and released.[140] Of the 939 tried, only 85 (or 9 per cent) were acquitted or dismissed and around half (437 or 47 per cent) were initially brought to court because they were found destitute or wandering. Paralleling the British model of liberal intervention, the juvenile court was a paternalistic assessment of poverty rather than a court of justice, mirroring the gendered authority of the nuclear family. The juvenile justice system remained particularly vulnerable to budget cuts, individual incompetence and chequered expansion, but by the 1940s it had been established in both law and practice that the government and civil society had a right to intervene and that poverty and crime were mutually intertwined.

Probation and Auxiliary Services

In 1940 the chief inspector of certified schools argued that only the basic structures of the juvenile court were in place without sufficient investment in expert services, such as social workers or child psychologists, who could offer advice based on their scientific understanding of the child and its circumstances.[141] Perhaps influenced by the new social work ideas emerging at the Sir Dorabji Tata Graduate School of Social Work, Bombay, he rejected the idea of the 'innate wickedness' of the child but reiterated that it was the responsibility of the court to establish whether 'misbehaviour' was caused by poverty or bad company.[142] This was not a new idea and the need for a probation service was recognised by the superintendent of the Tanjore borstal in his evidence to the Indian Jails Committee (IJC), but it was not until the 1930s that an attempt was made to bring this to reality.[143] In Madras the term encompassed probation officers who could arrange pre-trial custody, gather information regarding the child's family and environment, and supervise children after release or those sentenced to probation instead of incarceration.[144]

Probation officers were to be sufficiently literate to produce monthly reports on heath, conduct and progress.[145] Their character was of primary importance, and they were to be 'a respectable man of some social position' with 'great interest in children' who was required 'to take the boy under his wing'.[146] It was argued that

> one of the best ways of effecting the reformation of a child offender is to place him under the continuous supervision of some person possessing strength of character and sound judgment, who will keep himself in touch with the child, understands his difficulties and give him advice whenever needs, assist him in procuring work, and generally directs and influence his conduct for good.[147]

These could be parents or other 'suitable persons' within the family, or other authority figures and members of the professional classes such as members of municipal councils, village headmen, police officers or recognised philanthropic societies. If no voluntary assistance could be found, then paid probation officers were used, following the model employed by the highly commended Madras Borstal Association and DPAS. These probation officers were to be paid at the rank of a police sub-inspector, funded by the government but supervised by the MCAS.[148] The use of the metaphors of the extended family was applied not only to the probation officers themselves but also to the MCAS, who were to act 'not as officials but as their big brothers and sisters'.[149]

The expansion of probation services was intended to support rather than subvert the family. Before a case was heard in the juvenile court:

> ... enquiries are made by the Probation Officer concerning the juvenile offender's parents, school work, environment, character etc and parents are interviewed. The parents in many cases attend the court on the day of hearing and the case is disposed of in a manner calculated to conduce to the welfare of the boy or girl.[150]

While rhetorically the welfare of the child was the paramount concern, in practice if parents were traced, reinforcing the authority of the family meant that being 'restored to parents' was regarded as the best option.[151] Mr Palani, the MCAS probation officer, supported the parents at home; for example, in 1936 he visited twenty-three boys on probation, and found parents willing to cooperate by reporting 'the conduct of the boys at home, and ask our help if any difficulties arise with the boy'.[152] The boys club unofficially accepted 'uncontrollable boys brought by their parents' but 'in such cases the parents pay the cost of maintenance of those boys' to ensure parental responsibility continued.[153] Other 'uncontrollable' boys were briefly kept in a boys remand home as a deterrent to bad behaviour before being restored to the parents.[154] Probation was not so much the embodiment of state parental control, but was managed, staffed, funded and constructed by social reformers using the rhetoric of the child's familial network. It also appears to have been successful, and it was 'found that there was no difficulty in finding employment for the boys, who had received an excellent training and were desired as employees'.[155]

The probation officer in Madras City was the ideal, rather than typical, situation. The case of a twelve-year-old girl Pappamma from Dindigul demonstrated that for many children this bore little relation to their experience. Pappamma was convicted of theft and transported by two uniformed policemen to Chingleput Senior Certified School for four years.[156] The case became public when the MCAS complained to the chief inspector of certified schools that Pappamma was kept in jail for two months awaiting trial, in 'flagrant breach of the MCA'. In particular, Rule 55 specified that girls should not be detained in police custody and Rule 54 mentioned that children should not be detained in an adult jail. The MCAS requested that the government remind magistrates of 'the right method of dealing with children', which included the avoidance of punitive language such as 'convict' but instead used the terms of 'care and protection' or 'welfare and reformation'.[157] In Pappamma's case, although an apology was issued, the magistrate claimed that it had taken a month to discover her relatives and that she had been under the direct custody of the jail superintendent. This was not unusual given the lack of auxiliary services, particularly for those awaiting trial, but demonstrated the multiple layers of exclusion experienced by some children and the differences between the urban and rural situations.[158]

The difficulties of juvenile justice at a distance from the urban centres were further demonstrated in 1936 when the Home Department requested details from district magistrates as to the local provision of pre- and post-trial probation care for destitute children.[159] By 1936 Anantapur district had tried no cases under the MCA, and Ramnad had none under Clause 29, although children awaiting trial were placed in the care of an unspecified 'well-intentioned or interested person of good character'. In most of the northern, Telegu-speaking districts (for example, Nellor or Chittor), there was little evidence of the MCA and no pre-trial provision. In western areas of the presidency (for example, Mangalore, Coimbatore and Calicut), most district magistrates claimed to be taking action, and there was awareness of the terms of the act while parents were relied on for bail. The south of the presidency and areas surrounding Madras City were much more engaged with the juvenile justice provision. In North Arcot there were seventeen gentlemen (officials and non-officials) approved for remand care by the inspector-general of prisons, two in Trichinopoly, and in Salem and Shevapet stations all police officers above or of the rank of sub-inspector. The district magistrates of Malabar and Madura expressed a desire to improve but stressed the problems faced with adult overcrowding.

In South Arcot the children were left in the custody of non-uniformed police officers; the children in Guntur were kept in the main jail in separate cells. The local village headman also featured as the probation officer in all but name in a variety of areas throughout the presidency (South Arcot, Guntur, Chittor, East Godavari and Tinnevelly), while the DPAS was involved in pre-trial and post-incarceration care in North Arcot and Nellore. The MCA, for all its universalistic intentions, was not equal in implementation and the protection and rights offered to children were greater in the areas surrounding the centres of political power. Existing figures of authority such as the police, headmen and parents were central to the expansion of juvenile justice in rural areas, in contrast with the personal networks of philanthropic middle-class individuals in Madras City.

Boys Club

In 1936 the MCAS had the care of fifty-four boys on probation and ran three night schools in Vepery, Choolai and Royapuram with forty-three, forty-seven and fifty-four boys, respectively.[160] An additional ninety-four boys were brought to the MCAS remand home by the police as 'found wandering and uncontrollable' but were 'restored to their respective parents' and were 'being supervised and helped to find work' by the probation officer.[161] Similarly, in 1937 the MCAS had ninety boys on probation, supervised by two probation officers because of their 'vagabond life', and often because these boys had absconded from home. If the parents were discovered, the boys were returned to them if they were 'respectable people'.[162] Stretched resources meant that regularly engaging with the boys together was an effective way to support children, and one of the more successful schemes run by the MCAS was the boys club that supervised boys (seventy-two in 1932; sixty-eight in 1931), including board and lodging for thirty-eight boys in 1932.[163] Boys clubs were for 'ex-children of Certified Schools who have no homes to go to' and were intended for 'a different type of boy' to those who attended night school and associated with 'undesirable people', although in practice little difference was made.[164] The increased interest in non-institutional care in conjunction with other voluntary groups such as the DPAS was driven primarily by financial considerations, but they were also a way to regulate, support and train boys while allowing them to remain within their own communities and families.¹⁶⁵ Boys clubs were held in corporation school buildings.¹⁶⁶ Teachers were both salaried and voluntary workers, and activities were free for the juvenile members. Generally, funding was raised through dramas enacted by the boys themselves and from subscriptions of members of the society. To aid their work, the probation officers also used voluntary workers such as Rover Scouts.

The club functioned with the boys reporting to the probation officer on a Sunday, and the CPM received periodic progress reports. Boys clubs provided leisure activities, for example, a party in September 1932 with sweets, informal talks and a lecture by the National Health Association. It provided training opportunities, and the probation officers were able to secure employment for the boys in a number of prestigious weaving companies, as bookbinders and compositors, as Tramway Company conductors, as buglers and in domestic work. To assist this, the club established a workshop that undertook vehicle repairs and manufactured iron and steel goods such as gates, windows and dustbins.¹⁶⁷ Journals, for example *Stri Dharma*, were used to secure public cooperation in purchasing these articles as a means 'to uplift and reform and make useful citizens of these young lads', a further call on middle-class philanthropic sensibilities as well as rehabilitation through capitalist endeavour.¹⁶⁸ This probation work grew through the 1930s so that by 1935 the boys club housed 127 boys and the newly formed Girls Club had 5 girls.¹⁶⁹ In 1937 Dorothy Jinarajadasa requested additional financial support from the Home Department, the work being severely limited by lack of funds and trained probation officers.¹⁷⁰ The MCAS proposed dividing Madras City into five areas, each with a probation officer, in addition to a city-wide woman probation officer who was employed to facilitate the operation of the Immoral Traffic Act. An alternative scheme to establish children 'left helpless without work or shelter' as a self-sustaining village community reflected new pedagogical and penological ideas but was too costly and radical to be implemented.¹⁷¹

Conclusion

The implementation of the MCA was slow and patchy, but by 1940 some progress had been made even if the numbers involved remained small. This was evidenced in the establishment of the MCAS, and then in the gradual expansion of the juvenile courts and a variety of probation services. The practice across the presidency might not have reached the required ideal set out in the MCA or Juvenile Court Rules, but by 1940 it was generally accepted by magistrates and officials that children required a system of justice that was to be fundamentally different from adults, in space and in personnel, as well as in opportunities for reform. This was based on the idea of the vulnerable child in need of protection, the child as uniquely malleable and reformable and the child as the object of welfare, a worthy investment in the future life of the nation. There was little distinction between those perceived as actual or potential delinquents, and juvenile crime and poverty were regarded as mutually reinforcing. Both the legislative foundation and the experience of implementation contributed to a system based on welfare, not justice, and there was no real discussion of the rights of children to legal representation, of children as legal subjects with a voice or even discussion of limited criminal responsibility on account of their immaturity. All the court programmes were based on the assumption that with good management and strong examples, and the chance of productive labour, the child could be disciplined into a good adult contributor.

The personnel and management of the court's auxiliary services, honorary magistrates and the probation service were generally supervised by the MCAS. The voluntary organisations—MCAS, MSPC, boys clubs—relied heavily on public donations of money, but also time, although the government was prepared to fund the basic maintenance of the children in the boys club and remand homes. The close relationships between civil society and the state and the general consensus on the child and the role of the state with limited disagreement over detail are all the more remarkable against a background of bitter and even violent political tensions, particularly following the development of a mass anti-colonial movement after 1919, but also with the increasingly bitter localised caste and identity politics of the south and the tensions between and within the Justice Party and the Congress. Instead, there seems to have been the emergence of what in the European context Donzelot called 'the social': a depoliticised and consensual area of the increasing regulation of the family, participated in by legislators, officials, the judiciary, expert professionals and by an increasingly active and vocal voluntary sector, often associated with the women's movement.[172] As a result of dyarchy, this was a predominantly Indian space, although many have argued that this reflects the ascendency of bourgeois values within the liberal state and philanthropic middle class attempts to control working-class families for the future of the nation and advance their own economic and social interests.[173] Although a wealthy, well-educated and elite group, social class seems an overly simplistic explanation and the expansion of 'the social' as an arena of action seems rather to have been founded on the networks and interrelationships of a small number of individuals.[174] There were noticeable connections between the officials of the Law (Education) and Home Departments and the members of the WIA, MCAS and MSPC. These individuals, too, were linked to wider social and political reform movements, particularly the Theosophical Society, Indian National Congress and Justice Party, who cooperated together, again despite the fraught nature of Madras politics in the MLC.[175] The MCAS, for example, was based within the WIA headquarters and incorporated many prominent politicians and ICS officials on their management committee. The enhanced status of the lady honorary magistrates and expansion of the juvenile court was closely linked to the careers, family connections and personalities of individuals such as Mrs Dorothy Jinarajadasa, Dr Muthulakshmi Reddi and Mrs Stanford. The conspicuous role of these women demonstrated the way children could be used to further the cause of women's participation in the public sphere, and the gendered way in which children were perceived as still tied to the home, family, private and domestic spheres.

The family remained the centre of care, protection and education for the child, even when the state or civil society actors were involved. The most decisive factor in practical intervention remained the existence and respectability of the parents. While it was acknowledged that outsiders—teachers, doctors, probation officers—had a role in supporting the parents to adequately care for their children, removing children from the family was the last resort, and the family was perceived to be a site of rehabilitation rather than a threat. When intervention was unavoidable because the child was shown to be without parents, care for the child was facilitated by a variety of civil society activists who perceived themselves as operating within the family structure. The structure of the juvenile court mirrored the nuclear family, being designated a 'parental enquiry' with the salaried male presidency judge helped by the nurturing and maternal care of the lady honorary magistrate, while the probation officer was seen almost as a member of the extended family. Just as Nehru perceived himself as the uncle of the nation, the child was acted upon by the uncles and aunties of civil society groups who imagined themselves in terms of kinship relations rather than as an interventionist force. Although the state had a role in ensuring that every child had adequate care and protection, the family remained the primary site of authority and nurture in the life of the child, and intervention only happened when the parents explicitly failed. Despite acting on behalf of the state, and being funded by it, those who did intervene claimed that authority not as representatives of the state but as part of the extended national family.

7

Defining Childhood

Sexual Parameters of Childhood

The regulation of the sexual behaviour of children and sexual maturity as a boundary of childhood became a particular focus of controversy during the 1920s. Two distinctive issues demanded political attention in the Madras Presidency: the campaign to end the *devadasi* system of temple prostitution and the subsequent drive to end the immoral traffic of girls and women for prostitution, and the controversies over the age of marriage and age of consent for sexual relations. Although these two disputes have a slightly different, and indeed changing, focus, they speak to the discursive construction of childhood and normative childhood behaviour, with a focus on innocence, vulnerability and sexual maturity and the development or strengthening of new ideas about what a child is, was and could be. These controversies helped to define the parameters of childhood in discursive and biological terms and highlighted the many views existing in society about what the state's role should be in relation to the child.

The chapter approaches the controversies around the age of consent and the role of *devadasi*s through the angle of childhood and children's rights rather than seeing them only as women's issues, or eliding women and children as vulnerable. This is not to downplay the existing feminist historiography which highlights women's sexuality as a central point of disagreement between male patriarchies, whether colonial, liberal or nationalist, although Mrinilini Sinha emphasises how often nationalist and colonial approaches coalesced around a particular construction of respectable womanhood.[1] Sinha also establishes 1928 as a moment when Indian women began to express their own concerns around ideas of citizenship, often articulated within the vocabulary of liberal universalism.[2] This public assertion of women's rights was a response to the international outcry surrounding Katherine Mayo's book *Mother India*, and a number of bills to increase the age of consent in the Central Legislative Assembly in Delhi. Furthermore, Mytheli Sreenivas argues that in south India, the modernity of the Tamil nation was increasingly defined by conjugal relations, and defining the role of the wife within the family was important to the self-proclaimed modernity of the Tamil ruling classes.[3] However, gender relations is only one aspect of this story, and this chapter shows that it was the intersection between gender *and* age that was so contested.

Ishita Pande has argued that the Child Marriage Restraint Act (CMRA) of 1929 was a moment of change for children's rights in India, a distinctive point when numerically defined age became a more significant legal boundary than communal identity.[4] Certainly, the new legislation of the 1920s reflected changing global humanitarian constructions of childhood, and global changes in the age of consent intimately tied to continuing imperial practices across a number of imperial sites.[5] However, these universalising ideas about the child also intersected with ongoing debates around modern childhood occurring at the local level. This controversy remains firmly rooted in the debates, politics, personal networks and social structures of the Madras Presidency. The debate was one of many about the role and nature of childhood and state responsibility for children, and situating it within the context of other state interventions for children, whether health, justice or education, detailed in the rest of this book, reveals the complex crossovers, personal networks and shared ideas of the family, the state and the child across these issues. Discussions around consent, innocence, sexual morality, sexual maturity and the numerical definition of the boundary between childhood and adulthood both informed and were informed by these wider debates. This is rarely recognised in the existing literature, which remains categorised in terms of sexuality or education or juvenile justice with very limited recognition of the ways in which these discourses impacted each other.[6] These definitions of childhood were shaped too by the limited opportunities afforded by dyarchy as legislators sought to give local meaning to globally accepted

Legislating to Protect Children

The age of consent controversy was one of the most distinctive moments in the 1920s, achieving more global and national attention than any other social legislation. It culminated in the CMRA, 1929, which limited the age of marriage to fourteen for girls and eighteen for boys, implemented from 1 April 1930. This was a dyarchical law instituted in Delhi for the whole of British India and, as Sumita Mukherjee has shown, it demonstrated the willingness of Indian legislators to address social issues, carving out a space where only they had the legitimacy to regulate the lives of children.[7] It built on previous legislation, including the 1891 Age of Consent Act that raised the age of consent for sexual intercourse, both within and outside marriage, to twelve for boys and girls. The issue resurfaced in a number of private members' bills in 1922, 1925 and 1927, each attempting to modify the legislation by raising the age of consent or marriage; amending the age for extramarital sex; reconsidering the definition of rape and strengthening the penalties for those who transgressed the law.[8] These bills were pushed by liberal Indian social reformers; the British government in Delhi was cautious and only agreed to the CMRA after extensive public consultation, but also when they judged that the damage to their international reputation was a more significant risk than the danger of upsetting conservative public opinion, who often highlighted Queen Victoria's Proclamation of 1868 and the promise not to interfere in personal law.[9] A select committee was established in 1927 under the leadership of Sir Moropant Joshi, home member for the Central Provinces, with a remit to consult widely, and this report formed the basis of the 1929 legislation.[10] The attitudes and opinions expressed in this public consultation are the evidence base for this chapter. The committee comprised fourteen members, including A. Ramaswami Mudaliyar, member of the Madras Legislative Council (MLC) and later president of the Corporation of Madras, and Mrs M. O'Brieri Beadon, superintendent of the Victoria Government Hospital Madras, as well as other prominent figures such as the founder of the All-Indian Women's Conference Mrs Rameshwari Nehru. The committee received written responses to a questionnaire, which was supplemented with oral interviews and additional written submissions. The submissions from the Madras Presidency comprised two volumes of 500 pages and these provide a detailed insight into the views of the educated elite and those engaged in forming policy, campaigning or administering justice.

Running parallel to this was the campaign to end the *devadasi* system of temple prostitution, whereby young girls were dedicated to a deity at a local temple where they were trained in the religious and artistic traditions of the temple, but were often forced to perform sexual favours for male devotees. This was particularly common in the south of India. In 1922, a resolution was introduced into the Legislative Assembly in Delhi which supported legislation to prohibit the traffic of minor girls.[11] This led to the Indian Criminal Law Amendment Act, 1924, which altered the Criminal Codes so that minor girls could be rescued and rehabilitated, explicitly in line with the local Children Acts and emphasising the role of the guardian in protecting the girl child from physical and moral contamination. In 1926, the MLC took another approach with the introduction of the Madras Hindu Religious Endowments Act, ultimately passed in 1929, which attempted to undercut the economic foundations of the system by changing the use and ownership of the *inam* lands that were dedicated to the temple and used as a source of income. Finally, the 1930 Madras Prevention of Dedication Bill outlawed the dedication of young women, of whatever age, to the temple. This gradual process of reform kept the issue of consent and sexual morality within the sphere of public debate, and it was often mentioned in the Joshi Committee evidence.

The regulation of temple prostitution intersected with international concerns about the immoral trafficking of women and children. The Madras Suppression of Immoral Traffic Act was introduced into the MLC in October 1928, receiving assent from the governor in February 1930. The debates surrounding this act and the various amendments during the 1930s reflected both global humanitarian concerns around prostitution and the local applicability of such issues. This built on the *devadasi* legislation but included a more general focus on prostitutes and regulation of brothels, amended in 1930 to increase the regulation of the family and in 1940 to increase police potential for intervention.[12] This legislation clearly converged with the Madras Children Act, 1920, particularly around the institutional networks of the juvenile court and rescue homes, and reflected the debates on the regulation of licit and illicit sexual practices at the international level, even as it elided the categories of women and children again. The concern around marriage and prostitution meant that sexual innocence and sexual maturity remained key aspects of the wider debates and constructions of childhood within the Madras Presidency. These debates were also influenced by nationalist, feminist and imperial concerns around the regulation of normative conjugality and the centrality of monogamous marriage as a respectable form of conjugal and domestic behaviours.[13]

Defining Characteristics of the Child

The strong views aired in these debates about the boundaries and definitions of childhood, particularly in terms of consent, provide another lens through which to analyse contemporary views of childhood circulating in the presidency. Ideas about modern childhood were fluid, changing and contingent, reflecting changing global norms and the experience of governance, centring on the particular characteristics of childhood that ultimately needed adult protection. Physical maturity was a centrepiece of the controversies over the sexual boundaries of childhood. This had traditionally centred around puberty, with cohabitation expected within sixteen days of the girl's first menstruation. This equation of menstruation with physical maturity, giving 'custom' or religious-legal definitions a biological foundation, formed the basis of most religious opposition to the legislative changes.[14] A few submissions to the Joshi Committee reflected on the impact on the child-wife's body, and the report argued that early intercourse 'wrecks the physical system of the girl', sacrificing them to a 'life as long lingering misery'.[15] However, the horrifying biomedical details associated with the rape of Phulmoni, which was so central to the campaigns of the 1890s, were rarely present.[16] While specifics of injuries were submitted by female medical practitioners, witnesses such as Dr E. E. Tusker of the Wesleyan Mission Hospital, Chingleput or Dr Elizabeth Broges of the Victorian Memorial Women's and Children's Hospital, Bellary District, sex itself was infrequently mentioned, with much more emphasis on the long-term impact on health through sexually transmitted disease, early maternity and childbirth.[17] The high infant mortality rate, frequency of birth defects and the impact of childbearing on youthful bodies was a source of significant concern, but even those who contested the link between puberty and the ability to bear children rarely doubted the sexual capability of the child-wife after puberty.[18] Of course, there was no discussion of sexual maturity for males; puberty remained a boundary only for girls, even though the age of marriage for males was raised to eighteen.[19]

A corresponding number of concerns were raised about the psychological impact of early sexual intercourse, although never in the context of trafficking and prostitution. Mrs M. Rama Bai Madhave Rau argued that 'almost all such girls have lost their cheerfulness and vitality and seem to be incapable of either deriving any benefit from life or of themselves contributing to it'.[20] This idea of vitality became a recurring theme, linked to a medical discourse around mental ill-health. The trauma of early intercourse or rape, particularly by older husbands, had psychological manifestations, while childbirth was perhaps seen as a more natural process. Dr Anna Thomas, who worked in Maternity and Child Welfare, cited the case of a thirteen-year-old Brahmin girl brought by her concerned husband who was physically injured, but 'the poor girl was trembling and the shock was so much, that she had to be treated for several days before she came to herself'.[21] Miss L. Krishnabai argued that child-wives were 'weak, nervous, and susceptible to all kinds of ailments', while Mrs A. Lakshmi Pathi claimed that they were vulnerable to 'nervous debility, nervous breakdown or TB'.[22] Likewise, Dr Muthulakshmi Reddi argued girls were more likely to develop nervous troubles, sleeplessness and dyspepsia, impacting a girl's 'nerves and mental outlook'.[23] Not only medics but Mr Vannia Nadar Ramaswami of the Cosmopolitan Club, Ramnad, also mentioned mental fright, attempted suicide and mental derangement, while as an advocate C. Veeragahavier pointed out that 'invariably, a healthy girl, bright of eye, and cheery and active, after consummation, becomes languid and drooping and inert and morbid … one has to look at the number of girls that are said to be possessed, to be assured of the factor that they are only nervous wrecks, the result to the shock of sexual strain'.[24] This reflected a new global interest in normative psychological development and the trauma induced when this was interrupted, which fitted with the interest in educational development seen in Chapter 3. It echoed wider patterns of the recognition of the link between mental and physical health in the interwar years, and perhaps drew from earlier discourses around the links between women and hysteria.[25] That said, it was a significant change to emphasise early sexual activity, even within monogamous marriage, as the source of mental trauma and an aberration in a child's emotional and psychological development.

Concerns about the child-wife's intellectual maturity to cope with sex were closely entangled with her physical capability as a mother and her emotional and intellectual capability to run a household or to care for her own children.[26] This linked to wider concerns about the educational impact of early marriage. As Chapters 1, 2 and 3 have demonstrated, education was fast becoming a normative aspect of childhood, and while elementary education rarely lasted beyond twelve years old and was only infrequently available to girls, there was concern that marriage prevented continued education by removing the child-wife from school, and that the insufficiently educated child-wife was unable to adequately manage a family. The Joshi report itself highlighted the need for girls' education, particularly as a means to socially uplift and a reflection of women's increased desire to participate in public life.[27] This was reflected in the submissions, although a number of more conservative respondents feared that education for girls would destabilise the established social order.[28] Most contributors wanted to extend or deepen girls' education to allow them to become better wives and mothers, with a greater understanding of nutrition, hygiene and household management, and this reflected the gendered curriculum encouraged for most girls.[29] The advocate C. Veeragahavier argued that education was necessary so that women could become 'helpmates to their husbands, both in the interests of the family and of the nation', promoting a liberal idea of companionate marriage, which would contribute to national progress.[30] The boundaries between adulthood and childhood were entangled with discursive tropes of marriage and education, which assumed the two were incompatible, and this was reinforced by the experience of fathers such as M. A. Srinivasa Iyengar, whose daughter and son-in-law lived with the family so that she could finish her education, but this had such a detrimental impact on her health that her schooling was abandoned.[31]

The idea of the child as a learner intertwined with the modern idea that childhood was also a time of happiness and irresponsibility, a time of 'freedom and joy of youth'.[32] Shreemati Kamalabai Lakshmana Rao, a magistrate in Tinnevelly, suggested that 'twelve is the age of a playing child—of a happy girlhood'.[33] This was juxtaposed with the idea of responsibility: 'the short period of care-free and happy girlhood' was discussed in contrast with 'the cares and anxieties of a home and children'.[34] The removal from school impacted the intellectual life of these 'bright gems' but also their ability to manage 'the proper duties and responsibilities of wifehood and motherhood'.[35] Mrs Malati Patwardhan, honorary general secretary of the Women's Indian Association (WIA), contrasted that the 'young unmarried girls are bright, cheerful and healthy, while young girls who are married or are mothers with children look careworn and unhappy and undeveloped'.[36] This overtly emotional representation of childhood again highlighted premature ageing as these children failed to follow a normative development pattern. The emphasis on education reflects a wider interest in the notion of intelligent consent, and the age at which girls could understand the social and moral implications of their actions.[37] This weighed heavily on the minds of the Joshi Committee and featured in the questionnaire. Ishita Pande has argued that the idea of consent itself needs historicised, based in liberal political theory about individual subjectivity, seen in individual rights, choice, justice and physical integrity, crucially tied up with the distinction between child and adult.[38] Consent was numerically defined because of the imperatives of modern governance, rooted in imperial power relations as well nationalist and feminist constructs of the girl-child as an ideal citizen and a willing guardian of a moral order.[39] Even defining consent, and making it legally binding, required a recognition of scientifically defined normative patterns of development that pushed against religious traditions while remaining infused with a moralising agenda. Nonetheless, the recognition that 'consent' involved an act of reason, a deliberate understanding of the physical and moral consequences of sexual intercourse and an element of informed choice began to recognise the individual personhood of the girl-child as separate from the family.[40]

Different aspects were emphasised in the evidence, usually linked to 'due realisation of consequences'.[41] Both reformers and conservatives were concerned that while girls could have a 'voice' in the selection of a partner, only parents understood the long-term considerations of character and good family rather than the short-term attractions of good looks and stylish dressing.[42] The primary concern was that girls were unable to understand the consequences of extramarital sex on their reputation and marriage prospects and would lead to a life of prostitution.[43] This inability to judge moral and social consequences meant that girls 'in the heat of passion or solitude of seduction may give her ready consent to the ravisher without weighing the consequences of her act', and that even within marriage she would be unable to resist excessive demands from her husband, in both cases situating blame and responsibility with the girl.[44] The regulation of extramarital sex was not only a way to regulate girls' sexual practices and reinforce heteronormative, monogamous conjugality but was seen as a protective measure that would directly influence the regulation of *devadasi*s in the Madras Presidency.[45] For Rao Bahadur M. Chengayya Pantalu Garu, the commissioner of the Hindu Religious Endowments Board, the concept of intelligent consent provided legal protection for young *devadasi*s from the consequences of acts that they could not be deemed to have validly consented to because it assumed that sex with a stranger below this age meant rape.[46] The intersection of these issues shows how a significantly politicised debate could be used to promote a wide variety of reformist causes.

The notion of intelligent consent was often linked to the other legal boundaries of childhood, particularly the ability to hold and administer property. M. A. Srinivasa Iyengar argued that 'while for every other matter relating to a girl, she is considered incompetent to contract before she attains 18 years I wonder why in sexual matters alone, the most important thing in her life, she should be considered competent to give either her will or consent'.[47] The dissonance with the Indian Majority Act, 1875, and the Indian Contract Act, 1872, was a common complaint particularly, though not exclusively, among lawyers while the report itself contrasted the 'disposal of property' with the 'disposal of one's own person'.[48] This complaint revealed not only a familiarity with the legal contradictions but a widespread unease with the variety of legal boundaries of the minority.[49] It also filtered into the discussions around *devadasi*s, with Dr Mian Sir Muhammad Shafi using his speech in the Council of State to highlight the inconsistencies between property ownership and legal guardianship.[50] The discrepancies had particular resonance in Madras in the context of the Religious Endowments Act, 1929, centred on guaranteeing the livelihood and property ownership of the *devadasi* community as a means of securing their economic self-sufficiency.[51] The parameters of childhood for girls as well as boys were not merely defined by sexual maturity but were deeply entangled with other legislative boundaries, including labour, property and education, some operating at an all-Indian level, but mainly closely intertwined with the legislative politics and governance of the presidency.

Defining Modern Childhood

Sexual innocence was one of the clear markers of childhood. Satadru Sen has shown that accusations of sexual precocity which were levelled by British imperialists, and later white feminist-imperialists such as Katherine Mayo, were intended to both undermine the moral standing of Indian adults by failing to protect children, and meant that these prematurely adult children were never fully childlike, and therefore unable to achieve full adulthood.[52] These assumptions were contested by Indian nationalists and feminists, and it was in this area that the claim to control children's bodies was most pronounced. This was intimately connected to the desire by colonial officials, civil society activists and Indian policymakers to regulate appropriate sexual activity within the broadly agreed parameters of monogamous conjugality that was deemed both respectable and modern.[53] Within the Madras discourses of the 1920s, sexual innocence had physical and intellectual implications, as noted earlier, but this was predominantly a moral boundary. There was a tacit agreement that the married child was regarded as an adult after she had moved to the marital home and the marriage had been consummated—the act of consummation was the moment when the boundary to adulthood was crossed. This suggested that adulthood and childhood were two distinctive and bounded spheres, with a distinctive moment of transition between them. Even at an early age this was legal and expected, even as the numerical implications of that boundary were contested.

It was in the sphere of illicit or immoral sexual activity that the concept of childhood innocence was most actively deployed, partly as a foil to accusations of Indian sexual precocity.[54] Within the anti-trafficking and *devadasi* campaigns, the end of sexual innocence was seen as a particular 'sin against humanity', which transcended national and racial boundaries based on a global moral order, often emanating from Victorian moral values that saw childhood sexuality as transgressive and threatening.[55] In the Legislative Assembly debates of 1927, almost every speaker used the terms innocent, pure and helpless interchangeably and frequently, denoting dependence but also humanitarian and religious moral imperatives, which made sex outside marriage a more heinous and emotionally charged crime, even though the girls in question were the same age as their compatriots who were legally married. In her motion opposing the dedication of girls to temples, Dr Muthulakshmi Reddi argued that

> the most pathetic, the most regrettable and the most revolting nature of this custom is that the training for the immoral trade begins from these girls even from their childhood, that is, at an age when they cannot think and act for themselves. As a certain good lady has so feelingly remarked 'it was as wax, a little, tender innocent child in the hands of a wicked power when the fashioning process began'.[56]

In other words, the traffickers and the priests at temples used children specifically because they were malleable and impressionable, lacking the intellectual resources to query these 'unhealthy and superstitious notions'.[57] The moral repugnance was reinforced by their physical beauty; it was 'the most good looking and the most intelligent children of a family' who were given to temples.[58] This fitted wider global discourses that equated innocence with beauty and with whiteness, emphasising the cute lovability of the child.[59] In these terms hypothetically 'virtuous and loyal wives, affectionate mothers and useful citizens are slowly introduced into an evil life which subjects them to very painful, very debilitating, disfiguring and most contagious disease in addition to all the horrors of a prostitutes' life'.[60] Not only did this deprive the individual and nation of their future potential, but their physical disfigurement also signified their lost moral standing. What is more, as with children raised in hijra households, early sexual experience characterised these children both as victims and as a dangerous source of contagion.[61] These girls became 'mental, moral and physical wrecks'; the opposite of innocence was framed not as maturity but as immorality, which precluded the possibility of future redemption. Nonetheless, these girls had their innocence forcibly removed, which meant that their rescue or rehabilitation was more justifiable because their original motives were good, reinforcing gendered and class stereotypes about the innate immorality of the ordinary prostitute.[62] While marriage might prove a threat to physical and mental health, it was the moral health of the girls which was threatened by illicit sexuality—this informed policy on trafficking, on the age of consent outside marriage and also meant that girls who were sexually active forfeited their right to protection as children under the Madras Children Act, 1920 (MCA) as seen in Chapter 5.

Within this moral order, if childhood ended with sexual activity, then this should happen within closely defined, demonstrably respectable conjugal relations. This meant that the identity of the sexual partner was important. As Ashwini Tambe has pointed out, sex with an illegitimate stranger was morally more repugnant than sex with a legitimate stranger, a legally married husband.[63] Comparative ages were also important. Accordingly, the most problematic sexual partners were older male devotees who visited *devadasi*s at temples; these fitted into wider concerns about older men but also about the orientalist figure of the lecherous, over-sexualised Brahmin, an emotive trope that campaigners were prepared to use to promote their own agendas, even if specific examples were unclear.[64] The trope of the older man raping his child-wife received public attention during the Phulmoni case in 1889 and certainly received most international and reforming opinion, an effective rhetorical tool to inspire disgust and engender sympathy while also undoubtedly reflecting the plight of many child wives.[65] This remained a source of concern during the 1920s, particularly for children who became second or third wives.[66] However, perhaps in response to the criticism of Katherine Mayo and others, the submissions centred much more on the over-enthusiasm of younger husbands who were distracted from their studies and infected by youthful exuberance and passion, with older men positioned as the exception.[67] This reflected anxieties about adolescent sexuality but was rendered understandable as within the normal development of the adolescent body.

Though the legal contrast between adulthood and childhood, or majority and minority, was becoming more clearly established, within the context of sexual relations, there was some early interest in adolescence as a liminal life stage, and a recognition by a minority of the respondents that the break between childhood and adulthood was a gradual one. R. S. Subbalakshmi noted the immediacy of the transition: 'The pleasures of boyhood and girlhood are completely denied to them. After childhood comes all of a sudden manhood and womanhood to them. Or rather, the responsibilities of grown-up men and women are thrust on them.'[68] This reflected her observations as the headmistress of Lady Willingdon

Training College, Madras, but also her personal history as a child widow. Similarly, Miss E. Lazarus noted that

> while the Europeans have a distinct childhood, girlhood and womanhood period, where in each has full development and functioning of the instincts, play, muscular and thought processes, in India it is a great jump from childhood and womanhood with only an intervening period of a year or two only for girlhood.[69]

This concept of girlhood or youth as a distinctive life stage, still categorised by elements of playfulness and irresponsibility, and particularly suitable for education, was a relatively new concept on the subcontinent.[70] In these terms, puberty was a biological change that occurred during a wider time of physical, emotional and intellectual change, variously described as 'the impressionable and joyous period of maidenhood', a time of 'freedom and joy of girlhood'.[71] Noticeably, it was women activists who were most likely to raise these concerns in their evidence.

Adolescence could also be a threat. Children were safe and easily regulated; framed as asexual, they were in need of protection while adults had regulated sexual behaviours, constrained by domestic limits and heteronormative conjugal relations. Adolescents, by contrast, were much more characterised by changing and unregulated sexual instincts, potentially deviant and threatening. Mrs Gauri Sankunni, the superintendent of the Government Secondary and Training School for Women, recognised that for her students aged fifteen or sixteen 'the world is a shifting phenomenon full of fun and frolic and she is hardly sensible of the fundamental value of the sex instinct in her and its wonderful sanctity'.[72] This disjunction between physical desire and understanding of the consequences characterised both girls and boys so that the 'desire to cohabit is like hunger and thirst—a natural instinct. It does not wait till the maturity of the mind and understanding is reached', making emergent sexuality a thing to be feared.[73] For some, such as Govindoss Chathoorbhoojdoss, sexual desire was natural and inevitable and 'it is within the experience of every citizen, male or female, how two school children, irrespective of any age, satisfy their passion wherever possible by cohabiting secretly with the children of oppose sex or their own sex'.[74] The 'precocious sexual instinct in our youth' was variously attributed to early marriage, natural development or to the experience of modern life, with a number of respondents referring to 'free and fashionable youths' or 'young people's own curious minds filled by the giddy pleasures of sex'.[75] This endangered the young people themselves, seriously impacting their educational prospects. While parents increasingly desired a modern education for their children, schools, colleges and hostels—places where the youth could congregate in close proximity—were the focus of particular anxiety about illicit sexual relations.[76] While parents of girls feared the reputational damage of extramarital sex, the parents and educators of boys feared 'abnormal' sexual practices, particularly homosexuality, masturbation and disease-carrying prostitutes.[77]

This new, though legally unrecognised, category of youth required regulation by adults but hints at a recognition that the boundaries between childhood and adulthood were messier and blurred in social reality than in theory. Unregulated youthful sexual experiences could be contained through education, but the threat of scandal was ever-present, a threat to the reputation of young people and their families.[78] This could be combatted through surveillance by parents and schools, by committing to a life of Brahmacharya, celibacy and self-denial, by sex education and by the free availability of birth control.[79] Early marriage was seen by some, such as S. Varadachariar, as a way to calm or 'steady' the 'waywardness or laxity' of youth, the wife providing the young man with a sexual outlet within the bounds of legality, the domestic sphere and marital sex, thereby putting another burden on these young child-wives.[80] The sexual practices of young adults could be couched as either a cause or consequence of early cohabitation, but for both it reinforced the moral dangers posed by what was perceived to be a natural or inevitable process of sexual awakening and the need for these to be regulated by both the family and the state into acceptable conjugal relations.

Local Reformulations of Global Ideas

The control of adolescent sexuality was not only an Indian problem but also reflected global concerns. A number of respondents, particularly judges, referred to the work of the American progressive social reformer Ben B. Lindsey who co-authored *The Revolt of Modern Youth* with Wainwright Evans in 1925. Lindsey's work is credited with being central to emergent ideas about adolescence in America, particularly the argument that while girls were sexually mature, they continued to require the protection of the state and their parents because they lacked the 'intellectual restraint and sophistication of maturity' to make informed choices.[81] Rather than engaging with the progressive solutions suggested by Lindsey, the respondents used this to highlight the threat to (specifically) Hindu families of the immorality of Western, especially American, society and the need for more control over emergent female sexuality.[82] These well-read, professional men, from a range of political opinions, engaged with these concerns in the American context, partly as a rejoinder to Mayo, partly reflecting the cultural nativism of the nationalism movement, but also claiming a shared humanity, a universal development sequence which was, in itself, a radical claim to global equality and shared humanity. As seen in earlier chapters (Chapter 3), the claim to a shared development sequence was a significant challenge to the racial hierarchies intrinsic to colonial rule, but on the basis of similarity, not difference.

The concern about adolescence and juvenile sexuality mirrored anxieties about the impact of modernity on traditional Indian social structures and its implications for societal decline, even as those structures only reflected the social practices of the upper castes. While many of the contributors supported modern education for their own daughters or for other high caste girls, there was concern about the changing pace of modern life and its impact on the physical and moral health of children. This was the Indian manifestation of a global problem, modernity linked to the 'advancing materialism of the west' with the young being particularly susceptible.[83] These changes physically impacted the rich, and therefore high caste, girls living in urban areas where they were more likely to be educated, have good diets and avoid physical work. More than that, they had access to 'various unnatural modes of modern life', such as cinemas, theatres and novels, 'mischievous privileges' that were perceived to induce puberty earlier and meant that they 'drifted ... from their old and traditional habits'.[84] Respondents felt that modern life induced in the young 'an intolerable spirit of unmanageable, individualist, pleasure-seeking restlessness and revolutionary rowdyism' that threatened the existing social order.[85] Of particular concern was the breakdown in traditional hierarchies of authority and the decline in the joint family as a support system.[86] This intergenerational anxiety was not new but intersected with colonial and nationalist ideas about race, eugenics and appropriately gendered behaviours, as well as professional claims to scientific modernity. Importantly, they reflected concerns about upper-caste youths, having little relevance to those without the resources or leisure to access these new temptations.

The League of Nations emerged as a particularly significant hub for information exchange, setting a new tone for global consensus on social issues. While the state remained the centre for demographic and bio-political control, Ashwini Tambe argues that this was the first time that populations across the globe were regarded as 'knowable and governable' by an international or non-state body, setting a precedent for a number of international organisations after 1945.[87] Moreover, while the league cemented the political power of the European colonial powers, it also provided a new space in which information could be exchanged and where, in terms of social policy, new discourses emerged that reflected the ideas of state- and non-state actors. The league and its departments provided a space to contest and resist the racial hierarchies of the colonial powers by promoting a universalising language of equality and compassion for children, as well as demonstrating the priority of western categories and concerns, which showed the colonial heritage of modern humanitarianism.[88] Within these constraints, there slowly emerged a consensus that the age of consent for sexual relations should be broadly comparable irrespective of borders. This informed the push for legislative alignment between Great Britain and the different provinces of British India so that 'the highest considerations of justice and morality', which were in these terms necessarily universal, would be evident.[89]

The global anti-trafficking campaign was at the forefront of the movement to standardise the age of consent across the globe, largely because global exchanges of women and children required similar boundaries to police and enforce.[90] In 1922, when Dr H. Gour introduced his anti-*devadasi* resolution, he referred directly to the league, arguing that the resolution was a direct result of the Convention against Trafficking, the local application of a global principle.[91] Changing Sections 372 and 373 of the Indian Penal Code (IPC) was intended to protect the rights of women and children, but was also impacted by the ratification by India of International Convention regarding the traffic in women and children and the passing of Children's Acts in Bengal and Madras, which were themselves based on English law (see Chapter 5). This was supported by

Sir Devadasi Prasad Sarvadhikary in the Imperial Legislative Council, who argued that international consistency was important, particularly in the case of kidnapping. Importantly, this established the principle that the boundaries of child protection should transcend racial, national and particularly communal boundaries. In these terms, this universal standard was being inhibited by the Government of India in Delhi because of their hesitation to legislate, and should instead be based on 'humanitarian opinion' and on Indian membership of the League of Nations, which meant that her domestic institutions should be subject to the 'scrutiny of the world'.[92] While perhaps based on the normative moral judgements of the Western world, it gave Indians another way of contesting colonial rule through participation in global bodies and reliance on international authority.[93]

The Geneva Declaration on the Rights of the Child, 1924, was referred to both as part of the Joshi submissions and in the debates over *devadasis*. By framing their responses within the terminology of the rights of the child, the Tamil-educated elite demonstrated a familiarity with global notions of children's rights and a willingness to reference the universal applicability of these principles and to use the idea of international authority to strengthen their position, as noted in earlier chapters.[94] The Joshi report itself was framed in terms of the 'best interests of the children', a nod to the language of the Geneva Declaration.[95] A number of respondents couched their submissions in terms of 'cannons of justice and fair play' or the need for education to ensure that 'the girls understand their own [unspecified] rights and privileges'.[96] This dual concept that rights were inalienable *and* were guaranteed by the international community based on a set of universalising norms was particularly apparent in the trafficking discourse, which relied on a conception of a common humanity whose responsibility was wider than the nation state.[97]

Dr Muthulakshmi Reddi was particularly conversant in children's rights standards and argued that children should be protected 'in the interest of humanity and in the interest of the sacred rights of children'.[98] She highlighted

> the principles of which were agreed to by all civilised nations: 'men and women of all nations recognising that mankind owes the child the best that

it has to give, declare and accept it is their duty that beyond and above all considerations of race, nationality or creed, the child must be given the means request for its normal development, both material and spiritually'.⁹⁹

This applied to all children, even those living as *devadasi*s, on the basis of both justice and humanity, referencing both their innate rights and their vulnerability.¹⁰⁰ Additionally, she claimed that the child's protection was the responsibility of state intervention, with the rights of vulnerable children guaranteed by 'every right-minded person, from every parent and above all, from the state, because it is the duty of the state'.¹⁰¹ These were not rhetorical flourishes but were a clear example of using international human rights standards to inform local policy and action, particularly significant because Reddi was the deputy president of the MLC and fully aware of the possibilities within its jurisdiction.

These global controversies were also distinctly local and were rooted in the distinctive politics and civic activism of the Madras Presidency as well as the experience of political devolution and the articulation of new political subjectivities in response. The submissions to the Joshi Committee were submitted as a local cohort, and reflected the experiences of the presidency, while the legislation on immoral traffic and on *devadasi*s was passed in the MLC, as legislators integrated universal principles into the local decision-making process and legislation. The fledgling Dravidian movement was keen to stress the differences in social conditions from the north, with the Justice Party and Self-Respect campaigners such as Periyar E. V. Ramasami using social legislation around the family and gender politics to articulate the new identity politics of Tamil nationalism, and the discussions on children often played into these wider debates.¹⁰² The splits within the local Congress party undermined their claim to represent all of India, with many of the more socially conservative responses to the Joshi Committee and the question of *devadasi*s coming from Congress legislators such as S. Satyamurthi.¹⁰³ The Joshi submissions also reflected the globally networked nature of the Madras elite, whose personal contacts and information exchanges extended across the globe, often bypassing Delhi and London. T. R. Venkatarama Sastri, for example, demonstrated detailed knowledge of institutions such as the New York Society for the Prevention of Cruelty to Children, White Cross and the Social Purity League, as well as infant mortality rates in the John Hopkins

Hospital, Baltimore.[104] This reflects what Sarah Hodges calls 'the discursive traces and practical networks of the global circulation of a scientific modernity', the Indian educated elite using these information exchanges both for the quality of knowledge exchanged and to evidence their own modernity.[105]

The most influential civil society networks in Madras centred around the WIA and the Theosophical Society, with interjections from the Justice Party as well as the Indian National Congress. While Dr Reddi was the most internationally distinctive voice, she was supported by a wide range of women who claimed a particular role as nurturers and guardians of children's rights, using this to establish their roles in the public sphere as with the juvenile courts (Chapter 6). These included campaigners and activists, such as Mrs Malati Patwardhan, honorary general secretary of the WIA or Mrs Alamelu Magathavarammal, an honorary magistrate in Madras, as well as social workers, doctors and youth workers. These women were disproportionately well-educated, wealthy and high caste, and took the opportunity afforded by the Joshi Committee to articulate views in the public sphere, which separated them from mainstream nationalism as well as Western feminism.[106] This was not a distinctive moment but rather the most public element within a trajectory of women's articulation of children's rights across a range of social policy areas, including education and juvenile justice. These were not powerless women but were part of a globally-networked middle-class elite, which, as Mrinalini Sinha has shown, prioritised a conception of the liberal bourgeois citizen-subject and the state as the instigator of modern scientific forms of governance.[107] S. Anandhi also argues that they were very quickly co-opted within the wider Dravidian movement.[108] But that is not to underestimate the role they claimed for themselves or the distinctive ways in which they heard, formulated and implemented ideas within the Madras context.

The Role of the State in Policing Sexuality

In the sphere of sexual politics, the modern state assumed a number of complementary and intertwined roles, protecting vulnerable children, defining the boundaries of sexual maturity and enforcing these through measures such as the registration of marriage, managing the reproductive capacity of populations and investing in children as future citizens.[109]

As demonstrated in the previous chapters, there was a growing recognition of the state's duty to intervene if parents failed to provide adequate care and protection for their children, and an awareness that measures such as midwifery, schooling, public nurseries and child welfare services were a contribution to 'the physical, intellectual and social welfare of the country' as well as the individual.[110] The eventual decision to legislate on the age of marriage rather than consent reflected concerns about interference in the private lives of the population, the difficulty of enforcing an unstable and contested boundary of puberty and a tacit reflection of the low educational levels of the people, which meant that a numerical boundary was easier to manage, even though birth registration remained problematic. In practice, the legal changes could only be traced in the registration of marriage, and the increase in marriages in the six months preceding the implementation of the legislation was discreetly ignored.

The relationship between the state and family authority was complex and changing. Ashwini Tambe has argued that the state took on a role as a surrogate parent, assuming the anxieties and control usually associated with the birth parents.[111] The evidence from the Madras Presidency suggests that this overstates and simplifies this relationship. Rather, state actors were more likely to frame themselves as avuncular, working within the legal, social and even emotional boundaries of the family unit, distinctively qualified to intervene because of their modern training and approach but only exercising this power as a matter of last resort. This encouraged a less combative approach to the family. A number of respondents suggested that older members of the household should be punished if the legislation was broken because a young couple could only cohabit 'with the active connivance of the parents', while there was continued concern over the role of grandmothers in promoting traditional marriage practices.[112] In general, however, there was a recognition that parental decisions were tied by social convention, and that if they arranged an inappropriate match, this was inadvertent and benign, an understandable mistake.[113] The fear that the boys' parents would be offended and cancel the marriage was a key source of anxiety for parents, and many felt that they had little choice, even if they were also concerned about the health of their children.[114] This reflected the girl's economic potential as a contributor to the household economy but also the significant cost of the dowry to the natal family.[115] These constraints on parental actions were widely acknowledged by even the most ardent reformers who manifested a continued and overt reluctance to intervene in contravention of parental authority.

The state might have been reluctant to intervene in the parental decisions regarding heteronormative conjugality, but this parental right was withdrawn when the children were engaged in what was perceived to be immorality as a result of parental choice.[116] While there was limited support for women prostitutes who were regarded as responsible for their life choices, there was outrage that young girls should be exposed to a life of prostitution and vice, particularly 'at a time when she is unable to decide for herself'.[117] This referenced a perceived universal human principle that parents had primary responsibility for their vulnerable charges, and that parents who failed in their parental duty to protect their children from immorality had seceded their parental rights (see Chapter 5).[118] The targets were the parents who dedicated their daughters as a response to poverty or in lieu of a debt to the god, retired *devadasi*s who dedicated their own biological or adopted infant daughters or mothers who were prostitutes.[119] Girls brought up in these surroundings had little choice, and it was generally accepted that 'the State has to do its duty to these children' because the parents had forfeited their rights to that relationship.[120] Indeed others such as the lawyer—and later politician—Muhammad Ali Jinnah, argued that the state should step in and forcibly remove children in these circumstances, if necessary, by bypassing the usual legal procedure.[121] The changes to the Code of Criminal Procedure in 1924 increased the power of local magistrates to both 'rescue minor girls' and to 'make them over to suitable guardianship'.[122] The care of these rescued girls was then the responsibility of the police, the criminal courts and later the structures of the juvenile courts. This was supplemented by a number of civil society bodies. Rescue homes were generally financed by local and municipal boards, but managed by a variety of voluntary organisations.[123] These organisations included the Madras Children Aid Society, the Seva Sadan, the Society for the Protection of Children and the Avvai home in Madras City, along with mission societies such as the Salvation Army, professional social workers or kinship care within the extended family.[124] These homes were intended to provide for the 'care, treatment, instruction and maintenance of girls', although their rehabilitative potential was limited: the girls could be cared for and become productive members of society, but their innocence was irretrievable and they occupied a liminal space as not-quite child and not-quite adult.[125]

The modern state was responsible for protecting the vulnerable, and producing healthy future citizens who would contribute to the nation state. Early cohabitation was a threat to this, not because it threatened the health of young mothers but because it was perceived to impact the life chances of their potential male offspring, raising the possibility of a 'weak impoverished and debilitated population'.[126] This meant that much of the debate was framed in overtly eugenic terms. This was intended to refute Mayo's polemic, but also revealed wider racial anxieties about the 'future physical vitality of the Indian Nation'.[127] Sarah Hodges has shown how the eugenic movement intersected with the feminist and birth control movements in the presidency.[128] The debates over child marriage revealed another international exchange of information, and the familiarity with which the respondents on both sides of the debate used this pseudo-scientific language of nation-building, as well as the modern, global language of contraceptive choice, shows the extent and diversity of their networks.[129] While high infant-mortality rates were generally attributed by the conservatives to poverty and poor nutrition, medical officers such as Dr (Mrs) Lazarus used their evidence to make a case for enhanced child welfare provision to support and nurture both the small infants born and the child-adults who had birthed them.[130] If early marriage was perceived to threaten the racial strength of Indians, the much less numerous—though politically significant—offspring of the *devadasi*s were also a perceived threat to the health of the future nation, particularly as a result of sexually transmitted disease.[131] Eugenics therefore provided a platform for Western-educated Indians to both contest the notions of racial hierarchy and the civilisational backwardness of journalists such as Katherine Mayo, and to implement governmental strategies based on the regulation of health, the restriction of non-monogamous sexuality and the promotion of respectable conjugality under the guise of 'the blossom of national regeneration'.[132]

The CMRA and *devadasi* legislation was primarily aimed at controlling the sexuality of upper-caste women. As noted in earlier chapters, the dyarchical state's structures of governmentality drew heavily from previous colonial policies and were predicated on notions of communal difference, often on the lines of caste. The Joshi report itself emphasised that in the Madras Presidency, Brahmins and Vaisyas were 4 per cent of the population, and that early marriage was largely a high caste problem.[133] This was recognised in the submissions; for example, T. Rangachariar argued that early marriage was fashionable among Brahmins, but they comprised significantly less than 10 per cent of the population.[134] A disproportionate number of both male and female respondents were also Brahmin, reflecting higher levels of Western education among these groups, but also the dominance of middle-class Brahmins in constructing ideas about womanhood and childhood within the nationalist movement. Early marriage was used by Brahmins as a way of proving the purity of caste, another means of buttressing the distinctiveness of the community.[135] Within the Madras Presidency, the hegemony of the upper castes was being challenged by the non-Brahmin Justice movement as the dominant political party, and by the radical reformulation of marriage that was beginning through the Self-Respect movement.[136] This was one part of a wider campaign for a more egalitarian society, which positioned the social practice and political influences within the south of India as distinctive from the Congress-dominated north.

More significantly, child marriage was not a social justice issue that impacted the vast majority of the population. There was clear evidence that castes such as *mudaliar*s and *chettiar*s married long after puberty, while the average for the labouring classes for girls was the ages of eighteen–twenty, perhaps because puberty was delayed because of hard work and lower levels of nutrition.[137] The submissions became part of a discourse of resistance to upper-caste dominance, and there was opposition to enshrining in legislation what was already the reality for the majority.[138] Like sati 100 years earlier, child marriage claimed international and national—and indeed historiographical—interest disproportionate to its impact and, as a specifically high-caste concern, was assumed to stand for the whole of India.[139] This in itself reveals the ways in which normative childhoods were imagined by a particular group eager to maintain its world view, as well as political dominance; the social practices of a powerful caste minority being claimed as representative of the nation and its children.[140] The continuing failure to take this seriously reinforced the discursive power of Brahmin childhoods as normative, very similar to the educational discourses too (Chapters 1 and 2).

Conclusion

The move to numerically define childhood in law by regulating the age of marriage informed, and was informed by, other discourses of childhood within the Madras Presidency. In particular, it intersected with other debates about the responsibility of the state towards vulnerable children and with a growing consensus among the educated elite that all children progressed along a broadly similar development sequence, irrespective of race or community. The respondents to the Joshi Committee show how widespread and mutually constitutive these ideas were.

During the 1920s, childhood became yet another category for the state to delineate and regulate as part of the numerous controversies over sexuality and sexual practices. This was informed by global humanitarian discourses centred around the League of Nations and the anti-trafficking campaigns, as well as the participation of a wide variety of men and women in local social reform endeavours as honorary magistrates, teachers and doctors. Importantly, while these fraught disputes were colonial, global and nationalist, it was south Indians operating at the level of the presidency or municipality who pushed through legislation and who aimed to implement it, making ideas relevant to the local context. The new role of the modern state was, therefore, intimately tied to the devolution of power to Indians, and this was a further area of social change in which elite Indians carved out opportunities within the bounds of dyarchical law where they could intervene within the family and protect children, in turn strengthening their own reputations. As with education and juvenile justice, this established patterns and assumptions of governance for the governing elite, which would continue after 1947.

Many of the individuals operating at the fringes of the state were women. As with the juvenile courts, women were keen to establish child-saving and education for girls as spaces in which they were uniquely positioned to contribute, carving out a unique space for themselves within the public sphere. While state and civil society intervention was never couched in overtly avuncular terms, it appears that these elite individuals sought to accommodate familial constraints and practices but also to regulate them, operating within the bounds of the extended family as uncles and aunties rather than assuming an overtly surrogate parental role. Both policymakers and civil society activists were much more prepared to intervene to regulate illicit sexuality or sexual practices defined as immoral in order to promote a version of conjugal domesticity that would contribute to nation-building. At the same time, by critiquing traditional social practices, these individuals established their own position as modern experts. Conversely, while the claim to be modern was central to the self-definition of the respondents, activists and legislators, the new material and cultural opportunities afforded by modernity were seen to be a particular threat to the normal development of the young.

The age of marriage and *devadasi* controversies reveal the caste-based nature of governance in the presidency and the dominance of upper caste concerns as normative. The CMRA symbolised the power of the upper castes to define and set the policy agenda and to define childhood through the lens of their own concerns. Despite frequent attention to the wide variety of experiences, the upper-caste experience was the only one that mattered, either for marriage or for the experience of adolescence. The debates over trafficking and the age of marriage thus became a site where other visions of the nation could be formulated and emphasised, for example, the tensions between the Dravidian south and the dominance of Delhi and Calcutta in the formulation of social policy.

The debates provided another space in which to develop ideas about the nature of childhood. With the passing of the CMRA, sexual maturity became a clear boundary in legal terms. Furthermore, by emphasising innocence, the distinction between childhood and adulthood became a moral boundary, signified and embodied by the sexual activity of children, whether legitimate or outwith the regulation of normative practices. At the same time, there was growing recognition of adolescence as a distinctive and liminal life stage, a discourse not fully developed but one that contested the absolutism of the division between adult and child even at the moment at which it was enshrined in law. Sexual maturity was therefore not tied to physical maturity but intimately connected to the mature mind, with intellectual ability and moral capacity as a marker of adulthood, despite the significant concern in educational discourses about the protection of children's bodies. The dominance of adult, albeit Indian, voices is significant here. No children contributed to the committee and there were no testimonies from child *devadasi*s about their experiences or opinions. The next chapter cannot remedy this but seeks to show another perspective on attitudes to childhood through the attempt to listen to their voices, recognising their agency and experience.

8

Remembering Childhoods

Childhood Memories in Autobiographies

This chapter sits juxtaposed with the rest of the book by considering a number of its recurring themes through an entirely different and more personal archival material—the autobiographical memories of adults who were children during the 1920s, 1930s and 1940s.[1] By considering the embodied actions and memories of children, the chapter foregrounds children as historical actors and claims that historians need to not only consider adult-led initiatives to improve children's lives or regulate their identities and behaviours but to consider the complex, uneven and gradual ways in which ideas about childhood, the state and the community evolved in social practice and in the everyday. This deepens our understanding of the difference between the realities of social relationships on the ground as opposed to the ways that the lives of poor children were imagined by the avuncular elite.

A close reading of a wide range of autobiographies provides an opportunity to reflect on the impact of new modern views about childhood and the child as an individual, rights-bearing future citizen. The memoirs offer an alternative lens through which to analyse new modern practices of governmentality, the introduction of modern educational structures and to assess the relationship between new forms of knowledge transmission in the school and existing authority and knowledge structures within the home, workplace and community. This in turns helps us to interrogate further the contested ways in which new identities were formed and old ones were reformulated. In particular, the chapter begins to uncover how children negotiated their emerging individual selfhood alongside their allegiance to their peers, and their attempts to find personal meaning in identities that adult society imposed on them, particularly caste and gender. Autobiographies, as more intimate sources than those used in the previous chapters, also allow us some small, fragmentary insights into the affective and educational relationships within the family, considering how kinship relations functioned in practice rather than how they were assumed to function in state and civil society discourse. These perspectives were intrinsically linked to the author's choice of life writing as a genre. How these adult writers sought to represent their own childhoods and relationships was closely connected to their political commitment to the ideas of universal childhood and individual agency as a basis for progress and nation-building. The memoirs created a space for the writers to articulate and evaluate their changing ideas about childhood through their own remembered experiences rooted in the specific context of family and school life, and also gave them the opportunity to explore their aspirations for children and state intervention in post-colonial India.

The previous chapters suggest that the idea of the modern child, encompassing universally shared characteristics, was becoming hegemonic in state and civil society practice in south India. By contrast, the multiple autobiographical memories of south Indian childhoods together provide a fragmentary and imperfect alternative perspective, rooted in what Rukmini Sen calls *pratyaha* or the everyday life-worlds of children.[2] Rather than extrapolating from the micro-histories of one or two individuals, this chapter draws on the memoirs of 55 individuals, selected because the authors were born between 1910 and 1940 and lived their childhoods in south India, loosely defined as the Tamil-, Telugu-, Kannada- and Malayalam-speaking areas. All have been accessed in English; the vast majority were published by the writers themselves or posthumously by their families, while a minority were located in formal archives or were published in translation. Four of the Dalit autobiographies were translated and published in Britain as part of a wider Dalit literature project; these have been supplemented by two further volumes of Dalit literature edited by K. Satyanarayana and Susie Tharu.[3] There are eight Dalit or adivasi autobiographies consulted (14 per cent of the total), while almost half (twenty-two: 40 per cent) were written by Brahmins, a reflection of upper-caste dominance of education rather than their proportion of the population. Nine (16 per cent) were written by women from a number of caste backgrounds. While experiences of childhood are a very small proportion of most texts, which generally detail successful careers in politics and education, they are used here to foreground children as historical actors, even as their voices are mediated through adult memories.

Reflecting on Individual Childhoods: Methodological Observations

A key aspect of modern understandings of childhood is to see the child as an individual, rational, rights-bearing future citizen in a direct relationship with the state through its governmental structures. This has contemporary resonance, as historians of childhood continue to grapple with the methodological challenges, or even desirability, of accessing children's voice and agency in the past, and wrestle with the fragmented evidence of their embodied experiences and the difficulty of re-presenting this in a meaningful way, while negotiating the contemporary focus on children's rights with its emphasis on children's participation.[4] This danger of representing the subaltern voice in 'our own image', as autonomous, self-reflective subjects expressing their opinions in the language of the academe is not an unfamiliar challenge in the South Asian context.[5] It is not helpful to read autobiographies as the voices of children, but at the same time it is important to recognise that they offer an alternative emphasis to the sources produced by the state, a perspective on everyday life as interactive, and categories as fluid.[6] In conversing with these muted voices, interrogating them and thereby identifying other norms, structures and experiences of social identity, this chapter will articulate perspectives that act 'alongside' more conventional speech, not reducing the past to binaries of silence–speech and action–inaction.[7] Instead, this reflects the need to search for possibilities, entanglements and accommodations within the archive, increasing the visibility of children as not only active agents of historical change but also as legitimate participants, responding to, shaping and initiating historical processes.[8] Within this, it is important not to prioritise the child-as-individual as more significant than the child-in-community, however varied and changing these communities were, but to recognise that agency and age are relational and contextual, reflective and constitutive of unequal relations of power, even as it is expressed and remembered through the pen of often now powerful adults.

Autobiographical memory as a category of life histories is usually assumed to be a genre particularly linked to the emergence of individual subjectivity and to Enlightenment perceptions of the self as a rational individual, and the focus on childhood experience is often seen to reflect a crucial element of that process. This is clearly the case for many Western and Bengali traditions of autobiographical writing.[9] By contrast, south Indian autobiographies appear explicitly written to 'excise the self', and the writers use their personal stories to reflect the wider social and cultural change they have witnessed.[10] The individual life is used by the authors as a public source and as 'a background canvas to portray these wider events', described by the writer A. N. Sattanathan as 'social history written as a life', not intended to be comprehensive but in the teacher K. Santhanam's terms, 'snapshots form a person in a boat moving along the river of Indian history'.[11] The writers claim the authority and legitimacy to remember because they use the 'idiom of non-uniqueness', claiming that their lives are representative of wider historical processes.[12] In A. P. J. Kalam's words, his narrative becomes 'a story of national aspiration and of co-operative endeavour' written as a life story.[13] This also reflects constructions of Tamil individuality, or *tanittuvam*, which Mattison Mines argues recognises the self as a public individual and social being or self-in-society, a different emphasis to more individualist Bengali or Western ideas of the self.[14] Within this broad framing, the difference between the individual and the collective is contingent, reflecting age, caste and gender hierarchies, and social circumstances and affective relations.[15] As Rukmini Sen has highlighted, life writing provides an insight into how individuals, particularly women and lower classes, construct their own meanings out of the 'relational process of everyday life', the self lived in a constantly changing community.[16]

Significantly, the choice of autobiography as a literary genre also reflects the author's commitment to modern values and a shift 'to a temporality of newness and vibrancy' in contrast to a static past.[17] A. R. Venkatachalapathy argues that Tamil autobiographies are explicitly structured around a binary of the difference between *antha kalam/intha kalam*, or 'those days/these days', which demonstrates social transformation, often between the binaries of tradition and modernity, agency and passivity.[18] For example, the judge K. Veeraswami describes the 'chasm between my boyish days and now'.[19] This contributes to a narrative that is both nostalgic for a lost, traditional childhood and is 'rooted in Nehruvian optimism about the transformative possibilities of nationhood'.[20] In these terms, children as future citizens have the potential to transform a forward-looking, independent India, contrasting the past with both the childhoods of the present and the writer's own educated adulthood. The child is constructed as a memory of an un-modern era, indicative of a symbolic progression to adulthood and modern understandings and ways of looking at the world. Childhood memories thus serve as a 'narrative tool of de-familiarisation' to emphasise a past that no longer exists but is based on a particular claim to reliability because events are remembered through the innocent gaze of the child.[21]

The Child in the Community

The autobiographical memories of the child as a member of the community, rather than as an individual in a direct relationship with the state, show that contemporary understandings of modern childhood were more complex than the state discourses would allow. Authors recounted detailed personal experiences but were often more interested in their place in relation to other children than in the emergence of an individual selfhood. Play was viewed as a collective experience and children were described variously as 'gangs', 'a forgotten herd', 'a happy bunch' or even 'the damned pack of crows'.[22] This could involve siblings, cousins or friends in the wider community, sometimes across caste boundaries.[23] Collective activity was reflected in a variety of unstructured activities: boys appear to have spent their leisure time outdoors climbing trees, picking wild berries and flying kites together.[24] K. Sreenivasan's recollections included complicated competitive games with mango seeds and group swimming in the big irrigation wells.[25] Other team sports included cricket and football as well as more traditional games such as *chinni dandu*.[26] The groups also frequently included animals, again highlighting both the difference from adult life and the modern association between childhood, nature, the primitive and the savage.[27] These animals were either integrated into the group or became replacement companions, including anything from grasshoppers through chameleons and birds to more domesticated animals, such as peacocks, cats and dogs, or even exotic animals such as a monkey or elephant for the very rich.[28] Festivals, in particular the south Indian celebrations of Deepavali and Pongal, also provided distinctive moments for children to play and share sweets across the wider village community, often across religious divisions.[29] This memory of intercommunal harmony was influential to the world view of men like P. C. Alexander, later governor of Tamil Nadu then Maharashtra, fitting into a wider Nehruvian narrative that intolerance was a learned response to adult intervention.[30] When leisure time was spent alone, it usually involved reading; literacy and a modern education beginning the evolution towards a more modern individual sense of self that culminated in the rational, educated adult.[31]

The idea of children playing harmoniously together 'in those days' is overly romanticised, as the authors sought to rationalise the post-partition context and come to terms with the communal and political upheavals of the 1940s. While the sweet treats and observance of community performances seem to have been enjoyed by all, the provision of entertainment by marginal communities—such as dancing by cowherds or fishermen, Muslim wrestling or epics provided by storytelling castes—appears to have reinforced both the child's sense of belonging and their awareness of communal difference.[32] Play was also gendered, with girls playing at home, often engaging in gendered role-play which reflected women's roles in a rural community, acting out marriage festivals and domestic and agricultural chores while their brothers and cousins explored outside.[33] Social conventions also limited the ability to play freely in surprising ways—the Dalit woman Viramma remembered her freedom to roam with her companions and suggested that richer children, particularly from higher castes, had a much more restrictive and propriety-bounded experience of childhood despite her experience of early pressure to contribute to the family income.[34] Children negotiated these simultaneously fragile yet rigid boundaries on a daily basis; Viramma, for example, was employed in domestic labour in a local Reddi house and afterwards played with the higher caste girls who lived there. She remembered:

> I played at being a dog for them and ran around on all fours while they chased me, laughing, with sticks in their hands. They often asked me to tell them stories: I knew a lot more than they did.[35]

Ruby Lal has demonstrated how 'playfulness' blurred the binaries between juvenile and adult, work and play, and was used to contest the established structures of power at home and in school.[36] Here the girls used role-play to both infringe caste distinctions *and* reinforce village power relations, using the Dalit child as not fully human, but also affirming her individual capabilities as a storyteller, actress and competent worker. It was in these small-scale interactions that difference and similarity were learned, reaffirmed and transgressed.

Knowledge Transmission to the Young

The introduction of legislation at the presidency level and the implementation of compulsory education schemes at the municipal level suggested growing support for the idea that all children should be formally educated within a state-regulated school in order to fulfil their obligations as future citizens (see Chapters 1 and 2). This reflected the normative ideas that the child was malleable, that their primary identity and activity was that of a learner and that learning should take place within the school where children could be disciplined into being economically productive. The autobiographical memories help to unpick how this functioned in practice, although the writers themselves were unrepresentative for a while within the Madras Presidency—only 33 per cent of boys aged between five and fifteen years were in school in 1931, and nearly 90 per cent of the authors continued to tertiary education.[37] Many were the first generation of their family, and even of their village, to be formally educated to even the secondary level. This self-identity as 'schoolchild', though rarely formally acknowledged by the writers, not only enabled their own social progression and gave them the literary skills and contacts required to record their childhood experiences but also differentiated them from their peers from a very young age.

The narrative distinction between those days/these days is mirrored in the clear binary between the *pial*, or village school, with its large classes, informal control and rote learning representative of traditional schooling that was the experience of the majority, and the routine, material resources and enlightened discipline associated with more modern secondary education.[38] The material life of the school reinforced this, the desks, slates, 'extensive playgrounds and shady avenues of trees' of the secondary schools contrasted with the palm leaf documents and literacy learned through drawing letters in the sand in the *pial* school.[39] The perceived backwardness of the *pial* school was enhanced by the frequent presence of younger siblings, the local school effectively functioning as a hub for childcare, often populated by junior caregivers rather than individual learners.[40] By contrast, the skills and routines learned in the modern secondary schools contributed to the explicit belief of many of the autobiographers as adults that education was essential to nation-building and was the primary solution to inequality and that they personally embodied the success of this social reform.[41] Furthermore, many of the memoirs were written by politicians or teachers with the purpose of claiming an authentic opinion on educational policy at the time of writing on the basis of their own experience of success and ability to 'reproduce more faithfully and more intimately the social conditions, the facilities, the opportunities, the problems and the values that existed then'.[42]

The widening of access to the elementary school provided a new form of temporal and spatial authority and regulated the unmodern family into new routines. The space given to describing the details of elementary education, including the minutiae of individual lessons and memories of teachers, provides some indication of its prominence in children's daily lives.[43] The school also introduced new authority figures into the children's lives, whose status was established because they were waged, because they had been formally trained in modern pedagogy and because they held disciplinary power in the classroom. These elementary teachers, often the only embodiment of the modern state at the village level, were vividly remembered as 'young', disciplinarian and enthusiastic.[44] Reflecting the priorities of the Public Instruction Department, they reinforced their teaching with extra-curricular activities, such as boy scouts, physical education and drill.[45] Sport was often used as a pedagogical tool to regulate boys' bodies into the correct forms of masculine behaviour, encouraging teamwork and sportsmanship.[46] This was remembered only in terms of hatred or ridicule, while the pedagogical value was contested by parents as 'silly acrobatics' or 'a meaningless waste of time'.[47] Support for the educational reforms of the 1920s appears to have been more contested at the local level than the official sources indicate.

Not all teachers conformed to this modern pattern; many others were remembered as semi-literate and inclined to excessive physical punishment: Sargunam, for example, remembered the village teacher as 'old' and 'tardy in mental stature, but unduly rotund in the middle', again linking physical and mental agility.[48] Particularly scathing were the brothers R. K. Narayan and R. K. Laxman, whose antipathy towards their intellectually lazy teachers directly contrasted with their father, an intelligent, modernising secondary teacher.[49] Most beloved were a third category of men who 'had an absolute passion to teach and mould a young mind' and were remembered as a 'lasting influence', to whom the author owed a 'special debt' because of their pedagogical and pastoral care.[50] Characterised formulaically as 'a gentleman and a scholar', these teachers were respected as an integral part of the village community, a powerful figure respected by the children 'as kind and considerate', but also by the, mainly illiterate, adult population because they could mediate with state officials. These men derived their authority from their training and education, but also from their integration into the local community as avuncular figures, ready to work with, rather than against, parents to secure the best of opportunities for their children.

If, as argued in Chapters 1 and 2, the normative child in school was male and upper caste, this priority of access and assumption of accessibility was reflected in the content of the curriculum. In general, the autobiographers recorded memories of tedious rote learning at the elementary level.[51] Occasionally this was supplemented by images or with object lessons based on the local environment, most notably aerospace engineer Kalam's transformative experience of watching the seabirds flying.[52] A different group remembered stories, often moral tales, which fired their juvenile imagination—the heroic tales of Arjuna, Robin Hood and Napoleon, for instance.[53] The cartoonist R. K. Laxman had particularly detailed memories, amongst them his emotional response as a child to a Kannada poem about a pet parrot being eaten by a cat.[54] Laxman also recounted in vivid detail the Telegu/Kannada moral tale of the honesty and self-sacrifice of the virtuous cow Punyakoti and the story of the Honest Woodcutter, which he claimed was 'the other equally unforgettable poem known to all educated Kannadigas of that era', while the teacher Narasimhaiah received the Punyakoti story at school prize-giving.[55] The memories of these popular stories may have been reinforced in adulthood through south Indian folklore, but they reveal how moral values and character traits such as honesty were intentionally inculcated throughout various aspects of the curriculum. Additionally, they reveal a curriculum in which tropes, ideas and even animals are particularly linked to heroic male, Hindu and Brahminical understandings of education and the world. These predominantly rural and pastoral stories reinforced caste, racialised, gendered and socio-economic hierarchies within the classroom, delegitimising the home experience of many children and their stories and traditions and undermining their right to be in the classroom while underlining the normative practices of upper-caste lives.[56]

The shared experience of schooling reinforced generational hierarchies and created a new institutionalised identity as a community of learners among an otherwise disparate group.[57] For a number of authors, it encouraged the solidarity of all children in opposition to the adult authority of the teachers, and the Dalit writer C. Kesayan remembers the 'unjust exercise of authority by elders' (often within his caste) as central to his experience of childhood.[58] Within the classroom, the authority of the teacher was questioned, not in dramatic confrontation but in the everyday decisions of children and their attempts, perhaps unconsciously, to undermine adult authority through the 'weapons of the weak'.[59] The *guru* and philosopher Nitya Chaitanya Yati reflected that it was 'normal and healthy' for a child 'not to conform', with adult power undermined through mimicry and laughter, enacted through caricatures on the blackboard, graffiti and practical jokes.[60] There were recollections of whispered conversations, of throwing paper darts and pieces of chalk and fighting, memories of collective enterprise reinforcing the camaraderie of the group.[61] When, for example, Sattanathan played a practical joke on the teacher, he received the silent support of all his fellow students, relying on their silence for protection and depending on their mutual antipathy, despite the variety of caste backgrounds and usual lack of social interaction, and in the process discovered 'the thrill of mischief and the risk of punishment'.[62] Once again, being a member of a community of children appears to have been particularly significant here.

More conscious decisions to contest schooling, for example through truancy, are recorded less often, perhaps because the autobiographers were themselves the most compliant children or keen to portray themselves as such.[63] Yati, for example, had his attendance marked and followed the school timetable for meals but otherwise absconded to the fields, while the novelist R. K. Narayan missed the detested drill class the previous Friday, despite knowing he would be punished when Monday came.[64] Of minor significance in themselves, these incidents gave children the illusion of agency in a world of school where adults retained control over the daily details of life as well as the intended direction of the children's life. At the same time, the decision to conform—either through fear of punishment, a genuine commitment to education or a personal inclination to comply— was also a rational, and more common, decision, though less discussed in hindsight. In most cases, overt resistance was only a possibility for children who already fitted the implicitly normative category of a schoolchild, in other words a healthy, high caste, Tamil-speaking Hindu boy (see Chapter 2); for other groups the risk was too high. The silences are important; those who refused to attend school as a result of alienation from peers or the curriculum, who struggled academically or with the formal environment of the school, or who had no opportunity to attend as a result of economic and social pressures, leave little written trace.

Two-thirds of children remained outside the reach of formal school education altogether, either because they needed to contribute to the family income or because the education provided was deemed unsuitable for their future prospects, either as artisans, unskilled labourers or as girls destined for early marriage.[65] These children left no literary evidence, and of the autobiographers only Viramma was completely unschooled, her memoirs collected and recorded by the anthropologists Josiane and Jean-Luc Racine.[66] The new association between the school, intellectual plasticity and normative childhoods in the minds of legislators, activists and teachers, and ultimately the autobiographers themselves, meant that these 'working children' increasingly appear as a transgressive category, as workers and therefore insufficiently childlike, as contributors and so insufficiently dependent.[67] By constructing education and work or 'child labour' as mutually exclusive and by increasingly defining childhood by participation in formal education, policymakers—and often historians too—ignored the lives of the majority who combined both.[68] A number of authors engaged in agricultural work on a seasonal basis, for example, in the betel leaf plantation, paddy harvest or the brick kilns.[69] Sattanathan reflected both on his 'special privilege as an educated person', which meant he could help his family calculate the wages and produce, and his happiness as a younger boy when delegated to keep birds from the harvest— 'a delightful change for the little boy from school'.[70] Kalam recounted his exhaustion but also pride in being 'a working boy at eight' as he contributed to the family income by fitting his newspaper delivery job around his school schedule.[71] Often these activities were remembered not as a failure of the family to provide but as enhancing the child's feelings of self-worth as a contributor.[72]

The need to work was particularly apparent for children from marginalised groups. Many girls participated in domestic duties: looking after the house and the younger children or even producing handicrafts to sell.[73] The first female Badga politician, Akkamma Devi, recalled learning her lessons outside the school building while caring for her baby brother and the impact on her mother's workload when she secured a place at the local convent school.[74] All the Dalit autobiographies detail unskilled work by children; for example, K. A. Gunasekaran sold mangos or neem seeds or collected dung as fuel from the bullock carts outside the cinema.[75] Regardless of background, the autobiographers situate childhood work as a feature of 'those days', often to demonstrate the comparatively privileged position of the modern children of 'these days', ignoring the continuing presence of child labour in south India.[76] Despite its recognisable flaws, all see modern education as the primary solution to inequality, a universal norm of childhood and an important aspect of nation-building, claiming an authentic opinion on the basis of their own lived experience while remaining loyal to family choices at the time.[77]

Learning Difference

Although a child might attend school, it did not mean that they felt they belonged there. The varied access to modern education, as well as the varied experiences within the classroom, undermined the equalising claims of modern education, which upheld universal notions of the modern child as unmarked by difference and equal before the law. However, this universalist myth had continuing political potential. One aspect of this was that childhood has also been constructed as a time when it is 'easier' to interact across boundaries and 'walk in the shoes of the recognised Other'.[78] In his collection of academic autobiographies of childhood, M. Karlekar argues that 'one of the great joys of childhood is that one is blissfully unaware of the tensions and problems of the adult world', children being unconscious of financial responsibility, but also of the political implications of identity and difference.[79] This perception that children are less aware of, or better able to transcend, adult boundaries of class, caste, race and gender reinforces the association of childhood with political innocence, irresponsibility and a primitive understanding of power structures in ways that reflect colonial constructions of savagery, primitive peoples and civilisational hierarchies.[80] It ignores the ways in which children experienced, learned, contested and contributed to categories of difference such as gender, religion and caste. However, this view was widely held among the educated Indian elites in the post-independence period and children as 'future citizens' were perceived to be the solution to communal discord. The idea of childhood as a time of harmony proved a powerful motivator for a number of authors; for example, the former chief justice of Tamil Nadu recollected 'those days' of 'amity' 'irrespective of their caste, creed, community or religion', a nostalgic memory of a harmonious past that as a contemporary public figure Veeraswami was keen to recreate.[81]

Religious tolerance was remembered most distinctively by the former president of India A. P. J. Abdul Kalam, who was schooled by his father, the local imam, in the Qu'ran in the early morning and then attended the village school. Kalam details his personal experience of religious discrimination by a schoolteacher in both his autobiographies, recounting that in the fifth standard a new teacher separated him from his friend after noticing the material symbols of their religion—the Muslim cap and the Hindu sacred thread. In the first account the father of his friend, who was an orthodox Brahmin, rebuked the teacher 'that he should not spread the poison of social inequality and communal intolerance in the minds of innocent children'.[82] In the second account, his own father and the local Catholic priest accompanied their Hindu friend and confronted the teacher with their concern that intolerance was allowed to 'infect the minds of the youngest members of society'.[83] While the two versions demonstrated subtle differences, not unlike the retelling of oral history, they also re-emphasised Kalam's personal belief that discrimination is a learned behaviour and that the plasticity and naivety of children's minds both provided the potential to overcome prejudice and made them uniquely susceptible to imbibing it. This was a strategic use of a childhood memory to validate a policy agenda of intercommunal harmony and educational access for all, based on the claim to the authenticity of the child's voice and memory as apolitical. In general, however, there were only limited references in the autobiographies to interracial or religious tensions, largely reflecting the small numbers of Muslims and the indigenisation of mission work in the presidency.[84]

While for some adults the school was remembered as a place of companionship and collective solidarity as children, for others the school emerges in the recollections as a space in which children came to learn the practical implications of their identity. If, in the minds of policymakers, the normative child at school was implicitly a high-caste Hindu boy, and all others were categorised into recognisable educational communities, it is unsurprising that this was reflected in the experiences of the children. What is more, it was often this experience of difference that was intimately tied to the author's motivations for recording their childhood. For those who fit within that normative category, the school was the place where high-caste children such as Nataraja Guru were confronted with the implications of their privileged status, cutting across bonds of childhood friendship.[85] High-caste children played games with their peers but began to realise that they were an 'educational aristocracy', a position reinforced symbolically by the material culture of the classroom, including stools near the teacher, palmyra leaf mats and ceremonial silver coins on special occasions.[86]

These experiences of difference continued outside the classroom. The Dalit activist Thumbadi Ramaiah remembers the Jain storekeepers' fear of pollution, handing the children their baskets on a pole through the window, and who 'if their children played with us, they would drag them away, slap them for their insolence and make them wash their arms and feet before entering the house'.[87] He comments, 'We did not understand all this and stood watching in stunned silence,' recalling both incomprehension and humiliation on the part of all the children involved. This was part of a wider pattern in which highly educated, now self-consciously modern adults reflected on ways that they had subconsciously assumed loyalties to community, village and family within the framework of the caste system. Reminiscing about childhood became for them a space in which they could distance themselves from previous behaviours and express their discomfort. Sreenivasan, from a wealthy Gounder family, considered the extent to which 'every child in the village, including myself, absorbed these social values as part of one's nature, without being aware of it'.[88] As a child this made him unwilling to question the hypocrisy of his beloved grandfather, who refused to eat the food cooked by his low-caste mistress.

Similarly, Subramaniam, from a dominant Vellalar caste, remembered that the stigma of untouchability was evidenced in all aspects of village life 'and naturally the children carried on this tradition'.[89] A. M. N. Chakiar provides a particularly interesting example. After a long and successful career, his memoirs recount how, at the age of eleven years, he and his siblings were thrown out of his high-caste Namputiri family and were forced to become lower-caste Chakiars after his father's alleged extra-marital affair and subsequent suicide. Significantly, it was only after retirement that he felt emotionally able to revisit this experience.[90] Though the modern legislators, councillors and civic activists sought to ignore caste identity, identifying poverty and lack of parents as a more modern way to intervene in children's lives, caste relationships continued to structure the life experience of almost all children. These everyday experiences were incomparably more painful for children from minorities.

The school was, for many, a microcosm of the wider social relations, particularly for girls. Gender differences informed all aspects of childhood, and girls' experiences of play, marriage and home life reflected gendered constructions of their appropriate roles, often reinforced by socialisation within the home.[91] Despite this, a number of male writers mention the attendance of girls in the local village school, and only four remember that girls were specifically excluded.[92] This suggests that female education was perhaps more widespread than realised and that the *pial* school was perhaps better attended by girls than the literature would suggest, although whether attendance was sufficiently long-lived to encourage basic numeracy and literacy is unclear. Only nine of the autobiographies were authored by women, reflecting their limited access to formal education and the perceived insignificance of their public lives. Those who did write were exceptional; women such as Dr Muthulakshmi Reddi or Akkamma Devi were both educated at the university level, became involved in politics and were notable pioneers of women's rights. In both cases, this reflected their personal ambitions and the insistence of their reforming fathers, despite maternal concerns about the impact on their marriage prospects.[93] For them, as for women such as the feminist social worker M. Subbamma, a memoir was a campaigning tool, an opportunity to use their own experience to enable or advocate social change, explicitly 'a torch to show the way and provide the light in the darkness of ignorance, inequality and lack of education'.[94] Testimonies of their own childhoods provided women with an authentic voice in the highly politicised debates surrounding formal education and child marriage, debates which continued during the 1970s and 1980s as the women began to record their stories.[95] This drew from a longer tradition of high-caste Bengali women who used their life stories to campaign for an increase in the age of consent.[96] However, while the female writers, such as Subbamma and Viramma, record more details of marriage, sex and children than their male contemporaries, there remains a conscious veiling of private life from the public gaze, fitting with the wider constraints of Tamil autobiographical writing.[97]

Dalit Memories of Childhood as a Genre of Resistance

Women were not the only group who explicitly used memories of childhood to highlight the inequities of the past and to advocate for social reform. A. N. Sattanathan, for example, wrote his autobiography as part of his wider work campaigning for the rights of other backward castes.[98] These memoirs offer an insight into the histories of groups under-represented or even 'silenced' in the traditional archive, even though mediated by time and later personal experience.[99] Dalit writers, in particular, use autobiographies as another genre of resistance, as the record of collective struggle to contest their erasure from history.[100] Ravikumar and D. R. Nagaraj argue that Dalits use autobiographies to 'stake a claim to a public voice and to self-respect', both destabilising current and historical social relations by portraying the underlying common humanity of the Dalit community as complicated equals rather than 'objects of compassion', and encouraging a positive construction of Dalit selfhood among the community itself.[101] To some extent the memories are used as a 'collective biography', in which the individual's experience of oppression is representative of the history of the wider Dalit community—Bama, writing her autobiographical novel *Karukku* in the 1990s, recounts the 'pain and trauma of being treated as an untouchable', which was both intensely personal and a 'common experience that binds individual Dalits together'.[102] But to see Dalit memories only as representative of the community is to de-historicise their lives still further, and it is crucial to remember that the memories recorded are both a private and a collective source, a portrayal of the changing and tangled relationship between the individual and the local community, as the writers portray themselves as relational within the multiple subjectivities of gender, nation, race and class.[103] As Sharmila Rege argues, the individual writings are used not to symbolise the community but to build a cumulative insight into Dalit experiences.[104] It is particularly important, however, not to perpetuate the assumption that Dalit and lower-caste perspectives are marginal or exceptional because they are less frequently recorded. As noted earlier with the age of consent controversies (Chapter 4), the marriage patterns of a small and unrepresentative minority were deemed to characterise the experience of all. Given the preponderance of Dalit and low-caste children in numerical terms, it is justifiable to assume that it was *their* experience that was more likely to be representative.

Lower-caste or Dalit children who were allowed to access schooling were subject to systematic humiliation when they attended, often from the teaching staff. They were frequently forced to sit outside on the verandah or to supplement their learning with chores such as collecting firewood, encouraging the children to truant.[105] Gunasekaran remembered deliberate humiliation when he received his scholarship forms:

> Even now it hurts to think about those times when we had to stand up in front of the others in the class, shrinking and cringing. They would reinforce caste identities by labelling us *Pallars*, *Parayars* and *Chakiliyars* in front of our friends who never knew what caste was.[106]

Despite his father being a teacher, discrimination was further underlined by the midday meals provided to poor pupils, although only in exchange for dung cakes or firewood, and by the lengths his father had to go to get the scholarship form signed by the higher-caste village headman.[107] Sattanathan, a Sudra who was later chair of the 1971 Other Backward Caste Commission, remembered the Brahmin teachers' attitudes of condescension and contempt, notwithstanding their own poor socio-economic status.[108] He recalled his orthodox Brahmin Tamil teacher, an 'obscene petty tyrant' who would 'taunt' lower-caste pupils when they made a mistake, impacting his academic performance.[109] Elayaperumal, a Dalit, remembered his Brahmin teacher asking another pupil to mark his work, fearing caste pollution if he touched his slate.[110] His comment, 'Though I felt hurt, I did not have the strength or courage to raise my voice,' illustrates the power of hegemonic norms and the difficulties in contesting discrimination when combined with other relationships of power as teacher–pupil or adult–child. In these memories, the school emerges as a site where children learnt the implications of identity in everyday interactions with other communities, and where modern forms of governmentality—forms, free meals, scholarships—reinforced boundaries and solidified caste groups into educational communities.

The school was situated within the wider caste relationships of the village and ultimately subject to them. R. Kumar argues that recording experiences of discrimination was part of a strategic attempt by Dalit activists to 'convert the Dalit sorrows into assets' by highlighting examples of daily discrimination as typical.[111] They were also framed as a pivotal moment of self-discovery, a 'new understanding' and almost as the moment when innocence about adult society and hierarchies was lost.[112] Gunasekaran was beaten on a number of occasions when visiting relatives, being unaware of much stricter policing of caste boundaries in rural areas.[113] L. Elayaperumal revealed that his father died from cholera after the Panchayat Board officers refused to spray their houses or provide inoculations in their neighbourhood but accepted his fate as the only possibility of economic security.[114] Kamal Pokkudan 'learnt something new' when he realised that members of the Gandhian Harijan Welfare Committee maintained purity-based separation and required him to pay for his tea by dropping his coins in water and recalled the threat of violence when he unthinkingly shared a glass of buttermilk.[115] His memories were characterised by a fear of unconsciously transgressing caste boundaries, by the memory of betrayal and by his decision to run away. Similarly, Rettamalai Srinivasan progressed well academically at his school in Coimbatore but constantly 'pondered over the pain of not even being able to play with other children' through fear of revealing his Dalit background.[116] While children appear to have been aware of their caste identity in the familiar environment of family and community, learning the practical implications of difference was a difficult experience that often contributed to their politicisation and social activism and the decision to record their life stories. However, while children often infringed social norms and identities, especially in their friendships, it appears to be the adolescent and adult voices that explicitly questioned these power structures.[117]

The painful process of learning categories and becoming aware of difference and the searing memory of discrimination remained with many of the writers forever.

Family Life and Relationships

The autobiographical memories of family life and relationships reflect many of the methodological challenges already encountered. A number were written specifically to pass knowledge through the family, individuals writing so that their children and grandchildren were aware of their life story, keeping alive their own memory but also highlighting how different their experience of childhood was.[118] Jagannath Mohanty, as a pedagogue, argued:

> My objective in writing this book was to show the children the life and society during my childhood days. I wanted them to know how children particularly in the village grew up then, what difficulties they faced, what joy and sorrow they experienced, who was there to act as their guide and philosopher on life's puzzling path.[119]

Despite the reticence to share personal details, this last section will tease out memories of the adult influences on young lives, with a particular focus on affective relationships and the transmission of knowledge within the family.

Among the policymakers and civic activists of the provincial and municipal government, there was widespread ambivalence towards the Indian family. As became clear in the earlier chapters, the Indian family was increasingly subjected to the state's coercive gaze and took on new symbolic meanings as the object of reform or bastion of tradition, usually according to the class and educational levels of the family in question. Of particular importance was the dominance of the father and this was reinforced in the recorded memories. The father was portrayed as an authority figure, often a source of spiritual comfort and guidance, usually revered and respected for their intellect and leadership and a contributor of non-demonstrative affection.[120] The educationist and freedom fighter T. S. Avinashilingam, for example, recalled that his father 'loved his family and children deeply, but did not hesitate to correct them when wrong'.[121] This may reflect reality or may represent what Judith Walsh argues was a textual formula in which filial obedience and traditional deference to paternal authority were important.[122] Equally, the criticism expressed by Ramarau and Sattanathan of their harshly disciplinarian fathers and lack of personal freedom was unusual but still demonstrated the pre-eminent status of the father as the decision-maker within the family.[123] The mother had a different role, usually described as a source of emotional support, hard work and self-sacrificing piety, often poorly educated but long remembered as the affective hub of the family.[124] Yet, while autobiographical memory can hint at broad themes, the parallel autobiographies of the brothers R. K. Narayan and R. K. Laxman reveal very different experiences of affective relationships within the family and provide a necessary reminder of how uniquely personal each life story is.

The nuclear, patriarchal family assumed new symbolic and practical importance during the 1920s and 1930s in state and civil society discourse. By contrast, in the memories of children, it was often the role and authority of the extended family that was of particular significance. Grandparents were recalled as repositories of secular and religious wisdom on account of their age, experience and piety.[125] A number of grandmothers had the final decision over school attendance and were responsible for introducing the child to the alphabet and early numeracy, as well as religious storytelling.[126] For many men, their grandmothers were remembered as a particular source of emotional comfort and love during childhood, often as allies in defiance of male authority.[127] While affective relationships are less often remembered by women, grandmothers and widowed great-aunts were also important in socialising younger women into appropriately gendered forms of behaviour, including pre-marital chastity or sex education.[128] Viramma, for instance, remembered her first menstruation when she was confined indoors for eleven days:

> ... in the evenings, a group of old and young women, including Arayi's and Nagamma's grandmothers, would come and sit near the *tinnai* [or verandah] and sing funny, rude songs. By their singing, they were teaching me what was in store and how my husband would 'use' my body.

Interestingly, she comments that while she received explicit education about sex, themes such as pregnancy and childbirth were never mentioned.[129]

Uncles, and to a lesser extent aunts, were another significant group within the extended family who exercised significant control over children's lives, although never at the expense of paternal authority. The attention took a variety of forms: financial, emotional and practical and often included active participation in the decision-making about a child's future.[130] Both Laxman and Siddalingaiah were enrolled in school by their uncles, apparently without the prior consent of their parents.[131] It was Raghuramaiah's 'uncles who were proud that we were the first educated girls in the family' and her mother's younger sister who was her primary caregiver in her early years.[132] Often when children moved for education from village to town, it was an uncle or member of the extended family like an older sister who provided accommodation and practical support.[133] Sreenivasan, a member of a high-caste Nair family, remembered family decisions made by his fifteen uncles under the control of his grandfather, although he suspected that the conclusions reached had often been decided beforehand by his aunts, while Yati remembers that his mother and six aunts cared for all fifteen cousins together.[134] Gunasekaran, a Dalit folk artist, remembered the disputes between his parents because of the allowance sent by his father to support his nephew through medical school, even to the detriment of their family budget.[135] Similarly, many of his childhood memories come from his time in the countryside, staying with his *periyamma* (mother's elder sister) and *cinnamma* (mother's younger sister).[136] Nijalingappa, the chief minister of Karnataka, also recalled the twin influences of his mother's aunt and his teacher's older sister in his character formation.[137] These practical and affective relationships were not formally recognised in either state policy or practice, reflecting late colonial anxieties about the non-traditional family and a preference for the modern formulation of the nuclear family.[138] Perhaps though these civic activists and politicians claimed this avuncular authority for themselves. Previous chapters have demonstrated the extent to which Indian state actors and civil activists constructed for themselves a form of avuncular authority that worked in parallel to the authority of parents with the children's best interests at heart and encouraged the use of 'uncle' and 'auntie' as non-familial terms of respect.[139] The autobiographies reveal how significant avuncular authority was within the family, and how easily others could claim that mantle without contesting the position of the father.

These avuncular relationships were not only biological but could also encompass the local schoolteacher. A number of children from artistic castes were also raised in the *guru–sishya* tradition, under the tutelage of a parent or *guru* who assumed pseudo-parental authority.[140] Others remember similar avuncular figures within the local community who greatly influenced their lives. The writer Jagannath Mohanty, for example, remembered Sadhubhai, a local teacher and political activist who was regarded as the village mediator but also kept the children supplied with biscuits, dates and stories.[141] Sundaram recalled his close relationship with the Brahmin pandit, who became 'like an elder brother', investing time in walking and talking politics.[142] These individuals were not always well educated; the former president Kalam described in detail the emotional support and inspiration provided by his mentor Ahmed Jallaluddin and the local newspaper vendor Samsuddin, but were remembered as significant influences on the young child's emotional and intellectual life.[143]

The family, trade guild and community also played a significant role in training children in the practical skills of a trade and socialising them into the identities, traditions and hierarchies of an artisanal community.[144] This was particularly significant for women, who had much more limited access to formal schooling. Often members of the extended family provided practical support and care for children but were especially important as storytellers, socialising children into family values and traditions, whether religious, moral or secular.[145] Many authors remember 'the old Tamil songs and stories' and their impact on the imagination and 'the aesthetic life' of the child.[146] Sreenivasan noted the impact of observing a routine of communal prayer:

> Every Hindu child absorbs the myths, the traditions, the superstition and the morality along with his or her mother's milk. Participation in ritual and ceremonials is so much a part of one's life from very early childhood that they enter the subconscious.[147]

While as adults many of the authors became more critical of their earlier religious practices as they received a secular education, they nonetheless recognised the social value of religious storytelling and rituals as a collective experience that affirmed the child's place in the community, both strengthening a sense of belonging and re-emphasising the authority of the older generation.[148] Yati recounted his grandmother reading the Bhagavad Gita in the evening:

> Children gave up their pranks and grownups stopped gossiping. All sat and listened to the sonorous recitation of grandmother who was gifted with a musical voice. I did not understand what she was reading, but I liked the calm atmosphere and the picturesque setting of the evening prayer.[149]

Forms of oral knowledge transmission were often associated with people who were perceived to be socially inferior, such as older widows, servants or lower castes, and even grandparents were perceived to be outdated in a modernising world.[150] Increasingly, the schoolchild became both a source of family pride and economic potential and a threat to the generational hierarchies of knowledge within the family, as the religious and experiential wisdom of the elders gave way to the modern scientific knowledge of youth. The association with 'those days' of grandparents, religiosity, emotion and a pedagogy based on repetition was also positioned in stark contrast to 'these days' of a modern education system and the rational, progressive world of the modern child. Often it was the authors themselves who played an ambivalent role as the primary drivers of change, the pioneers in accessing education and new opportunities, committed as adults to furthering this modernising agenda of education for all, but now aware, looking back, that life had changed irreparably and of the social losses that had occurred in the process.

It is important not to over-valorise the family and to recognise the extent to which it reflects the nostalgic memory of authors who were now themselves grandparents. For many children, especially those living in poverty, the evidence from the previous chapters suggests that the home was a space of disorder and unpredictable tensions. A number of writers detail instances of domestic violence, particularly the Dalit autobiographers, reflecting the strains that poverty caused in relationships: Mogalli Ganesh recalled that his father was so cruel that all three of his wives committed suicide, while N. K. Hanumanthaiah remembered his father's alcoholism and physical abuse of his mother.[151] However, only a few chose to record familial tension or to see themselves as the victim.[152] This is more a reflection of the nature of autobiographies as source material and the desire to portray the outward respectability of the family than an unproblematic representation of the past.[153] Viramma described a life that to the outsider was defined by labour, hunger and poverty, but for her it was characterised by friendship, 'happiness' and 'days of games and laughter'.[154] In the context of contemporary street children, Balagopalan's research has revealed the fluidity of boundaries between 'home' or the 'streets'; the continuing ties with the natal home, particularly mothers, and the complex intertwining of violence and tenderness in many impoverished households.[155] The desire to categorise children in legislative terms as either safe or at risk; either in danger or secure; either dangerous or conformist and the increasing distinction between the modern and the traditional family appear to reflect the imperatives and priorities of modern governmentality rather than the lived experiences of most children.

Conclusion

A detailed analysis of autobiographical memories foregrounds children as historical actors and as contributors to historical processes, such as the expansion of modern education, and highlights the differing ways in which children negotiated, supported and resisted pre-existing social structures and identities. The legislation of the earlier chapters and the new principles and norms of international discourses surrounding the child promised a universal standard of modern childhood, in which the child was unmarked by difference and equal before the law. Yet the personal memories of childhood suggest that the child was rarely viewed as an individual, and the experience of inequality and social hierarchy continued to impact all aspects of life. In particular, modern schooling was advocated for its transformational possibilities, but in practice the attitudes of teachers, the content of the curriculum and interrelationships between peers often meant that it reinforced, rather than contested, existing structures of domination. The autobiographies reveal how caste, religion and gender operated as traditional forms of social organisation and were expanded through the operation of modern power and within modern institutions to perpetuate the power of upper-caste men. They also show how that power was managed and negotiated by children in their everyday life-worlds. The assumption of education's transformative potential was, in itself, an indicator of privilege, a failure to recognise the discursive and structural limitations faced by the disadvantaged, which meant that policymakers were not forced to confront their own social advantages.

Personal memories also add a new depth to our understanding of the family. They contribute another, albeit fragmentary, perspective on the sources already used, showing that the policymakers, bureaucrats and civil society activists whose words form the basis of much of this book often oversimplified the authority and knowledge transmission structures at the family level. Importantly, they largely ignored the role of grandparents in grounding the children within the extended family and contributing to emotional security and a sense of belonging. At the same time, the state drew on avuncular metaphors that were already familiar to the children and to the village community, both in the form of school teachers, biological uncles and aunts and older adults acting in a mentoring capacity, showing the wide range of individuals involved in the child's education and socialisation. These figures rarely contested the authority of the father, but worked with him to exercise protective control over children's lives. My suggestion is that this was an assumed norm of village and family life, and perhaps unwittingly influenced the policymakers themselves as they came to imagine their own role in the formation of social policy.

The memoirs detail the reality, and often bitterness, of social difference and emphasise in multiple small but cumulative ways how social distinctions of caste, gender and religion were a central and defining feature of childhood. This impacted how and why the authors chose to share their life stories and helps to explain why the memories of a small minority remain dominant. Childhood memories had contemporary political resonance at the time of writing, either to push a modernising agenda, to reinforce the contemporary idea of the child as a future citizen intimately connected to the success of the new nation or to remember childhood experiences of discrimination as a genre of resistance, part of a longer life story that contested structures of oppression. Operating within a convention of writing to show social change while veiling the private, the autobiographies hinted at how ideas about childhood were changing in post-colonial India and suggested the beginnings of change at a grassroots level in the 1920s and 1930s. This highlighted the continued limitations of state power and alluded to the firm commitment of all the writers to modern concepts of childhood as central to the functioning of the modern state.

Conclusion

Children, Childhood and the Growth of the Avuncular State in South India

The post-independence Indian Constitution of 1950 is often assumed to have fundamentally altered the relationship between the child and the state. This book demonstrates that many of the principles contained within it, for example, access to elementary education for all children as a right guaranteed by the state (Article 45), were part of a much longer trajectory of social legislation. Instead, the 1920s and 1930s were a time of radical change in regard to childhood in India. This reflected discursive and political changes at a national and global level but was linked most clearly to the devolution of power to Indians at a local and provincial level. What is more, these moderate Indian elites were prepared to use the limited powers granted to them under the 1919 and then 1935 Government of India Acts to significantly rethink and change the relationship between the child, the family and the state.

Imagining Childhood, Improving Children

The 1920s and 1930s was the era when the idea of childhood as a universal social category distinct from adulthood, which deserved state protection and investment, became widely accepted by the south Indian political elite. This particularly reflected the elite interest in modern childhood as a universal global formation, accepting a particular view of modern childhood as normative. This commitment to a universal norm precluded any discussion that the meaning of the term 'modern' could be reinterpreted or reformulated or have different meanings in different times and spaces. This failure to interrogate the universality of a particular mode of childhood at an intellectual level perpetuated the dominance of one idea as universal and continues to inform attitudes towards childhood within India even today.

Within this broad framing certain aspects of modern childhood were particularly important and marked children as distinct from, rather than inferior to, adults. The first was the assumption that the child was uniquely malleable, that the proper place for the child was in school and that the primary identity of the child was as a learner. The school became the primary space for the interaction between the child and the state, the place where citizenship was learned and performed. The emphasis on free and compulsory education, the interest in new forms of pedagogy, the provision of food and medical inspection of children in the school and the reformation of children through disciplined regimes of vocational education and time-keeping all reaffirmed the dominance of particular forms of knowledge and knowledge transmission. This de-legitimised other forms of pedagogy, excluding schools outside the purview of the state, and introduced new power structures into the lives of children, which precluded the family and their world view. This was reinforced by widely held beliefs that located sexual maturity not only in the physical body of the child but in their intellectual maturity and moral capacity to understand the consequences of their actions. These strands contributed to a universalising discourse around the normal development of the child's mind, a pattern threatened when the child engaged in acts—such as sexual intercourse, crime or economic labour—not usually associated with these normative forms of childhood behaviour. At the same time, it meant that the childhoods of the vast majority of children, who remained in the labour force or at home, were characterised as a failure.

Children were also defined by their physical vulnerability. This informed the debates on safe travel to school, as well as the intimate details of nutrition in the elementary schools and certified schools. Children's bodies were regulated into correct forms of being and doing, particularly within the classroom, and the body became central to the learning process as children learned to physically dominate their environment and learn through active play. The interest in establishing paediatrics as a distinctive medical discipline, the eugenic attention paid to infant mortality and neonatal health of infants born to young mothers, and the focus on the physical measurements of the child as an indication of malnutrition were significant indicators of a new emphasis on the healthy body of the child as important to the production of a healthy nation. In all three cases, the child's body could be rendered legible through statistics. The protection of the vulnerable child's body was a clear modern trope, which influenced policies as divergent as the rescue of *devadasi* girls from a life of prostitution to a focus on pedagogical theories in the school and reformatory, which emphasised reward and the regulation of young bodies into new routines of love and self-control rather than corporal punishment. Yet even as the boundary between childhood and adulthood became conceptually more important, its numerical definition and legal status in terms of justice, education and sexual relations remained contested and changing, and differed according to the community and sex of the child.

The Indian child was imagined in debates as both valuable and vulnerable, evidencing a number of different, not always compatible, perspectives. This bound each child into a direct relationship with the state. There was frequent and explicit acknowledgement of the child as a future citizen, a valuable investment whose future loyalty and behaviour could be ensured through adequate disciplining. To become competent adults, children required basic literacy and numeracy to fulfil the administrative functions of civic life, as well as a healthy body, either economically productive or successfully reproductive, but also, particularly after 1935, a sense of loyalty and identity as belonging to the Indian nation state. Children thus merited government and municipal attention on the basis of their future potential as citizens. There was also increasing recognition of the child as having rights as an individual, with a legitimate call on the state's resources, enhanced because they had a right to protection as vulnerable. Although more often used as a rhetorical tool than as a motivator for government policy, the genealogy of the modern idea of the 'best interests of the child' can be traced in the South Asian context to the participation of Indians in government, not only among intellectuals and experts but at the level of local civil society.

The idea of the child as a rights-bearing individual has been linked to the capacity of children to be agents of historical change, to actively impact their surroundings. This recognition of children's opinions and actions only rarely impacted the adult decision-makers, for example, in the discussion over acceptable food choices and interesting textbooks.

Occasionally an individual child appears in the historical records, such as Gullipalli Yerrayya, who is recorded in the colonial archives because he queried the terms of his imprisonment at the Bellary Junior Certified School.[1] Similarly adults recalling their childhoods in their autobiographies remember distinctive moments of decision, or instances when children fulfilled, resisted or distorted the plans of adults in authority through truancy, mimicry or outstanding exam grades. There is growing, albeit limited, recognition that children are historical actors, have distinctive voices who can contribute to historical processes, who act and are not merely acted upon. This is historically significant because it reveals another dimension to our understanding of the way power was constructed and functioned in India and suggests that state, particularly colonial, power was perhaps more limited than many of its proponents believed. Only by looking at the fragmentary evidence of children themselves can historians really begin to understand the impact of adult actions and appreciate the limitations of discursive constructions of modern childhood in the lives of real children. Adult memories of childhood, for example, suggest that the home and family life, particularly the role of the extended family, was much more complicated and a much richer source of practical, emotional and religious education than the government sources would suggest. Additionally, they suggest that children moved flexibly between languages and belief and loyalty structures, which they participated in but did not attempt to intellectually reconcile, again complicating our perceptions of the power of new modern forms of governance and knowledge.[2] Dalit and female writers, in particular, often use autobiographies as a way of emphasising that their experiences of childhood were equally valid. At the same time, however, it should never be assumed that children acted only as rational, autonomous agents. More often, the autobiographies show the emotional impact of events and the child acting, playing and being part of a wider community, variously including peers, animals and family members. And indeed for some groups the claim to represent the experience of a marginalised community is intentionally more significant than the claim to represent an individual life.

All these ideas about childhood and about the normal child were predicated on a notion of the child with universally shared characteristics. However, when policies aimed at this child were implemented, it becomes clear that 'the child' imagined by officials, politicians and civil society activists was an upper caste, wealthy, able-bodied, Tamil-speaking, unmarried Hindu boy. This was reinforced in the pedagogical methods, the content of the curriculum and the decision to allow parents to choose an educational institution and pay school fees. It is seen most clearly in the extensive debates surrounding child marriage, respondents providing two volumes of evidence to the Joshi Committee on the details of a marriage form which, a number admitted, was only relevant to a very small percentage of the population but was held to be normative in the local, national and global imagination. To fail to fit this definition of a child was to be 'not quite' a child, and meant that many of the policies failed to reflect the circumstances and limitations of daily life. This was not merely reflective of the 'unevenness' of educational or social welfare provision.[3] Rather, children outside this implicit normative definition were categorised by communities, which reflected social identities such as gender, caste, language and religion. Belonging to one of these marginalised educational communities frequently became a more significant indicator of children's experience, opportunities and boundaries than age or immaturity. Often the school, the key site of modern childhoods, became the place where children learned that difference.

The assumption of a normative Indian childhood as modern, distinct from the ideal of Western childhood but still equal, shows the confidence with which the Indian elite was able to interact with these universalising ideas—a good example of the interactive universalism that Sarkar advocates.[4] But this did not make policies towards children any more inclusive but rather reinforced the 'non-modernity' and continuing inferiority of the rest of the population. Most schemes initiated by state actors were targeted toward these disadvantaged communities, and many were premised on a new identity, that of the 'poor child', which conveniently conflated socio-economic disadvantage, the likelihood of conflict with the law and rhetorical assumptions of sympathy.[5] This led to a curious juxtaposition, whereby the child was imagined as a high caste male while the targeted poor child was provided opportunities that were demonstrably and explicitly inferior, preventing the poor child from ever obtaining this normative standard. When compulsory education was introduced in Madras City, the schools directly managed by the Madras Corporation explicitly aimed to provide for the poorest sections of the population by choosing food types based on the normal diet of the poor rather than increasing the nutritional level. The education provided aimed to deliver basic literacy, numeracy and citizenship skills that would enable the production of more disciplined citizens, but there was no corresponding commitment to an education of sufficient standard to enable social progression, and any suggestion of this was resisted. Similarly, in juvenile justice discourses, the difference between delinquent and destitute children was discursively important, although it had little practical effect on whether individual children entered the probation system or were sent to certified schools. The focus on poverty, often rather than structural inequalities based around gender or caste, was used to highlight the failures of the adults from these communities but without the possibility of change. As the autobiographies of A. P. J. Abdul Kalam, M. Subbamma, A. N. Sattanathan, K. A. Guneskaran and others so poignantly suggest, the institutions of the state, particularly the school, became the place where marginal identities were learned, reinforced and internalised by many children. Intervention was intended to maintain, not destabilise, the social order.

The State and the Child

The emergence and impact of particular understandings of the child, the citizen and the family were linked to the changing form and nature of the state itself. This book argues that dyarchy should be considered on its own terms as a form of state power, not just teleologically through the assumption of eventual political independence. Dyarchy was undoubtedly a limited, and generally unpopular, political compromise and Indians remained constrained by the overarching power of both Delhi and London. However seeing dyarchy only as transitional and as a failure of nationalist aspirations ignores that the transferred departments, although politically insignificant, were the government departments that were most interested in children. The colonial binaries of the 'public' and the 'private' had much less relevance when Indians were in power; rather, the era was characterised by fundamental changes in the relationship between Indian society and state power.[6] Crucially, in the departments that dealt with children and in the municipal councils, the state was Indian in personnel, ideas, character, motivation and even budgetary responsibility. This was enhanced by the 1935 reforms. The new forms of government and schemes to divide communities and target interventions were driven by the governmental needs and desires of changing Indian governments, intimately linked to the communal electoral system established in 1919 and to pragmatic decisions of governance. While this does not dispute the political rejection of British imperialism by almost all the Indians cited in this book, it questions its relevance in this context. This also raises questions about the nature of political devolution that requires work on other presidencies and other target communities. While the nationalist elite was beginning to articulate new visions of the post-colonial state, the *practice* of self-government at the level of province and municipality changed how Indians perceived the role and function of the state in society, encouraging a commitment to a socially interventionist state, which would continue to inform the welfare and planning policies of a newly independent India.

This move to moderate Indian control meant that most state intervention in children's lives operated within 'the social': a consensual, depoliticised sphere distinct from the realm of political contest. This consensual sphere was located at the intersection between the state, the family, the administration, expert professionals and an increasingly active and vocal voluntary sector, often associated with the women's movement.[7] Although funding decisions were scrutinised along party lines and there was some limited political conflict about details, most decisions—for example, compulsory education—received broad support across the legislatures and in the realm of experts and civil society. While issues like the age of marriage remained fiercely debated and highly politicised, even the respondents to the Joshi Committee—and certainly those working to stop the trafficking of children—operated within the same discursive boundaries. Within the transferred subjects such as welfare, education and juvenile justice, there was surprisingly little reference to the British Raj or racial theory, and very little disagreement between Indians. Too often historians have studied social reform in the late colonial period to delineate another aspect of the political sphere, which was characterised by bitter confrontation, violence, a rejection of imperial hypocrisy and a superior claim to modern, liberal citizenship through national self-determination. Every sphere in life is assumed to be influenced by both colonial power and opposition to it, and all actions, reformist or otherwise, are seen in terms of hostility to colonial governmentality and a colonial rule of difference based primarily on racial superiority. Focusing on the social—whether social reform, child protection or education—as merely political obscures the growth of consensual decision-making and misunderstands the importance of changing governmental structures, particularly in the provinces. It was equally significant, however, that while there were many and frequent commitments to act on behalf of children, there was often no interest in implementing them and even less commitment to adequately funding these schemes. Saving children might have been important to the modern self-identity of the elite policymakers, but it was rarely matched with the political will to make difficult decisions over budgets, expenditure and increasing taxation.

Children were constructed as objects of social action at the mercy of a number of organisations with overlapping goals and visions.[8] Although a wealthy, well-educated and elite group, this was not merely the expansion of the middle classes' control of the poor. Instead, there is evidence of specific alliances and networks of Indian 'child savers' who had different agendas, whether of feminism, religious philanthropy, progressive pedagogy or nationalism. They shared a common understanding that liberal intervention was both legitimate and necessary. Practical and financial support was provided from organisations such as the MCAS, the Theosophists, the WIA, honorary magistrates, pedagogues, political parties (both the Justice Party and the Congress), the trade union movement, city councillors and officials. The entangled and interconnected organisational and personal networks of the child savers facilitated the emergence of consensual decision-making and the growth and acceptance of a universal ideal. It is important to notice how many of these activists were women. Although women were only occasionally elected politicians, they used their advocacy of children's issues to carve out a space for themselves in the public sphere that they could claim was distinctly gendered. This built on traditionally gendered ideas about women as caregivers and uniquely suited to understand children, a role particularly associated with the honorary magistrates and the domestic structures of the juvenile court. This was enhanced by the number, and prominence, of women in the medical and teaching professions who were willing to contribute to public discourse on the basis of their expertise. And while policy was made and driven forward in the chambers of the Legislative Council and the Municipal Corporation and in discussion with officials, Indian experts became increasingly important. These professionals claimed a right to be heard and to contribute to policy on the basis of their specialist scientific knowledge and modern education. By the interwar years, they included pedagogues, psychologists, paediatricians, magistrates, criminologists, penal reformers, anti-trafficking experts and statisticians, as well as doctors, teachers and medical inspectors. This formed an important aspect of the governmental claim to modernity and to govern on the basis of modern scientific evidence.

The emergence of this new construction of the modern state and its relationship with the child was also influenced by changing global discourses. Indian experts and policymakers drew on international agreements to prioritise the 'best interests of the child'. They participated in new international organisations, based on global anti-trafficking measures or progressive pedagogy and criminology, which facilitated comparisons between nation states and claimed universal features for children regardless of geographical space. Similarly, they were influenced by legislation introduced in Britain, such as the Children Act, 1908, and used this to form the basis for new legislation in the Madras context, such as the Children's Act. Again, this reflected the personal networks of social reformers and experts who, as global participants, transferred knowledge and ideas between diverse sites across the world, including Geneva, Sydney and Cape Town, as well as Delhi, Calcutta and London. The assertion of universality for the Indian child was used to bolster the Indian middle classes' claim to a full share, as equals, in the perceived modernity of the West and to cement their position as equal scientific experts on the global stage. In view of the current anxieties surrounding global child rights legislation (and the UNCRC in particular), the historical participation of Indians in these networks, and in the formulation of universal ideas about the child, demonstrates that child rights legislation was not a colonial imposition. It was instead a global process in which Indians participated from the outset, claiming to be equals, and which had an impact in south India as early as the 1920s, as Indians used these ideas to inform legislative and practical interventions in children's lives, using the power granted to them under the constitutional reforms.

The State and the Family

The child as distinct from the family, rather than a resource of the family, is central to modern views of childhood and the state. New legislation enabled intervention into the domestic sphere in unprecedented ways, potentially justifying the removal of children 'in danger' from their parents. The underlying principle of compulsory schooling was intended to force parents to send their children to school, preventing them from contributing to the family income and introducing the teacher as an alternative authority figure in their lives. The introduction of welfare measures such as midday meals was philanthropic but included a claim to responsibility for the child in areas that had previously been the preserve of the family. Even in the previously private sphere of marriage, parents lost the right to marry their girl-children after puberty, being constrained by the legal age limits of the Child Marriage Restraint Act. However, while changes to sexual maturity and *devadasi* laws proved contentious because they interfered with spheres of influence previously regarded as under religious authority, there is little evidence that anyone queried the new claims to authority and responsibility made by the dyarchical Indian state. There was little attempt to limit the interventionist power of state actors, perhaps because as part of 'the social' and as 'Indian' they were non-threatening, perhaps because of a wider commitment to these ideas among the governing classes.

During the nineteenth century, colonial administrators and Christian missionaries sought to 'orphan' children, removing them from families because of the perceived damaging impact of native nurture. As scientific discourses of racial hierarchy became more politically important, the nature of the native as inherently flawed and incapable of reform became more discursively prominent, and the Indian home was seen as a site of danger and threat. While nationalists and social reformers tried to reclaim the middle-class Indian home, as private and outside the gaze of the state, there remained deep unease about domestic influences, such as older females and religious devotion, particularly within the poor home. These were seen as undermining the growth of modern rational education. There was a clear distinction between politicians, teachers and civil society actors—who shared anxieties about the working class or the poor home as backward—and the professional experts. Those reformers who claimed authority based on rational scientific expertise—pedagogues, nutritional experts or doctors like Dr Muthulakshmi Reddi—were decisively more dismissive of the home and the family as sites of scientific unreason and threat to children's health, educational attainment and morals, than those who were politically accountable, such as city councillors, or those who worked with children on a daily basis. In practice, this meant that the Public Health Department, backed by extensive quantitative analysis, was noticeably more prepared to enforce its opinion than the Education or Home Departments.

The assertion of a new relationship between the state and the child, and the characterisation of the Indian home and family in terms of 'lack', was more important in rhetoric than in practical reality. Despite the claims of the schemes, only 5,000 children received food at schools, while parental choice was quickly re-established when the scheme to assure equality of educational access through abolishing school fees in Madras City was abandoned in 1932. Attendance committees established to enforce compulsory education lacked adequate resources and, apparently, even the desire to seriously challenge parents who opposed sending their children to school. In moments of confrontation, the authority of the parents remained intact. Care was taken to respect Muslim educational views, and the age for compulsory education varied according to the community. This was evidenced most clearly in the reaffirmation of parental choice in arranging marriages, despite the changing legal requirements of age. Additionally, the existence of parents was the key determinant of whether a child who appeared before the juvenile courts was taken into care in the certified schools, regardless of criminal responsibility or socio-economic distress. Corporal punishment or fines continued to be the preferred means of control. The authority of parents was rarely questioned in practice.

My argument here is that we need to formulate a new understanding of the state and how it functioned, and my suggestion is that we need to see this state as having aspired to be 'avuncular': the new welfare state claimed authority to act in the best interests of the child and pragmatically recognised the limits of using that authority. This contrasts with the more aggressive paternalism of the colonial state. Many of the autobiographies demonstrated the role of uncles and aunts in the lives of children: they provided another source of authority; they were involved in financial and educational decisions regarding the child; and they accepted responsibility for the growth of the child but worked with, rather than challenged, the authority of the father. Very often these uncles were also remembered as educated, modern and professional and were particularly associated with the child's move from rural to urban areas for secondary education. The Tamil language includes a number of terms for aunts and uncles differentiated by their sex and relationship to parents. The terms themselves (*periyappa, chitappa, periamma, chithi* as big-father, small-father, big-mother, small-mother, respectively) reflect both their significance in Tamil culture and the near-parental responsibility of the role.

Nehru, as the prime minister of independent India, explicitly conceptualised his own relationship with the nation's children as that of *chacha*, or uncle. This embodied his authority, but also the familiar and the familial, in conscious opposition to the detachment of the colonial state.[9] The identification gave legitimacy to intervention, yet honoured the cultural allegiances of both nuclear and extended families, without challenging the position of the family patriarch. Balakrishnan argues that a relationship-based approach to state intervention similar to that of *chacha* is necessary for the progress of children's rights after 2000. This envisages the state as 'distant but familiar' and blurs the line between the private and the public.[10] It also complicates the assumption that state intervention should be seen as state paternalism or the state acting as a 'surrogate parent'.[11] My argument is that while 'avuncular' was not used explicitly as a term, the evidence from educational, juvenile justice and medical discourses is that social reformers during the 1920s and 1930s— who were, of course, Nehru's contemporaries—can be seen in similar terms. The sentiment was echoed in the Madras Corporation in 1931 when, to laughter across the chamber, a Justice Party councillor asked: 'Have they not any Godfathers in this Council?'[12] State and civil society actors—warders, teachers, legislators, local councillors, pedagogues, probation officers and health inspectors—claimed authority to intervene in the lives of individual children through welfare legislation. Yet they implicitly saw themselves in kinship terms as uncles and aunties, characterising themselves as part of the extended national family rather than as an interventionist Indian state. This appears to have been the case for experts, for those in paid employment by the state and for those acting in a voluntary or philanthropic capacity. This allowed them to respect the ultimate authority of the parents while claiming a particular role as familial in contrast to the more formal rule of the British Raj, which prioritised detached justice rather than relationships and negotiation. The assumption of limited political power by moderate Indians in the 1920s and 1930s thus set patterns of state behaviour and governance that were both distinctively modern and distinctively Indian and which continued to inform the state's relationship with children well past political independence.

Notes

Introduction

1. http://www.un-documents.net/gdrc1924.htm (accessed 10 September 2022).
2. Vivianna Zelizer, *Pricing the Priceless Child: The Changing Social Value of Children* (Princeton: Princeton University Press, 1994), 209.
3. Olga Nieuwenhuys, 'Editorial: Is There an Indian Childhood?', *Childhood* 16, no. 2 (2009): 147–53.
4. Michael Freeman, 'Children's Rights as Human Rights: Reading the UNCRC', in *Palgrave Handbook of Childhood Studies*, ed. Jens Qvortrup, William A. Corsarao and Michael-Sebastian Honig (Basingstoke: Palgrave Macmillan, 2009); Olga Nieuwenhuys, 'From Child Labour to Working Children's Movements', in *Palgrave Handbook of Childhood Studies*, ed. Qvortrup, Corsarao and Honig; Krishna Kumar, 'Childhood in a Globalising World', *Economic and Political Weekly* 41, no. 38 (23 September 2006).
5. Sarada Balagopalan, *Inhabiting Childhood: Children, Labour and Schooling in Postcolonial India* (London: Palgrave Macmillan, 2014).
6. Sarada Balagopalan, 'Introduction: Children's Lives and the Indian Context', *Childhood* 18, no. 3 (2011); Ali Khan, *Representing Children: Power, Policy and the Discourse on Child Labour in the Football Manufacturing Industry of Pakistan* (Oxford: Oxford University Press, 2007); Olga Nieuwenhuys, 'Global Childhood and the Politics of Contempt', *Alternatives* 23, no. 3 (1998).

7. Films: Garth Davis, *Lion* (2016); Danny Boyle, *Lion* (2016); Danny Boyle, *Slumdog Millionaire* (2008); and Nila Madhab Panda, *I Am Kalam* (2011). For an analysis of this, see Anto Thomas Chakramakkil, 'The Polemics of Real and Imagined Childhood(s) in India', *International Research in Children's Literature* 11, no. 1 (2017).
8. Phillipe Aries, *Centuries of Childhood* (London: Jonathan Cape, 1962); Chris Jenks, *Childhood* (London; New York: Routledge, 1996), 23.
9. See, for example, Balagopalan, *Inhabiting Childhood*; Nieuwenhuys, 'Global Childhood'; Deepak Kumar Behera, ed., *Childhoods in South Asia* (New Delhi: Pearson Longman, 2007), 151.
10. Balagopalan, *Inhabiting Childhood*; Urvashi Misri, 'Child and Childhood: A Conceptual Construction', in *The Word and the World: Fantasy, Symbol and Record*, ed. Veena Das (New Delhi: Sage, 1986); Patricia Uberoi, *Freedom and Destiny: Gender, Family and Popular Culture in India* (New Delhi: Oxford University Press, 2006); Vijayalakshmi Balakrishnan, *Growing Up and Away: Narratives of Indian Childs, Memory, History and Identity* (Delhi: Oxford University Press, 2011).
11. Sudhir Kakar, *The Inner World: A Psycho-analytic Study of Childhood and Society in India* (Delhi: Oxford University Press, 1981).
12. Carol A. Breckenridge and Peter Van Der Veer, *Orientalism and the Postcolonial Predicament: Perspectives on South Asia* (Philadelphia: University of Pennsylvania Press, 1993), 25.
13. Satadru Sen, 'Notes on Juvenilia', in *Traces of Empire: India, America and Post-Colonial Cultures* (New Delhi: Primus Books, 2014); Qvortrup, 'Childhood as a Structural Form', in *Palgrave Handbook of Childhood Studies*, ed. Qvortrup, Corsarao and Honig.
14. Hia Sen, *'Time-Out' in the Land of Apu: Childhoods, Bildungsmoratorium and the Middle Classes of Urban West Bengal* (Wiesbaden: Springer, 2014).
15. Ishita Pande, 'Coming of Age: Law, Sex and Childhood in Late Colonial India', *Gender and History* 24, no. 1 (April 2012): 205–30. Contrast this with the histories of education, such as Nita Kumar, *Lessons from Schools: The History of Education in Banaras* (New Delhi: Sage Publications, 2000); or Zazie Bowen and Jessica Hinchy, 'Introduction: Children and Knowledge in India', *South Asian History and Culture* 6, no. 3 (2015): 317–29.
16. Nicholas Stargardt, 'German Childhoods: The Making of a Historiography', *German History* 16, no. 1 (1998): 12; Behera, *Childhoods in South Asia*.
17. Jane Humphries, 'Childhood and Child Labour in the British Industrial Revolution', *Economic History Review* 66, no. 2 (2013): 395–418; Karen

Vallgårda, *Imperial Childhoods and Christian Mission: Education and Emotions in South India and Denmark* (Basingstoke: Palgrave Macmillan, 2015), 32; Peter Stearns, *Childhood in World History*, 2nd ed. (Abingdon: Routledge, 2011); Kumar, *Lessons from Schools*, 105, 186; Supriya Goswami, *Colonial India in Children's Literature* (New Delhi; London: Routledge, 2012); Bowen and Hinchy, 'Introduction', 319.

18. Kim Wagner and Ricardo Roque, *Engaging Colonial Knowledge: Reading European Archives in World History* (Basingstoke: Palgrave Macmillan, 2012), particularly the introduction.
19. Antoinette Burton, 'Thinking beyond the Boundaries: Empire, Feminism and the Domains of History', *Social History* 26, no. 1 (2001): 67. In terms of children's history, see David Oswell, *The Agency of Children: From Family to Global Human Rights* (Cambridge: Cambridge University Press, 2013).
20. Dipesh Chakrabarty, *Habitations of Modernity: Essays in the Wake of Subaltern Studies* (Delhi: Permanent Black, 2002), 105.
21. For further reading, see Ishita Pande, 'Power, Knowledge, and the Epistemic Contract on Age: The Case of Colonial India', *American Historical Review* 125, no. 2. (2020): 407–17; Veena Das, 'Voices of Children', *Daedalus* 118, no. 4 (Fall 1989): 285; Misri, 'Child and Childhood', 131; Balagopalan, *Inhabiting Childhood*, 56, 83; Ruby Lal, *Coming of Age in Nineteenth-Century India: The Girl-Child and the Art of Playfulness* (Cambridge: Cambridge University Press, 2013); Veena Das, *Life and Words: Violence and the Descent into the Ordinary* (Berkeley: University of California Press, 2007), 6; Kaisa Vehkalahti, 'Sentimental Histories: Emotions in the Historical Representation of Childhood' (European Social Science History Conference, 2008). For wider reading, see Gyandendra Pandey, 'Voices from the Edge: The Struggle to Write Subaltern Histories', in *Mapping Subaltern Studies and the Postcolonial*, ed. Vinayak Chaturvedi (London: Verso, 2000), 281–88, 296; Ranajit Guha, 'Chandra's Death', in *Subaltern Studies 5* (New Delhi: Oxford University Press, 1987), 167–202.
22. Durba Ghosh, *Sex and the Family in Colonial India: The Making of Empire* (Cambridge: Cambridge University Press, 2006), 22.
23. Heidi Morrison, *Childhood and Colonial Modernity* (Basingstoke: Palgrave Macmillan, 2015).
24. Clare Anderson, *Subaltern Lives: Biographies of Colonialism in the Indian Ocean World 1780–1920* (Cambridge: Cambridge University Press, 2012); Majid Siddiqi quoted in O'Hanlon in Chaturvedi, *Mapping Subaltern Studies*, 87.

25. Nieuwenhuys, 'Editorial', 151.
26. Satadru Sen, *Colonial Childhoods: The Juvenile Periphery of India 1850–1945* (London: Anthem, 2005).
27. David Pomfret, *Youth and Empire: Trans-colonial Childhoods in British and French Asia* (Stanford: Stanford University Press, 2015).
28. Vallgårda, *Imperial Childhoods*, 2. Further reading for white children in empire: E. M. Collingham, *Imperial Bodies: The Physical Experience of the Raj 1800–1947* (Cambridge, MA: Polity, 2001); Elizabeth Buettner, *Empire Families: Britons and Late Imperial India* (Oxford: Stanford University Press, 2004); for Indian children: Satadru Sen, 'The Orphaned Colony: Orphanage, Child and Authority in British India', *Indian Economic Social History Review* 44 (2007): 463–88; Karen Vallgårda, 'Between Consent and Coercion: Danish Missionaries and Tamil Parents in Late Nineteenth Century South India', *Review of Development and Change* 14, nos. 1–2 (2006).
29. Sen, *Colonial Childhoods*, 10, 137; Sen, 'The Orphaned Colony'.
30. Vallgårda, 'Between Consent and Coercion', 100; Sudipa Topdar, 'The Corporeal Empire: Physical Education and Politicising Children's Bodies in Late Colonial Bengal', *Gender and History* 29, no. 1 (2017): 176–97.
31. For age of consent, see Tanika Sarkar, *Hindu Wife, Hindu Nation: Community, Religion and Cultural Nationalism* (New Delhi: Paul's Press, 2001); Mrinalini Sinha, *Specters of Mother India: The Global Restructuring of an Empire* (Durham: Duke University Press, 2006). For the expansion of colonial governmentality, see Samiksha Sehrawat, *Colonial Medical Care in North India: Gender, State and Society c. 1830–1920* (Oxford: Oxford University Press, 2013); U. Kalpagam, 'Colonial Governmentality and the Public Sphere in India', *Journal of Historical Sociology* 15, no. 1 (March 2002).
32. We see this particularly in debates over women, Partha Chatterjee, *Nation and Its Fragments* (Princeton: Princeton University Press, 1993). See also Ann L. Stoler, *Carnal Knowledge and Imperial Power: Race and the Intimate in Colonial Rule* (Berkley: University of California Press, 2002); Swapna Banerjee, 'Debates on Domesticity and the Position of Women in Late Colonial India', *History Compass* 8, no. 6 (2010).
33. Jacques Donzelot, *The Policing of Families: Welfare versus the State* (London: Hutchison, 1979); Victor Bailey, *Delinquency and Citizenship: Reclaiming the Young Offenders, 1914–18* (Oxford: Clarendon Press, 1987); David Garland, *Punishment and Welfare* (Aldershot: Gower, 1985).
34. Ashis Nandy, *Intimate Enemy: Loss and Recovery of Self under Colonialism* (Delhi: Oxford University Press, 1993); Partha Chatterjee, *Nationalist Thought*

and the Colonial World: A Derivative Discourse? (London: Zed Books, 1986); Vasanthi Raman, 'The Diverse Life-Worlds of Indian Childhood', in *Family and Gender: Changing Values in Germany and India*, ed. Margrit Pernau, Imtiaz Ahmed and Helmut Reifeld (New Delhi: Sage, 2003).

35. David Arnold, *Science, Technology and Medicine in Colonial India*, vol. 5 (Cambridge: Cambridge University Press, 2000).
36. Kalpagam, 'Colonial Governmentality'; Sarah Hodges, *Contraception, Colonialism and Commerce: Birth Control in South India 1920-1940* (Aldershot: Ashgate, 2008).
37. Arnold, *Science, Technology and Medicine*, 15.
38. Sunil Amrith, *Decolonising International Health: India and Southeast Asia, 1930-65* (Basingstoke: Palgrave MacMillan, 2006).
39. See, for example, Kumari Jayawardena, *The White Woman's Other Burden: Western Women and South Asia during British Colonial Rule* (New York; London: Routledge, 1995); Hodges, *Contraception, Colonialism and Commerce*; Jana Tschurenev, *Empire, Civil Society, and the Beginnings of Colonial Education in India* (Cambridge: Cambridge University Press, 2019); Georgina Brewis, '"Fill Full the Mouth of Famine": Voluntary Action in Famine Relief in India 1896-1901', *Modern Asian Studies* 44, no. 4 (2010): 887-918.
40. See Balagopalan, 'Introduction'; Ishita Pande, '"Listen to the Child": Law, Sex, and the Child Wife in Indian Historiography', *History Compass* 11, no. 9 (2013).
41. Dominique Marshall, 'The Construction of Children as an Object of International Relations', *International Journal of Children's Rights* 7 (1999): 103–47. See also Linda Mahood, *Feminism and Voluntary Action: Eglantyne Jebb and Save the Children 1876–1928* (Basingstoke: Palgrave Macmillan, 2009), 199; Daniel Gorman, 'Empire, Internationalism, and the Campaign against the Traffic in Women and Children in the 1920s', *Twentieth Century British History* 19, no. 2 (2008): 188; Ashwini Tambe, 'The State as Surrogate Parent: Legislating Non-marital Sex in Colonial India, 1911–1929', *Journal of the History of Childhood and Youth* 2, no. 3 (2009).
42. Pomfret, *Imperial Childhoods*, ch. 7.
43. L. Gordon, 'The Perils of Innocence, or What's Wrong with Putting Children First', *Journal of the History of Childhood and Youth* 1, no. 3 (2008): 331–50.
44. See, for example, Hodges, *Contraception, Colonialism and Commerce*; Jana Tschurenev, 'Women, Early Childhood Education, and Global Reform Movements: New Perspectives on Colonial and National Education in India', *Südasien-Chronik - South Asia Chronicle* 7 (July 2017): 425–48; Carolien

Stolte and Harald Fischer-Tiné, 'Imagining Asia in India: Nationalism and Internationalism (ca. 1905–1940)', *Comparative Studies in Society and History* 54, no. 1 (2012): 65–92; Harald Fischer-Tiné, Stefan Huebner and Ian Tyrrell, eds., *Spreading Protestant Modernity: Global Perspectives on the Social Work of the YMCA and YWCA, 1889–1970* (Honolulu: University of Hawaii Press, 2020).

45. Judith M. Brown, *Modern India: The Origins of an Asian Democracy* (Oxford: Oxford University Press, 1985), 234.
46. For a wider analysis of dyarchy, see Eleanor Newbigin, *The Hindu Family and the Emergence of Modern India: Law, Citizenship and Community* (Cambridge: Cambridge University Press, 2012); James Chiriyankandath, '"Democracy" under the Raj: Elections and Separate Representation in British India', in *Democracy in India*, ed. Niraja Gopal Jayal (Oxford: Oxford University Press, 2001), 59; Sehrawat, *Colonial Medical Care*, 49–51; Eleanor Newbigin, Ornit Shani and Stephen Legg, 'Introduction: Constitutionalism and the Evolution of Democracy in India', *Comparative Studies of South Asia, Africa and the Middle East* 36, no. 1, special issue (May 2016): 42–43.
47. Arvind Elangovan, 'Constitutionalism, Political Exclusion, and Implications for Indian Constitutional History: The Case of Montagu Chelmsford Reforms (1919)', *South Asian History and Culture* 7, no. 3 (2016): 271–88. In field of education, see Taylor C. Sherman, 'Education in Early Postcolonial India: Expansion, Experimentation and Planned Self-help', *History of Education* 47, no. 4 (2018): 504–20.
48. Sehrawat, *Colonial Medical Care*, 61, 112; Brown, *Modern India*, 293. A good example is the case of medical research: Pratik Chakrabarti, '"Signs of the Times": Medicine and Nationhood in British India', *Osiris* 24, no. 1 (2009): 188–211.
49. M. Bhagavan, *Sovereign Spheres: Princes, Education and Empire in Colonial India* (New Delhi: Oxford University Press, 2003).
50. Hodges, *Contraception*, 151; Sehrawat, *Colonial Medical Care*, 49–51.
51. For a broader imperial perspective, see Shurlee Swain, 'A Motherly Concern for Children: Invocations of Queen Victoria in Imperial Child Rescue Literature', in *Children, Childhood and Youth in the British World*, ed. Shirleen Robinson and Simon Sleight (Basingstoke: Palgrave, 2016), 27–40; Sukanya Banerjee, *Becoming Imperial Citizens: Indians in the Late-Victorian Empire* (Durham: Duke, 2010); Upendra Baxi, 'Introduction', in *The Juvenile Justice System in India: From Welfare to Rights*, ed. Ved Kumari, 2nd ed. (Oxford: Oxford University Press, 2004), xiv–xv.

52. Sarada Balagopalan, 'Rationalising Seclusion: A Preliminary Analysis of a Residential Schooling Scheme for Poor Girls in India', *Feminist Theory* 11, no. 3 (2010): 304.
53. Sen, *Colonial Childhoods*, 49. See also Sudipa Topdar, 'Duties of a "Good Citizen": Colonial Secondary School Textbook Policies in Late Nineteenth-Century India', *South Asian History and Culture* 6, no. 3 (2015): 430; Sanjay Seth, *Subject Lessons: The Western Education of Colonial India* (Durham: Duke University Press, 2007); Uberoi, *Freedom and Destiny*, 103–04; K. Vallgårda, K. Alexander and S. Olsen, 'Emotions and the Global Politics of Childhood', in *Childhood, Youth and Emotions in Modern History, National, Colonial and Global Perspectives*, ed. Stephanie Olsen (Basingstoke: Palgrave Macmillan, 2015).
54. Jessica Hinchy, *Governing Gender and Sexuality in Colonial India, the Hijra, c. 1850–1900* (Cambridge: Cambridge University Press, 2019).
55. Mytheli Sreenivas, *Wives, Widows, Concubines: The Conjugal Family Ideal in Colonial India* (Bloomington: Indiana University Press, 2008).
56. Banerjee, 'Debates on Domesticity'.
57. Indrani Chatterjee, ed., *Unfamiliar Relations: Family and History in South Asia* (New Brunswick: Rutgers University Press, 2004).
58. These roles themselves were defined according to age, sex and relationship to parents: *mama, mami, atthai, attimbar, periyappa, periyamma, chitthappa, chitti, machchan, machinitchi*.
59. See, for example, Tambe, 'The State as Surrogate Parent'.
60. See Balakrishnan, *Growing Up and Away*, 13; Neera Burra, *Born Unfree: Child Labour, Education and the State in India* (Oxford: Oxford University Press, 2006); Leigh Denault, 'The Home and the World: New Directions in the History of the Family in South Asia', *History Compass* 12, no. 2 (2014): 101–11; Satadru Sen, 'Health, Race and Family in Colonial Bengal', in *Children, Childhood and Youth in the British World*, ed. Robinson and Sleight, 144–60, 155; Ritu Menon, '*Parens Patriae*: Exercising Patriarchal Prerogative in Post-Partition India', in *Challenging the Rule(s) of Law: Colonialism, Criminology and Human Rights in India*, ed. Kalpana Kannabiran and Ranbir Singh (London: Sage, 2008).
61. Balakrishnan, *Growing Up and Away*, 82–99, 209.
62. Sen, *Colonial Childhoods*.
63. Balagopalan, *Inhabiting Childhood*, 77. Myron Weiner, *The Child and the State in India* (New Jersey: Princeton University Press, 1991); Kannabiran and Singh, eds., *Challenging the Rule(s) of Law*, 183, 191. Weiner argues that

this was a deliberate strategy to maintain pre-existing social hierarchies; this is a powerful argument but I do not have sufficient evidence for it here.

64. C. A. Bayly, 'Afterword', in *Trans-colonial Modernities in South Asia*, ed. Michael Dodson and Brian Hatcher (London: Routledge, 2012), 231–48. By contrast, when Bengal is taken to represent the whole, see Swapna Banerjee, 'Blurring Boundaries, Distant Companions: Non-kin Female Caregivers for Children in Colonial India', *Paedagogica Historica* 46, no. 6 (2010): 775–88.

65. For wider reading on the social structures of the Madras Presidency, see David Washbrook, *The Emergence of Provincial Politics: the Madras Presidency 1870–1920* (Cambridge: Cambridge University Press, 1976); Eugene Irschick, *Dialogue and History: Constructing South India, 1795–1895* (Berkeley: University of California Press, 1994); Mattison Mines, *Public Faces, Private Voices: Community and Individuality in South India* (Berkeley: University of California Press, 1994); C. J. Baker and D. A. Washbrook, *South India: Political Institutions and Political Change 1880–1940* (Delhi: Macmillan, 1975); Christopher Baker, *Politics of South India 1920–1937* (Cambridge: Cambridge University Press, 1976).

66. Baker, *Politics of South India*, ix. For wider reading, see Washbrook, *Emergence of Provincial Politics*, 206; Eugene Irschick, *Politics of Tamil Revivalism in the 1930s* (Madras: Cre-A, 1986); Marguerite Barnett, *Politics of Cultural Nationalism in South India* (New Jersey: Princeton University Press, 1976); Hodges, *Contraception, Colonialism and Commerce*.

67. For wider reading on language politics, see Sumathi Ramaswamy, *Passions of the Tongue: Language Development in Tamil India, 1891–1970* (Berkeley: Cambridge University Press, 1997); Velcheru Narayana Rao, David Shuman and Sanjay Subrahmanyam, *Textures of Time: Writing History in South India 1600–1800* (Delhi: Permanent Black, 2001).

68. For wider reading on radical politics, see Sarah Hodges, 'Revolutionary Family Life and the Self Respect Movement in Tamil South India, 1926–49', *Contributions to Indian Sociology* 39, no. 2 (2005): 251–77; Eliza Kent, *Converting Women: Gender and Protestant Christianity in Colonial South India* (Oxford: Oxford University Press, 2004); Hodges, *Contraception, Colonialism and Commerce*; S. Anandhi, 'Women's Question in the Dravidian Movement c. 1925–1948', in *Women and Social Reform in Modern India*, ed. Sumit Sarkar and Tanika Sarkar, vol. 2 (New Delhi: Permanent Black, 2007); Sreenivas, *Wives, Widows, Concubines*.

69. See, particularly, Rupa Viswanath, 'Spiritual Slavery, Material Malaise: "Untouchables" and Religious Neutrality in Colonial South India', *Historical*

Research 83, no. 219 (February 2010). Rupa Viswanath, 'Rethinking Caste and Class: "Labour", the "Depressed Classes", and the Politics of Distinctions, Madras 1918–1924', *International Review of Social History* 59 (2014): 1–37. Within this book, the classification 'Dalit' will be used in all but primary source quotations, because of the political connotations of classifications Adi-Dravida, Adi-Andhra, Backward Castes, Harijans, Untouchables or Pariahs.

70. Baker, *Politics of South India*, 6. By comparison, the population of Great Britain in the 1921 census was 42.8 million.
71. Kenneth McPherson, *'How Best Do We Survive?' A Modern Political History of the Tamil Muslims* (London: Routledge, 2010).

Chapter 1

1. For a discussion of the all-India level see Parimala Rao, ed., *New Perspectives in the History of Indian Education* (New Delhi: Orient Blackswan, 2014).
2. Sarada Balagopalan, 'Constructing Indigenous Childhoods: Colonialism, Vocational Education and the Working Child', *Childhood* 9, no. 1 (2002): 19–34.
3. For a wider discussion of the history of education see Catriona Ellis, 'Perspectives on the History of Colonial Education', in *Global Education Systems: Handbook of Education Systems in South Asia*, ed. Padma M. Sarangapani and Rekha Pappu (Singapore: Springer, 2020). Also see, Deepak Kumar, Joseph Bara, Nadita Khadria and Radha Gayathri, eds., *Education in Colonial India: Historical Insights* (New Delhi: Manohar, 2013); Nigel Crook, ed., *The Transmission of Knowledge in South Asia* (Delhi: Oxford University Press, 1996), 19; Sabyasachi Bhattacharya, ed., *The Contested Terrain: Perspectives on Education in India* (London: Sangam Books, 1998); Rao, *New Perspectives*.
4. Barnita Bagchi, 'Connected and Entangled Histories: Writing Histories of Education in the Indian Context', *Paedagogica Historica* 50, no. 6 (2014): 817; Joseph Bara, 'Colonialism and Educational Fragmentation in India', in *Contested Terrain*, ed. Bhattacharya, 125–70; Latika Chaudhary, 'Determinants of Primary Schooling in British India', *Journal of Economic History* 69, no. 1 (2009).
5. IOR: L/PJ/6/1592, file 2941, D. Swamikannu Pillai, 19 December 1918.
6. Tamil Nadu State Archives (TNSA): GO644 Home (Education) Department 31 May 1920, 16 April 1919.

7. British Library (BL): V10750 Madras Parliament Transactions: Compulsory Elementary Education Act, 2nd Reading of Bill 17 April 1915.
8. Schools: total 29,848, government 208, municipal boards 564, local board institutions 6,330, private aided 19,072, unaided 3,674. IOR: L/PJ/6/1592, file 2941, Swamikannu Pillai, 19 December 1918.
9. IOR: V/27/862/4 Educational Survey Madras Presidency 1924.
10. IOR: V/27/862/4.
11. 'Lakh' is a unit followed in the South Asian numbering system, where 1 lakh = 100,000.
12. IOR: L/PJ/6/1592, file 2941, TNSAL: MLC Debates 29 March 1920, 690.
13. TNSAL: MLC Debates 29 March 1920, 698.
14. TNSAL: MLC Debates 29 March 1920, 700.
15. IOR: L/PJ/6/1592, file 2941, Minute of Dissent 28 May 1920.
16. Rao, *New Perspectives*.
17. IOR: L/PJ/6/1592, file 2941, Select Committee 21 July 1920.
18. TNSAL: MLC Debates 15 November 1921, 1387.
19. NLS: IP/25/PJ.3 DPI 1934–35, 1.
20. For a wider discussion of this, see Nita Kumar, *The Politics of Gender, Community and Modernity: Essays on Education in India* (New Delhi: Oxford University Press, 2007).
21. TNSA: GO1951 Law & Education (LE) 8 June 1925.
22. TNSA: GO882 LE 17 May 1926.
23. Harry Hendrick, *Children, Childhood and English Society, 1880–1990* (Cambridge: Cambridge University Press, 1997), 5.
24. IOR: L/PJ/6/1592, file 2941, Madras Elementary Education Act 1920, ch. 1, sec. xiii, 28 September 1920, 23.
25. IOR: L/PJ/6/1592, file 2941, 28 September 1920, 22–23. The lack of ability to define age was recognised in other reports. IOR: V/24/3705 Report of the Director of Public Health (DPH), Madras, 1921, 1. See also Timothy Alborn, 'Age and Empire in the Indian Census, 1871–1931', *Journal of Interdisciplinary History* 30, no. 1 (Summer 1999): 61–89.
26. TNSA: GO1193 LE 7 October 1922. DPI 9 September 1922.
27. TNSA: GO1440 LE 28 November 1922. DPI 27 October 1922.
28. TNSA: GO1951 LE 8 June 1925.
29. TNSA: GO882 LE 17 May 1926.
30. TNSA: GO2070 LE 17 June 1922; GO 882 LE 17 May 1926.
31. TNSA: GO1193 LE 7 October 1922; Memo 8 July 1922.

32. TNSA: GO1193 LE 7 October 1922.
33. C. J. Baker, 'Leading Up to Periyar: The Early Career of E. V. Ramaswami Naicker', in *Leadership in South Asia*, ed. B. N. Pandey (New Delhi: Vikas, 1977), 501–24.
34. TNSA: GO1193 LE 7 October 1922.
35. NLS: IP/25/PJ.3 DPI 1921–22, 59.
36. TNSA: GO1901 LE 3 November 1925 Elementary Education Survey Report 1924–25.
37. BL: Mss Eur E221/44 Evidence to the Hartog Commission: R. S. Subbalkshmi Ammal; Dr Muthulaksmi Reddi.
38. Seth, *Subject Lessons*, 129.
39. NLS: IP/25/PJ.3 DPI 1919–20; Sita Anantha Raman, *Getting Girls to School: Social Reform in the Tamil Districts, 1870–1930* (Chennai: Stree, 1996); Rao, *New Perspectives*; Kumar, *Politics of Gender, Community and Modernity*.
40. NLS: IP/25/PJ.3 DPI 1926–27, 113.
41. Kumar, *Politics of Gender, Community and Modernity*.
42. S. Paik, *Dalit Women's Education in Modern India: Double Discrimination* (Abingdon: Routledge, 2014).
43. NLS: IP/25/PJ.3 DPI 1936–37, Quinquennium 1932–33 to 1936–37, 88, 1927–28 to 1931–32, 83; Nicholas Dirks, *Castes of Mind: Colonialism and the Making of Modern India* (Princeton: Princeton University Press, 2001); Ronald Inden, *Imagining India* (Bloomington: Indiana University Press, 2000).
44. Seth, *Subject Lessons*, 119–25; see also U. Kalpagam, *Rule by Numbers: Governmentality in Colonial India* (London: Lexington Books, 2014), for a general overview.
45. TNSA: GO1938 LE 10 November 1925 Malabar; GO1901 LE 3 November 1925 Trichinolopoly, Ramnad District.
46. IOR: L/PJ/6/1592, file 2941, 30 September 1920, 87.
47. IOR: L/PJ/6/1592, file 2941, 28 September 1920, 76.
48. Parna Sengupta, *Pedagogy for Religion: Missionary Education and the Fashioning of Hindus and Muslims in Bengal* (Berkeley: University of California Press, 2011).
49. IOR: L/PJ/6/1592, file 2941, 30 September 1920, 85.
50. TNSA: GO1901 LE 3 November 1925 Tinnevelly; Madras Corporation Archives (MCA): Proceedings 30 March 1938, 22.
51. McPherson, 'How Best Do We Survive?', 5.
52. McPherson, 'How Best Do We Survive?', 140.

53. BL MssEur E221/44 Hartog Evidence: Mrs Muzeruddin.
54. NLS: IP/25/PJ.3 DPI Quinquennium 1916–17 to 1921–22, 35, 66. Mentions GO329 Home (Education) 17 March 1919, GO886 Home (Education) 07 August 1920, GO28 LE 6 January 1922.
55. TNSAL: MLC Debate 16 November 1921, 1457–58.
56. BL V 12547 Hartog Commission on Education (Interim Report of Indian Statutory Commission), 377.
57. Viswanath, 'Rethinking Caste and Class', 29.
58. TNSAL: Debate 30 October 1931, 130.
59. For a wider reading, see Chatterjee, *Nations and Its Fragments*; Kalpagam, 'Colonial Governmentality'.
60. IOR: V/27/860/88-/97 1892–1940 amendments, app. 17.
61. NLS: IP/25/PJ.3 DPI Quinquennium 1916–17 to 1921–22, 35, DPI 1935–36, 18, 29.
62. NLS: IP/25/PJ.3 DPI Quinquennium 1916–17 to 1921–22, 67; Deepa Sreenivas, 'Telling Different Tales: Possible Childhoods in Children's Literature', *Childhood* 18, no. 3 (2011); Krishna Kumar, *Political Agenda of Education: A Study of Colonialist and Nationalist Ideas* (New Delhi: Sage Publications, 1991).
63. NLS: IP/25/PJ.3 DPI 1932–33 to 1936–37, 139.
64. NLS: IP/25/PJ.3 DPI 1930–31, 19; DPI, 1933–34, 15.
65. Kent, *Converting Women*; Kumar, *Political Agenda of Education*.
66. NLS: IP/25/PJ.3 DPI 1921–22, 65.
67. NLS: IP/25/PJ.3 DPI Quinquennium 1921–22 to 1926–27, 127.
68. NLS: IP/25/PJ.3 DPI Quinquennium 1916–17 to 1921–22, 35, 67.
69. NLS: IP/25/PJ.3 DPI 1919–20, 66.
70. Viswanath, 'Rethinking Caste and Class', 29–35.
71. BL: V12547, MssEur E221/44 Hartog Evidence: S. H. Slater.
72. BL MssEur E221/44 Hartog Evidence: Slater, 44.
73. TNSAL: Debate 19 March 1923, 2585–92.
74. TNSAL: MLC Debate 29 March 1920, 688.
75. IOR: L/PJ/6/1592, file 2941, 28 September 1920, 21.
76. IOR: L/PJ/6/1592, file 2941.
77. BL: A. P. Patro, *Studies in Local Self-Government, Education and Sanitation* (Madras: G. A. Natesan & Co. 1910), 5, 138–140; IOR: L/PJ/6/1592, file 2941, MLA Debates 19 March 1920, 695.
78. IOR: L/PJ/6/1592, file 2941, 701–02.

79. Prashant Kidambi, *The Making of an Indian Metropolis: Colonial Governance and Public Culture in Bombay, 1890-1920* (Farnham: Ashgate, 2007).
80. IOR: L/PJ/6/1592, file 2941, Select Committee Evidence, 8-9; 16 April 1919; TNSAL: MLA Debate 28 January 1939, 71-78. See also Irschick, *Politics of Tamil Revivalism*, 230.
81. TNSA: GO868 LE 21 July 1922 Note 20 June 1922.
82. TNSA: GO868 LE 21 July 1922 District Educational Officer 24 May 1925.
83. TNSA: GO868 LE 21 July 1922 Correspondence: 23 May 1922, 19 May 1922, 5 June 1922, 30 June 1922, 15 June 1922.
84. TNSA: GO868 LE 21 July 1922.
85. TNSA: GO951 LE 8 June 1925 Correspondence, 26 March 1924, 30 April 1924, 6 June 1924, 8 June 1925, 3 September 1924, 23 August 1924.
86. IOR: L/PJ/6/1592, file 2941, MLA Debate 30 September 1920, 101.
87. TNSAL: MLA Debates 29 March 1920, 689.
88. TNSA: GO1465 LE 16 October 1923.
89. TNSAL: MLA Debates 19 March 1923, 2582-86, 2597, 2603; BL MssEur E221/44 Hartog Evidence: Nityandanda Mudaliar, 2, Dr Muthulakshmi Reddi.
90. TNSA: GO779 LE 17 April 1935, question and response 27 February 1935.
91. IOR: L/PJ/6/1592, file 2941, Debates 28 September 1920, 74.
92. IOR: L/PJ/6/1592, file 2941, Select Committee 21 July 1920.
93. NLS: IP/25/PJ.3 DPI 1931-32, Quinquennium 1927-28 to 1931-32.
94. IOR: L/PJ/6/1592, file 2941, Select Committee 21 July 1920.
95. IOR: L/PJ/6/1592, file 2941, Debates MLA 28 September 1920, 23-24, 72-73, Select Committee Report: Minute of Dissent N. Subba Rao; TNSAL: MLA Debates 15 November 1921, 1383, 1385.
96. NLS: IP/25/PJ.3 DPI 1930-31, 23.
97. TNSA: GO951 LE 8 June 1925. Divisions are local authority wards or areas.
98. MCA: Proceedings 3 February 1925.
99. MCA: Proceedings 20 January 1925, 13; TNSA: GO951 LE 8 June 1925.
100. MCA: Proceedings 20 January 1925, 14.
101. MCA: Proceedings 14 May 1925, 183-87.
102. MCA: Proceedings 28 March 1925, 16 April 1926, 20, 8 May 1926, 62, 7 September 1925, 49, 8 May 1926, 60, 63-69.
103. MCA: Proceedings 23 September 1930.
104. MCA: Proceedings 28 March 1933, 27
105. MCA: Proceedings 24 August 1926, 48, 13 October 1924, 336, 7 September 1926, 50.

106. MCA: Proceedings 11 April 1927, 16 April 1928, 23 September 1930, 24 July 1931, 121, 124, 130.
107. MCA: Proceedings 8 May 1926, 49.
108. MCA: Proceedings 8 May 1926, 50–53, 11 April 1927, 26 August 1927.
109. TNSA: MLC Debates 30 March 1931, 119, 126.
110. MCA: Proceedings 24 July 1931, 121, 124, 130.
111. Post-independence: Kumari, *The Juvenile Justice System in India*, 41; A. B. Bose, *The State of Children in India: Promises to Keep* (New Delhi: Manhor, 2003), 206.
112. MCA: Proceedings 11 April 1927.
113. IOR: V/27/860/97 Madras Educational Rules 1940, 28; TNSAL: MLA Debates 21 November 1919, 185.
114. IOR: V/27/862/4, TNSA: GO1440 LE 28 November 1922: A. P. Patro 18 June 1922, Sir Ahamad Thamby Maricair 6 October 1922, GO 2070 LE 5 December 1925 Conjeeveram Council 30 September 1925.
115. TNSAL: MLC Debates 19 March 1923, 2598, 2600–01.
116. BL MssEur E221/44 Hartog Evidence: Missionary Education Council of South India, 6.
117. IOR: L/PJ/6/1592, file 2941, Note 7 April 1919; J. M. Sen, *History of Elementary Education in India* (Calcutta: Book Company, 1933).
118. IOR: L/PJ/6/1592, file 2941, Statement 7 April 1919: first conviction 10 rupees to maximum 100 rupees, or imprisonment for third and subsequent convictions.
119. TNSA: GO2070 LE 17 June 1922.
120. TNSAL: MLC Debate 29 March 1920, 691. See also Balagopalan, *Inhabiting Childhood*, ch. 2.
121. TNSAL: MLC Debate 30 September 1920, 90.
122. TNSAL: MLC Debate 29 March 1920.
123. IOR: L/PJ/6/1592, file 2941, 9 June 1919.
124. IOR: L/PJ/6/1592, file 2941, 16 April 1919.
125. IOR: L/PJ/6/1592, file 2941, MLC Debate 26 July 1920, 8.
126. IOR: L/PJ/6/1592, file 2941, MLC Debate 30 September 1920, 89, 1459–60.
127. IOR: L/PJ/6/1592, file 2941, MLC Debate 28 September 1920, 78, 30 September 1920.
128. IOR: L/PJ/6/1592, file 2941, MLC Debate 30 September 1920.
129. See also Sengupta, *Pedagogy for Religion*.
130. Balagopalan, *Inhabiting Childhood*.
131. MCA: Proceedings 15 July 1925, 233.

Chapter 2

1. MCA: Proceedings 4 June 1943, 4; TNSA: GO1437 LE 10 October 1942.
2. TNSA: GO2268 LE 9 December 1926.
3. MCA: Proceedings 25 November 1941, 9.
4. MCA: Proceedings 31 May 1932, 10. Gokhale (1866–1915) was a moderate leader of the Indian National Congress (INC), famous for his attempt to introduce compulsory elementary education at an all-India level in 1911.
5. TNSA: GO951 LE 8 June 1925.
6. TNSA: GO951 LE 8 June 1925, Letter 15 April 1925.
7. TNSA: GO951 LE 8 June 1925, 3.
8. MCA: Proceedings 28 March 1924, 477, 482; Short Proceedings 28 March 1924, 143.
9. MCA: Proceedings 28 March 1924, 477.
10. MCA: Proceedings 20 May 1930.
11. MCA: Proceedings 28 March 1924, 490.
12. MCA: Proceedings 28 March 1924, 485.
13. MCA: Proceedings 28 March 1924, 476, 488.
14. MCA: Proceedings 28 March 1924, 482–95; 17 February 1931, 25; 3 March 1931, 27. See also B. Cohen and S. Ganguly, 'Introduction: Regions and Regionalism in India', *India Review* 13, no. 4 (2014).
15. Marshall, 'The Construction of Children as an Object of International Relations'.
16. MCA: Proceedings 28 March 1924, 499.
17. MCA: Proceedings 18 March 1935, 19, 20.
18. MCA: Proceedings 28 March 1924, 484.
19. MCA: Proceedings 28 March 1924, 477.
20. MCA: Proceedings 27 September 1938, 23; 19 November 1935, 60.
21. MCA: Proceedings 30 March 1938, 6.
22. MCA: Proceedings 1 December 1936, 37.
23. A number of people have written on the idea of the 'good citizen', for example, Topdar, 'Duties of a "Good Citizen"'; or Sen, *Colonial Childhoods*.
24. MCA: Proceedings 1 December 1936, 36.
25. MCA: Proceedings 1 December 1936, 36–37; 7 July 1937, 24, 32.
26. MCA: Proceedings 7 July 1937, 27–28.
27. MCA: Proceedings 7 July 1937, 26.
28. MCA: Proceedings 19 November 1935, 52.

29. Kumar, *Lessons from Schools*, 192; Bowen and Hinchy, 'Introduction'.
30. MCA: Proceedings 30 March 1938, 17, 19; 30 February 1938, 50–57.
31. MCA: Proceedings 13 December 1935, 61.
32. MCA: Proceedings 24 January 1939, 32.
33. MCA: Proceedings 24 January 1939, 36.
34. MCA: Proceedings 24 January 1939, 35.
35. MCA: Proceedings 24 January 1939, 35; 28 October 1942, 9.
36. MCA: Proceedings 29 November 1939, 16.
37. MCA: Proceedings 29 November 1939, 30; 25 February 1931, 3.
38. MCA: Proceedings 14 November 1939, 42–43.
39. MCA: Proceedings 1 December 1931, 27.
40. MCA: Proceedings 7 February 1933, 40; 31 August 1937, 56.
41. MCA: Proceedings 1 December 1931, 33–35; 4 December 1934, 47; 8 October 1935, 47, 54; 31 August 1937, 55–56. For a wider discussion of Dravidian nationalism and language politics, see Ramaswamy, *Passions of the Tongue*.
42. MCA: Proceedings 8 August 1933, 68; 22 December 1936, 54; 31 August 1937, 49; TNSA: GO1908 Education 10 September 1936.
43. MCA: Proceedings 4 December 1934, 41–47.
44. MCA: Proceedings 1 December 1931, 31; 31 August 1937, 53–54.
45. MCA: Proceedings 1 December 1931, 35; A. R. Venkatachalapathy, *In Those Days There Was No Coffee: Writings in Cultural History* (New Delhi: Yoda Press, 2006), 153.
46. MCA: Proceedings 1 April 1931; 7 September 1931, 38, 39; 18 November 1939, 15–18. McPherson, 'How Best Do We Survive?'.
47. MCA: Proceedings 20 January 1925, 14; TNSA: GO951 LE 8 June 1925, Letter 23 August 1924.
48. TNSA: GO2268 LE 9 December 1926.
49. TNSA: GO951 LE 8 June 1925. Divisions are local authority wards/areas.
50. MCA: Proceedings 3 February 1925.
51. MCA: Proceedings 20 January 1925, 13; TNSA: GO951 LE 8 June 1925.
52. MCA: Proceedings 20 May 1930.
53. MCA: Proceedings 20 May 1930.
54. MCA: Proceedings 5 May 1937, 27.
55. MCA: Proceedings 17 February 1931, 24; 9 December 1936, 38–39; 31 March 1937, 96–97; 17 March 1938, 11.
56. MCA: Proceedings 18 November 1939, 11.
57. MCA: Proceedings 29 July 1934; 23 February 1939; 18 November 1939; 3 February 1941.

Notes

58. MCA: Proceedings 27 September 1938, 15.
59. MCA: Proceedings 28 March 1933; 29 March 1933; 9 December 1936; 17 March 1938, 11, 15; 29 July 1941, 23–33.
60. MCA: Proceedings 14 May 1925, 183–84.
61. MCA: Proceedings 22 July 1925, 352.
62. TNSA: GO2268 LE 9 December 1926, Scheme for the Extension of Free and Compulsory Education, 4.
63. MCA: Proceedings 25 November 1925, 352.
64. TNSA: GO1951 LE 8 June 1925; GO2268 LE 9 December 1926; MCA: Proceedings 22 July 1925.
65. MCA: Proceedings 30 October 1930 Attendance Committee Rules.
66. MCA: Proceedings date missing 1929.
67. MCA: Proceedings date missing 1929.
68. MCA: Proceedings 25 February 1931, 3.
69. MCA: Proceedings 25 February 1931, 3.
70. TNSA: GO 2268 LE 9 December 1926.
71. MCA: Proceedings 13 November 1931, 4; 28 March 1933, 29; BL: J. M. Sen, *History of Elementary Education in India* (Calcutta: Book Company, 1933).
72. MCA: Proceedings 13 November 1931; 1 December 1931, 25.
73. MCA: Proceedings 30 March 1928, 2.
74. IOR: L/PJ/6/1592, file 2941, MLC Debate 28 September 1920, Select Committee, 21 July 1920, 69.
75. TNSA: GO951 LE 8 June 1925, Letter 15 April 1925; GO2268 LE 9 December 1926, Letter DPI 15 October 1924.
76. MCA: Proceedings 7 September 1931, 35.
77. MCA: Proceedings 1 April 1931, 38.
78. MCA: Proceedings 1 April 1931, 39.
79. MCA: Proceedings 1 April 1931, 21–23, 38–42; 19 September 1935, 43.
80. MCA: Proceedings 14 May 1925, 184; 30 March 1938, 18.
81. MCA: Proceedings 18 November 1939, 39.
82. MCA: Proceedings 13 October 1924, 235; 8 December 1924, 61; 13 November 1931; 14 May 1925, 184; 30 March 1938, 18; 18 November 1939, 39.
83. Balagopalan, 'Constructing Indigenous Childhoods', 27.
84. Kumar, *Lessons from Schools*.
85. MCA: Proceedings 13 November 1931.
86. NLS: IP/25/PJ.3 DPI Reports; TNSA: GO329 Home (Education) 17 March 1919; GO886 Home (Education) 07 August 1920; GO28 LE 06 January 1922.

87. MCA: Proceedings 16 April 1928.
88. For further reading see Hodges, 'Revolutionary Family Life'.
89. MCA: Proceedings 5 May 1937.
90. MCA: Proceedings 30 June 1939, 44–47; 18 November 1939, 14.
91. MCA: Proceedings 25 October 1938, 40.
92. MCA: Proceedings 31 March 1937, 113.
93. MCA: Proceedings 28 March 1939, 35.
94. MCA: Proceedings 25 October 1938, 38.
95. MCA: Proceedings 25 February 1931.
96. MCA: Proceedings 18 February 1932, 2. Personal experience of this is recounted by K. A. Gunasekaran, *The Scar* (Hyderabad: Orient Blackswan, 2009).
97. MCA: Proceedings 28 March 1924, 488.
98. MCA: Proceedings 14 May 1925, 187; 8 December 1942, 16–19.
99. MCA: Proceedings 18 October 1932; 4 July 1933, 42–43.
100. MCA: Proceedings 1 December 1931.
101. MCA: Proceedings 19 September 1927.
102. MCA: Proceedings 31 March 1937, 114; 1 December 1931.
103. MCA: Proceedings 19 September 1927.
104. MCA: Proceedings 19 September 1927.
105. MCA: Proceedings 19 September 1927.
106. MCA: Proceedings 3 August 1928.
107. MCA: Proceedings 19 September 1927.
108. Balagopalan, 'Constructing Indigenous Childhoods'.
109. MCA: Proceedings 9 December 1936.
110. MCA: Proceedings 19 January 1937; 4 October 1938, 44.
111. MCA: Proceedings 31 March 1937, 100–01.
112. 'Anna' was a unit formerly used in British India, where 1 *anna* = 1/16th of a rupee.
113. MCA: Proceedings 18 November 1939, 4.
114. MCA: Proceedings 29 November 1939, 4; 18 November 1939, 31, 8; 29 November 1939, 10–11.
115. Balagopalan, *Inhabiting Childhood*.
116. MCA: Proceedings 29 November 1939, 7.
117. MCA: Proceedings 23 August 1938, 37; 14 November 1939, 46; 18 November 1939, 19.
118. Parimala V. Rao, '"Promiscuous Crowd of English Smatterers": The "Poor" in the Colonial and Nationalist Discourse on Education in India, 1835–1912', *Contemporary Education Dialogue* 10, no. 2 (2013): 223–48.

119. Parimala V. Rao, *Beyond Macaulay: Education in India, 1780–1860* (Abingdon: Taylor & Francis, 2019), emphasises this point in the context of the nineteenth century.
120. MCA: Proceedings 27 January 1925; 31 December 1924; TNSA: GO951 LE 8 June 1925, Letter 27 September 1925.
121. Seth, *Subject Lessons*; NLS: IP/25/PJ.3 DPI Reports, Quinquennial Reports.
122. MCA: Proceedings 27 January 1925, 19–22.
123. MCA: Proceedings 4 August 1928.
124. MCA: Proceedings 4 August 1928.
125. MCA: Proceedings 30 March 1938, 2–22.
126. MCA: Proceedings 19 March 1931, 21, 24; MCA: Proceedings 6 October 1938, 14.
127. See, for example, Chatterjee, *Nation and Its Fragments*; Raman, *Getting Girls to School*; Tim Allender, *Learning Femininity in Colonial India, 1820–1932* (Manchester: Manchester University Press, 2016). The best overview is Shenila Khoja-Moolji, *Forging the Ideal Educated Girl: The Production of Desirable Subjects in Muslim South Asia* (Oakland, California: University of California Press, 2018).
128. MCA: Proceedings 1 December 1931, 19; 30 January 1938, 7.
129. Urvashi Butalia, *The Other Side of Silence: Voices from the Partition of India* (London: Hurst & Company, 2000).
130. MCA: Proceedings 16 April 1929.
131. MCA: Proceedings 1 April 1931, 47.
132. MCA: Proceedings 1 April 1931, 46–49; 12 February 1932, 26–29.
133. MCA: Proceedings 12 February 1932, 29.
134. MCA: Proceedings 31 March 1937, 109–12.
135. MCA: Proceedings 13 April 1939, 39.
136. MCA: Proceedings 18 November 1939, 5.
137. MCA: Proceedings 18 November 1939, 21, 27.
138. NLS: IP/25/PJ.3 DPI 1936–37, Quinquennium, 1932–33 to 1936–37, 107.
139. MCA: Proceedings 23 March 1939, 34. 1939: Corporation 137 Elementary Schools, 39,000 pupils.

Chapter 3

1. For a full discussion, see Tschurenev, *Empire, Civil Society, and the Beginnings of Colonial Education*.

2. A good summary of the ways in which colonial education changed over time, both in content and priority, can be found in Tim Allender, 'Learning Abroad: The Colonial Educational Experiment in India, 1813–1919', *Paedagogica Historica* 45, no. 6 (2009): 727–41. For a general summary of colonial education, see Tschurenev, *Empire, Civil Society, and the Beginnings of Colonial Education*; and Rao, *Beyond Macaulay*.
3. For secondary reading, see Kumar, *Political Agenda of Education*, 300; Seth, *Subject Lessons*; G. Viswanathan, *Masks of Conquest: Literary Study and British Rule in India* (London: Faber & Faber, 1989), 101; Thomas Metcalf, *Ideologies of Raj* (Cambridge: Cambridge University Press, 1998). An overview can be found at Ellis, 'Perspectives'.
4. NLS: Indian Statutory Commission, *Report*, vol. 1 (London, May 1930), 402.
5. Kumar, *Political Agenda of Education*.
6. For a discussion of indigenous education, see Dharampal, *The Beautiful Tree: Indigenous Indian Education in the Eighteenth Century* (New Delhi: Bilia, 1983); Rao, *Beyond Macaulay*, ch. 2.
7. Kumar, *Lessons from Schools*, ch. 4; M. Manchanda, 'Contested Domains: Reconstructing Education and Religious Identity in Sikh and Arya Samaj Schools in Punjab', in *New Perspectives*, ed. Rao.
8. Kumar, *Politics of Gender*, 37; Padma Sarangapani, *Constructing School Knowledge: An Ethnography of Learning in an Indian Village* (New Delhi: Sage, 2003), 170; Kumar, *Lessons from Schools*, 69.
9. S. R. Karnataka, 'Child-Centred Education', *Educational India*, February 1937, 293.
10. P. K. Banerjee, 'The Aim of Education', *Educational India*, October 1935, 129; C. Swamikannu Paul, 'New Ideals in Education', *Educational India*, February 1936; Dr M. Siddalingaiya, 'Modern Developments in Educational Practice', *Educational India*, May–June 1937, 405.
11. Parna Sengupta, 'An Object Lesson in Colonial Pedagogy', *Society for Comparative Study of Society and History* (2003); William Glover, 'Objects, Models, and Exemplary Works: Educating Sentiment in Colonial India', *Journal of Asian Studies* 64, no. 3 (2005): 539–66.
12. For further reading, consider Barnita Bagchi, Eckhardt Fuchs and Kate Rousmaniere, eds., *Connecting Histories of Education: Transnational and Cross-Cultural Exchanges in (Post) Colonial Education* (Oxford; New York: Berghahn Books, 2014); Jana Tschurenev, 'Inequality, Difference, and the Politics of Education for All', *South Asia Chronicle*, August 2018; M. Mann,

ed., *Shantiniketan-Hellerau: New Education in the 'Pedagogic Provinces' of India and Germany* (Heidelberg: Draupadi, 2015).
13. P. Kallaway, 'Conference Litmus: The Development of a Conference and Policy Culture in the Interwar Period', in *Transformations in Schooling: Historical and Comparative Perspectives*, ed. K. Tolley (New York: Palgrave MacMillan, 2007), 123. Report New Education Fellowship: Visit of Delegation to India, *Educational India*, April 1937; *Educational India*, January 1938, 277.
14. Eckhart Fuchs, 'The Creation of New International Networks in Education: the League of Nations and Educational Organisations', *Paedagogica Historica* 43, no. 2 (April 2007): 199–209.
15. *Educational India*, 1 July 1934.
16. *Educational India*, March 1935: D. S. Gordon, Assistant Professor of Education, Mysore University, or T. Vyas, principal of New Era School, Bombay, *Educational India*, July 1934: Ismail, Dewan of Mysore.
17. Mrs D. Subhadra Chenciah, 'Right Training in the Infant Stage', *Educational India*, December 1936, 211, March 1935, Women's Page; Mrs K. Satthianadhan, 'Corner for Women', *Educational India*, September 1938.
18. *Educational India*, August 1934.
19. G. S. Krishnayya, 'Some Lessons from Negro Education', *Educational India*, November 1934.
20. Moga, 'First Steps in Vernacular Education, Suggestions for Improvement', staff training course, October–December 1935, *Educational India*, May–June 1936, 416.
21. Swamikannu Paul, 'New Ideals', 294.
22. B. V. Subbarao, 'State and Education', *Educational India*, February 1935, 255.
23. Moga, 'First Steps', 416.
24. A. Bagshaw, 'The Place of Beauty in Education', *Educational India*, November 1934, 167.
25. Ismail, 'Mass Education', *Educational India*, July 1934, 20.
26. B. Ramchandra Rao, 'The Need for a New Orientation in Education', *Educational India*, September 1935.
27. P. Venkata Rao, 'Pedagogics of Regional Geography', *Educational India*, February 1935, 297–98.
28. N. K. Venkateswaran, 'The Three Kinds of Teaching', *Educational India*, January 1935; N. Kuppuswami Avengar, 'The Declared Aim of Education', *Educational India*, January 1937, 254.

29. NLS: IP/25/PJ.3, almost all DPI Reports 1920s and 1930s. See also H. C. Buck, 'An Interpretation of Physical Education', *Educational India*, July 1934; A. B. Van Doren, eds., *Fourteen Experiments in Rural Education: Some Indian Schools Where New Methods Are Being Tested* (Calcutta: Association Press, 1928), 23, 46–47, 64, 93.
30. Van Doren, *Fourteen Experiments*, 80.
31. M. Venkatarangaiya, 'Mahatma Gandhi's Educational Views', *Educational India*, September 1937.
32. IOR: V/27/860/10 Lillian De Lissa, 'Infant Education', Report of the Imperial Education Conference (1924), 75.
33. D. S. Gordon, 'New Education: What It Means', *Educational India*, March 1935.
34. IOR: R/2/511/185: 'New Psychology and the Curriculum', Theme of New Education Conference, 1929.
35. Krishnayya, 'Some Lessons', 5.
36. Anon., 'Education and Environment', *Educational India*, September 1934, 104; Moga, 'First Steps', 420.
37. S. R. Diddi, 'General Methods of Teaching', *Educational India*, February 1937, 298.
38. C. Swamikannu Paul, 'Intelligence Tests', *Educational India*, January 1935, 251.
39. M. S. Srinivasa Sarma, 'The Roots of Educational Reform: A Study in Pedagogical Handicaps', *Educational India*, December 1936, 215.
40. Article reprinted from *Schoolmaster* on 'Treatment of Backward Children in England', *Educational India*, September 1937, 226; Jal J. Nanavaty, 'The Backward Child', *Educational India*, April 1939, 345.
41. Sarma, 'The Roots of Educational Reform', 218.
42. Mathew Thomson, *Psychological Subjects: Identity, Culture and Health in Twentieth-Century Britain* (Oxford: Oxford University Press, 2006); Sarah Hodges, ed., *Reproductive Health in India: History, Politics, Controversies* (Hyderabad: Orient Longman, 2001).
43. Gordon, 'New Education: What It Means', 327–28; Bagshaw, 'The Place of Beauty in Education', 165; M. R. Sakhare, 'Intelligence', *Educational India*, April 1937, 367.
44. K. T. Paul, 'Introduction', in *Fourteen Experiments in Rural Education: Some Indian Schools Where New Methods Are Being Tested*, ed. Van Doren (Calcutta: Association Press, 1928).
45. Editorial, *Educational India*, July 1934, 22; C. B. Krishna Sastry, 'Vernaculars as Media of Instruction', *Educational India*, July 1934; Bagchi, 'Connected and Entangled Histories'.

46. NLS IP/25/PJ.3 DPI Quinquennium 1927–28 to 1931–32, 96.
47. Editorial on Wardha, *Educational India*, November 1937, 173–75.
48. BL 8355.de.68 1937 All India National Education Conference, *Proceedings* (1937), 4.
49. Simone Holzwarth and Veronica Oelsner, 'Re-defining Work and Education as a Means to National Self-Determination: A Comparative Study of Gandhian India and Peronist Argentina', in *New Perspectives*, ed. Rao.
50. Venkatarangaiya, 'Mahatma Gandhi's Educational Views', 83.
51. Zakir Hussain on Wardha, *Educational India*, January 1939.
52. K. N. Pasupathi, 'The Wardha Scheme', *Educational India*, April 1939, 353; N. Kuppuswami Ayengar, 'Wardha Scheme: Confusion of Thought as to What Is Revolutionary in It and What Is Not', *Educational India*, May and June 1939, 415.
53. C. Swamikannu Paul, 'Educational Experiments: Bholpur Experiment', *Educational India*, August 1934, 70. For a wider discussion of Tagore, see C. Kupfer, 'Isolation or Connection? Tagore's Education towards the Universal as Pedagogical Province', in *Shantiniketan*, ed. Mann; Tanika Sarkar, *Rebels, Wives, Saints: Designing Selves and Nations in Colonial Times* (London: Permanent Black, 2009).
54. IOR: R/2/511/185 World Conference on New Education, 1929.
55. Editorial, *Educational India*, July 1934.
56. Subbarao, 'State and Education', 254.
57. *Educational India*, October 1934, 143.
58. Swamikannu Paul, 'Intelligence Tests', 251.
59. Gordon, 'New Education: What It Means', 328; Nagaraja Rao, 'The Individual Method', 110; IOR: V/27/860/10 Imperial Education Conference, 1923, 80.
60. S. David Malaiperuman, 'Training Our Emotions', *Educational India*, August 1939, 250; Sundar Raj Naidu, 'The New Education', *Educational India*, August 1939.
61. Venkateswaran, 'Three Kinds of Teaching', 257; N. K. Venkateswaran, 'Three Axioms of Education', *Educational India*, June 1935, 420.
62. M. Srinivasa Sarma, 'Attitudes—Their Formation: The Heart of the Educational Process', *Educational India*, October 1935, 129; M. S. Srinivasa Sarma, 'The Modern Trend in Teaching Methods: The Foundations of Educational Reconstruction', *Educational India*, April 1938; Nagaraja Rao, 'The Individual Method', 111; Chenciah, 'Right Training', 211.

63. Venkateswaran, 'Three Axioms of Education', 420.
64. M. Srinivasa Sarma, 'The Test of Educational Efficiency', *Educational India*, 1935, 342.
65. D. Krishnayya, 'Infant Teaching', *Educational India*, October 1935, 218.
66. Sir Jehangir C. Coyajee, 'Some Thoughts on Education', *Educational India*, August 1934; T. Vyas, 'Education and New Psychology', *Educational India*, March 1935, 334; Dr James Kulpathi, 'Character through Emotion-Education', *Educational India*, December 1936, 130.
67. M. Srinivas Sarma, 'Children's Misdeeds: Their Psychology', *Educational India*, February 1937, 286.
68. Sarma, 'Attitudes—Their Formation', 127; Valerie Walkerdine, *Schoolgirl Fictions* (London: Verso, 1990), 203.
69. Sarma, 'Children's Misdeeds', 285.
70. Venkateswaran, 'The Three Kinds of Teaching'; Sarma, 'Children's Misdeeds', 285; NLS: IP/MA.14 *Education in India*, 1936–37, 12.
71. A. S. Venkataraman, 'Corporal Punishment in Schools', *Educational India*, March 1939; Chenciah, 'Right Training', 212–13.
72. Sarma, 'Children's Misdeeds', 288.
73. Sarma, 'Test of Educational Efficiency', 1935, 341.
74. NLS IP/MA.14 *Education in India*, 1936–37, 16–17.
75. Sarma, 'Test of Educational Efficiency', 340; M. S. Srinivasa Sarma, 'Discipline and School Life: Need for Self-Control', *Educational India*, January 1939, 248.
76. This has been written about extensively; see, for example, Hendrick, *Children, Childhood and English Society*.
77. An analysis of the life of K. Satthaianandhan reveals much about the interaction of Indian elites in global networks of educational knowledge transfer, the activities of elites and limitations on ambition and action. See Barnita Bagchi, 'Tracing Two Generations in Twentieth-Century Indian Women's Education through Analysis of Literary Sources: Selected Writings by Padmini Sengupta', *Women's History Review* 29, no. 3 (2020): 465–79.
78. Mrs K. Satthianandhan, 'Our Women's Page: Education for Mothers of Daughters', *Educational India*, October 1936; Anon., 'Education and Environment', 104.
79. K. Sattianadhan, 'Our Women's Page', *Educational India*, February 1935, 35, October 1936, 153; A. Bagshaw, 'Comparative Study of Education', *Educational India*, June 1934, 211; G. S. Krishnayya, 'The Social Approach in Education', *Educational India*, November 1937, 172.

80. Chenciah, 'Right Training'; Pradip Kumar Bose, 'Sons of the Nation: Child Rearing in the New Family', in *Texts of Power: Emerging Disciplines in Colonial Bengal*, ed. Partha Chatterjee (Minneapolis: University of Minnesota Press, 1995); Allender, *Learning Femininity*.
81. Sarma, 'Attitudes—Their Formation', 127. For a wider discussion of colonial masculinities, see Mrinalini Sinha, *Colonial Masculinity: The 'Manly Englishman' and the 'Effeminate Bengali' in the Later Nineteenth Century* (Manchester: Manchester University Press, 2005); Chatterjee, *Nation and Its Fragments*.
82. Sarma, 'The Roots of Educational Reform'; Venkateswaran, 'The Three Kinds of Teaching', 257.
83. Walkerdine, *Schoolgirl Fictions*, 203–10.
84. Moga, 'First Steps', 416.
85. Chenciah, 'Right Training', 211; Gordon, 'New Education: What It Means', 329.
86. P. K. Banerjee, 'Caning in Schools', *Educational India*, April 1936, 371–72; Ismail, 'Mass Education', 20; Krishnayya, 'Some Lessons'; Sidhanta, Editorial, *Educational India*, July 1937, 22; Banerjee, 'The Aim of Education', 129–33.
87. Swamikannu Paul, 'Educational Experiments in India', *Educational India*, July 1934, 13.
88. M. Dapaepe, 'Belgian Images of the Psycho-Pedagogical Potential of the Congolese during the Colonial Era, 1908–1960', *Paedagogica Historica* 45, no. 6 (December 2009).
89. Krishnayya, 'The Social Approach in Education'; N. L. Kitroo and D. N. Dhar, 'Curriculum for Elementary Education', *Educational India*, August 1937.
90. This latter would reflect Srivastava's work on the Doon School in the post-independence era, Sanjay Srivastava, *Constructing Post-Colonial India: National Character and the Doon School* (London: Routledge, 1998).
91. Chatterjee, *Nation and Its Fragments*.
92. Zakir Hussain, 'The Wardha Education Scheme', *Educational India*, January 1938, 248; Satish Chandra M. Joshi, 'The Suggestible Child', *Educational India*, January 1939, 355.
93. M. A. Mazumdar, 'Young India', *Educational India*, April–June 1938, 397.
94. Chenciah, 'Right Training', 212.
95. Editorial, October 1934, 142; Public Opinion, V. S. Srinivasa Satstri, *Educational India*, September 1934, 114; Bagshaw, 'Comparative Study', 211.
96. A. V. Matthew, 'Parental Attitude', *Educational India*, August 1936, 56; M. M. Masilamani, 'Home and School Influences', *Educational Review*, 1915, 427;

Sarma, 'The Roots of Educational Reform', 218; A. S. Venkataraman, 'Talking Down to Children: Quite a Wrong Approach', *Educational India*, July 1934; Masilamani, 'Home and School Influences', 427; Banerjee, 'Caning in Schools'.
97. Masilamani, 'Home and School Influences', 426.
98. P. Levine, ed., *Gender and Empire* (Oxford: Oxford University Press, 2007); Sen, *Colonial Childhoods*.
99. Sarma, 'The Roots of Educational Reform', *Educational India*, December 1936.
100. G. Ramachandra Rao, Review R. A. Lyster, 1936, 'Hygiene of the School', *Educational India*, March 1937; A. S. Venkataraman, 'Do Teachers Require to Be Trained?', *Educational India*, July 1934, 1.
101. G. S. Krishnayya, Review Article, 'What the Home Can Do', *Educational India*, April 1939; Paresh Chandra Sen from *The Teacher's Journal*, *Educational India*, August 1934, 74.
102. Nandini Chandra, *The Classic Popular: Amar Chitra Katha, 1967–2007* (New Delhi: Yoda Press, 2008).
103. Kitroo and Dhar, 'Curriculum for Elementary Education'; G. S. Krishnayya, 'Home Discipline Made Easy', *Educational India*, December 1938.
104. Editor Answers, *Educational India*, December 1934.
105. For wider reading, see Sengupta, 'An Object Lesson'; Seth, *Subject Lessons*; Srivastava, *Constructing Post-Colonial India*.
106. See also Balagopalan, *Inhabiting Childhood*.
107. NLS: IP/25/PJ.3 DPI Quinquennium 1927–28 to 1931–32, 4, 119.
108. Raman, *Getting Girls to School*, 213.
109. BL: ORW.1988.a.1738, International Women's Year Celebration Committee Tamil Nadu, *Some Illustrious Women of India: With Special Reference to Tamilnadu* (Madras: Asian Book, 1975).
110. Raman, *Getting Girls to School*, 109.
111. Geraldine Forbes, *Women in Modern India* (Cambridge: Cambridge University Press, 2006), 57–60; BL: MssEur F221/44 Hartog Evidence.
112. NLS: IP/25/PJ.3 DPI Quinquennium 1927–28 to 1931, 101.
113. BL: MssEur F220/224 KN Brockway, Marjorie Sykes, *Unfinished Pilgrimage: The Story of Some South Indian Schools*.
114. St Christopher's Training School: http://scced.edu.in/about-us/ (accessed 25 August 2015).
115. MssEur F220/224, 2.

116. See Allender, *Learning Femininity*, in particular the section on Isabel Brander. For a more global view, see Joyce Goodman, "'Their Market Value Must be Greater for the Experience They Had Gained"; Secondary School Headmistresses and Empire, 1897–1914 in *Gender, Colonialism and Education: The Politics of Experience*, ed. Joyce Goodman and Jane Martin (London: Woburn Press, 2002), 547–59; Avril Powell, 'Challenging the 3Rs: Kindergarten Experiments in Colonial Madras', in *Memory, Identity and the Colonial Encounter in India: Essays in Honour of Peter Robb*, ed. E. Rashkow, S. Ghosh and U. Chakrabarti (New Delhi: Taylor & Francis, 2017).
117. IOR: Q/13/5/4, Conference with the Education Committee, Calcutta, 16 January 1929, 23; Mahima Manchanda, 'Contested Domains: Reconstructing Education and Religious Identity in Sikh and Arya Samaj Schools in Punjab', in *New Perspectives*, ed. Rao; Allender, *Learning Femininity*.
118. NLS: IP/25/PJ.3 DPI Quinquennium 1932–33 to 1936–37, 114.
119. NLS: IP/25/PJ.3 DPI Quinquennium 1927–28 to 1931–32, 101.
120. NLS: IP/25/PJ.3 DPI Quinquennium 1932–33 to 1936–37, 96.
121. MssEur F220/224, 353.
122. MssEur F220/224, 50–58.
123. NLS: IP/25/PJ.3 DPI Quinquennium 1927–28 to 1931–32; BL: MssEur 221/44.
124. Mathew Thomson, *The Problem of Mental Deficiency: Eugenics, Democracy and Social Policy in Britain, c. 1870–1959* (Oxford: Oxford University Press, 1998).
125. NLS: IP/25/PJ.3: DPI Quinquennium 1927–28 to 1931–32, 97–101.
126. This was referenced at St Christophers. BL: MssEur F220/224, 58; and IOR: V/25/867/1 Corrie Gordon, 'Child Education: Scheme of Work for the First Five Classes' (Madras: Teachers College, Saidapet, 1930), 4.
127. NLS: IP/25/PJ.3: DPI Quinquennium 1932–33 to 1936–37, 114; IP/MA.14, *Education in India*, 1930–31, 52.
128. BL: MssEur F220/224 p37–38, 222/222, 8.
129. Kristine Alexander, 'The Girl Guide Movement and Imperial Internationalism during the 1920s and 1930s', *Journal of the History of Childhood and Youth* 2, no. 1 (2009): 37–63.
130. BL: MssEur F220/224, 40.
131. BL: MssEur F220/224, 39, 47; Mss 220/222, 6; IOR: V/25/867/1 Gordon, 'Child Education', 36.

132. BL: MssEur F220/224, 73.
133. BL: MssEur F220/222, Pamphlet Training for Home Life, 3, 8; MssEur F220/224, 104.
134. IOR: V/25/867/1 Gordon, 'Child Education', 2.
135. See, for example, M. Hancock, 'Home Science and the Nationalization of Domesticity in Colonial India', *Modern Asian Studies* 35, no. 4 (2001): 871–903.
136. IOR: V/25/867/1 Gordon, 'Child Education', 26.
137. BL: MssEur F220/224, 114.
138. Sarangapani, *Constructing School Knowledge*, app. A; Robin Alexander, *Culture and Pedagogy: International Comparisons in Primary Education* (Oxford: Blackwell, 2001), 307.
139. The archives and history are a key part of the publicity for this school, and the claim to originality and longevity contribute to its eligibility for funding and support. See http://www.childrensgardenindia.org (accessed 22 October 2014).
140. The Krishnamurti School was started in 1918 by Annie Besant, and relocated to Mandanapalle, Madras Presidency, in 1931 under the Principal G. V. Subba Rao.
141. Children's Garden School Society (CGS):*'Let None Be Like Another': Report of Children's Garden Society 1937–2007* (Chennai, 2007), 11.
142. CGS: *'Let None Be Like Another'*, 42.
143. For a brief overview see Powell, 'Challenging the 3Rs'.
144. CGS: Extract from 1939–40 school brochure, in *'Let None Be Like Another'*, 22, 25.
145. CGS: *'Let None Be Like Another'*, 24.
146. Lakshmi Viswanathan, *Ellen Sharma's Kindergarten System: Pioneering Pre-primary Education in India* (Chennai: Seawaves Printers, 2007).
147. CGS: Annual Inspection September and October 1944, CGS Annual Report, 1945–46, 23.
148. CGS: Appeal by Directors, 'A School for the Little Ones, Mylapore, Madras', *'Let None Be Like Another'*, 21.
149. CGS: *'Let None Be Like Another'*, 11.
150. M. S. Rajalakshmi, *Under the Banyan Tree*, trans. Miss Choodamani (Chennai, n.d.).
151. Rajalakshmi, *Under the Banyan Tree*.
152. Viswanathan, *Ellen Sharma's Kindergarten System*, 55, 57.

153. Rajalakshmi, *Under the Banyan Tree*.
154. Rajalakshmi, *Under the Banyan Tree*.
155. In this they mirrored other middle-class educators, seen, for example, in Vallgårda, *Imperial Childhoods*.
156. CGS: Annual Report 1938, 13.
157. CGS: Ellen and V. N. Sharma, *Work by Principals 1942–43* (self-published, 27 March 1943), 5.
158. CGS: 'Let None Be Like Another', 9.
159. Interview with retired teacher G. Saradambal 6 July 1999; Viswanathan, *Ellen Sharma's Kindergarten System*, 53.
160. CGS: Ellen Sharma Letter, 8 September 1937, in 'Let None Be Like Another', 3.
161. CGS: 'Let None Be Like Another', 24.
162. Rajalakshmi, *Under the Banyan Tree*.
163. CGS: 1939–40 brochure: 'Let None Be Like Another', 14.
164. Viswanathan, *Ellen Sharma's Kindergarten System*, 42–49.
165. CGS: Annual Report, 1945–46, 20.
166. Viswanathan, *Ellen Sharma's Kindergarten System*, 298.
167. CGS: Annual Report, assumed to be 1943, 7.
168. CGS: V. N. Sharma and E. Sharma, 'An Appeal', Madras, 1937, in 'Let None Be Like Another', 13.
169. CGS: Ellen Sharma, 'The Public and the School', Financial Statement, 1940–41, 7.
170. CGS: Annual Report, 1938, 13.
171. CGS: Ellen Sharma Letter, 8 September 1937, 3.
172. CGS: Leaflet *Information for Parents*, undated, probably mid-1940s.
173. CGS: 'Let None Be Like Another', 32.
174. Viswanathan, *Ellen Sharma's Kindergarten System*, 26.
175. Anne Logan, 'Policy Networks and the Juvenile Court: The Reform of Youth Justice, c. 1905–1950', *Crime and Misdemeanours* 3, no. 2 (2009).
176. Sarangapani, *Constructing School Knowledge*, 257.

Chapter 4

1. MCA: Proceedings 11 March 1930.
2. Sehrawat, *Colonial Medical Care*, xlviii.
3. S. Amrith, 'Food and Welfare in India, c. 1900–1950', *Comparative Studies in Society and History* 50, no. 4 (2008): 1010–35.

4. Hodges, *Contraception, Colonialism and Commerce*, 9; Mark Harrison, *Public Health in British India: Anglo-Indian Preventative Medicine, 1859–1914* (Cambridge: Cambridge University Press, 1994), 228; B. R. Siegel, *Hungry Nation: Food, Famine and the Making of Modern India* (Cambridge: Cambridge University Press, 2018).
5. The relationship between Western and Indian medicine was a complicated one, and the nationalist movement in the 1920s and 1930s both championed Indian medicine and was deeply ambivalent about it. Pratik Chakrabarti, *Western Science in Modern India: Metropolitan Methods, Colonial Practices* (Delhi: Permanent Black, 2004); Arnold, *Science, Technology and Medicine*; Poonam Bala, ed., *Medicine and Colonialism: Historical Perspectives in India and South Africa* (London: Pickering and Chatto, 2014). Of particular note is the argument that Western medicine only really reached 'colonial enclaves' and the big cities, not the whole population. Poonam Bala, *Medicine and Medical Policies in India: Social and Historical Perspectives* (Lanham: Lexington Books, 2007).
6. Amrith, *Decolonising International Health*.
7. Sinha, *Specters of Mother India*.
8. Robert Balogh, 'Feeding Workers in Colonial India 1919–1947', in *Food Culture Studies in India*, ed. S. Malhotra, K. Sharma and S. Dogra (Singapore: Springer, 2021); Sehrawat, introduction to *Colonial Medical Care*.
9. BL: 'School Medical Inspection in India', *Lancet* (16 August 1913), 508.
10. BL: 'School Medical Inspection in India', *Lancet* (23 August 1913), 597.
11. BL: 'Notes from India on Madras Presidency', *Lancet* (19 March 1921).
12. Sujata Mukherjee, 'Disciplining the Body? Health Care for Women and Children in Early Twentieth-Century Bengal', in *Disease and Medicine in India: A Historical Overview*, ed. Deepak Kumar (New Delhi: Tulika, 2001); Barbara Ramusack, 'Women's Hospitals And Midwives in Mysore, 1870–1920', in *India's Princely States: People, Princes and Colonialism*, ed. Waltraud Ernst and Biswamoy Pati (Abingdon: Routledge, 2007).
13. NLS: IP/25/PJ.3 DPI Report 1927–28; IOR: V/24/3705 DPH 1926, 66.
14. NLS: IP/QA.7 Annual Report of the Public Health Commissioner with the Government of India (PHC) 1928, 122.
15. IOR: V/26/845/2 Central Advisory Board of Health, *Medical Inspection of School Children and Teaching of Hygiene in Schools Joint (Jolly) Committee* or *Jolly Report 1941* (New Delhi, 1942), 2. On Poonamalle, see IOR: V/24/3706 DPH, 1938, 1939, 1941; much of this scheme was funded by the Rockefeller Foundation.

16. IOR: V/26/845/2: Jolly Report.
17. MCA: Annual Report of the Health Officer, Corporation of Madras (COM Health Report), 1918, 4; Proceedings 13 December 1922.
18. MCA: Proceedings 20 February 1923, 36–37.
19. NLS: IP/QA.7 PHC 1923, 130.
20. MCA: COM Health Report 1939, 2.
21. For a discussion of colonial governmentality and the creation of the colonial subject, see Sehrawat, *Colonial Medical Care*, xlix–xlvii; Harrison, *Public Health in British India*, 3. See Hodges, *Contraception, Colonialism and Commerce*, 26–27, on the impact of dyarchy.
22. Bernard Harris, *The Health of the Schoolchild: A History of School Medical Service in England and Wales* (Buckingham: Oxford University Press, 1995), 61; Hendrick, *Children, Childhood and English Society*; Donzelot, *The Policing of Families*; R. Cooter, *In the Name of the Child* (Abingdon: Routledge, 2013).
23. MCA: Proceedings 11 April 1933, 4, 14; 23 September 1924, 259.
24. MCA: COM Health Report 1939, 32.
25. NLS: IP/26/HB.3 COM Health Report 1919, 5.
26. MCA: COM Health Report 1926, 87.
27. IOR: V/24/3705 DPH 1927, 36.
28. Topdar, 'The Corporeal Empire', 2.
29. Nagendranath Gangulee, *Health and Nutrition in India* (London: Faber & Faber, 1939), 33.
30. Siegel, *Hungry Nation*, 4.
31. IOR: V/24/3705 DPH 1927, 44.
32. IOR: V/24/3705 DPH 1927, 36.
33. Newman quoted in IOR: V/26/845/2: Jolly Report, 26.
34. NLS: IP/26/HB.3 COM Health Report 1919, 4.
35. IOR: V/26/845/2: Jolly Report, 7.
36. MCA: Proceedings 13 December 1935, 12–1396.
37. MCA: Proceedings 13 December 1935, 12–13.
38. NLS: IP/26/HB.3 COM Health Report 1919, 4.
39. NLS: IP/26/HB.3 COM Health Report 1927, 27.
40. MCA: COM Health Report 1926.
41. MCA: Proceedings 28 March 1924, 493; 28 March 1939, 35–36; NLS: IP/25/PJ.3 DPI Report 1929–30, 34.
42. MCA: COM Health Report 1926, 99.
43. MCA: COM Health Report 1926, 91.
44. MCA: COM Health Report 1937.

45. IOR: V/26/845/2: Jolly Report, 14.
46. MCA: Proceedings 25 November 1925, 352; IOR: V/24/3705 DPH 1930, 36; 1931; 1938, 36.
47. MCA: Proceedings 1 December 1936, 22–23.
48. NLS: IP/QA.7 PHC 1925, 178; IP/26/HB.3 COM Health Report 1920, 5–6.
49. NLS: IP/26/HB.3 COM Health Report 1921, 4.
50. MCA: Proceedings 2 February 1937; 30 March 1938, 9. See also V. R. Muraleedharan, 'Rural Health Care in Madras Presidency: 1919–39', *Indian Economic and Social History Review* 24, no. 3 (1987): 31–33.
51. MCA: Proceedings 1 December 1936, 23.
52. MCA: Proceedings 12 September 1939, 32.
53. MCA: Proceedings 18 November 1939, 15, 30; 29 November 1939.
54. NLS: IP/26/HB.3 COM Health Report 1921, 3.
55. Donzelot, *The Policing of Families*; Garland, *Punishment and Welfare*.
56. MCA: COM Health Report 1936–37, 23.
57. MCA: COM Health Report 1937, 33.
58. IOR: V/24/3705 DPH 1927, 41.
59. MCA: Proceedings 29 March 1933, 13; 19 November 1937, 26–28; Sehrawat, *Colonial Medical Care*.
60. IOR: V/24/3705 DPH 1929, 34; MCA: Proceedings 23 September 1924, 257.
61. Harrison, *Public Health in British India*; Amrith, 'Food and Welfare in India'; David Arnold, 'The Medicalisation of Poverty in Colonial India', *Historical Research* 85, no. 229 (August 2012).
62. TNSAL: MLC Debates 31 March 1927, 1414. Dr Muthulakshmi Reddi was the first Indian woman to train at a medical college in India (1907) and on graduation in 1912 became the first woman house surgeon in the Government Maternity and Ophthalmic Hospital. As a social reformer, she was involved in the Women's Indian Association, was nominated to the Madras Legislative Assembly as a female representative in 1927 and was elected to deputy president where she continued to campaign for women and children's rights.
63. For a history of paediatrics as a discipline, see Elizabeth M. R. Lomax, *Small and Special: The Development of Hospitals for Children in Victorian Britain* (London: Wellcome Institute for the History of Medicine, 1996); C. P. Bansal and Sailesh Gupta, 'The Past Half Century of Indian Academy of Pediatrics (IAP)', *Indian Paediatrics* 50, no. 1 (2012): 39–48.
64. TNSAL: MLC Debates 31 March 1927, 1415.
65. Hodges, *Contraception, Colonialism and Commerce*, 10.

66. Sen, *Colonial Childhoods*.
67. TNSAL: MLC Debates 31 March 1927, 1417.
68. TNSAL: MLC Debates 31 March 1927, 1419.
69. R. Jeffery, *The Politics of Health in India* (Berkeley: University of California Press, 1988).
70. David C. Sloane, 'A (Better) Home Away from Home: The Emergence of Children's Hospitals in an Age of Women's Reform', *Designing Modern Childhoods: History, Space, and the Material Culture of Children* (New Brunswick: Rutgers University Press, 2008), 42–60.
71. Bala, *Medicine and Colonialism*; Sehrawat, *Colonial Medical Care*, xlviii–xlix; Hodges, *Contraception, Colonialism and Commerce*, 1.
72. TNSAL: MLC Debates 31 March 1927, 1415.
73. TNSAL: MLC Debates 31 March 1927, 1423–24.
74. TNSAL: MLC Debates 31 March 1927, 1424.
75. MCA: Proceedings 29 April 1922; Jeffery, *Politics of Health*; Arnold, 'Medicalisation of Poverty'; Harrison, *Public Health in British India*.
76. NLS: IP/QA.7 PHC, 178.
77. NLS: IP/QA.7 PHC 1926, 66.
78. NLS: IP/QA.7 PHC 1926.
79. NLS: IP/QA.7 PHC 1938, 26; 1939, 33; John Farley, *To Cast Out Disease: A History of the International Health Division of the Rockefeller Foundations* (Oxford: Oxford University Press, 2004).
80. See also V. R. Muraleedharan, 'Diet, Disease and Death in Colonial South India', *Economic and Political Weekly* 29, no. 1 (January 1994): 55–63; D. Arnold, 'Discovery of Malnutrition and Diet in Colonial India', *Indian Economic and Social Review* 31, no. 1 (1994): 1–26; Josep L. Barona, 'Nutrition and Health: The International Context during the Interwar Crisis', *Social History of Medicine* 21, no. 1 (2008): 87–105.
81. IOR: V/26/845/2: Jolly Report, 14.
82. Robert Wright, 'Keratomalacia in Southern India', *British Journal of Ophthalmology* 6, no. 4 (1922): 164, 175; MCA: Proceedings 11 February 1930; 26 March 1930.
83. Arnold, 'The Medicalisation of Poverty'.
84. Catriona Ellis, '"If You Cannot Feed the Body of a Child You Cannot Feed the Brain": Education and Nutrition in Late Colonial Madras', *South Asia: Journal of South Asian Studies* 44, no. 1 (February 2021), DOI: 10.1080/00856401.2021.1862497.

85. MCA: Proceedings 18 November 1939.
86. IOR: V/24/3705 DPH 1922, 34.
87. MCA: Proceedings 8 March 1938, 28.
88. James Vernon, *Hunger: A Modern History* (Cambridge, MA: Belknap Press, 2007), 160.
89. MCA: COM Health Report 1926, 98.
90. Cooter, *In the Name of the Child*; Hendrick, *Children, Childhood and English Society*.
91. NLS: IP/26/HB.3 COM Health Report, 1920, 15; Report of Child Welfare Scheme, 1919–1920.
92. MCA: Proceedings 29 June 1923; 13 November 1931; 19 September 1939, 8.
93. TNSA: GO244 LE 17 February 1927; GO1519 LE 1 November 1923; GO1189 LE 18 July 1924.
94. MCA: Proceedings 28 March 1924, 477.
95. MCA: Joint Conference Tax & Finance, Education Committees 11 March 1925, Proceedings 28 March 1924, 477; 25 March 1925; 30 April 1925; 24 August 1926. IOR: V/27/860/11 GOI Memorandum on the Progress of Education in British India 1916 and 1926 (1928).
96. MCA: Proceedings 3 May 1935, 4.
97. MCA: Proceedings 4 January 1938, 5; COM Health Report, 1937, 38.
98. MCA: Proceedings 1939, 35.
99. MCA: Proceedings 9 February 1943; 15 April 1943; 24 November 1943, 2.
100. Harris, *Health of the Schoolchild*, 6.
101. Christine Piper, 'Moral Campaigns for Children's Welfare in the Nineteenth Century', in *Child Welfare and Social Policy: An Essential Reader*, ed. Harry Hendrick (Bristol: Policy Press, 2005), 20.
102. A. R. Ruis, '"The Penny Lunch Has Spread Faster than the Measles": Children's Health and the Debate over School Lunches in New York City, 1908–1930', *History of Education Quarterly* 55, no. 2 (May 2015): 195.
103. Vernon, *Hunger*, 160.
104. Barona, 'Nutrition and Health', 88.
105. Harris, *Health of the Schoolchild*, 25.
106. S. Williamson, *The Vaccination Controversy: The Rise, Reign, and Fall of Compulsory Vaccination for Smallpox* (Liverpool: Liverpool University Press, 2007).
107. TNSA: GO1508 LE 1 August 1927.

108. TNSA: GO748 LE 12 May 1924; GO106 LE 25 January 1926.
109. TNSA: GO748 LE 12 May 1924.
110. TNSA: GO748 LE 12 May 1924.
111. TNSA: MLC Debate 18 March 1927 in GO1508 LE 1 August 1927; GO1899 LE 3 October 1927.
112. TNSA: LE 7 November 1927, Question 763; GO106 LE 25 January 1926; GO4600 LE 16 October 1926; MCA: Proceedings 16 March 1927.
113. TNSA: LE 7 November 1927, Question 763.
114. TNSA: GO1899 LE 2 November 1931; GO106 LE 25 January 1926; LE 7 November 1927, Question 763, including Draft Answer 29 August 1927. MCA: Proceedings 16 March 1927, 1 January 1932.
115. IOR: Madras Public Health Act 1939, Act 4 of 1944.
116. MCA: Proceedings 16 March 1927, 39.
117. MCA: Proceedings 30 March 1927, 40.
118. MCA: Proceedings 29 April 1927.
119. MCA: Proceedings 26 March 1928; 25 February 1931, 44–46. See also L. Mahood, *Policing Gender, Class and Family: Britain 1850–1940* (London: UCL Press, 1995); Garland, *Punishment and Welfare*.
120. MCA: Proceedings 31 March 1937, 91.
121. MCA: Proceedings 29 November 1939, 10; 6 October 1938; 23 April 1939, 42; 29 March 1930.
122. Cooter, *In the Name of the Child*.
123. IOR: L/PJ/6/1796, file 1677.
124. IOR: L/PJ/6/1796, file 1677.
125. MCA: Proceedings 22 September 1931, 43.
126. MCA: Proceedings 22 September 1931, 47.
127. MCA: Proceedings 19 September 1939, 19; Hendrick, *Children, Childhood and English Society*.
128. MCA: Proceedings 28 March 1939, 41; Amrith, 'Food and Welfare in India', 1011.
129. MCA: Proceedings 22 September 1931, 50.
130. MCA: Proceedings 22 September 1931, 49.
131. IOR: L/PJ/6/1796, file 1677.
132. Viswanath, 'Rethinking Caste and Class'.
133. MCA: Proceedings 28 March 1939, 39.
134. Amrith, 'Food and Welfare in India', 1024.
135. MCA: Proceedings 26 March 1930.

136. MCA: Proceedings 11 March 1930; 15 July 1930; 26 March 1930.
137. MCA: Proceedings 8 May 1926, 72.
138. MCA: Proceedings 24 August 1926, 41.
139. MCA: Proceedings 21 January 1927, 34; 28 March 1927, 36; 25 February 1931, 3; 18 March 1935, 17.
140. MCA: Proceedings 18 March 1935, 20.
141. MCA: Proceedings 17 March 1938, 14.
142. TNSA: GO244 LE 17 February 1927; 17 January 1927; MCA: Proceedings 22 September 1931, 42–44; 25 February 1931, 46; 9 September 39, 12, 29; Gangulee, *Health and Nutrition in India*.
143. MCA: COM Health Report 1926, 82.
144. BL: MssEur E221/44, Hartog Evidence: Slater.
145. IOR: V/26/845/2: Jolly Report, 7; MCA: Proceedings 11 March 1930; 26 March 1930; 1 December 1936, 26; 30 March 1938, 4; TNSA: GO1508 LE 1 August 1927, Debate 18 March 1927; Gangulee, *Health and Nutrition in India*, 7.
146. James H. Mills and Satadru Sen, *Confronting the Body: The Politics of Physicality in Colonial and Post-Colonial India* (London: Anthem, 2004); Topdar, 'Corporeal Empire'.
147. MCA: Proceedings 28 March 1939, 38.
148. Vernon, *Hunger*, 161.
149. MCA: Proceedings 30 March 1938, 2–7; W. R. Aykroyd, *Notes on Food and Nutrition Policy in India* (New Delhi: GOI, 1944).
150. MCA: Proceedings 26 March 1930.
151. MCA: Proceedings 19 September 1939, 9, 14; 29 September 1931, 48; 22 September 1931.
152. MCA: Proceedings 15 July 1930; 22 September 1931, 42–48; 29 January 1943; 3 December 1935; 17 December 1935; 21 March 1938, 17; 19 September 1939, 11.
153. MCA: Proceedings 28 March 1939, 41.
154. MCA: Proceedings 7 March 1939; 28 March 1939.
155. Gangulee, *Health and Nutrition in India*, 80, 213. A longer discussion of Aykroyd's research can be found in Ellis, 'If You Cannot Feed the Body of a Child'.
156. Barona, 'Nutrition and Health'.
157. MCA: Proceedings 28 March 1939; 14 March 1939, 12; 28 March 1939, 38.
158. MCA: Proceedings 28 March 1939, 40.

159. For a discussion of ethical experimentation in the West and the use of vulnerable groups such as children, see W. Bynum, 'Reflections on The History of Human Experimentation', in *The Use of Human Beings in Research: With Special Reference to Clinical Trials*, ed. F. Spicker, I. Alon, A. De Vries and H. Tristram Engelhardt Jr (Dordrecht: Kluwer Academic Publications, 1988), 29–46; or J. Goodman, A. McElligot and L. Marks, *Useful Bodies: Humans in the Service of Medical Science in the Twentieth Century* (Baltimore: John Hopkins University Press, 2003).
160. MCA: Proceedings, 43–44.
161. MCA: Proceedings 15 July 1930.
162. MCA: Proceedings 16 July 1930.
163. MCA: Proceedings 26 March 1930; 15 July 1930.
164. Chakrabarti, *Western Science in Modern India*.
165. MCA: Proceedings 15 July 1930.
166. MCA: Proceedings 15 July 1930; 28 March 1939, 40.
167. MCA: Proceedings 28 March 1939, 40–41.
168. MCA: Proceedings 15 July 30; 14 March 1939.
169. MCA: Proceedings 15 July 1930; 14 March 1939; 28 March 1939, 42.
170. MCA: Proceedings 15 July 1930, 17; 19 September 1939, 7, 12, 16. See discussion in Muraleedharan, 'Diet, Disease and Death', 60.
171. MCA: Proceedings 15 July 1930; 19 September 1939.
172. MCA: Proceedings 15 July 1930.
173. MCA: Proceedings 15 July 1930. In particular, Dr Syed Niyamatullah and Mrs Hannen Angelo.
174. MCA: Proceedings 15 July 1930; Hendrick, *Children, Childhood and English Society*.
175. Vernon, *Hunger*, 180.
176. MCA: Proceedings 14 March 1932; 18 May 1932; 29 January 1943; 19 January 1943; 10 August 1942; 31 August 1942; 12 November 1942, 3–4.
177. MCA: COM Health Report 1926, 62.
178. MCA: COM Health Report 1937, 4; 1938, 41; 1939.
179. MCA: 'Note on Infant Mortality and on the Work Done under the Corporation Child-Welfare Scheme for One Year, Ending Sept 1915', COM Health Report 1915–16.
180. MCA: Proceedings 15 July 1930.
181. MCA: Proceedings 19 September 1939, 7.
182. IOR: V/26/845/2: Jolly Report, 6–7, 17.

Chapter 5

1. Laurent Fourchard, 'Lagos and the Invention of Juvenile Delinquency in Nigeria, 1920–60', *Journal of African History* 47 (November 2006): 115–37; R. S. Rastogi, 'Prevention and Treatment of Juvenile Delinquency in India', *Canadian Journal of Corrections* 2 (1959); Gautam Chatterjee, *Child Criminals and the Raj: Reformation in British Jails* (New Delhi: Askhaya Publications, 1995).
2. Stephanie Olsen, 'Adolescent Empire: Moral Dangers for Boys in Britain and India, c. 1880–1914', in *Juvenile Delinquency and the Limits of Western Influence, 1850–2000*, ed. Heather Ellis (Basingstoke: Palgrave Macmillan, 2014), 36.
3. Anand Yang, *Crime and Criminality in British India* (Tucson, Arizona: University of Arizona, 1985); Anand Yang, 'Disciplining "Natives": Prisons and Prisoners in Early Nineteenth Century India', *South Asia* 10, no. 2 (1987): 29–45; David Arnold, 'The Colonial Prison: Power, Knowledge and Penology in Nineteenth-Century India', in *Subaltern Studies 8*, ed. David Arnold and David Hardiman (Delhi: Oxford University Press, 1994).
4. NLS: IP/25/PJ.4 *Report of the Chingleput Reformatory School*, Madras 1891–92, 1.
5. NLS IP/25/PJ.4 *Report of the Chingleput Reformatory School*, Madras 1898, 11.
6. Sen, *Colonial Childhoods*; Nandy, *The Intimate Enemy*; Olsen, 'Adolescent Empire'. A good example would be Sir Louis Stuart, Indian Empire Society, former chief judge of Oudh in Lt-Col F. A. Barker, *Modern Prison System of India: A Report to the Department* (London: Macmillan & Co., 1944), appendix.
7. Sen, *Colonial Childhoods*, 10.
8. Garland, *Punishment and Welfare*; Bailey, *Delinquency and Citizenship*; Pamela Cox and Heather Shore, *Becoming Delinquent: British and European Youth 1650–1950* (Dartmouth: Ashgate, 2002).
9. Herbert Lou, *Juvenile Courts in the US* (Chapel Hill: University of North Carolina, 1927), 5.
10. Baxi, 'Introduction', 10.
11. IOR: *Report of the Indian Jails Committee 1919–20* (House of Commons Records, 1921), 29, 31, 33, 201, 35, (henceforth IJC).
12. Clarke Hall, *The State and the Child*, in IOR: IJC, 196.

13. IOR: IJC, 193.
14. IOR: IJC, 197.
15. IOR: IJC, 196–97.
16. Mahood, *Policing Gender, Class and Family*, 12.
17. IOR: IJC, 142, 179; Sen, *Colonial Childhoods*, 55.
18. IOR: IJC, 204.
19. Sen, *Colonial Childhoods*, 38–39.
20. IOR: IJC, 193, 196.
21. IOR: L/PARL/2/407 A–Madras, IJC Evidence, 309.
22. IOR: IJC, 198.
23. IOR: L/PARL/2/407 A–Madras, IJC Evidence, 170; Sen, 'Orphaned Colony', 44, 463–88; Vallgårda, 'Between Consent and Coercion'.
24. Sarkar, *Hindu Wife, Hindu Nation*; Sinha, *Spectres of Mother India*.
25. Saint Nihal Singh, *Making Bad Children Good: A Plea for an Indian Juvenile Court* (Madras: Mount Road, 1910).
26. Cumming, foreword to *English Borstal System: A Study in the Treatment of Young Offenders*, by S. Barman (London: P. S. King & Son, 1934), 16, 35, 58, 76, 406.
27. Olsen, 'Adolescent Empire'; Sen, *Colonial Childhoods*, 11.
28. Pande, 'Coming of Age', 222.
29. Pande, 'Coming of Age'.
30. Chris Leonards, 'Border Crossings: Care and the Criminal Child' in *Becoming Delinquent*, ed. Cox and Shore; Marshall, 'The Construction of Children as an Object of International Relations', 104; Dominque Marshall, 'Children's Rights in Imperial Political Cultures: Missionary and Humanitarian Contributions to the Conference of the African Child of 1931', *International Journal of Children's Rights* 12 (2004): 273–318; Mahood, *Feminism and Voluntary Action*, 199.
31. NLS: LN.IV.2 (30), League of Nations: *Institutions for Erring and Delinquent Minors, Child Welfare Committee* (Geneva, 1934); Tambe, 'The State as Surrogate Parent'.
32. Clifford Manshardt, *Delinquent Child in India* (Bombay: D. B. Taraporevala & Sons, 1939); also, *Indian Journal of Social Work*, https://www.tiss.edu/view/6/research/the-indian-journal-of-social-work/ (accessed 11 June 2020).
33. Manshardt, *Delinquent Child*, 13.
34. Manshardt, *Delinquent Child*, 17, 38, 57.

35. Manshardt, *Delinquent Child*, 91.
36. Manshardt, *Delinquent Child*, 110, 115, 123, 173, 213, 230.
37. Manshardt, *Delinquent Child*, 268.
38. Manshardt, *Delinquent Child*, 100–05, 255.
39. In Britain: Cox and Shore, *Becoming Delinquent*, 187. In India: Newbigin, *The Hindu Family*.
40. Manshardt, *Delinquent Child*, 262.
41. Manshardt, *Delinquent Child*, 293–95.
42. Olga Nieuwenhuys, 'Keeping Asking: Why Childhood? Why Children? Why Global?', *Childhood* 17, no. 3 (2010); Balagopalan, *Inhabiting Childhood*.
43. IOR: L/PJ/6/1686, file 4040.
44. IOR: L/PJ/6/1686, file 4040, 4; Madras Borstal Schools Act, 1926 IOR/L/PJ/6/1902, file 1134: March 1925–September 1926.
45. Other Children Acts followed: Bengal, 1922; Bombay, 1924; Central Provinces, 1928; Pondicherry, 1928; Delhi, 1941; Mysore, 1943; Travancore, 1945; Cochin, 1946; and East Punjab, 1949.
46. TNSAL: MLC Debates 14 March 1918, 451, 455.
47. TNSAL: MLC Debates 14 March 1918, 453–54.
48. TNSAL: MLC Debates 14 March 1918, 452, 455.
49. TNSAL: MLC Debates 14 March 1918, 455.
50. TNSAL: MLC Debates 14 March 1918, 453.
51. TNSAL: MLC Debates 15 March 1920, 600; MLC Debates 19 November 1919.
52. TNSAL: MLC Debates 15 March 1920, 594, 600.
53. TNSAL: MLC Debates 15 March 1920, 591.
54. TNSAL: MLC Debates 15 March 1920, 590.
55. TNSAL: MLC Debates 14 March 1918, 451.
56. Arnold discusses this in more detail in David Arnold, 'Vagrant India: Famine, Poverty, and Welfare under Colonial Rule', in *Cast Out: Vagrancy and Homelessness in Global and Historical Perspective*, A. L. Beier and Paul Ocobock (Athens: Ohio University Press, 2008), 117–39.
57. TNSAL: MLC Debates 15 March 1920, 600.
58. TNSAL: MLC Debates 15 March 1920, 600; 14 March 1918, 451, 457, 458.
59. TNSA: GO2245 Home 12 September 1936 Chief Inspector of Certified Schools 14 May 1936.
60. TNSA: GO1427 LE 15 July 1935.
61. TNSA: GO2610 Home 12 July 1937.

62. TNSAL: MLC Debates 14 March 1918, 451.
63. Newbigin, *The Hindu Family*; Sreenivas, *Wives, Widows, Concubines*.
64. TNSAL: MLC Debates 15 March 1920, 599.
65. TNSAL: MLC Debates 15 March 1920, 598; Raman, *Getting Girls to School*.
66. Mahood, *Policing Gender, Class and Family*; Hinchy, *Governing Gender and Sexuality*.
67. Hodges, *Contraception, Colonialism and Commerce*.
68. Pande, 'Coming of Age'.
69. TNSAL: MLC Debates 15 March 1920, 593.
70. TNSAL: MLC Debates 15 March 1920, 601.
71. TNSAL: MLC Debates 27 January 1932, 232.
72. TNSAL: MLC Debates 27 January 1932, 232; GO902 28 June 1932 LE Annual Report for 1931.
73. TNSAL: MLC Debates 27 January 1932, 233.
74. TNSAL: MLC Debates 27 January 1932, 234.
75. TNSAL: MLC Debates 3 September 1936, 761.
76. TNSA: GO2245 Home 12 September 1936 T. G. Rutherford 7 July 1936.
77. TNSA: GO2160 Home 6 September 1943.
78. TNSA: GO2160 Home 6 September 1943.
79. TNSA: GO2160 Home 6 September 1943 Committee of Visitors Bellary 28 December 1942.
80. TNSA: GO2160 Home 6 September 1943 Chief Inspector of Certified Schools 13 January 43.
81. TNSA: GO2160 Home 6 September 1943 District Superintendent of Railway Police 17 July 1943 (italics mine).
82. TNSA: GO2160 Home 6 September 1943 Home Department 29 April 1943.
83. TNSA: GO5113 Home 26 April 1943.
84. TNSA: GO397 LE 16 March 1926.
85. TNSA: GO1376 LE 12 July 1927 MCA Report 1925; Alborn, 'Age and Empire'.
86. Dirks, *Castes of Mind*; Inden, *Imagining India*; Manshardt, *Delinquent Child*, 27.
87. TNSA: GO397 LE 16 March 1926.
88. NLS: IP/25/PJ.3 DPI 1919–20.
89. NLS: IP/25/PJ.3 DPI 1939–40.
90. TNSA: GO902 LE 28 June 1932–31; GO1354 Home 14 July 1936–35; GO1443 Home 26 June 1943–42.

91. TNSA: GO123 LE 28 January 1930, Letter 21 October 25.
92. TNSA: GO1354 Home 14 July 1936; GO1443 Home 26 June 1943.
93. Sen, *Colonial Childhoods*; Balagopalan, *Inhabiting Childhood*.
94. Kumari, *Juvenile Justice System in India*, 182; Weiner, *The Child and the State*; Kannabiran and Singh, *Challenging the Rule(s) of Law*, 182.
95. TNSA: GO2121 LE 11 December 1925, Question: 13 August 1925.
96. TNSA: GO1621 LE 16 September 1925; GO898 LE 17 May 1926.
97. NLS: IP/25/PJ.3 DPI 1922–23, 1923–24.
98. NLS: IP/25/PJ.3 DPI 1936–37, 1932–33 to 1936–37, 127.
99. TNSA: GO397 LE 16 March 1926.
100. BL: I.S.410/30 Bureau of Education, 'The Neglected and Delinquent Children and Juvenile Offenders in the States of Indian Union, 1949' (GOI Press, 1952), 16; IOR: L/PJ/6/1902, file 1134, The Madras Borstal Schools Act, 1926.
101. NLS: IP/25/PJ.3 DPI 1921–12, 1916–17 to 1921–22, 54.
102. NLS: IP/25/PJ.3 DPI 1922–23, 22.
103. TNSA: GO1234 LE 15 July 1925 Letter 8 November 1924; NLS: IP/25/PJ.3 DPI 1923–24.
104. TNSA: GO1234 LE 15 July 1925 Letter 8 November 1924 A. R. Knapp 29 January 1925.
105. TNSA: GO1234 LE 15 July 1925 V. T. Krishnamachariyar 8 November 1924.
106. TNSA: GO1234 LE 15 July 1925 A. P. Patro 29 January 1925.
107. NLS: IP/25/PJ.3 DPI1926–27, 1921–22 to 1916–27, 170.
108. NLS: IP/25/PJ.3 DPI 1919–20, 1939–40.
109. TNSA: GO902 LE 28 June 1932 MCA Report 1931.
110. Bailey, *Delinquency and Citizenship*; Mahood, *Policing Gender, Class and Family*.
111. TNSA: GO1376 LE 12 July 1927 MCA Report 1926, 4.
112. TNSA: GO1376 LE 12 July 1927 MCA Report 1926, 4.
113. IJC, 310, Littlehailes evidence.
114. Chatterjee, *Child Criminals and the Raj*, 21.
115. Nicola Sheldon, 'The Musical Careers of the Poor: The Role of Music as a Vocational Training for Boys in British Care Institutions 1870–1918', *History of Education* 38, no. 6 (2009): 747–59.
116. Trevor Herbert and Margaret Sarkissian, 'Victorian Bands and Their Dissemination in the Colonies', *Popular Music* 16, no. 2 (1997); Trevor Herbert, 'God's Minstrels', ch. 5 in *The British Brass Band: A Musical and Social History* (Oxford: Oxford University Press, 2000).

117. NLS: IP/25/PJ.3 DPI 1931–32, 1927–28 to 1931–32.
118. TNSA: GO1282 LE 24 June 1935 MCA Report 1934.
119. NLS: IP/25/PJ.3 DPI 1909; Rastogi, 'Prevention and Treatment of Juvenile Delinquency in India', 326.
120. For further reading on music and rehabilitation, see C. Ellis, 'The Trumpet and the Drum: Music and Reclaiming the Delinquent Child', in *Childhoods and Youth in India: Engagements with Modernity*, ed. Anandini Dar and Divya Kannan (New Delhi: Routledge, forthcoming).
121. TNSA: GO902 LE 28 June 1932 MCA Report 1931, 34.
122. Sen, *Colonial Childhoods*, 84; see also Balagopalan, *Inhabiting Childhood*.
123. Satadru Sen, 'Schools, Athletes and Confrontation: The Student Body in Colonial India', in *Confronting the Body*, ed. Mills and Sen; Pamela Cox, *Gender, Justice and Welfare* (Basingstoke: Palgrave Macmillan, 2003), 66; Abigail Wills, 'Delinquency, Masculinity and Citizenship in England 1950–1970', *Past and Present* 187 (May 2005).
124. IOR: L/PARL/2/407 A–Madras, IJC Evidence, 169.
125. NLS: IP/25/PJ.3 DPI 1921–22, 1916–17 to 1921–22, 1931–32 Mayhew Shield; TNSA: GO1376 LE 12 July 1927 MCA Report 1926.
126. TNSA: GO1032 LE 3 June 1926 MCA Report 1925.
127. IOR: L/PJ/6/1961, file 2014, 22.
128. TNSA: GO1354 Home 14 July 1936; GO1282 LE 24 June 1935 MCA Report 1934. Long been a metropolitan concerns, Mahood, *Policing Gender, Class and Family*, 123–36.
129. TNSA: GO1282 LE 24 June 1935 MCA Report 1934.
130. TNSA: GO2556 Home 12 June 1940 MCA Report 1939.
131. Mahood, *Policing Gender, Class and Family*; Cox and Shore, *Becoming Delinquent*.
132. TNSA GO1234 LE 15 July 1925; IOR: V/24/2278 MCA Report 1936; IOR: L/PARL/2/407-A, 142.
133. Sen, *Colonial Childhoods*, ch. 2.
134. IOR: L/PARL/2/407 A Evidence 4 January 1920, 104–05; Pande, 'Coming of Age'; Louise Jackson, *Child Sexual Abuse in Victorian England* (London; New York: Routledge, 2000); Sen, *Colonial Childhoods*, 68.
135. TNSA: GO801 LE 9 June 1923.
136. TNSA: GO801 LE 9 June 1923.
137. TNSA: GO1032 LE 3 June 1926 MCA Report 1925.
138. TNSA: GO902 LE 28 June 1932 MCA Report 1931, Letter 13 May 1932.

139. TNSA: GO902 LE 28 June 1932 MCA Report 1931.
140. TNSA: GO1282 LE 24 June 1935 MCA Report 1934.
141. James C. Scott, *Domination and the Arts of Resistance: Hidden Transcripts* (Yale: Yale University Press, 1990).
142. For extensive discussion of resistance by children in the reformatory, see Jenneke Christiaens, 'Testing the Limits: Redefining Resistance in a Belgian Boys' Prison, 1895–1905', in *Becoming Delinquent*, ed. Cox and Shore.

Chapter 6

1. Donzelot, *The Policing of Families*, 55; Bailey, *Delinquency and Citizenship*; Garland, *Punishment and Welfare*.
2. This often spilled over into social questions, such as the age of consent controversies discussed in Chapter 7, but these controversies were political in nature.
3. In the north Indian context, Watt considers the emergence of these ideas and their longer heritage in religious philanthropy. Carey Watt, *Serving the Nation: Cultures of Service, Association and Citizenship* (Oxford: Oxford University Press, 2005); Balagopalan, *Inhabiting Childhood*, 84.
4. Garland, *Punishment and Welfare*, 206; Ellis, *Juvenile Delinquency*. The 'introduction' questions the extent to which this reflects the constructed nature of 'the state' itself.
5. This is the traditional interpretation; see Sen, *Colonial Childhoods*, 49; but also Donzelot, *Policing of Families*, 163.
6. Logan, 'Policy Networks and the Juvenile Court'.
7. For further detail on the history of juvenile justice in India and the difference between a welfare, due process or participatory model, see Kumari, *The Juvenile Justice System in India*.
8. Balakrishnan, *Growing Up and Away*, 87.
9. Balakrishnan, *Growing Up and Away*, 209.
10. MSPC website: www.mspcchildrenhome.com (accessed 16 September 2022). Evidence of the society's activities comes from its correspondence with the government, their own archives being untraceable.
11. TNSA: GO673 LE 2 June 1922.
12. TNSA: GO673 LE 2 June 1922 MSPC Letter 24 March 1922.
13. TNSA: GO638 LE 8 April 1930 MSPC Letter 16 May 1929.
14. TNSA: GO673 LE 2 June 1922 MSPC Letter 27 May 1920. Dr Varadappa Naidu was a medical practitioner who funded the MSPC Orphanage. His

family continue to be significant contributors. See Raman, *Getting Girls to School*, 210.
15. TNSA: GO1684 LE 1 December 1923 DPI Budget 21 November 1922.
16. TNSA: GO433 LE 30 March 1925 Education Department 5 February 1925.
17. TNSA: GO2080 LE 5 November 1926.
18. TNSA: GO433 LE 30 March 1925 MSPC 27 February 1925.
19. TNSA: GO638 LE 8 April 1930 MSPC Report 16 May 1929.
20. TNSA: GO638 LE 8 April 1930 Education 27 May 1929.
21. TNSA: GO752 LE 28 April 1930 MSPC Letter 29 March 1930.
22. TNSA: GO227 Home 22 April 1936 Memo 22 April 1936.
23. TNSA: GO735 LE 11 April 1935.
24. TNSA: GO433 LE 30 March 1925 Mrs Stanford Letter 4 December 1924.
25. TNSA: GO433 LE 30 March 1925 WIA Letter 5 February 1925.
26. TNSA: GO433 LE 30 March 1925 Annie Besant Letter 24 October 1924.
27. Barbara Ramusack, 'Cultural Missionaries, Maternal Imperialists, Feminist Allies: British Women Activists in India 1865–1945', *Women's Studies International Forum* 13, no. 4 (1990): 309–21.
28. TNSA: GO433 LE 30 March 1925 Invitation 6 March 1925.
29. TNSA: GO2080 LE 5 November 1926 MSPC Memo 5 February 1925; GO 433 LE 30 March 1925 (italics mine).
30. TNSA: GO433 LE 30 March 1925 Letter Education Department 5 February 1925.
31. TNSA: GO946 LE 14 October 1926 Education Note 23 October 1926.
32. TNSA: GO433 LE 30 March 1925 Inspector-General of Prisons 20 July 1926; DPI 24 January 1925.
33. TNSA: GO2080 LE 5 November 1926 Letter 25 June 1925.
34. TNSA: GO946 LE 14 October 1926 MCAS Letter 23 October 1926.
35. TNSA: GO433 LE 30 March 1925 CPM Memo 4 February 1925.
36. TNSA: GO3893 Home 23 September 1940 Note 16 May 1940.
37. TNSA: GO2373 13 November 1929 MCAS Letter 27 October 1926.
38. TNSA: GO483 LE 15 March 1929.
39. TNSA: GO 621 LE 2 April 1929 MCAS Letter 27 November 1927.
40. TNSA: GO621 LE 2 April 1929 ICS Memo 1 December 1927.
41. TNSA: GO433 LE 30 March 1925 MCAS Letter 23 October 1926; GO621 LE 2 April 1929 Briefing 26 January 28; GO227 LE 16 February 32; GO2222 LE 22 November 1933; GO79 LE 9 January 1934.
42. TNSA: GO2082 LE 6 November 1926.

43. TNSA: GO621 LE 2 April 1929 H. Stuart Letter; GO 2100 LE 1 January 1927 GOI Note 24 May 1916.
44. TNSA: GO2080 LE 5 November 1926 MCAS Letter 23 October 1926; GO946 LE 14 October 1926; GO 2100 LE 1 January 1927.
45. TNSA: GO621 LE 2 April 1929 Memo 29 November 1927.
46. TNSA: GO621 LE 2 April 1929 Education Department 12 December 1927.
47. TNSA: GO2100 LE 1 January 1927.
48. TNSA: GO418 LE 1 March 1928; GO 139 LE 23 January 1929.
49. TNSA: GO1230 LE 23 June 1930 Education Department Letter 1 March 1928; GO483 LE 15 March 1929.
50. Women's Library: MCAS Seventh Annual Report, 1932.
51. Women's Library: MCAS Seventh Annual Report, 1932.
52. Weiner, *The Child and the State in India*; Rastogi, 'Prevention and Treatment', 324.
53. TNSA: GO433 LE 30 March 1925 CPM 18 December 1924.
54. TNSA: GO433 LE 30 March 1925 CPM 18 December 1924.
55. Louise A. Jackson, 'Care or Control? The Metropolitan Women Police and Child Welfare 1919–1969', *Historical Journal* 46, no. 3 (2003): 623–48.
56. TNSA: G0778 Home 23 February 1937 Madras Mail 17 February 1937.
57. TNSAL: MCAS Sixth Annual Report, year ending 1931. Published in *Stri Dharma*, 1932.
58. IOR: MssEur F341/182 *Stri Dharma* August–September 1934, 491.
59. GO1879 LE 17 September 1930.
60. GO1191 LE 22 August 1932 Inspector-General Police 9 June 1932, MCAS Letter 26 April 1932.
61. Women's Library: MCAS Seventh Annual Report, 1932.
62. TNSAL: MCAS Sixth Annual Report, year ending 1931.
63. For a wider discussion of the sexually active female child as both victim and social threat, see Jackson, *Child Sexual Abuse in Victorian England*.
64. TNSAL: MCAS Sixth Annual Report, year ending 1931.
65. TNSAL: MCAS Sixth Annual Report, year ending 1931.
66. TNSA: GO 78 Home 23 February 1937 Madras Mail 17 February 1937.
67. Michelle Elizabeth Tusan, 'Writing *Stri Dharma*: International Feminism, Nationalist Politics, and Women's Press Advocacy in Late Colonial India', *Women's History Review* 12, no. 4 (2003): 623–49; Gorman, 'Empire, Internationalism'.
68. TNSAL: *Stri Dharma*, 1932.

69. IOR: MssEur F341/30/2 Annual Report WIA 1933–34, 5, Geneva International Conference on Child Labour.
70. Anne Logan, '"A Suitable Person for Suitable Cases": The Gendering of Juvenile Courts in England, c. 1910–39', *Twentieth Century British History* 16, no. 2 (2005): 129–45; Radha Kumar, *The History of Doing* (London: Verso, 1993).
71. IOR: MssEur F341/186 WIA, Golden Jubilee Celebration, 1917–67 (Recollections and Reminiscences), MssEur F341/182 I. M. Dickinson, 'Children's Aid Society', in *Stri Dharma* 10, no. 11 (September 1927).
72. IOR: MssEur F341/30/2 WIA Reports 1930–31, 1931–32.
73. Pande, 'Coming of Age'; Sinha, *Specters of Mother India*.
74. IOR: MssEur F341/182 *Stri Dharma* August–September 1934, 489.
75. IOR: MssEur F341/186; IOR: ZD.9.b.31 Avvai home for orphans in Madras, 3.
76. IOR: MssEur F 341/72 Guild of Service Annual Report 1923.
77. IOR: W33/8063 Dr S. Muthulakshmi Reddy, 'My Experience as a Legislator' (Triplicane: Current Thought Press, 1930), 222, MssEur F341/186.
78. IOR: W33/8063, 223.
79. IOR: W33/8063, 224.
80. IOR: ZD.9.b.31.
81. IOR: MssEur F341/186, 71, 79.
82. WIA scholarships for ten girls in 1930. IOR: MssEur F341/186, 6.
83. IOR: MssEur F341/186 Reddi Address to WIA, 22; MssEur F341/30/2 WIA Annual Reports, 1934–36.
84. Women's Library: MCAS Seventh Annual Report 1932, 18.
85. TNSA: GO621 LE 2 April 1929.
86. TNSA: GO3893 Home 23 September 1940.
87. TNSA: GO2373 13 November 1929 MCAS Letter 27 October 1926; GO3893 Home 23 September 1940 Executive Committee 9 April 1940.
88. TNSA: GO946 LE 14 October 1926; GO3893 Home 23 September 1940 MCAS Letter 8 July 1940, MCAS Minutes 9 April 1940.
89. TNSA: GO433 LE 30 March 1925.
90. TNSA: GO4200 Home 15 October 1940 Remarks 24 May 1940.
91. TNSA: GO1428 LE 15 July 1935.
92. TNSA: GO433 LE 30 March 1925 CPM Letter 18 December 1924.
93. TNSA: GO433 LE 30 March 1925 CPM 18 December 1924.
94. TNSA: GO433 LE 30 March 1925 Letter 24 January 1925.

95. TNSA: GO397 LE 16 March 1926 Letter 18 May 1925.
96. TNSA: GO397 LE 16 March 1926 Police Note 6 July 1925, CPM 8 July 1925.
97. TNSA: GO397 LE 16 March 1926 DPI 10 June 1925.
98. TNSA: GO169 LE 5 February 1925.
99. TNSA: GO397 LE 16 March 1926 Third Presidency Magistrate 20 March 1926.
100. TNSA: GO397 LE 16 March 1926 CPM 30 April 1926.
101. TNSA: GO397 LE 16 March 1926 CPM Memo 16 March 1926.
102. TNSA: GO1879 LE 17 September 1930; GO 1191 LE 22 August 1932.
103. TNSA: GO433 LE 30 March 1925 Government of Bengal Judicial Branch 12 January 1925.
104. TNSA: GO397 LE 16 March 1926 Copy 3 November 26, based on information from Sydney, New South Wales, Australia.
105. Marshall, 'The Construction of Children as an Object of International Relations'; Alan Lester, 'Imperial Circuits and Networks: Geographies of the British Empire', *History Compass* 4, no. 1 (2006): 124–41; TNSA: GO 433 LE 30 March 1925 Undated Memo to C. P. Ramaswmi Aiyar.
106. IOR: L/PJ/6/1961, file 2014, Proceedings of the Third All-India Conference of Inspectors-General of Prisons, December 1927.
107. TNSA: GO2202 LE 28 October 1929 GOI Home Department No. F.168/29 dated 26 September 1929.
108. TNSA: GO2202 LE 28 October 1929 Proceedings of District Magistrate Tinnevelly.
109. TNSA: GO2202 LE 28 October 1929 Proceedings of District Magistrate Chingleput.
110. TNSA: GO2202 LE 28 October 1929 Proceedings of District Magistrate Tinnevelly.
111. TNSA: GO2202 LE 28 October 1929 Chief Inspector Certified Schools Ooty 24 October 1929.
112. TNSA: GO397 LE 16 March 1926 CPM Letter 12 March 1926.
113. TNSA: GO902 LE 28 June 1932 MCAS Report; GO2202 LE 28 October 1929 District Magistrate Tinnevelly.
114. TNSA: GO1545 LE 26 June 1934; GO 1282 LE 24 June 1935 MCA Certified Schools Report 1934.
115. TNSA: GO1428 LE 15 July 1935 Letter 17 April 1935.
116. TNSA: GO1428 LE 15 July 1935 Letter 7 May 1936, 25 May 1935, 9 June 1935.

Notes 291

117. TNSA: GO1428 LE 15 July 1935 (Section 44 (3)); GO3554 Home 15 December 1936.
118. Kumari, *Juvenile Justice System in India*.
119. IOR: V/24/2278 Annual Reports of Certified Schools 1935, 1936, 1942; TNSA: GO1032 LE 3 June 1926 1925 Report; GO1376 LE 12 July 1927; GO902 LE 28 June 1942.
120. TNSA: GO397 LE 16 March 1926 CPM Letter 3 February 1925.
121. TNSA: GO397 LE 16 March 1926 CPM Letter 18 May 1925.
122. TNSA: GO433 LE 30 March 1925 Undated Memo to C. P. Ramaswami Aiyar.
123. TNSA: GO2202 LE 28 October 1929 Proceedings of District Magistrate Tinnevelly 19 January 1928.
124. TNSA: GO902 LE 28 June 1932 MCAS Report.
125. IOR: L/PJ/6/1961 Memo Home Department 26 June 1940, CPM Remarks 24 May 1940, 'patient motherly' hearings; TNSA: GO4200 Home 15 October 1940 Madras Juvenile Court Rules.
126. Logan, "'A Suitable Person for Suitable Cases'".
127. TNSA: GO4200 Home 15 October 1940.
128. TNSA: GO4200 Home 15 October 1940, Madura, 29 May 1940.
129. TNSA: GO5112 Home 16 December 1940; GO Home 4200 15 October 1940; GO 4200 Home 15 October 1940 Chief Inspector Certified Schools 25 July 1940.
130. TNSA: GO4200 Home 15 October 1940 Chief Inspector Certified Schools 25 July 1940.
131. TNSA: GO4200 Home 15 October 1940 CPM Remarks 24 May 1940.
132. TNSA: GO4200 Home 15 October 1940 CPM 16 October 1940.
133. TNSA: GO4200 Home 15 October 1940 CPM 23 October 40, MCAS Memo 8 July 1940.
134. TNSA: GO4200 Home 15 October 1940 District Magistrate N. Arcot, Vellore 6 August 1940.
135. TNSA: GO4200 Home 15 October 1940 District Magistrate Madura 22 November 1940, Amended Rules of Juvenile Court 25 September 1940.
136. TNSA: GO4200 Home 15 October 1940.
137. TNSA: GO4306 Home 19 November 1942 District Magistrate Salem 10 November 1942.
138. TNSA: GO3364 Home 21 December 1943 District Magistrate Coimbatore 17 November 1943; GO4365 Home 28 October 1940; GO1324 Home 28 March 1942.

139. TNSA: GO4306 Home 19 December 1942 CPM Memo 2 November 1942.
140. TNSA: GO4306 Home 19 December 1942 CPM to Judicial Department 27 October 1943.
141. TNSA GO2556 Home 12 June 1940; GO4200 Home 15 October 1940 Chief Inspector 26 June 1940; Manshardt, *Delinquent Child in India*.
142. TNSA: GO2556 Home 12 June 1940.
143. IOR: L/PARL/2/407 A-Madras Jails Committee Evidence, 100.
144. TNSAL: MLC 15 March 1920 Debate, 598; TNSA: GO433 LE 30 March 1925.
145. TNSA: GO902 LE 28 June 1932.
146. IOR: L/PARL/2/407 A-Madras Jails Committee Evidence.
147. TNSA: GO2138 Home 4 June 1937 Memo 22 December 1936.
148. TNSA: GO433 LE 30 March 1925; GO902 LE 28 June 1932.
149. TNSA: GO433 LE 30 March 1925; IOR: MssEur F341/182 I. M. Dickinson, 'Children's Aid Society', *Stri Dharma* 10 (11 September 1927), 165.
150. TNSA: GO2138 Home 4 June 1937 Home Department Note 7 December 1935, 22 December 1936.
151. TNSA: GO2556 Home 12 June 1940; TNSAL: MLC 15 March 1920 Debate 597–98.
152. Women's Library: MCAS Seventh Annual Report, 1932, 14.
153. TNSA: GO778 Home 23 February 1937.
154. TNSA: GO2138 Home 4 June 1937 Note 18 January 1937.
155. IOR: L/PJ/6/1961, file 2014, 25.
156. TNSA: GO725 Home 19 February 1937 Detention Order, Madura Case 24 of 1936, P. Madhava Menon.
157. TNSA: GO725 Home 19 February 1937 MCAS Letter 13 March 1936.
158. TNSA: GO725 Home 19 February 1937 CPM Letter 19 March 1936.
159. TNSA: GO725 Home 19 February 1937. Includes separate submission from district magistrates according to area.
160. TNSA: GO2138 Home 4 June 1937 Chief Inspector Certified Schools 24 October 1936.
161. TNSA: GO2138 Home 4 June 1937 Chief Inspector 24 October 1936.
162. TNSA: GO2138 Home 4 June 1937.
163. TNSA: GO902 LE 28 June 1932 MCAS Report, 13.
164. TNSA: GO169 LE 5 February 1925; GO2138 Home 4 June 1937 Note to Finance Department 4 February 1937.
165. Chatterjee, *Child Criminals and the Raj*.

166. TNSA: GO778 Home 23 February 1937 MCAS 11th Annual Meeting.
167. TNSA: GO902 LE 28 June 1932 MCAS Report, 15.
168. TNSA: GO902 LE 28 June 1932 MCAS Report.
169. TNSA: GO2610 Home 12 July 1937 Certified Schools Report 1936.
170. TNSA: GO2138 Home 4 June 1937.
171. TNSA: GO2138 Home 4 June 1937 MCAS Note 27 February 1937.
172. Garland, *Punishment and Welfare*, 206; Donzelot, *Policing of Families*.
173. Donzelot, *Policing of Families*; Weiner, *The Child and the State*.
174. Logan, 'Policy Networks and the Juvenile Court'.
175. Sen, *Colonial Childhoods*.

Chapter 7

1. Sinha, *Colonial Masculinity*, 143, 172; Sarkar, *Hindu Wife, Hindu Nation*; Geraldine Forbes, *Women in Colonial India: Essays in Politics, Medicine and Historiography* (New Delhi: Chronicle Books, 2005).
2. Sinha, *Specters of Mother India*.
3. Sreenivas, *Wives, Widows, Concubines*, 89.
4. Pande, 'Coming of Age'.
5. 'Regulating Age of Consent in the British Empire', special issue, *Law and History Review* 38, no. 1 (2020): 143–279.
6. Ishita Pande, *Sex, Law, and the Politics of Age: Child Marriage in India, 1891–1937* (Cambridge: Cambridge University Press, 2020); and Kumar, *Politics of Gender, Community and Modernity*, would be good examples of this.
7. Sumita Mukherjee, 'Using the Legislative Assembly for Social Reform: The Sarda Act of 1929', *South Asia Research* 26, no. 3 (2006): 219–33.
8. IOR/L/PJ/6/1800 file 2083, Indian Criminal Law Amendment Act.
9. Tambe, 'The State as Surrogate Parent'.
10. IOR/L/PJ/7/158 Age of Consent (Joshi) Committee Report.
11. IOR/L/PJ/6/1800 file 2083, Indian Criminal Law Amendment Act.
12. IOR/L/PJ/6/1970 file 4632, Madras Suppression of Immoral Traffic Act, 1930. See as Amendment 1930 IOR L/PJ/7/2052, Amendment 1940 IOR/L/PJ/7/3930.
13. Sreenivas, *Wives, Widows, Concubines*.
14. Pande, 'Coming of Age'.
15. IOR/L/PJ/7/158 Age of Consent (Joshi) Committee Report, 102. Submissions from IOR/V/26/910/6: Evidence from Madras Dr (Mrs) Lazarus, 314, Mrs A. Lakshmi, 298.

16. Ishita Pande, 'Phulmoni's Body: The Autopsy, the Inquest and the Humanitarian Narrative on Child Rape in India', *South Asian History and Culture* 4, no. 1 (2013): 3.
17. IOR/V/26/910/6: Evidence from Madras Dr E. E. Tusker, 43, Dr Elizabeth Broges, 434.
18. IOR/V/26/910/6: Evidence from Madras C. Narayanaswami Reddi, 445.
19. For a more detailed study of boys, see Ishita Pande, 'Sorting Boys and Men: Unlawful Intercourse, Boy-Protection, and the Child Marriage Restraint Act in Colonial India', *Journal of the History of Childhood and Youth* 6, no. 2 (2013): 332–58.
20. IOR/V/26/910/7: Evidence from Madras Mrs M. Rama Bai Madhave Rau, 139.
21. IOR/V/26/910/7: Evidence from Madras Dr Anna Thomas, 518.
22. IOR/V/26/910/6: Evidence from Madras Miss L. Krishnabai, Mrs A. Lakshmi Pathi.
23. IOR/V/26/910/6: Evidence from Madras Dr Muthulakshmi Reddi, 365.
24. IOR/V/26/910/6: Evidence from Madras C. Veeragahavier, 501.
25. Roy Porter, *Madness: A Brief History* (Oxford: Oxford University Press, 2002).
26. IOR/V/26/910/6: Evidence from Madras Miss E. Lazarus, 562.
27. IOR/L/PJ/7/158 Age of Consent (Joshi) Committee Report, 119, 258.
28. IOR/V/26/910/6: Evidence from Madras T. Rangachariar, 108.
29. IOR/V/26/910/6: Evidence from Madras Dr U. Ram Rao, 4, P. Ramanathan, 154, Miss E. Lazarus, 562, R. S. Subbalakshmi, 115. For a wider reading, see Raman, *Getting Girls to School*; and Allender, *Learning Femininity in Colonial India*.
30. IOR/V/26/910/6: Evidence from Madras C. Veeragahavier, 507–10. For further reading, see Swapna Banerjee, *Men, Women and Domestics: Articulating Middle-Class Identity in Colonial Bengal* (New Delhi: Oxford University Press, 2004).
31. IOR/V/26/910/6: Evidence from Madras M. A. Srinivasa Iyengar, 402.
32. Vallgårda, *Imperial Childhoods*, writes extensively about this.
33. IOR/V/26/910/7: Evidence from Madras Shreemati Kamalabai Lakshmana Rao, 280.
34. IOR/V/26/910/7: Evidence from Madras Mrs Subba Rao, 127.
35. IOR/V/26/910/7: Evidence from Madras Mrs Gauri Sankummi, 135.
36. IOR/V/26/910/6: Evidence from Madras Mrs Malati Patwardhan, 95–96.

37. IOR/L/PJ/7/158 Age of Consent (Joshi) Committee Report, 186.
38. Pande, '"Listen to the Child"'; Kanika Sharma, 'Withholding Consent to Conjugal Relations within Child Marriages in Colonial India: Rukhmabai's Fight', *Law and History Review* 38, no. 1 (2020): 151–75.
39. Tambe, 'The State as Surrogate Parent', 410.
40. IOR/L/PJ/7/158 Age of Consent (Joshi) Committee Report, 179, 189.
41. Term used in the standard questionnaire. IOR/V/26/910/6: Evidence from Madras.
42. IOR/V/26/910/6: Evidence from Madras M. K. Acharya, 177, A. Parasurama Rao Garu, 414, L. R. Krishnaswamy, 470.
43. IOR/V/26/910/6: Evidence from Madras Dr Muthulakshmi Reddi, 361–62, President of Hindu Girls School, 537–40, M. Subramania Ayyar, 474.
44. IOR/V/26/910/6: Evidence from Madras Khan Bahadur M. Abdulla Ghattala, 426.
45. IOR/L/PJ/7/158 Age of Consent (Joshi) Committee Report, 191–92; see also Sreenivas, 'Creating Conjugal Subjects'.
46. IOR/V/26/910/6: Evidence from Madras Rao Bahadur M. Chengayya Pantalu Garu, 83–84.
47. IOR/V/26/910/6: Evidence from Madras M. A. Srinivasa Iyengar, 401.
48. IOR/V/26/910/6: Evidence from Madras Mrs A. Lakshmi Pathi, 298, E. Raghave, Dr Muthulakshmi Reddi., 466.
49. See also Sreenivas, *Wives, Widows, Concubines*.
50. IOR/L/PJ/6/1800 file 2083, Indian Criminal Law Amendment Act, Council of State Debate, 19 September 1924, 11.
51. IOR/L/PJ/6/1800 file 2083, Madras Hindu Religious Endowments Act, 1926.
52. Sen, *Colonial Childhoods*, ch. 4.
53. Sreenivas, *Wives, Widows, Concubines*; Tambe, 'The State as Surrogate Parent', 395.
54. Tambe, 'The State as Surrogate Parent', 393.
55. Ishita Pande, 'Vernacularizing Justice: Age of Consent and a Legal History of the British Empire', *Law and History Review* 38, no. 1 (2020).
56. IOR/L/PJ/6/1800 file 2083, MLC Proceedings 4 November 1927, 416.
57. IOR/L/PJ/6/1800 file 2083, MLC Proceedings 4 November 1927, 416.
58. IOR/L/PJ/6/1800 file 2083, MLC Proceedings 4 November 1927, 417.
59. See Toby Rollo, 'The Color of Childhood: The Role of the Child–Human Binary in the Production of Anti-Black Racism', *Journal of Black Studies* 49, no. 4 (2018): 307–29; Vallgårda, *Imperial Childhoods*.

60. IOR/L/PJ/6/1800 file 2083, MLC Proceedings 4 November 1927, 417.
61. Hinchy, *Governing Gender and Sexuality*.
62. Mytheli Sreenivas, 'Creating Conjugal Subjects: Devadasis and the Politics of Marriage in Colonial Madras Presidency', *Feminist Studies* 37, no. 1 (2011): 68.
63. Tambe, 'The State as Surrogate Parent, 397.
64. See, for example, Ashok Malhotra, *Making British Indian Fictions: 1772-1823* (New York: Palgrave Macmillan, 2012).
65. Pande, 'Phulmoni's Body'.
66. IOR/V/26/910/6: Evidence from Madras S. Ramasami Iyer, 406.
67. IOR/L/PJ/7/158 Age of Consent (Joshi) Committee Report, 192.
68. IOR/V/26/910/6: Evidence from Madras R. S. Subbalakshmi, 115.
69. IOR/V/26/910/6: Evidence from Madras Miss E. Lazarus, 563.
70. Lal has written about girlhood and playfulness. Lal, *Coming of Age*.
71. IOR/V/26/910/7: Evidence from Madras Mrs M. Rama Bai Madhave Rau; 138 IOR/L/PJ/7/158 Age of Consent (Joshi) Committee Report, 258.
72. IOR/V/26/910/7: Evidence from Madras Mrs Gauri Sankunni,, 134.
73. IOR/V/26/910/6: Evidence from Madras T. M. Narasimha Charlu, 201.
74. IOR/V/26/910/6: Evidence from Madras Govindoss Chathoorbhoojdoss, 384.
75. IOR/V/26/910/6: Evidence from Madras Letter U. P. Krishnamacharya, 219.
76. IOR/V/26/910/6: Evidence from Madras Brahma Shri K. G. Natesa Sastrigal, 546; See also Sneha Krishnan, 'Where Do Good Girls Have Sex? Space, Risk and Respectability in Chennai', *Gender, Place and Culture* 28, no. 7 (2020): 1–20.
77. IOR/V/26/910/7: Evidence from Madras S. S. Setlur, 538; IOR/L/PJ/6/1970 file 4632, Bill for Suppression of Brothels and Immoral Traffic, Bill 16 of 1928, MLC Proceedings, 10 October 1928, Dr B. S. Mallayya, 12.
78. IOR/V/26/910/6: Evidence from Madras Justice Ramesam, 352.
79. See, for example, IOR/V/26/910/6: Evidence from Madras Mr Justice Ramesam, 354, Govindoss Chathoorbhoojdoss, 386, Pandit S. S. Anandam, 396.
80. IOR/V/26/910/6: Evidence from Madras Mr S. Varadachariar, 386, T. R. Venkatarama Sastri, 566.
81. IOR/V/26/910/6: Evidence from Madras Brahma Shri K. G. Natesa Sastrigal, 250.
82. IOR/V/26/910/6: Evidence from Madras Justice Ramesam, 342, T. R. Venkatarama Sastri, 566.

83. IOR/V/26/910/7: Evidence from Madras Vannia Nadar Ramaswami, 354.
84. IOR/V/26/910/7: Evidence from Madras Pracharka Sabha, 206, M. R. R. Y. N. Natesa Ayyar, 163; IOR/V/26/910/6: Evidence from Madras Medical Sub-Committee of the Madras Branch of the Social Hygiene Committee, 526, C. Vencata Subbramiah, 126, Mr R. Vira Raghava Sarma, 389.
85. IOR/V/26/910/6: Evidence from Madras Letter U. P. Krishnamacharya to Governor of Madras.
86. IOR/V/26/910/7: Evidence from Madras Miss Zimha Lazarus, 539.
87. Ashwini Tambe, 'Climate, Race Science and the Age of Consent in the League of Nations', *Theory, Culture and Society* 28, no. 2 (2011): 122–23.
88. Pande, 'Coming of Age', 217.
89. IOR/L/PJ/6/1800 file 2083, Discussion at Simla 1924, 707; Indian Criminal Law Amendment Bill, 14 February 1924.
90. Tambe, 'Climate, Race Science and the Age of Consent', 121.
91. IOR/L/PJ/6/1800 file 2083.
92. IOR/L/PJ/6/1800 file 2083, Resolution V. Ramdas Pantulu, 12 September 1927.
93. IOR/L/PJ/6/1970 file 4632, Minutes of Dissent F. E. James, 13 September 1929, 12.
94. Geraldine H. Forbes, 'Women and Modernity: The Issue of Child Marriage in India', *Women's Studies International Quarterly* 2, no. 4 (1979): 407–19.
95. IOR/L/PJ/7/158 Age of Consent (Joshi) Committee Report, 169; IOR/V/26/910/6: Evidence from Madras M. Chengayya Pantalu Garu, 91.
96. IOR/V/26/910/7: Evidence from Madras Shreemati Kamalabai Lakshmana Rao, 270, Miss G. Samuel, 329; IOR/L/PJ/7/158 Age of Consent (Joshi) Committee Report, 116–17.
97. IOR/V/26/910/6: Evidence from Madras Mrs Margaret E. Cousins, 570; IOR/L/PJ/6/1970 file 4632, Bill for Suppression of Brothels and Immoral Traffic, MLC Proceedings, 10 October 1928, 9.
98. IOR/L/PJ/6/1970 file 4632, Bill for Suppression of Brothels and Immoral Traffic, MLC Proceedings, 10 October 1928, 9.
99. IOR/L/PJ/6/1800 file 2083, MLC Proceedings, 5 November 1927, 514.
100. IOR/L/PJ/6/1800 file 2083, MLC Proceedings, 5 November 1927, 514.
101. IOR/L/PJ/6/1800 file 2083, MLC Proceedings, 5 November 1927, 514.
102. Hodges, 'Revolutionary Family Life'.
103. Anandhi, 'Women's Question in the Dravidian Movement', in *Women and Social Reform in Modern India*, ed. Sarkar and Sarkar.

104. IOR/V/26/910/6: Evidence from Madras T. R. Venkatarama Sastri, 568.
105. Hodges, *Contraception, Colonialism and Commerce*.
106. Sinha, *Specters of Mother India*.
107. Mrinalini Sinha, 'Mapping the Imperial Social Formation: A Modest Proposal for Feminist History', *Signs: Journal of Women in Culture and Society* 25, no. 4 (Summer 2000): 1081.
108. Anandhi, 'Women's Question in the Dravidian Movement'.
109. David Arnold, 'Official Attitudes to Population, Birth Control and Reproductive Health in India 1921–1946', in *Reproductive Health in India*, ed. Hodges.
110. IOR/V/26/910/6: Evidence from Madras M. A. Srinivasa Iyengar, 401.
111. Tambe, 'The State as Surrogate Parent'.
112. IOR/V/26/910/6: Evidence from Madras Mrs Alamelu Mangathavarammal, 310; Evidence from Madras C. V. Viswantatha Sastro, 50, Dr (Mrs) Lazarus, 320, C. Veeragahavier, 514; IOR/V/26/910/7: Evidence from Madras Rajkumar S. N. Dorai Rajah, 326, Dr Anna Thomas, 529.
113. IOR/V/26/910/6: Evidence from Madras C. V. Anatakrishna Aiyar, 50, U. P. Krishnacharaya, 212.
114. IOR/V/26/910/6: Evidence from Madras V. Ramadas Pantulu, 22, C. Viswantha Sastri, 33, S. Ramasami Iyer, 406–07.
115. IOR/V/26/910/6: Evidence from Madras Mrs Malati Patwardhan, 95.
116. IOR/L/PJ/6/1970 file 4632, Bill for Suppression of Brothels and Immoral Traffic, MLC Proceedings 31 January 1930.
117. IOR/L/PJ/6/1800 file 2083, Resolution re Prohibition of Traffic in Minor Girls, 27 February 1922, 1912.
118. IOR/L/PJ/6/1800 file 2083, Criminal Law Amendment Act 1924, MLC Proceedings, 28 October 1927, 1135–40.
119. IOR/L/PJ/6/1800 file 2083, Resolution re Prohibition of Traffic in Minor Girls, 27 February 1922, 1912.
120. IOR/L/PJ/6/1970 file 4632, Bill for Suppression of Brothels and Immoral Traffic, MLC Proceedings, 31 January 1930, 8; IOR/L/PJ/6/1800 file 2083, MLC Debate, 5 November 1927, 521, Resolution re Prohibition of Traffic in Minor Girls, 27 February 1922, 2602.
121. IOR/L/PJ/6/1800 file 2083, Indian Criminal Law Amendment Bill, MLC Debate, 15 September 1924.
122. IOR/L/PJ/6/1800 file 2083, Indian Criminal Law Amendment Bill, MLC Proceedings, 15 September 1924, 3442.

123. IOR/L/PJ/6/1970 file 4632, Bill for Suppression of Brothels and Immoral Traffic, MLC Proceedings, 10 October 1928, 8; Minutes of Dissent F. E. James, 13 September 1929, 12.
124. IOR/L/PJ/6/1970 file 4632, Bill for Suppression of Brothels and Immoral Traffic, MLC Proceedings, 10 October 1928, 2, 7; IOR/L/PJ/6/1800 file 2083, Resolution re Prohibition of Traffic in Minor Girls, 27 February 1922, 2606.
125. IOR/L/PJ/6/1970 file 4632, Bill for Suppression of Brothels and Immoral Traffic, MLC Proceedings, 10 October 1928, 4.
126. IOR/V/26/910/6: Evidence from Madras P. Ramanathan, 154; IOR/V/26/910/7: Evidence from Madras Dr Anna Thomas, 517.
127. IOR/V/26/910/7: Evidence from Madras Rao Bahadu M. R. Ramaswami Sivan, 245.
128. Sarah Hodges, 'Indian Eugenics in an Age of Reform', in *Reproductive Health in India*, ed. Hodges.
129. IOR/V/26/910/6: Evidence from Madras P. Ramanathan, 157.
130. IOR/V/26/910/6: Evidence from Madras Dr (Mrs) Lazarus, 314, Dr C. S. Govinda Pillai, 322.
131. IOR/L/PJ/6/1800 file 2083, MLC Proceedings, 5 November 1927, 515.
132. IOR/L/PJ/6/1800 file 2083, MLC Proceedings, 28 October 1927, 1131; see also Sreenivas, 'Creating Conjugal Subjects',72–73.
133. IOR/L/PJ/7/158 Age of Consent (Joshi) Committee Report, 57.
134. IOR/V/26/910/6: Evidence from Madras Dewan Bahadur T. Rangachariar, 105.
135. C. J. Fuller and Haripriya Narasimhan, 'Marriage, Education, and Employment among Tamil Brahman Women in South India, 1891–2010', *Modern Asian Studies* 47, no. 1 (2013): 60.
136. Sreenivas, *Wives, Widows, Concubines*; Hodges, 'Revolutionary Family Life', 79–83.
137. IOR/V/26/910/6: Evidence from Madras Mrs Alamelu Mangathavarammal, 312.
138. IOR/V/26/910/6: Evidence from Madras S. V. Ramaswamy Mudalier, 328; IOR/V/26/910/7: Evidence from Madras Mr S. Subramania Moopanar, 328.
139. Forbes, 'Women and Modernity'; Lata Mani, 'Production of an Official Discourse on Sati in Early Nineteenth-Century Bengal', in *Women and Social Reform*, ed. Sarkar and Sarkar.
140. Pande, 'Listen to the Child'.

Chapter 8

1. For an overview of childhoods in south India as remembered in autobiographies, see C. Ellis, 'Remembering Pre-independence Childhoods in South India: Interrogating Autobiographies and Identities', *Social History* 44, no. 2 (2019): 202–28.
2. R. Sen, 'Remembering the Prayahik (Daily): "De"familiarising Familial Social History through Memoirs', in *Pratyaha: Everyday Lifeworlds Dilemmas, Contestations and Negotiations*, ed. P. Ray and Nandini Ghosh (Delhi: Primus Books, 2015).
3. M. Dasan, V. Pratibha, P. Pampirikunnu and C. S. Chandrika, eds., *Oxford Indian Anthology of Malayalam Dalit Writing* (Oxford: Oxford University Press, 2012); Ravikumar and R. Azhagarasan, eds., *Oxford Indian Anthology of Tamil Dalit Writing* (Oxford: Oxford University Press, 2012); K. Satyanarayana and S. Tharu, eds., *Steel Nibs Are Sprouting: New Dalit Writing from South India* (New Delhi: HarperCollins, 2013); S. Tharu and K. Satyanarayana, eds., *No Alphabet in Sight: New Dalit Writing in South India* (New Delhi: Penguin Books, 2011).
4. See, for example, 'Rethinking the History of Childhood', special issue, *American Historical Review* 125, no. 4 (October 2020).
5. For subaltern studies see, for example, Dipesh Chakrabarty, 'Postcoloniality and the Artifice of History: Who Speaks for "Indian" Pasts?', in 'Imperial Fantasies and Postcolonial Histories', special issue, *Representations*, no. 37 (Winter 1992): 1–26.
6. R. Sen, 'Reading the *Social* in Autobiographies: A Glimpse into Everyday Life and History', in *Knowing the Social World: Perspectives and Possibilities*, ed. N. Jayaram (Hyderabad: Orient BlackSwan, 2017).
7. Butalia, *The Other Side of Silence*, 279.
8. Wagner and Roque, *Engaging Colonial Knowledge*.
9. For the Bengali situation, see R. C. P. Sinha, *The Indian Autobiographies in English* (New Delhi: S. Chand & Co., 2013); K. Hansen, *Stages of Life: Indian Theatre Autobiographies* (Wimbledon, London: Anthem Press, 2011).
10. Venkatachalapathy, *In Those Days*.
11. K. Santhanam, *Looking Back: Memoirs of K. Santhanam* (Mumbai: Bharatiya Vidya Bhavan, 2001), 6; A. N. Sattanathan, *Plain Speaking: A Sudra's Story*, ed. Uttara Natarajan (Oxford: Permanent Black, 2007).
12. Venkatachalapathy, *In Those Days*, 175; U. Kumar, 'Subjects of New Lives: Reform, Self-Making and the Discourse of Autobiography in Kerala',

in *Different Types of History*, ed. B. Ray (Delhi: Pearson Longman, 2009), 307.
13. A. P. J. Kalam and Arun Tiwari, *Wings of Fire: An Autobiography* (Hyderabad: Universities Press, 1999), xv.
14. Mines, *Public Faces, Private Voices*, 149.
15. Mines's argument is an attempt to counter the work of Dumont and earlier colonial theorists who only see Indian society structured in terms of caste, that is, in collective and not as individuals.
16. Sen, 'Reading the *Social*', 294.
17. U. Kumar, *Writing the First Person: Literature, History and Autobiography in Modern Kerala* (Bangalore: Permanent Black, 2016), 19, 230.
18. Venkatachalapathy, *In Those Days*, 173; Kumar, *Writing the First Person*, 315.
19. K. Veeraswami, *The Perils to Justice: A Judge Thinks Aloud* (Calcutta: Eastern Law House, 1996), 351; Hansen, *Stages of Life*, 38–39.
20. Sen, *Traces of Empire*, 91.
21. Kumar, *Writing the First Person*, 260; Morrison, *Childhood and Colonial Modernity*, 122.
22. N.C. Yati, *Love and Blessings: The Autobiography of Guru Nitya Chaitanya Yati*, ed. Peter Oppenheimer (Varkala: Narayana Gurukula, 2000), 2; A. P. J. Abdul Kalam, *My Journey: Transforming Dreams into Actions* (Delhi: Rupa, 2013); Viramma, J. Racine and J.-L. Racine, *Viramma: Life of an Untouchable* (London: Verso, 1997), 39; M. Ganesh, 'My Grandfather Had a Wish', in *Steel Nibs Are Sprouting*, ed. Satyanarayan and Tharu, 275.
23. Kalam, *My Journey*, 52; J. Mohanty and S. Mohanty, *In Quest of Quality Education and Literature: An Autobiography* (Delhi: Deep & Deep Publications, 2006), 5.
24. R. K. Narayan, *My Days: A Memoir* (Oxford: Picador, 1974), 45; R. K. Laxman, 'Through the Coloured Glass', in *Past Forward: Six Artists in Search of Their Childhood*, ed. Gowri Ramnarayan (New Delhi: Oxford University Press, 1997), 38; K. R. R. Sastry, *Reminiscences of a Jurist* (Madras: Jupiter, 1963).
25. K. Sreenivasan, *Climbing the Coconut Tree: A Partial Autobiography* (Delhi: Oxford University Press, 1980), 43.
26. S. Nijalingappa, *My Life and Politics* (Delhi: Vision Books, 2000), 57n.
27. Sen, 'The Orphaned Colony', 463–488.
28. Sreenivasan, *Climbing the Coconut Tree*, 42; Laxman, 'Through the Coloured Glass', 37, 39; Kalam, *My Journey*, 52; K. P. S. Menon, *Many Worlds:*

An Autobiography (Calcutta: Oxford University Press, 1965), 9; H. Raman, *Daughter of the Mountains* (Madras: East West Books, 1993), 43–44; Narayan, *My Days*, 21–24.

29. Nijalingappa, *My Life*, 18–20; Mohanty and Mohanty, *In Quest of Quality Education*, 26; K. L. Raghuramaiah, *Hurricane: Autobiography of a Woman* (Delhi: Chanakya Publications, 1993), 8; C. Subramaniam, *Hand of Destiny: Memoirs* (Bombay: Bharatiya Bhavan, 1993), 36; P. S. Sundaram, *Simple Simon: An Autobiography* (Madras: Nirmala Sundaram, 1997), 13, 16; Sattanathan, *Plain Speaking*, 25; Gunasekaran, *The Scar*, 4, 20.

30. P. C. Alexander, *Through the Corridors of Power: An Insider's Story* (Delhi: Harper Collins India, 2004), 51–55.

31. Narayan, *My Days*, 58–60; R. K. Laxman, *The Tunnel of Time* (New Delhi: Penguin, 1971), 2–3.

32. R. V. M. G. Ramarau, *Of Men, Matter and Me* (London: Asia Publishing House, 1961), 15–21. Santha Rama Rau, *Gifts of Passage* (London: Victor Gollancz, 1961), 3–4; Menon, *Many Worlds*, 26; A. M. N. Chakiar, *The Last Smārtha Vichāram: A Victim's Reminiscences* (Madras: Padma C. Menon, 1998), 77.

33. Viramma, *Viramma*, 4, 5, 14; Krishnabai Nimbkar, *Smrutika: The Story of My Mother as Told by Herself* (self-pub., Pune, 1988).

34. Viramma, *Viramma*, 14.

35. Viramma, *Viramma*, 8.

36. Lal, *Coming of Age in Nineteenth-Century India*, 207.

37. NLS: *Report on Public Instruction in the Madras Presidency* (1927–28 to 1931–32), 83.

38. M. J. Sargunam, *An Autobiography* (Coimbatore: Palaniandavar Printers, 1978), 5–6, 11; Subramaniam, *Hand of Destiny*, 37–39; B. A. Sayeed, *My Life, A Struggle* (Madras: Academy of Islamic Research, 1983), 12; Kalam, *My Journey*, 35; Laxman, *Tunnel of Time*, 10; Mohanty and Mohanty, *In Quest of Quality Education*, 30–44; C. Narasimhaiah, *'N for Nobody': Autobiography of an English Teacher* (Delhi: B. R. Publishing Corporation, 1991), 4–10; Narayan, *My Days*, 44; N. Guru, *Autobiography of an Absolutist* (Fernhill: Gurkula Publishing House, 1989), 2–9; Nijalingappa, *My Life*, 16–21; K. M. Panikkar, *An Autobiography* (Delhi: Oxford University Press, 1954), 3–4; Sattanathan, *Plain Speaking*, 29–49; Veeraswami, *The Perils to Justice*, 7.

39. Sattanathan, *Plain Speaking*, 36; Alexander, *Through the Corridors of Power*, 61; S. Muthulakshmi Reddi, *Autobiography* (self-pub., Madras, 1964), 3;

Sreenivasan, *Climbing the Coconut Tree*, 39. For further discussion of school buildings, see Ellis, 'Remembering Pre-independence Childhoods', 388.

40. For example, Mohanty and Mohanty, *In Quest of Quality Education*; Sundaram, *Simple Simon*.
41. A. K. Samban, *Autobiography of Prof. A. K. Samban* (Madras: Sri Maruthi Graphics, 1994), 19.
42. Morrison, *Childhood and Colonial Modernity*, 102, 122. See also C. Ellis, 'Climbing the Coconut Tree: Three South Indians Use Their Personal Memories of Colonial Education to Influence the Decolonization of Education after Independence', in *Decolonization's and Education New Polities and New Men*, ed. Marcelo Caruso and Daniel Maul (Berlin: Peter Lang, 2020); quote from Mohanty and Mohanty, *In Quest of Quality Education*, xiv.
43. Mohanty and Mohanty, *In Quest of Quality Education*, 33; Sundaram, *Simple Simon*, 41–43; Laxman, *Tunnel of Time*, 10–14.
44. Subramaniam, *Hand of Destiny*, 38; Santhanam, *Looking Back*, 13.
45. Narayan, *My Days*, 44–45; Subramaniam, *Hand of Destiny*, 39; M. Subbamma, *Fearless Feminist: An Autobiography of a Social Revolutionary* (Hyderabad: Booklinks Corp., 1994), 24; Alexander, *Through the Corridors of Power*, 62.
46. See, for example, H. Fischer-Tiné, 'Fitness for Modernity? The YMCA and Physical Education Schemes in Late Colonial South Asia (circa 1900–40)', *Modern Asian Studies* 53, no. 2 (2019): 512–59; Mills and Sen, *Confronting the Body*.
47. Narayan, *My Days*.
48. Sargunam, *Autobiography*, 5; Alexander, *Through the Corridors of Power*, 61; Narasimhaiah, 'N for Nobody'; Sattanathan, *Plain Speaking*, 50; Nijalingappa, *My Life*, 21; K. Das, *My Story* (Delhi: Sterling Paperbacks, 1988), 21; Veeraswami, *Perils to Justice*, 7; Chakiar, *Last Smārtha Vichāram*, 90; Reddi, *Autobiography*, 3.
49. Laxman, *Tunnel of Time*, 4, 10–12; Narayan, *My Days*, 8.
50. Mohanty and Mohanty, *In Quest of Quality Education*, 30–31; Nijalingappa, *My Life*, 6; T. M. Mahadevan, *A Philosopher Looks Back* (Delhi: Bharatiya Vidya Bhavan, 1982), 11.
51. See, for example, N. G. Ranga, *Fight for Freedom: Autobiography of N. G. Ranga* (Delhi: S. Chand, 1968), 10–11; Chakiar, *Last Smārtha Vichāram*, 44; Vaidyanathan, *Thoughts and Reminiscences* (Chetput: Ananda Books, 1986), 9; Sattanathan, *Plain Speaking*, 50; Mohanty and Mohanty, *In Quest of Quality Education*, 31.

52. A. P. J. Abdul Kalam, http://www.abdulkalam.com/kalam/theme/jsp/guest/myprofile.jsp (accessed 6 November 2015).
53. Sundaram, *Simple Simon*, 41–43.
54. Laxman, *Tunnel of Time*, 10, 12.
55. Laxman, *Tunnel of Time*, 10–14; Narasimhaiah, 'N for Nobody', 5.
56. See contemporary work, including Sreenivas, 'Telling Different Tales', 316–32.
57. Laxman, *Tunnel of Time*, 10–12; Narayan, *My Days*, 8.
58. C. Kesavan, 'Jeevithasamaram', in *Steel Nibs Are Sprouting*, ed. Satyanarayana and Tharu, 261.
59. S. Humphries, *Hooligans or Rebels? An Oral History of Working-Class Childhood and Youth, 1889–1939* (Oxford: Basil Blackwell, 1981); James C. Scott, *Weapons of the Weak: Everyday Forms of Peasant Resistance* (Yale: Yale University Press, 1985); Ellis, 'Remembering Pre-independence Childhoods', 392.
60. Das, *My Story*, 18, 19, 39; Siddalingaiah, *Ooru Keri: An Autobiography* (Bangalore: Sahitya Akademi, 2003); Rau, *Gifts of Passage*, 10; Yati, *Love and Blessings*, 22. See also H. Bhabha, 'Of Mimicry and Man: The Ambivalence of Colonial Discourse', *October* 28 (1984): 125–33.
61. Laxman, *Tunnel of Time*, 11; Narayan, *My Days*, 10; Sreenivasan, *Climbing the Coconut Tree*, 39; Ramarau, *Of Men, Matter and Me*, 10.
62. Sattanathan, *Plain Speaking*, 90.
63. Sattanathan, *Plain Speaking*, 40–46; Reddi, *Autobiography*, 1; Gunasekaran, *The Scar*, 17–18.
64. Yati, *Love and Blessings*, 20; Narayan, *My Days*, 41–42, 51.
65. For more detail, see Kumar, *Lessons from Schools*.
66. Viramma, *Viramma*.
67. Balagopalan, 'Constructing Indigenous Childhoods'.
68. Balagopalan, *Inhabiting Childhood*.
69. Mohanty and Mohanty, *In Quest of Quality Education*, 17–18; Narasimhaiah, 'N for Nobody', 5. Gunasekaran, *The Scar*, 23, 30, 34, 84.
70. Sattanathan, *Plain Speaking*, 57–58.
71. Kalam, *My Journey*, 23–26.
72. Sreenivas, 'Telling Different Tales', 316–32, here 331. See also, A. Davin, *Growing Up Poor: Home, School and Street in London 1870–1914* (London: Rivers Oram Press, 1996), 41.
73. Nimbkar, *Smrutika*, 18–20; Kalam, *My Journey*, 52; Gunasekaran, *The Scar*, 203.

74. Raman, *Daughter of the Mountains*, 3, 9, 13, 18–19.
75. Gunasekaran, *The Scar*.
76. Burra, *Born Unfree*.
77. Morrison, *Childhood and Colonial Modernity*, 102, 122.
78. Raman, *Daughter of the Mountains*, 35; Sen, *Traces of Empire*, 80.
79. M. Karlekar and R. Mukherjee, eds., *Remembered Childhood* (Oxford: Oxford University Press, 2010), 134.
80. A. Nandy, *Traditions, Tyranny and Utopias* (Delhi: Oxford University Press, 1992), 57.
81. Veeraswami, *The Perils to Justice*, 4.
82. Kalam, *Wings of Fire*, 8–9.
83. Kalam, *My Journey*, 33–39.
84. 'The lack of Muslim autobiographies probably reflects the small numbers of Muslims throughout the presidency and the complications of their language policies.' See Kenneth McPherson, *'How Best Do We Survive?': A Modern Political History of the Tamil Muslims* (London: Routledge, 2010). Only 7 per cent of population. Alexander, *Through the Corridors of Power*. See also N. Etherington, ed., *Missions and Empire: Oxford History of the British Empire Series* (Oxford: Oxford University Press, 2005). On racial discrimination check the JSH article.
85. Guru, *Autobiography*, 9.
86. Vaidyanathan, *Thoughts and Reminiscences*, 16; Chandy, *Quest of Community*, 10; Yati, *Love and Blessings*, 28; Subbamma, *Fearless Feminist*, 20.
87. T. Ramaiah, 'Manegara: Excerpts', trans. Maitreyi Karnoor, in *Steel Nibs Are Sprouting*, ed. Satyanarayana and Tharu, 190.
88. Sreenivasan, *Climbing the Coconut Tree*, 18.
89. Subramaniam, *Hand of Destiny*, 35; Menon, *Many Worlds*, 23.
90. Chakiar, *Last Smārtha Vichāram*, 115, 146.
91. For a wider discussion, see Kumar, *Politics of Gender*.
92. Panikkar, *An Autobiography*, 3; Santhanam, *Looking Back*, 13; Subramaniam, *Hand of Destiny*, 38; Kalam, *My Journey*, 35; M. Arjunamani and M. Dhanasekar, *Tale of a Tamil Widow* (Rockhampton: Central Queensland University Publishing, 2001), 7; Das, *My Story*, 13; Mohanty and Mohanty, *In Quest of Quality Education*, 32; Guru, *Autobiography*, 2; Raghuramaiah, *Hurricane*, 25; Subbamma, *Fearless Feminist*, 10.
93. Reddi, *Autobiography*, 5–7.
94. Subbamma, *Fearless Feminist*, 5.

95. Reddi, *Autobiography*, 5–7. For an extensive discussion of Subbamma, *Fearless Feminist*, see Ellis, 'Climbing the Coconut Tree'.
96. Bagchi, 'Two Lives'; R. Gayathri, 'Silent Voices: Women's Perceptions about Self and Education in Late Nineteenth-Century India', in *New Perspectives*, ed. Rao.
97. Nimbkar, *Smrutika*, 20; Subbamma, *Fearless Feminist*, 10–14; Raman, *Daughter of the Mountains*, 63; Raghuramaiah, *Hurricane*; Das, *My Story*; Viramma, *Viramma*, 32.
98. A particularly good example is Sattanathan, *Plain Speaking*, 4.
99. Dasan et al., *Oxford Indian Anthology*, 181.
100. David Arnold and Stuart Blackburn, eds., *Telling Lives in India: Biography, Autobiography and Life History* (Delhi: Permanent Black, 2004), 15.
101. Dasan et al., *Oxford Indian Anthology*; D. R. Nagaraj, *The Flaming Feet and Other Essays: The Dalit Movement in India* (London: University of Chicago Press, 2011), 211; Ravikumar, 'Introduction', in Gunasekaran, *The Scar*; Sreenivasan, *Climbing the Coconut Tree*, 271. See also B. M. Puttaiah, 'Does Dalit Literature Need Poetics?', in *Steel Nibs Are Sprouting*, ed. Satyanarayana and Tharu, 347–68; Satyanarayana and Tharu, *Steel Nibs Are Sprouting*, 44–65.
102. Hansen, *Stages of Life*, 308, refers to Bama's *Karukku*.
103. U. Kumar, 'Autobiography as a Way of Writing History: Personal Narratives from Kerala and the Inhabitation of Modernity' in *History in the Vernacular*, ed. P. Chatterjee and R. Aquil (Delhi: Permanent Black, 2008); Balagopalan, 'Introduction: Children's Lives', 291–97, here 295.
104. Sharmila Rege, *Sociology of Gender: The Challenge of Feminist Sociological Knowledge* (New Delhi: Sage, 2003).
105. Siddalingaiah, *Ooru Keri*; Das, *My Story*, 43.
106. Gunasekaran, *The Scar*, 5 (italics mine).
107. Gunasekaran, *The Scar*, 9, 18.
108. Sattanathan, *Plain Speaking*, 32.
109. Sattanathan, *Plain Speaking*, 52.
110. L. Elayaperumal, 'The Flames of Summer' ['Cithirai Neruppu'], trans. D Venkataramanan, in *Oxford Indian Anthology*, ed. Ravikumar and Azhagarasan, 184.
111. Ravikumar and Azhagarasan, *Oxford Indian Anthology*; R. Kumar, *Dalit Personal Narratives: Reading Caste, Nation and Identity* (Hyderabad: Orient Blackswan, 2010).

112. K. Pokkudan 'My Life, Ende Jeevitham', in *Oxford Indian Anthology*, ed. Dasan et al., 185.
113. Gunasekaran, *The Scar*, 21, 25, 43, 51, 81.
114. Elayaperumal, 'Flames of Summer', 185.
115. P. Pokkudan, 'My Life, *Ende Jeevitham*', in *Oxford Indian Anthology*, ed. Dasan et al., 186–87.
116. R. Srinivasan, 'A Brief History of my Life', in *Oxford Indian Anthology*, ed. Ravikumar and Azhagarasan, 177.
117. Chakiar, *Last Smārtha Vichāram*, 27; C. Walikar, 'On a Raft Made of Entrails', trans. S. Jayasrinivasa Rao, in *Steel Nibs Are Sprouting*, ed. Satyanarayana and Tharu, 83–93.
118. Ramarau, *Of Men, Matter and Me*, 7. Chakiar, preface to *Last Smārtha Vichāram*; Sayeed, *My Life, a Struggle*.
119. Mohanty and Mohanty, *In Quest of Quality Education*.
120. Kalam, *My Journey*, 4; Sattanathan, *Plain Speaking*, 28; Amjad Ali Khan, 'Speaking Strings', in *Past Forward*, ed. Ramnarayan, 48–50; Laxman, *Tunnel of Time*; Narayan, *My Days*; Yati, *Love and Blessings*, 7.
121. T. S. Avinashilingam, *The Sacred Touch: An Autobiography* (Bombay: Bharatiya Vidya Bhavan, 1986), 44.
122. Walsh, *Growing Up in British India*, 25–27; Gopal Ram, *Rhythm in the Heavens: An Autobiography* (London: Secker & Warburg, 1957), x.
123. Ramarau, *Of Men, Matter and Me*, 8; Sattanathan, *Plain Speaking*, ch. 2.
124. Kalam, *My Journey*, 46–52; Sattanathan, *Plain Speaking*, 15; Raman, *Daughter of the Mountains*; Avinashilingam, *Sacred Touch*, 44.
125. Sattanathan, *Plain Speaking*, 42; Chakiar, *Last Smārtha Vichāram*.
126. Narayan, *My Days*, 12; Panikkar, *An Autobiography*, 3.
127. Sattanathan, *Plain Speaking*, 15; Das, *My Story*; Narayan, *My Days*; Avinashilingam, *Sacred Touch*, 43; Panikkar, *An Autobiography*, 3; Ramarau, *Of Men, Matter and Me*, 10.
128. Subbamma, *Fearless Feminist*, 22; Viramma, *Viramma*. For a more detailed discussion, see Lal, *Coming of Age*.
129. Viramma, *Viramma*, 32 (italics mine).
130. Raghuramaiah, *Hurricane*, 27; Sayeed, *My Life*, 12; Nijalingappa, *My Life*, 22; Sastry, *Reminiscences of a Jurist*, 3; Sundaram, *Simple Simon*, 12; Das, *My Story*; Chakiar, *Last Smārtha Vichāram*, 115–16; Ramarau, *Of Men, Matter and Me*, 74. See also Walsh, *Growing Up in British India*.

131. Laxman, *Tunnel of Time*, 7; Siddalingaiah, *Ooru Keri*, 11.
132. Raghuramaiah, *Hurricane*, 4.
133. Panikkar, *An Autobiography*, 6; Subramaniam, *Hand of Destiny*, 37; Vaidyanathan, *Thoughts and Reminiscences*, 10–11; Kalam, *My Journey*.
134. Sreenivasan, *Climbing the Coconut Tree*, 12–14, 35–38; Yati, *Love and Blessings*, 2, 15.
135. Gunasekaran, *The Scar*, 64.
136. Gunasekaran, *The Scar*, 20–33, 34–39, 58.
137. Nijalingappa, *My Life*, 20.
138. See Hinchy, *Governing Gender and Sexuality*, on non-traditional families including Hijra lineage households.
139. Balakrishnan, *Growing Up and Away*.
140. V. Tendulkar, 'View from the Balcony', in *Past Forward*, ed. Ramnarayan; Interview with Semmangudi Srinivasa Iyer, 'Semmangudi Looks Back at 90', *Frontline* 15, no. 22 (24 October 1998); C. S. Lakshmi, *The Singer and the Song: Conversations with Women Musicians* (Delhi: Kali, 2000); M. S. Subbalakshmi, 'Songbird in Springtime', in *Past Forward*, ed. Ramnarayan.
141. Mohanty and Mohanty, *In Quest of Quality Education*, 24.
142. Sundaram, *Simple Simon*, 35.
143. Kalam, *My Journey*, 51–55; Kalam, *Wings of Fire*, 8.
144. Kumar, *Politics of Gender*.
145. Raghuramaiah, *Hurricane*, 34; Sastry, *Reminiscences*, 2–3; Sreenivasan, *Climbing the Coconut Tree*, 58; Panikkar, *An Autobiography*, 4; Santhanam, *Looking Back*, 13; Avinashilingam, *Sacred Touch*, 43; Laxman 'Through the Coloured Glass', 40; Kalam, *Wings of Fire*, 8.
146. Narasimhaiah, '*N for Nobody*', 4; Sundaram, *Simple Simon*, 32–36; Sreenivasan, *Climbing the Coconut Tree*, 17; Rau, *Gifts of Passage*, 13; Nijalingappa, *My Life*, 20.
147. Sreenivasan, *Climbing the Coconut Tree*, 56.
148. Sreenivasan, *Climbing the Coconut Tree*, 54–55; Interview with Dr Muthulakshmi Reddi, 7 December 1930; Menon, *Many Worlds*, 4, 8; Ranga, *Fight for Freedom*, 4; Chakiar, *Last Smārtha Vichāram*, 59–61. See also Kumar, *Politics of Gender*.
149. Yati, *Love and Blessings*, 3.
150. Raghuramaiah, *Hurricane*, 33; Ranga, *Fight for Freedom*, 11–12; Ganesh, 'My Grandfather', 275.
151. A. Malagatti, 'The Bride', trans. S. R. Ramakrishna, in *Steel Nibs Are Sprouting*, ed. Satayanarayana and Tharu, 229; and N. Kz. Hanumanthaiah,

'Wedding Lamps on Holeya Street', trans. S. R. Ramakrishna, in *Steel Nibs Are Sprouting*, ed. Satayanarayana and Tharu, 386–88.
152. Sattanathan, *Plain Speaking*, 38, records his sister's experience of domestic violence; others record occasional violence.
153. Sen, *Traces of Empire*, 78.
154. Viramma, *Viramma*, 9.
155. Balagopalan, *Inhabiting Childhoods*, 45; Malagatti, 'The Bride', 229.

Conclusion

1. TNSA: GO2160 Home 6 September 1943, Committee of Visitors, Bellary, 28 December 1942.
2. Kumar, *Politics of Gender*.
3. Balagopalan, *Inhabiting Childhood*.
4. Sarkar, *Rebels, Wives, Saints*, 9.
5. Kannabiran and Singh, eds., *Challenging the Rule(s) of Law*, 195.
6. Newbigin, *The Hindu Family*, 2.
7. Garland, *Punishment and Welfare*; Donzelot, *Policing of Families*.
8. Cox, *Gender, Justice and Welfare*, 7, 13, 168.
9. Ranabir Samaddar, 'Crimes, Passion and Detachment: Colonial Foundations of the Rule of Law', in *Challenging the Rule(s) of Law*, ed. Kannabiran and Singh, 451–62.
10. Balakrishnan, *Growing Up and Away*, 99, 220–21.
11. Ritu Menon, '*Parens Patriae*: Exercising Patriarchal Prerogative in Post-Partition India', in *Challenging The Rules (s) of Law: Colonialism, Criminology and Human Rights in India*, ed. Kannabiran, Kalpana and Ranbir Singh (New Delhi: SAGE Publications Inc., 2008), 286.
12. MCA: Proceedings 1 April 1931, 39.

Bibliography

Archives

British Library, India Office Records (London)

All-India Conference of Inspectors-General of Prisons, December 1927.
All-India National Education Conference 1937.
Bureau of Education Publications.
Central Advisory Board of Health. *Medical Inspection of School Children and Teaching of Hygiene in Schools Joint Committee*, 1941.
Educational Survey Madras Presidency 1924.
Indian Jails Committee 1919–20: Official Report, Evidence and Submissions from the Madras Presidency.
Indian Statutory Commission: Auxiliary Report on Education. Hartog Commission 1929. Official Report, Evidence and Submissions from the Madras Presidency.
Imperial Education Conference 1923, 1924.
Judicial and Public Department Files: 1920–40.
Madras Educational Rules. Editions 1908–40.
Report of the Age of Consent. Joshi Committee: Report, Evidence and Submissions from the Madras Presidency 1928–29.
Report of the Director of Public Health, Madras 1921–48.
World Conference on New Education 1929.

British Library, India Office Records (Non-Government Organisations)

Teachers College, Saidapet.
St Christopher's Training School, Vepery.

Stri Dharma.
Women's India Association Reports 1917–67.
Educational India.

Madras Corporation Archives (Chennai)

Proceedings 1923–44.
Annual Report of Health Officer 1914–44.

National Library of Scotland (Edinburgh)

Indian Statutory Commission. *Report of the Indian Statutory Commission.* London, May 1930.
Annual and Quinquennial Reports of Director of Public Instruction. Madras Presidency, 1890–1940.
Education in India: Annual Reports of Education in India 1925–41.
Annual Reports of the Public Health Commissioner with the Government of India, 1922–45.
Report of the Chingleput Reformatory School, Madras 1890–1909.
League of Nations: Child Welfare Committee. Reports 1929–44.
Proceedings of the Central Advisory Board of Education in India, 1941–47.

Tamil Nadu State Archives (Chennai)

Law. Education. Department/Education Department File 1916–45.
Home Department Files 1936–43.
Report on the Working of the Madras Children Act and Administration of the Certified Schools, from Chief Inspector of Certified Schools 1925–49.

Tamil Nadu State Archives Library (Chennai)

Proceedings of the Madras Legislative Council, Madras Legislative Assembly 1915–45.

Women's Library (London)

Madras Children's Aid Society Seventh Annual Report 1932.

Published Works

Arundale, G. S. *The Bedrock of Education.* Madras: Theosophical Publishing House, 1924.

Aykroyd, W. R. *Notes on Food and Nutrition Policy in India*. New Delhi: Government of India, 1944.

Barker, Lt-Col F. A. *Modern Prison System of India: A Report to the Department*. London: Macmillan & Co., 1944.

Barman, S. *English Borstal System: A Study in the Treatment of Young Offenders*. London: P. S. King & Son, 1934.

Brander, Mrs. *Kindergarten Teaching in India: Stories, Object Lessons, Occupations, Songs and Games*. London: Macmillan and Co., 1899.

Carpenter, Mary. *Six Months in India*. Vol. 2. London: Longmans, Green & Co., 1868.

Children's Garden School Society. *'Let None Be Like Another': Report of Children's Garden Society 1937–2007*. Chennai: Seawaves Printers, 2007.

Clarke Hall, W. *The State and the Child*. London: Headley, 1917.

Gangulee, Nagendranath. *Health and Nutrition in India*. London: Faber & Faber, 1939.

International Women's Year Celebration Committee Tamil Nadu. *Some Illustrious Women of India: With Special Reference to Tamilnadu*. Madras: Asian Book, 1975.

Kalam, A. P. J. Abdul. *India 2020: A Vision for the New Millennium*. New York: Viking, 1998.

Lakshmi, C. S. *Mirrors and Gestures: Conversations with Women Musicians*. New Delhi: Kali, 2000.

———. *The Singer and the Song: Conversations with Women Musicians*. New Delhi: Kali, 2000.

Lou, Herbert. *Juvenile Courts in the US*. Chapel Hill: University of North Carolina, 1927.

Manshardt, Clifford. *The Delinquent Child in India*. Bombay: D. B. Taraporevala & Sons, 1939.

Moomaw, W. *Education and Village Improvement*. Mangalore: Oxford University Press, 1939.

Patro, A. P. *Studies in Local Self-Government, Education and Sanitation*. Madras: G. A. Natesan & Co., 1910.

Rajalakshmi, M. S. *Under the Banyan Tree*. Translated by Miss Choodamani. Chennai: Privately published by the school, n.d.

Sen, J. M. *History of Elementary Education in India*. Calcutta: Book Company College Square, 1933.

———. *Primary Education Acts in India—A Study*. Calcutta: YMCA, 1925.

Singh, Saint Nihal. *Making Bad Children Good: A Plea for an Indian Juvenile Court*. Madras: Mount Road, 1910.

Van Doren, A. B., ed. *Fourteen Experiments in Rural Education: Some Indian Schools Where New Methods Are Being Tested*. Calcutta: Association Press, 1928.
Wright, Robert. 'Keratomalacia in Southern India'. *British Journal of Ophthalmology* 6, no. 4 (1922): 164.

Autobiographies

Alexander, P. C. *Through the Corridors of Power: An Insider's Story*. New Delhi: Harper Collins India, 2004.
Appasamy, A. J. *A Bishop's Story*. Madras: Christian Literature Society, 1969.
Arjunamani, M., and M. Dhanasekar. *A Tale of a Tamil Widow*. Rockhampton: Central Queensland University Publishing, 2001.
Avinashilingam, T. S. *The Sacred Touch: An Autobiography*. Bombay: Bharatiya Vidya Bhavan, 1986.
Bhoothalingam, S. *Reflections on an Era: Memoirs of a Civil Servant*. Delhi: Affiliated East-West Press, 1993.
Chakiar, A. M. N. *The Last Smārtha Vichāram: A Victim's Reminiscences*. Madras: Padma C. Menon, 1998.
Chandy, K. K. *Quest of Community and Dynamic Non-violence*. Delhi: CiSRS, 1990.
Chockalingam, K. *Memoirs of the Last Sheriff of Madras*. Chennai: K. Chockalingam, 1997.
Das, Kamala. *My Story*. New Delhi: Sterling Paperbacks, 1988.
Gunasekaran, K. A. *The Scar [Vadu]*. Translated by V. Kadambari from Tamil. Hyderabad: Orient Blackswan, 2009.
Iyengar, B. K. S., John J. Evans and Douglas Abrams. *Light on Life: The Journey to Wholeness, Inner Peace and Ultimate Freedom*. London: Rodale International Ltd, 2005.
Kalam, A. P. J. Abdul. *My Journey: Transforming Dreams into Actions*. Delhi: Rupa, 2013.
Kalam, A. P. J. Abdul, and Arun Tiwari. *Wings of Fire: An Autobiography*. Hyderabad: Universities Press, 1999.
Keshava, N. *Autobiography of N. Keshava MP*. Bangalore: Vichara Sahitya Private Ltd, 1984.
———. *The Tunnel of Time*. New Delhi, India: Penguin, 1998.
Mahadevan, T. M. P. *A Philosopher Looks Back*. Bombay: Bharatiya Vidya Bhavan, 1928.

Menon, K. P. S. *Many Worlds: An Autobiography*. Calcutta: Oxford University Press, 1965.

Mohanty, Jagannath, and Suhansu Mohanty. *In Quest of Quality Education and Literature: An Autobiography*. New Delhi: Deep & Deep Publications, 2006.

Narasimhaiah, C. *'N for Nobody': Autobiography of an English Teacher*. Delhi: B. R. Publishing Corporation, 1991.

Narayan, R. K. *My Days: A Memoir*. 2nd ed. Oxford: Picador, 1974.

Nataraja Guru. *Autobiography of an Absolutist*. Fernhill: Gurkula Publishing House, 1989.

Nayanar, E. K. *My Struggles: An Autobiography*. New Delhi: Vikas, 1982.

Nijalingappa, S. *My Life and Politics: An Autobiography*. Delhi: Vision Books, 2000.

Nimbkar, Krishnabai. *Smrutika: The Story of My Mother as Told by Herself*. Self-published, Pune, 1988. BL: MssEur F 341/125.

Panikkar, K. M. *An Autobiography*. Translated by K. Krishnamurthy from Tamil. Delhi: Oxford University Press, (1954) 1977.

Raghuramaiah, K. Lakshmi. *Hurricane: Autobiography of a Woman*. Delhi: Chanakya Publications, 1993.

Ram, Gopal. *Rhythm in the Heavens: An Autobiography*. London: Secker & Warburg, 1957.

Raman, Hema. *Daughter of the Mountains*. Madras: East West Books, 1993.

Ramarau, R. V. M. G. *Of Men, Matter and Me*. London: Asia Publishing House, 1961.

Ramnarayan, Gowri. *Past Forward: Six Artists in Search of their Childhood*. New Delhi: Oxford University Press, 1997.

Ranga, N. G. *Fight for Freedom: Autobiography of N. G. Ranga*. Delhi: S. Chand, 1968.

Ranganathan, S. R. *A Librarian Looks Back: An Autobiography of Dr S. R. Ranganathan*. New Delhi: ABC Publishing House, 1992.

Rao, V. K. R. V. *Partial Memoirs of V. K. R. V. Rao*. Edited by S. L. Rao. Delhi: Oxford University Press, 2002.

Rau, Santha Rama. *Gifts of Passage*. London: Victor Gollancz, 1961.

Reddi, Dr Muthulakshmi. Interview. 7 December 1930. IOR: MSS EUR F341/157.

———. *My Experience as a Legislator*. Tripicane: Current Thought Press, 1930. BL: W33/8063.

———. *Autobiography*. Self-published, Madras, 1964. IOR: MssEur F341/157.

Samban, A. K. *Autobiography of Prof. A. K. Samban: The Teacher Recipient UNESCO Award*. Madras: Sri Maruthi Graphics, 1994.

Santhanam, K. *Looking Back: Memoirs of K. Santhanam*. Mumbai: Bharatiya Vidya Bhavan, 2001.

Sargunam, M. J. *An Autobiography*. Coimbatore: Palaniandavar Printers, 1978.

Sastry, K. R. R. *Reminiscences of a Jurist*. Madras: Jupiter, 1963.

Sattanathan, A. N. *Plain Speaking: A Sudra's Story*. Edited by Uttara Natarajan. Oxford: Permanent Black, 2007.

Sayeed, Basheer Ahmed. *My Life, a Struggle: An Autobiography*. Madras: Academy of Islamic Research, 1983.

Sivananda, Swami. *Autobiography of Swami Sivananda*. Garhwal: Divine Life Society, 2009.

Sreenivasan, Kasthuri. *Climbing the Coconut Tree: A Partial Autobiography*. Delhi: Oxford University Press, 1980.

Srinivasa Iyer, Semmangudi. 'Semmangudi Looks Back at 90'. Interview, *Frontline* 15, no. 22 (24 October 1998).

Subbamma, Malladi. *Fearless Feminist: An Autobiography of a Social Revolutionary*. Hyderabad: Booklinks Corp., 1994.

Subramaniam, C. *Hand of Destiny: Memoirs. Vol 1: The Turning Point*. Bombay: Bharatiya Bhavan, 1993.

Sundaram, P. S. *Simple Simon: An Autobiography*. Madras: Nirmala Sundaram, 1997.

Swaminatha Iyer, U. V. *En Carittiram: The Story of My Life*. Translated by Kamil Zvelebil. Madras: Institute of Asian Studies, 1990.

Vadakkan, Joseph. *A Priest's Encounter with Revolution*. Bangalore: Christian Literature Society, 1974.

Vaidyanathan, P. *Thoughts and Reminiscences*. Chetput: Ananda Books, 1986.

Veeraswami, K. *The Perils to Justice: A Judge Thinks Aloud*. Calcutta: Eastern Law House, 1996.

Viramma, Josiane Racine, and Jean-Lus Racine. *Viramma: Life of an Untouchable*. Translated by Will Hobson from French. London: Verso, 1997.

Yati, Nitya Chaitanya. *Love and Blessings: The Autobiography of Guru Nitya Chaitanya Yati*. Edited by Peter Oppenheimer. Varkala: Narayana Gurukula, 2000.

Published Works, after 1947

Advani, Shalini. *Schooling the National Imagination: Education, English and the Indian Modern*. New Delhi: Oxford University Press, 2009.

Ahluwalia, Sanjam. *Reproductive Restraints: Birth Control in India, 1877–1947*. Chicago: University of Illinois Press, 2008.

Alborn, Timothy L. 'Age and Empire in the Indian Census, 1871–1931'. *Journal of Interdisciplinary History* 30, no. 1 (Summer 1999): 61–89.

Alexander, Kristine. 'The Girl Guide Movement and Imperial Internationalism during the 1920s and 1930s'. *Journal of the History of Childhood and Youth* 2, no. 1 (2009): 37–63.

Alexander, Robin. *Culture and Pedagogy: International Comparisons in Primary Education*. Oxford: Blackwell, 2001.

Allender, Tim. 'Learning Abroad: The Colonial Education Experiment in India, 1813–1919'. *Pedagogica Historica* 45, no. 6 (December 2009): 727–41.

———. *Learning Femininity in Colonial India, 1820–1932*. Manchester: Manchester University Press, 2016.

Amrith, Sunil. *Decolonising International Health: India and Southeast Asia, 1930–65*. Basingstoke: Palgrave MacMillan, 2006.

———. 'Food and Welfare in India, c. 1900–1950'. *Comparative Studies in Society and History* 50, no. 4 (2008): 1010–35.

Anderson, Clare. *Subaltern Lives: Biographies of Colonialism in the Indian Ocean World 1780–1920*. Cambridge: Cambridge University Press, 2012.

Aries, Phillipe. *Centuries of Childhood: A Social History of Family Life*. London: Jonathan Cape, 1962.

Arnold, David. 'Discovery of Malnutrition and Diet in Colonial India'. *Indian Economic and Social Review* 31, no. 1 (1994): 1–26.

———. *Police Power and Colonial Rule Madras 1859–1947*. Delhi: Oxford University Press, 1986.

———. *Science, Technology and Medicine in Colonial India*. Cambridge: Cambridge University Press, 2000.

———. 'The Medicalisation of Poverty in Colonial India'. *Historical Research* 85, no. 229 (August 2012): 488–504.

———. 'Vagrant India: Famine, Poverty, and Welfare under Colonial Rule'. In *Cast Out: Vagrancy and Homelessness in Global and Historical Perspective*, 117–39. Athens, Ohio: Ohio University Press, 2008.

Arnold, David, and Stuart Blackburn, eds. *Telling Lives in India: Biography, Autobiography and Life History*. Delhi: Permanent Black, 2004.

Arnold, David, and David Hardiman, eds. *Subaltern Studies 8: Essays in Honour of Ranajit Guha*. Delhi: Oxford University Press, 1994.

Babu, Sentil. 'Tamil Mathematical Manuscripts and the Possibility of a Social History of Mathematics Education in India'. *Trends in Mathematics Education Research* (2004): 75–102.

Bagchi, Barnita. 'Connected and Entangled Histories: Writing Histories of Education in the Indian Context'. *Paedagogica Historica* 50, no. 6 (2014): 813–21.

———. 'Tracing Two Generations in Twentieth-Century Indian Women's Education through Analysis of Literary Sources: Selected Writings by Padmini Sengupta'. *Women's History Review* 29, no. 3 (2020): 465–79.

———. 'Two Lives: Voices, Resources, and Networks in the History of Female Education in Bengal and South Asia'. *Women's History Review* 19, no. 1 (2010): 51–69.

Bagchi, B., Eckhardt Fuchs and Kate Rousmaniere, eds. *Connecting Histories of Education: Transnational and Cross-Cultural Exchanges in (Post-)Colonial Education.* Oxford; New York: Berghahn Books, 2014.

Bailey, Victor. *Delinquency and Citizenship: Reclaiming the Young Offenders, 1914–18.* Oxford: Clarendon Press, 1987.

Baker, C. J. *An Indian Rural Economy 1880–1955: The Tamilnad Countryside.* Oxford: Clarendon Press, 1984.

———. 'Leading Up to Periyar: The Early Career of E. V. Ramaswami Naicker'. In *Leadership in South Asia*, edited by B. N. Pandey, 501–24. New Delhi: Vikas, 1977.

———. *Politics of South India 1920–1937.* Cambridge: Cambridge University Press, 1976.

Baker, C. J., and D. A. Washbrook. *South India: Political Institutions and Political Change 1880–1940.* Delhi: Macmillan, 1975.

Bala, Poonam, ed. *Contesting Colonial Authority: Medicine and Indigenous Reponses in Nineteenth- and Twentieth-Century India.* Lanham: Lexington Books, 2012.

———, ed. *Medicine and Colonialism: Historical Perspectives in India and South Africa.* London: Pickering and Chatto, 2014.

———. *Medicine and Medical Policies in India: Social and Historical Perspectives.* Lanham: Lexington Books, 2007.

Balagopalan, Sarada. 'Constructing Indigenous Childhoods: Colonialism, Vocational Education and The Working Child'. *Childhood* 9, no 1 (2002): 19–34.

———. *Inhabiting Childhood: Children, Labour and Schooling in Postcolonial India.* Basingstoke: Palgrave Macmillan, 2014.

———. 'Introduction: Children's Lives and the Indian Context'. *Childhood* 18, no. 3 (2011): 291–98.

———. 'Rationalising Seclusion: A Preliminary Analysis of a Residential Schooling Scheme for Poor Girls in India'. *Feminist Theory* 11, no. 3 (2010): 295–308.

Balakrishnan, Vijayalakshmi. *Growing Up and Away: Narratives of Indian Childs, Memory, History and Identity*. Delhi: Oxford University Press, 2011.

Balogh, R. 'Feeding Workers in Colonial India 1919–1947'. In *Food Culture Studies in India*, edited by S. Malhotra, K. Sharma and S. Dogra, 119–37. Singapore: Springer, 2021.

Banerjee, Sukanya. *Becoming Imperial Citizens: Indians in the Late Victorian Empire*. Durham: Duke, 2010.

Banerjee, Swapna M. *Men, Women and Domestics: Articulating Middle-Class Identity in Colonial Bengal*. New Delhi: Oxford University Press, 2004.

———. 'Blurring Boundaries, Distant Comparisons: Non-kin Female Caregivers for Children in Colonial India in the Nineteenth and Twentieth Centuries'. *Paedagogica Historica* 46, no. 6 (2010): 775–88.

———. 'Debates on Domesticity and the Position of Women in Late Colonial India'. *History Compass* 8, no. 6 (2010): 455–73.

Bansal, C. P., and Sailesh Gupta. 'The Past Half Century of Indian Academy of Pediatrics. IAP'. *Indian Paediatrics* 50, no. 1 (2012): 39–48.

Barnett, Marguerite Ross. *The Politics of Cultural Nationalism in South India*. New Jersey: Princeton University Press, 1976.

Barona, Josep L. 'Nutrition and Health: The International Context during the Interwar Crisis'. *Social History of Medicine* 21, no. 1 (2008): 87–105.

Basu, Aparna. *The Growth of Education and Political Development in India, 1898–1920*. Delhi: Oxford University Press, 1974.

Bates, Crispin. *Subalterns and Raj*. Oxford: Routledge, 2007.

Behera, Deepak Kumar, ed. *Childhoods in South Asia*. New Delhi: Pearson Longman, 2007.

Bellenoit, Hayden. *Missionary Education and Empire in Late Colonial India, 1860–1920*. London: Pickering & Chatto, 2007.

Bhabha, Homi K. 'Of Mimicry and Man: The Ambivalence of Colonial Discourse'. *October* 28 (1984): 125–33.

Bhagavan, Manu. *Sovereign Spheres: Princes, Education and Empire in Colonial India*. New Delhi: Oxford University Press, 2003.

Bhattacharya, B. K. *Juvenile Delinquency and Borstals*. Calcutta: C. S. Sarket & Sons, 1962.

Bhattacharya, Sabyasachi, ed. *The Contested Terrain: Perspectives on Education in India*. London: Sangam Books, 1998.

Bhattacharya, Tithi. *The Sentinels of Culture: Class, Education and the Colonial Intellectual in Bengal 1848–85*. Oxford: Oxford University Press, 2005.

Bose, A. B. *The State of Children in India: Promises to Keep*. New Delhi: Manohar, 2003.

Bowen, Zazie, and Jessica Hinchy. 'Introduction: Children and Knowledge in India'. *South Asian History and Culture* 6, no. 3 (2015): 317–29.

Bradley, Kate. 'Inside the Inner London Juvenile Court c. 1909–1953'. *Crime and Misdemeanours* 3, no. 2 (2009): 37–59.

Breckenridge, Carol A., and Peter Van Der Veer. *Orientalism and the Postcolonial Predicament: Perspectives on South Asia*. Philadelphia: University of Pennsylvania Press, 1993.

Brewis, Georgina. '"Fill Full the Mouth of Famine": Voluntary Action in Famine Relief in India 1896–1901'. *Modern Asian Studies* 44, no. 4 (2010): 887–918.

Broome, Sarah K. 'Stri-Dharma: Voice of the Indian Women's Rights Movement 1928–1936'. History Theses Paper 57, Georgia State University, 2012.

Brown, Judith. *Modern India: The Origins of an Asian Democracy*. Oxford: Oxford University Press, 1985.

Buettner, Elizabeth. *Empire Families: Britons and Late Imperial India*. Oxford: Oxford University Press, 2004.

Bugge, Henriette. *Mission and Tamil Society, Social and Religious Change in South India, 1840–1900*. Richmond: Curzon Press, 1994.

Burra, Neera, ed. *Born Unfree: Child Labour, Education and the State in India*. Oxford: Oxford University Press, 2006.

Burton, Antoinette. *Dwelling in the Archive: Women Writing House, Home and History in Late Colonial India*. New Delhi: Oxford University Press, 2003.

———. 'Thinking beyond the Boundaries: Empire, Feminism and the Domains of History'. *Social History* 26, no. 1 (2001): 60–71.

Butalia, Urvashi. *The Other Side of Silence: Voices from the Partition of India*. London: Hurst & Company, 2000.

Bynum, W. 'Reflections on The History of Human Experimentation'. In *The Use of Human Beings in Research: With Special Reference to Clinical Trials*, edited F. Spicker, I. Alon, A. De Vries and H. Tristram Engelhardt Jr, 29–46. Dordrecht: Kluwer Academic Publications, 1988.

Chakrabarti, Pratik. *Western Science in Modern India: Metropolitan Methods, Colonial Practices*. Delhi: Permanent Black, 2004.

———. '"Signs of the Times" Medicine and Nationhood in British India'. *OSIRIS* 24, no. 1 (2009): 188–211.

Chakrabarty, Dipesh. *Habitations of Modernity: Essays in the Wake of Subaltern Studies*. Delhi: Permanent Black, 2002.

———. 'Postcoloniality and the Artifice of History: Who Speaks for "Indian" Pasts?' In 'Imperial Fantasies and Postcolonial Histories', special issue, *Representations* 37 (Winter 1992): 1–26.

Chakramakkil, Anto Thomas. 'The Polemics of Real and Imagined Childhood(s) in India'. *International Research in Children's Literature* 11, no. 1 (2017): 74–88.

Chandra, Nandini. *The Classic Popular: Amar Chitra Katha, 1967–2007*. New Delhi: Yoda Press, 2008.

———. 'The Pedagogic Imperative of Travel Writing in the Hindi World: Children's Periodicals, 1920–1950'. *South Asia: Journal of South Asian Studies* 30, no. 2 (2007): 293–325.

Chatterjee, Gautam. *Child Criminals and the Raj: Reformation in British Jails*. New Delhi: Akshaya Publications, 1995.

Chatterjee, Indrani. *Unfamiliar Relations: Family and History in South Asia*. New Jersey: Rutgers University Press, 2004.

Chatterjee, Partha. *Nation and Its Fragments*. Princeton: Princeton University Press, 1993.

———. *Nationalist Thought and the Colonial World: A Derivative Discourse?* London: Zed Books, 1986.

———, ed. *Texts of Power: Emerging Disciplines in Colonial Bengal*. Minneapolis: University of Minnesota Press, 1995.

Chaturvedi, Vinayak. *Mapping Subaltern Studies and the Postcolonial*. London: Verso, 2000.

Chaudhary, Latika. 'Determinants of Primary Schooling in British India'. *Journal of Economic History* 69, no. 1 (March 2009): 269–302.

———. 'Land Revenues, Schools and Literacy: A Historical Examination of Public and Private Funding of Education'. *Indian Economic Social History Review* 47, no. 179 (2010): 179–204.

Chiriyankandath, James. '"Democracy" under the Raj: Elections and Separate Representation in British India'. In *Democracy in India*, edited by Niraja Gopal Jayal, 39–63. Oxford: Oxford University Press, 2001.

Chisholm, Linda. 'The Pedagogy of Porter: The Origins of the Reformatory in the Cape Colony, 1882–1910'. *Journal of African History* 27, no. 3 (1986): 481–95.

Cohen, B., and S. Ganguly. 'Introduction: Regions and Regionalism in India'. *India Review* 13, no. 4 (2014): 313–20.

Cohn, Bernard. *Colonialism and Its Forms of Knowledge: The British in India*. New Jersey: Princeton University Press, 1996.

Collingham, E. M. *Imperial Bodies: The Physical Experience of the Raj 1800–1947*. Cambridge, MA: Polity, 2001.

Cooter, Roger. *In the Name of the Child*. Abingdon: Routledge, 2013.

Cox, Pamela. *Gender, Justice and Welfare: Bad Girls in Britain, 1900–1950*. Basingstoke: Palgrave Macmillan, 2003.

Cox, Pamela, and Heather Shore. *Becoming Delinquent: British and European Youth 1650–1950*. Dartmouth: Ashgate, 2002.

Crawford, Sally, and Carenza Lewis. 'Childhood Studies and the Society for the Study of Childhood in the Past'. *Childhood in the Past* 1, no. 1 (2008): 5–16.

Crook, Nigel, ed. *The Transmission of Knowledge in South Asia: Essays on Education, Religion, History, and Politics*. Delhi: Oxford University Press, 1996.

Dapaepe, Marc. 'Belgian Images of the Psycho-pedagogical Potential of the Congolese during the Colonial Era, 1908–1960'. *Pedagogica Historica* 45, no. 6 (December 2009): 707–25.

Das, Veena. *Life and Words: Violence and the Descent into the Ordinary*. Berkley: University of California Press, 2007.

———. 'Voices of Children'. *Daedalus: Another India* 118, no. 4 (Fall 1989): 262–94.

Dasan, M., V. Pratibha, Pradeepan Pampirikunnu and C. S. Chandrika, eds. *Oxford Indian Anthology of Malayalam Dalit Writing*. Oxford: Oxford University Press, 2012.

Davin, Anna. *Growing Up Poor: Home, School and Street in London 1870–1914*. London: Rivers Oram Press, 1996.

Denault, Leigh. 'The Home and the World: New Directions in the History of the Family in South Asia'. *History Compass* 12, no. 2 (2014): 101–11.

Dirks, Nicholas B. *Castes of Mind: Colonialism and the Making of Modern India*. Princeton: Princeton University Press, 2001.

Dharampal. *The Beautiful Tree: Indigenous Indian Education in the Eighteenth Century*. New Delhi: Bilia Impex Private Ltd, 1983.

Dodson, Michael S., and Brian A. Hatcher. *Trans-colonial Modernities in South Asia*. London: Routledge, 2012.

Donzelot, Jacques. *The Policing of Families: Welfare versus the State*. London: Hutchison University Library, 1979.

Dube, Saurabh, and Anupama Rao, eds. *Crime through Time*. New Delhi: Oxford University Press, 2013.

Elangovan, Arvind. 'Constitutionalism, Political Exclusion, and Implications for Indian Constitutional History: The Case of Montagu Chelmsford Reforms 1919'. *South Asian History and Culture* 7, no. 3 (2016): 271–88.

Ellis, Catriona. 'Climbing the Coconut Tree: Three South Indians Use Their Personal Memories of Colonial Education to Influence the Decolonization of Education after Independence'. In *Decolonization's and Education New Polities and New Men*, edited by Marcelo Caruso and Daniel Maul, 67–90. Berlin: Peter Lang, 2020.

———. 'Education for All: Reassessing the Historiography of Education in Colonial India'. *History Compass* 7, no. 2 (2009): 363–75.

———. '"If You Cannot Feed the Body of a Child You Cannot Feed the Brain": Education and Nutrition in Late Colonial Madras'. *South Asia: Journal of South Asian Studies* 44, no. 1 (February 2021). DOI: 10.1080/00856401.2021.1862497.

———. 'Perspectives on the History of Colonial Education'. In *Global Education Systems: Handbook of Education Systems in South Asia*, edited by Padma M. Sarangapani and Rekha Pappu, 363–89. Singapore: Springer, 2020.

———. 'Remembering Pre-independence Childhoods in South India: Interrogating Autobiographies and Identities'. *Social History* 44, no. 2 (2019): 202–28.

———. '"Snapshots" of the Classroom: Autobiographies and the Experience of Elementary Education in the Madras Presidency, 1882–1947'. In 'Childhoods in South Asia', special issue, *Childhood* 18, no. 3 (August 2011): 384–401.

———. 'The Trumpet and the Drum: Music and Reclaiming the Delinquent Child'. In *Childhoods and Youth in India: Engagements with Modernity*, edited by Anandini Dar and Divya Kannan. New Delhi: Routledge, forthcoming.

Ellis, Heather, ed. *Juvenile Delinquency and the Limits of Western Influence, 1850–2000*. Basingstoke: Palgrave Macmillan, 2014.

Etherington, Norman, ed. *Missions and Empire: Oxford History of the British Empire Series*. Oxford: Oxford University Press, 2005.

Farley, John. *To Cast Out Disease: A History of the International Health Division of the Rockefeller Foundations*. Oxford: Oxford University Press, 2004.

Fischer-Tiné, Harald. 'Fitness for Modernity? The YMCA and Physical-Education Schemes in Late-Colonial South Asia (circa 1900–40)'. *Modern Asian Studies* 53, no. 2 (2019): 512–59.

Fischer-Tine, Harald, and Caroline Stolte. 'Imagining Asia in India: Nationalism and Internationalism'. *Comparative Studies in Society and History* 54, no. 1 (2012): 65–92.

Fischer-Tiné, Harald, Stefan Huebner and Ian Tyrrell, eds. *Spreading Protestant Modernity: Global Perspectives on the Social Work of the YMCA and YWCA, 1889–1970*. Honolulu: University of Hawaii Press, 2020.

Forbes, Geraldine. 'Women and Modernity: The Issue of Child Marriage in India'. *Women's Studies International. Quarterly* 2, no. 4 (1979): 407–19.

———. *Women in Colonial India: Essays in Politics, Medicine and Historiography*. New Delhi: Chronicle Books, 2005.

———. *Women in Modern India*. Cambridge: Cambridge University Press, 2006.

Fourchard, Laurent. 'Lagos and the Invention of Juvenile Delinquency in Nigeria, 1920–60'. *Journal of African History* 47, no. 1 (2006): 115–37.

Fuchs, Eckhart. 'The Creation of New International Networks in Education: The League of Nations and Educational Organisations'. *Paedagogica Historica* 43, no. 2 (April 2007): 199–209.

Fuller, C. J., and Haripriya Narasimhan. 'Marriage, Education, and Employment among Tamil Brahman Women in South India, 1891–2010'. *Modern Asian Studies* 47, no. 1 (2013): 53–84.

Garland, David. *Punishment and Welfare*. Aldershot: Gower, 1985.

Ghosh, Durba. *Sex and the Family in Colonial India: The Making of Empire*. Cambridge: Cambridge University Press, 2006.

Glover, William. 'Objects, Models, and Exemplary Works: Educating Sentiment in Colonial India'. *Journal of Asian Studies* 64, no. 3 (2005): 539–66.

Goodman, Joyce, and Jane Martin. *Gender, Colonialism and Education: The Politics of Experience*. London: Woburn Press, 2002.

Goodman, Joyce, A. McElligot and L. Marks. *Useful Bodies: Humans in the Service of Medical Science in the Twentieth Century*. Baltimore: John Hopkins University Press, 2003.

Gordon, Linda. 'The Perils of Innocence, or What's Wrong with Putting Children First'. *Journal of the History of Childhood and Youth* 1, no. 3 (Fall 2008): 331–50.

Gorman, Daniel. 'Empire, Internationalism, and the Campaign against the Traffic in Women and Children in the 1920s'. *Twentieth Century British History* 19, no. 2 (2008): 186–216.

Goswami, Supriya. *Colonial India in Children's Literature*. New Delhi; London: Routledge, 2012.

Guha, Ranajit. 'Chandra's Death'. In *Subaltern Studies V*, 167–202. Oxford: Oxford University Press, 1987.

———. 'The Small Voice of History'. In *Subaltern Studies IX: Writings on South Asian History and Society*, edited by Ranajit Guha, 304–18. Oxford: Oxford University Press, 1997.

Hancock, M. 'Home Science and the Nationalization of Domesticity in Colonial India'. *Modern Asian Studies* 35, no. 4 (2001): 871–903.

Hansen, Kathryn. *Stages of Life: Indian Theatre Autobiographies*. Wimbledon, London: Anthem Press, 2011.

Harrington, Joel. *The Unwanted Child: The Fate of Foundlings, Orphans and Juvenile Criminals in Early Modern Germany*. Chicago; London: University of Chicago Press, 2009.

Harris, Bernard. *The Health of the Schoolchild: A History of School Medical Service in England and Wales*. Buckingham: Oxford University Press, 1995.

Harrison, Mark. *Public Health in British India: Anglo-Indian Preventative Medicine 1859–1914*. Cambridge: Cambridge University Press, 1994.

Haynes, Douglas, and Gyan Prakash, eds. *Contesting Power: Resistance and Everyday Social Relations in South Asia*. Delhi: Oxford University Press, 1991.

Hendrick, Harry, ed. *Child Welfare and Social Policy: An Essential Reader*. Bristol: Policy Press, 2005.

———. *Children, Childhood and English Society, 1880–1990*. Cambridge: Cambridge University Press, 1997.

Herbert, Trevor. *The British Brass Band: A Musical and Social History*. Oxford: Oxford University Press, 2000.

Herbert, Trevor, and Margaret Sarkissian. 'Victorian Bands and Their Dissemination in the Colonies'. *Popular Music* 16, no. 2 (1997): 165–79.

Heywood, Colin. *A History of Childhood: Children and Childhood in the West from Medieval to Modern Times*. Cambridge, MA: Polity Press, 2001.

Hinchy, Jessica. *Governing Gender and Sexuality in Colonial India, the Hijra, c.1850–1900*. Cambridge: Cambridge University Press, 2019.

Hodges, Sarah. *Contraception, Colonialism and Commerce: Birth Control in South India 1920–1940*. Aldershot: Ashgate, 2008.

———, ed. *Reproductive Health in India: History, Politics, Controversies*. Hyderabad: Orient Longman, 2001.

———. 'Revolutionary Family Life and the Self Respect Movement in Tamil South India, 1926–49'. *Contributions to Indian Sociology* 39, no. 2 (2006): 251–77.

Humphries, Jane. 'Childhood and Child Labour in the British Industrial Revolution'. *Economic History Review* 66, no. 2 (2012): 395–418.

Humphries, Stephen. *Hooligans or Rebels? An Oral History of Working-Class Childhood and Youth, 1889–1939*. Oxford: Basil Blackwell, 1981.

Inden, Ronald B. *Imagining India*. Bloomington: Indiana University Press, 2000.

Irschick, Eugene F. *Dialogue and History: Constructing South India, 1795–1895*. Berkeley: University of California Press, 1994.

———. *Politics of Tamil Revivalism in the 1930s*. Madras: Cre-A, 1986.

Jackson, Louise. *Child Sexual Abuse in Victorian England*. London; New York: Routledge, 2000.

———. 'Care or Control? The Metropolitan Women Police and Child Welfare 1919–1969'. *Historical Journal* 46, no. 3 (2003): 623–48.

James, Allison, Chris Jenks and Alan Prout. *Theorising Childhood*. Cambridge, MA: Blackwell Press, 1998.

Jayawardena, Kumari. *The White Woman's Other Burden: Western Women and South Asia during British Colonial Rule*. New York; London: Routledge, 1995.

Jeffery, Roger. *The Politics of Health in India*. Berkeley: University of California Press, 1988.

Jenks, Chris. *Childhood*. London; New York: Routledge, 1996.

Kakar, Sudhir. *The Inner World: A Psycho-analytic Study of Childhood and Society in India*. Delhi: Oxford University Press, 1981.

Kallaway, P. 'Conference Litmus: The Development of a Conference and Policy Culture in the Interwar Period with Special Reference to the New Education Fellowship and British Colonial Education in Southern Africa'. In *Transformations in Schooling: Historical and Comparative Perspectives*, edited by K. Tolley, 123–49. New York: Palgrave MacMillan, 2007.

Kalpagam, U. 'Colonial Governmentality and the Public Sphere in India'. *Journal of Historical Sociology* 15, no. 1 (March 2002): 35–58.

———. *Rule by Numbers: Governmentality in Colonial India*. London: Lexington Books, 2014.

Kamtekar, Indivar. 'A Different War Dance: State and Class in India 1939–1945'. *Past and Present* 176 (2002): 187–221.

Kannabiran, Kalpana, and Ranbir Singh, eds. *Challenging the Rule(s) of Law: Colonialism, Criminology and Human Rights in India*. New Delhi: SAGE Publications Inc., 2008.

Karlekar, Malavika, and Rundrangshu Mukherjee, eds. *Remembered Childhood: Essays in Honour of Andre Beteille*. Oxford: Oxford University Press, 2010.

Kent, Eliza F. *Converting Women: Gender and Protestant Christianity in Colonial South India*. Oxford: Oxford University Press, 2004.

Khan, Ali. *Representing Children: Power, Policy and the Discourse on Child Labour in the Football Manufacturing Industry of Pakistan*. Oxford: Oxford University Press, 2007.

Khoja-Moolji, Shenila. *Forging the Ideal Educated Girl: The Production of Desirable Subjects in Muslim South Asia*. Berkeley: University of California Press, 2018.

Kidambi, Prashant. *The Making of an Indian Metropolis: Colonial Governance and Public Culture in Bombay, 1890–1920*. Aldershot: Ashgate, 2007.

Krishnan, Sneha. 'Where Do Good Girls Have Sex? Space, Risk and Respectability in Chennai'. *Gender, Place and Culture* 28, no. 7 (2021): 999–1018.

Kumar, Deepak, Joseph Bara, Nadita Khadria and Radha Gayathri, eds. *Education in Colonial India: Historical Insights*. New Delhi: Manohar, 2013.

Kumar, Krishna. 'Childhood in a Globalising World'. *Economic and Political Weekly* (2006): 4030–34.

———. *Political Agenda of Education: A Study of Colonialist and Nationalist Ideas*. New Delhi: Sage Publications, 1991.

Kumar, Nita. *Lessons from Schools: The History of Education in Banaras*. New Delhi: Sage, 2000.

———. *The Politics of Gender, Community and Modernity: Essays on Education in India*. New Delhi: Oxford University Press, 2007.

Kumar, Radha. *The History of Doing*. London: Verso, 1993.

Kumar, Raj. *Dalit Personal Narratives: Reading Caste, Nation and Identity*. Hyderabad: Orient Blackswan, 2010.

Kumar, Udaya. 'Autobiography as a Way of Writing History: Personal Narratives from Kerala and the Inhabitation of Modernity'. In *History in the Vernacular*, edited by Partha Chatterjee and Raziuddin Aquil, 418–48. Delhi: Permanent Black, 2008.

———. 'Subjects of New Lives: Reform, Self-Making and the Discourse of Autobiography in Kerala'. In *Different Types of History*, edited by Bharati Ray, 299–327. Delhi: Pearson Longman, 2009.

———. *Writing the First Person: Literature, History and Autobiography in Modern Kerala*. Bangalore: Permanent Black, 2016.

Kumari, Ved. *The Juvenile Justice System in India: From Welfare to Rights*. 2nd ed. Oxford: Oxford University Press, 2004.

Lal, Ruby. *Coming of Age in Nineteenth Century India: The Girl-Child and the Art of Playfulness*. New Delhi: Cambridge University Press, 2013.

Lang, Sean. 'Drop the Demon *Dai*: Maternal Mortality and the State in Colonial Madras, 1840–1875'. *Social History of Medicine* 18, no. 3 (2005): 357–78.

Lester, Alan. 'Imperial Circuits and Networks: Geographies of the British Empire'. *History Compass* 4, no. 1 (2006): 124–41.

Levine, Philippa, ed. *Gender and Empire*. Oxford: Oxford University Press, 2007.

Lieten, G. K., Ravi Srivastava and Sukhadeo Thorat. *Small Hands in South Asia: Child Labour in Perspective*. New Delhi: Manohar, 2004.

Logan, Anne. '"A Suitable Person for Suitable Cases": The Gendering of Juvenile Courts in England, c. 1910–39'. *Twentieth Century British History* 16, no. 2 (2005): 129–45.

———. 'Policy Networks and the Juvenile Court: The Reform of Youth Justice, c. 1905–1950'. *Crime and Misdemeanours* 3, no. 2 (2009): 18–36.

Lomax, Elizabeth M. R. 'Small and Special: The Development of Hospitals for Children in Victorian Britain'. *Medical History*, supp. 16 (1996): 1.

Mahood, Linda. *Feminism and Voluntary Action: Eglantyne Jebb and Save the Children 1876–1928*. Basingstoke: Palgrave Macmillan, 2009.

———. *Policing Gender, Class and Family: Britain 1850–1940*. London: UCL Press, 1995.

Malhotra, Ashok. *Making British Indian Fictions: 1772–1823*. New York: Palgrave Macmillan, 2012.

Manjrekar, Nandini. 'Ideals of Hindu Girlhoods: Reading Vidya Bharati's *Balika Shikshan*'. *Childhood* 18, no. 33 (2011): 350–66.

Mann, M., ed. *Shantiniketan—Hellerau: New Education in the 'Pedagogic Provinces' of India and Germany*. Heidelberg: Draupadi, 2015.

Marshall, Dominique. 'Children's Rights in Imperial Political Cultures: Missionary and Humanitarian Contributions to the Conference of the African Child of 1931'. *International Journal of Children's Rights* 12, no. 3 (2004): 273–318.

———. 'The Construction of Children as an Object of International Relations: The Declaration of Children's Rights and the Child Welfare Committee of League of Nations, 1900–1924'. *International Journal of Children's Rights* 7 (1999): 103–47.

McPherson, Kenneth. *'How Best Do We Survive?': A Modern Political History of the Tamil Muslim*. London: Routledge, 2010.

Metcalf, Thomas. *Ideologies of Raj*. Cambridge: Cambridge University Press, 1998.

Mills, James H., and Satadru Sen. *Confronting the Body: The Politics of Physicality in Colonial and Post-Colonial India*. London: Anthem, 2004.

Mines, Mattison. *Public Faces, Private Voices: Community and Individuality in South India*. Berkeley: University of California Press, 1994.

Mishra, Shashi Bhushan. *Autobiography in Indian Writing in English*. Delhi: Adhyayan Publishers, 2004.

Misri, Urvashi. 'Child and Childhood: A Conceptual Construction'. In *The Word and the World: Fantasy, Symbol and Record*, edited by Veena Das, 198–215. New Delhi: Sage, 1986.

Morrison, Heidi. *Childhood and Colonial Modernity*. Basingstoke: Palgrave Macmillan, 2015.

———, ed. *The Global History of Childhood Reader*. London; New York: Routledge, 2012.

Mukherjee, Sumita. 'Using the Legislative Assembly for Social Reform: The Sarda Act of 1929'. *South Asia Research* 26, no. 3 (2006): 219–33.

Mukherjee, Sunjata. 'Disciplining the Body? Health Care for Women and Children in Early Twentieth-Century Bengal'. In *Disease and Medicine in India: A Historical Overview*, edited by Deepak Kumar, 198–215. New Delhi: Tulika, 2001.

Muraleedharan, V. R. 'Diet, Disease and Death in Colonial South India'. *Economic and Political Weekly* 29, no. 1 (January 1994): 55–63.

———. 'Rural Health Care in Madras Presidency: 1919–39'. *Indian Economic and Social History Review* 24, no. 3 (1987): 323–34.

Muttiah, S. *A Madras Miscellany: A Decade of People, Places and Potpourri*. Chennai: EastWest, 2011.

———, ed. *Madras Chennai: 400 Years Record of the First City of Modern India: The Land, the People and Their Governance*. Chennai: Palaiappa Brothers, 2008.

Nagaraj, D. R. *The Flaming Feet and Other Essays: The Dalit Movement in India*. London: University of Chicago Press, 2011.

Nandy, Ashis. *The Intimate Enemy: Loss and Recovery of Self Under Colonialism*. 7th ed. Delhi: Oxford University Press, 1993.

———. *Traditions, Tyranny and Utopias: Essays in the Politics of Awareness*. Delhi: Oxford University Press, 1992.

Newbigin, Eleanor. *The Hindu Family and the Emergence of Modern India: Law, Citizenship and Community*. Cambridge: Cambridge University Press, 2012.

Newbigin, Eleanor, Ornit Shani and Stephen Legg. 'Introduction: Constitutionalism and the Evolution of Democracy in India'. *Comparative Studies of South Asia, Africa and the Middle East* 36, no. 1, special issue (May 2016): 42–43.

Nieuwenhuys, Olga. 'Editorial: Is There an Indian Childhood?' *Childhood* 16, no. 2 (2009): 147–53.

———. 'Global Childhood and the Politics of Contempt'. *Alternatives* 23, no. 3 (1998): 267–89.

———. 'Keeping Asking: Why Childhood? Why Children? Why Global?' *Childhood* 17, no. 3 (2010): 291–96.

Olsen, Stephanie, ed. *Childhood, Youth and Emotions in Modern History, National, Colonial and Global Perspectives*. Basingstoke: Palgrave Macmillan, 2015.

Oswell, David. *The Agency of Children: From Family to Global Human Rights*. Cambridge: Cambridge University Press, 2013.

Paik, S. *Dalit Women's Education in Modern India: Double Discrimination*. Abingdon: Routledge, 2014.

Pande, Ishita. 'Coming of Age: Law, Sex and Childhood in Late Colonial India'. *Gender and History* 24, no. 1 (April 2012): 205–30.

———. '"Listen to the Child": Law, Sex, and the Child Wife in Indian Historiography'. *History Compass* 11, no. 9 (2013): 687–701.

———. 'Phulmoni's Body: The Autopsy, the Inquest and the Humanitarian Narrative on Child Rape in India'. *South Asian History and Culture* 4, no. 1 (2013): 9–30.

———. 'Power, Knowledge, and the Epistemic Contract on Age: The Case of Colonial India'. *The American Historical Review* 125, no. 2 (2020): 407–17.

———. *Sex, Law, and the Politics of Age: Child Marriage in India, 1891–1937*. Cambridge: Cambridge University Press, 2020.

———. 'Sorting Boys and Men: Unlawful Intercourse, Boy-Protection, and the Child Marriage Restraint Act in Colonial India'. *Journal of the History of Childhood and Youth* 6, no. 2 (2013): 332–58.

———. 'Vernacularizing Justice: Age of Consent and a Legal History of the British Empire'. *Law and History Review* 38, no. 1 (2020): 267–79.

Pandian, M. S. S. *Brahmin and Non-Brahmin: Genealogies of the Tamil Political Present*. New Delhi: Permanent Black, 2007.

Pati, Biswamoy, and Mark Harrison, eds. *Health, Medicine and Empire: Perspectives on Colonial India*. Hyderabad: Orient Longman, 2005.

Pomfret, David. 'World Contexts'. In *Cultural History of Childhood and Family in the Age of Empire*, edited by Colin Heywood, Elizabeth Foyster and James Marten, 190–227. Oxford: Oxford University Press, 2010.

———. *Youth and Empire: Trans-colonial Childhoods in British and French Asia*. Stanford: Stanford University Press, 2015.

Porter, Roy. *Madness: A Brief History*. Oxford: Oxford University Press, 2002.

Powell, A. 'Challenging the 3Rs: Kindergarten Experiments in Colonial Madras'. In *Memory, Identity and the Colonial Encounter in India: Essays in Honour of Peter Robb*, edited by E. Rashkow, S. Ghosh and U. Chakrabarti, 276–97. New Delhi: Taylor & Francis, 2017.

Powell, Avril A., and Siobhan Lambert-Hurley. *Rhetoric and Reality: Gender and the Colonial Experience in South Asia*. New Delhi: Oxford University Press, 2006.

Qvortrup, Jens, William A. Corsarao and Michael-Sebastian Honig, eds. *Palgrave Handbook of Childhood Studies*. Basingstoke: Palgrave Macmillan, 2009.

Raman, Sita Anantha. *Getting Girls to School: Social Reform in the Tamil Districts, 1870–1930*. Chennai: Stree, 1996.

Raman, Vasanthi. 'The Diverse Life-Worlds of Indian Childhood'. In *Family and Gender: Changing Values in Germany and India*, edited by Margrit Pernau, Imtiaz Ahmed and Helmut Reifeld, 84–111. New Delhi: Sage, 2003.

Ramaswamy, Sumathi. *Passions of the Tongue: Language Development in Tamil India, 1891–1970*. Berkeley: University of California Press, 1997.

Ramusack, Barbara M. 'Cultural Missionaries, Maternal Imperialists, Feminist Allies: British Women Activists in India 1865–1945'. *Women's Studies International Forum* 13, no. 4 (1990): 309–21.

———. 'Women's Hospitals and Midwives in Mysore, 1870–1920'. In *India's Princely States: People, Princes and Colonialism*, edited by Waltraud Ernst and Biswamoy Pati, 173–93. Abingdon: Routledge, 2007.

Rao, Parimala V. *Beyond Macaulay: Education in India, 1780–1860*. Abingdon: Oxford: Taylor & Francis, 2019.

———, ed. *New Perspectives in the History of Indian Education*. New Delhi: Orient Blackswan, 2014.

———. '"Promiscuous Crowd of English Smatterers": The "Poor" in the Colonial and Nationalist Discourse on Education in India, 1835–1912'. *Contemporary Education Dialogue* 10, no. 2 (2013): 223–48.

Rao, Velcheru Narayana, David Shuman and Sanjay Subrahmanyam. *Textures of Time: Writing History in South India 1600–1800*. Delhi: Permanent Black, 2001.

Rastogi, R. S. 'Prevention and Treatment of Juvenile Delinquency in India'. *Canadian Journal of Corrections* 2, no. 4 (1959): 324–41.

Ravikumar and R. Azhagarasan, eds. *Oxford Indian Anthology of Tamil Dalit Writing*. Oxford: Oxford University Press, 2012.

Rege, Sharmila. *Sociology of Gender: The Challenge of Feminist Sociological Knowledge*. New Delhi: Sage, 2003.

'Regulating Age of Consent in the British Empire'. Special issue, *Law and History Review* 38, no. 1 (2020): 143–279.

Richards, Jeffrey. *Imperialism and Music: Britain 1876–1953*. Manchester: Manchester University Press, 2001.

Robinson, Shirleen, and Simon Sleight. *Children, Childhood and Youth in the British World*. Basingstoke: Palgrave Studies in the History of Childhood, 2016.

Rollo, Toby. 'The Color of Childhood: The Role of the Child–Human Binary in the Production of Anti-Black Racism'. *Journal of Black Studies* 49, no. 4 (2018): 307–29.

Rudolph, Susanna, and Lloyd Rudolph, eds. *Reversing the Gaze: Amar Singh's Diary, A Colonial Subject's Narrative of Imperial India*. New Delhi: Oxford University Press, 2000.

Ruis, A. R. '"The Penny Lunch Has Spread Faster than the Measles": Children's Health and the Debate over School Lunches in New York City, 1908–1930'. *History of Education Quarterly* 55, no. 2 (May 2015): 190–217.

Saha, Jonathan. 'Everyday Violence in British India'. *History Compass* 9, no. 11 (2011): 844–53.

Sangari, Kumkum, and Sudesh Vaid, eds. *Recasting Women: Essays in Colonial History*. New Delhi: Kali for Women, 1989.

Sarangapani, Padma. *Constructing School Knowledge: An Ethnography of Learning in an Indian Village*. New Delhi: Sage, 2003.

———. 'Childhood and Schooling in an Indian Village'. *Childhood* 10, no. 4 (2003): 403.

Sarkar, Tanika. *Hindu Wife, Hindu Nation: Community, Religion and Cultural Nationalism*. New Delhi: Paul's Press, 2001.

———. *Rebels, Wives, Saints: Designing Selves and Nations in Colonial Times*. London: Permanent Black, 2009.

Sarkar, Sumit, and Tanika Sarkar, eds. *Women and Social Reform in Modern India: A Reader*. Indiana: Permanent Black, 2008.

Satyanarayana, K., and S. Tharu, eds. *Steel Nibs Are Sprouting: New Dalit Writing from South India*. New Delhi: HarperCollins, 2013.

Scott, James C. *Domination and the Arts of Resistance: Hidden Transcripts*. Yale: Yale University Press, 1990.

———. *Weapons of the Weak: Everyday Forms of Peasant Resistance*. Yale: Yale University Press, 1985.

Sehrawat, Samiksha. *Colonial Medical Care in North India: Gender, State, and Society c. 1830–1920*. Oxford Scholarship Online, 2013.

Sen, Hia. *'Time-Out' in the Land of Apu: Childhoods, Bildungsmoratorium and the Middle Classes of Urban West Bengal*. Berlin: Springer, 2014.

Sen, Rukmini. 'Reading the *Social* in Autobiographies: A Glimpse into Everyday Life and History'. In *Knowing the Social World: Perspectives and Possibilities*, edited by N. Jayaram, 280–98. Hyderabad: Orient BlackSwan, 2017.

———. 'Remembering the Prayahik (Daily): "De"familiarising Familial Social History through Memoirs'. In *Pratyaha: Everyday Lifeworlds Dilemmas, Contestations and Negotiations*, edited by P. Ray and Nandini Ghosh, 222–43. Delhi: Primus Books, 2015.

Sen, Satadru. 'A Juvenile Periphery: The Geographies of Literary Childhood in Colonial Bengal'. *Journal of Colonialism and Colonial History* 5, no. 1 (2004).

———. *Colonial Childhoods: The Juvenile Periphery of India 1850–1945*. London: Anthem Press, 2005.

———. 'The Orphaned Colony: Orphanage, Child and Authority in British India'. *Indian Economic Social History Review* 44, no. 4 (2007): 463–88.

———. *Traces of Empire: India, America and Post-Colonial Cultures*. New Delhi: Primus Books, 2014.

Sengupta, Parna. 'An Object Lesson in Colonial Pedagogy'. *Society for Comparative Study of Society and History* 45, no. 1 (2003): 96–121.

———. *Pedagogy for Religion: Missionary Education and the Fashioning of Hindus and Muslims in Bengal*. Berkeley: University of California Press, 2011.

Seth, Sanjay. *Subject Lessons: The Western Education of Colonial India*. Durham: Duke University Press, 2007.

Shah, A. M. *The Family in India: Critical Essays*. London: Orient Longman Ltd, 1998.

Sharma, Kanika. 'Withholding Consent to Conjugal Relations within Child Marriages in Colonial India: Rukhmabai's Fight'. *Law and History Review* 38, no. 1 (2020): 151–75.

Sheldon, Nicola. 'The Musical Careers of the Poor: The Role of Music as a Vocational Training for Boys in British Care Institutions 1870–1918'. *History of Education* 38, no. 6 (November 2009): 747–59.

Sherman, Taylor C. 'Education in Early Postcolonial India: Expansion, Experimentation and Planned Self-Help'. *History of Education* 47, no. 4 (2018): 504–20.

Siddalingaiah. *Ooru Keri: An Autobiography*. Translated by S. R. Ramakrishna from Kannada. Bangalore: Sahitya Akademi, 2003.

Siegel, B. R. *Hungry Nation: Food, Famine and the Making of Modern India*. Cambridge: Cambridge University Press, 2018.

Sinha, Mrinalini. *Colonial Masculinity: The 'Manly Englishman' and the 'Effeminate Bengali' in the Late Nineteenth Century*. Manchester: Manchester University Press, 2005.

———. 'Mapping the Imperial Social Formation: A Modest Proposal for Feminist History'. *Signs: Journal of Women in Culture and Society* 25, no. 4 (Summer 2000): 1077–82.

———. *Spectres of Mother India: The Global Restructuring of an Empire*. Durham: University Press, 2006.

Sinha, R. C. P. *The Indian Autobiographies in English*. New Delhi: S. Chand & Co., 2013.

Sloane, David C. 'A (Better) Home Away from Home: The Emergence of Children's Hospitals in an Age of Women's Reform'. In *Designing Modern Childhoods: History, Space, and the Material Culture of Children*, 42–60. New Brunswick: Rutgers University Press, 2008.

Spicker, F., I. Alon, A. De Vries and H. Tristram Engelhardt Jr., eds. *The Use of Human Beings in Research: With Special Reference to Clinical Trials*. Dordrecht: Kluwer Academic Publications, 1988.

Spivak, Gayatri. 'Can the Subaltern Speak?'. In *Marxism and the Interpretation of Culture*, edited by Cary Nelson and Lawrence Grossberg, 66–111. London: Macmillan, 1988.

Sreenivas, Deepa. 'Forging New Communities: Gendered Childhood through the Lens of Caste'. *Feminist Theory* 11, no. 3 (2010): 267–81.

———. 'Telling Different Tales: Possible Childhoods in Children's Literature'. *Childhood* 18, no. 3 (2011): 316–32.

Sreenivas, Mytheli. *Wives, Widows, Concubines: The Conjugal Family Ideal in Colonial India*. Bloomington: Indiana University Press, 2008.

———. 'Creating Conjugal Subjects: Devadasis and the Politics of Marriage in Colonial Madras Presidency'. *Feminist Studies* 37, no. 1 (2011): 63–92.

Srivastava, Sanjay. *Constructing Post-Colonial India: National Character and the Doon School*. London: Routledge, 1998.

Stargardt, Nicholas. 'German Childhoods: The Making of a Historiography'. *German History* 16, no. 1 (1998): 1–15.

Stearns, Peter. *Childhood in World History*. 2nd ed. Abingdon: Routledge, (2006) 2011.

Stewart, John. 'The Dangerous Age of Childhood': Child Guidance and the 'Normal' Child in Great Britain, 1920–50'. *Paedagogica Historica* 47, no. 6 (December 2011): 785–803.

Stoler, Ann Laura. *Along the Archival Grain: Epistemic Anxieties and Colonial Common Sense*. Princeton: Princeton University Press, 2009.

———. *Carnal Knowledge and Imperial Power: Race and the Intimate in Colonial Rule*. Berkeley: University of California Press, 2002.

———. *Race and the Education of Desire: Foucault's History of Sexuality and the Colonial Order of Things*. Durham; London: Duke University Press, 1995.

Swain, Shurlee, and Margot Hillel. *Child, Nation, Race and Empire: Child Rescue Discourse, England, Canada and Australia, 1850–1915*. New York: Palgrave Macmillan, 2010.

Tambe, Ashwini. 'Climate, Race Science and the Age of Consent in the League of Nations'. *Theory, Culture and Society* 28, no. 2 (2011): 122–23.

———. 'The State as Surrogate Parent: Legislating Non-marital Sex in Colonial India, 1911–1929'. *Journal of the History of Childhood and Youth* 2, no. 3 (2009): 393–427.

Tharu, S., and K. Satyanarayana, eds. *No Alphabet in Sight: New Dalit Writing in South India*. New Delhi: Penguin Books, 2011.

Thomson, Mathew. *Psychological Subjects: Identity, Culture and Health in Twentieth-Century Britain*. Oxford University Press on Demand, 2006.

———. *The Problem of Mental Deficiency: Eugenics, Democracy and Social Policy in Britain, c. 1870–1959*. Oxford: Oxford University Press, 1998.

Topdar, Sudipa. 'Duties of a "Good Citizen": Colonial Secondary School Textbook Policies in Late Nineteenth-Century India'. *South Asian History and Culture* 6, no. 3 (2015): 417–39.

———. 'The Corporeal Empire: Physical Education and Politicising Children's Bodies in Late Colonial Bengal'. *Gender and History* 29, no. 1 (2017): 176–97.

Tschurenev, Jana. *Empire, Civil Society, and the Beginnings of Colonial Education in India*. Cambridge: Cambridge University Press, 2019.

———. 'Inequality, Difference, and the Politics of Education for All'. *South Asia Chronicle* 8 (2018): 1–19.

———. 'Women, Early Childhood Education, And Global Reform Movements: New Perspectives on Colonial and National Education in India'. *Südasien-Chronik—South Asia Chronicle* 7 (July 2017): 425–48.

Tusan, Michelle Elizabeth. 'Writing *Stri Dharma*: International Feminism, Nationalist Politics, and Women's Press Advocacy in Late Colonial India'. *Women's History Review* 12, no. 4 (2003): 623–49.

Uberoi, Patricia. *Freedom and Destiny: Gender, Family and Popular Culture in India*. New Delhi: Oxford University Press, 2006.

Vallgårda, Karen. 'Between Consent and Coercion: Danish Missionaries and Tamil Parents in Late Nineteenth Century South India'. *Review of Development and Change* 14, nos. 1–2 (2006): 87–108.

———. 'Can The Subaltern Woman Run? Gender, Race and Agency in Colonial Missionary Texts'. *Scandinavian Journal of History* 39, no. 4 (2014): 472–86.

———. *Imperial Childhoods and Christian Mission: Education and Emotions in South India and Denmark*. Basingstoke: Palgrave Studies in the History of Childhood, 2015.

Vehkalahti, Kaisa. 'Sentimental Histories: Emotions in the Historical Representation of Childhood'. European Social Science History Conference (2008).

Venkatachalapathy, A. R. *In Those Days There Was No Coffee: Writings in Cultural History*. New Delhi: Yoda Press, 2006.

Vernon, James. *Hunger: A Modern History*. Cambridge, MA: Belknap Press, 2007.

Viswanath, Rupa. 'Rethinking Caste and Class: "Labour", the "Depressed Classes", and the Politics of Distinctions, Madras 1918–1924'. *International Review of Social History* 59, no. 1 (2014): 1–37.

———. 'Spiritual Slavery, Material Malaise: "Untouchables" and Religious Neutrality in Colonial South India'. *Historical Research* 83, no. 219 (February 2010): 124–45.

Viswanathan, Gauri. *Masks of Conquest: Literary Study and British Rule in India*. London: Faber & Faber, 1989.

Viswanathan, Lakshmi. *Ellen Sharma's Kindergarten System: Pioneering Pre-primary Education in India*. Chennai: Seawaves Printers, 2007.

Wagner, Kim A., and Ricardo Roque. *Engaging Colonial Knowledge: Reading European Archives in World History*. Basingstoke: Palgrave Macmillan, 2012.

Walkerdine, Valerie. *Schoolgirl Fictions*. London: Verso, 1990.

Walsh, Judith E. *Growing Up in British India: Indian Autobiographers on Childhood and Education under the Raj*. New York: Holmes & Meier, 1983.

Washbrook, David. *The Emergence of Provincial Politics: The Madras Presidency 1870–1920*. Cambridge: Cambridge University Press, 1976.

Watt, Carey. *Serving the Nation: Cultures of Service, Association and Citizenship*. Oxford: Oxford University Press, 2005.

Watts, Ruth. 'Breaking the Boundaries of Victorian Imperialism or Extending a Reformed "Paternalism"? Mary Carpenter and India'. *History of Education: Journal of the History of Education Society* 29, no. 5 (2000): 443–56.

Weiner, Myron. *The Child and the State in India*. New Jersey: Princeton University Press, 1991.

Whitehead, Clive. 'The Historiography of British Imperial Education Policy, Part I: India'. *History of Education* 34, no. 3 (2005): 315–29.

Williamson, S. *The Vaccination Controversy: The Rise, Reign, and Fall of Compulsory Vaccination for Smallpox*. Liverpool: Liverpool University Press, 2007.

Wills, Abigail. 'Delinquency, Masculinity and Citizenship in England 1950–1970'. *Past and Present* 187 (May 2005): 157–85.

Yang, Anand. *Crime and Criminality in British India*. Tucson, Arizona: University of Arizona, 1985.

———. 'Disciplining "Natives": Prisons and Prisoners in Early Nineteenth Century India'. *South Asia* 10, no. 2 (1987): 29–45.

Zelizer, Vivianna. *Pricing the Priceless Child: The Changing Social Value of Children*. Princeton: Princeton University Press, 1994.

Unpublished PhD Theses

Desideria, S. 'Dr Mrs S Muthulakshmi Reddi: Social Reform, Legislation and Women's Struggle for Political Space in the Madras Presidency. 1900–1947'. PhD thesis, Pondicherry University, October 2000.

Hindumathi, R. 'Management of Juvenile Delinquency in Tamil Nadu'. PhD thesis, Meenaskhi College for Women, October 2001.

Kbrathi, T. M. T. 'Child Welfare Administration in Tamil Nadu 1947–1967'. PhD thesis, Ethiraj College for Women, September 2007.

Lewis, Caroline. 'Establishing India: British Women's Missionary Organisations and their Outreach to the Women and Girls of India, 1820–1870'. PhD thesis, University of Edinburgh, 2014.

Rajasekaran, Premakumari. 'Social Welfare Administration in Madras Presidency'. PhD thesis, Presidency College, University of Madras, November 1997.

Srinivasan, M. 'History of the Government Juvenile Home, Ranipet 1923–1987'. PhD thesis, C. Abdul Hakeem College, January 1989.

Websites

Children's Garden School Society, Mylapore, http://childrensgarden.in/. Accessed 17 October 2022.

The Madras Society for the Protection of Children (MSPC), www.mspcchildrenhome.com. Accessed 17 October 2022.

A. P. J. Abdul Kalam, http://www.abdulkalam.com/kalam/theme/jsp/guest/myprofile.jsp. Accessed 17 October 2022.

St Christopher's Training College, http://scced.edu.in/. Accessed 17 October 2022.

UN Documents, Geneva Declaration of the Rights of the Child, http://www.un-documents.net/gdrc1924.htm. Accessed 17 October 2022.

Index

Adi-Dravida, 35, 62, 115, 142. *See also* Dalit
adolescent, 142, 192–93
adulthood, 16, 45, 96–97, 181, 186, 189, 191, 193, 204, 209, 213, 230, 232
Alexander, P. C., 210, 212
Ali, Sharifa Hamid, 94
all-India Age of Consent debates of 1929, 9, 180–204. *See also* CMRA
all-India Elementary Act of 1911, 26
All-India Women's Conference (AIWC), 94
American 'Children Charter' of 1931, 132
Angelo, Hannen, 120–21
animals, 209–10, 214, 233
aunts, 3, 18–19, 163, 179, 203, 224–25, 229, 240–41
autobiographies, childhood memories in, 8, 18, 23, 70, 228–29
   child as a community member, 209–11
   of dalits as a genre of resistance, 220–23
   differences in learning, 216–20
   family life and relationships, 223–28
   knowledge transmission to young, 211–16
   reflection of individual childhoods, 207–09
Avinashilingam, T. S., 223
Avvai Home, 165, 200
Aykroyd, Walter R., 110, 119–20, 122

Bama
   Karukku, 220
Basudev, C., 54, 62, 64–65, 117
Bellary Junior Certified School, 233
Besant, Annie, 74
birth control, 12, 193, 201
Bombay Children Act, 1922, 131
Borstal system, 147, 166
   English Borstal System, 129
   government-managed, 142
   Madras Borstal Association, 173
   Madras Borstal Schools Act, 1926, 132
   Tanjore, 148, 172
Boy Scouts, 12, 86, 93, 115, 147, 176, 212

Index 339

British Children Act, 1908, 132, 150, 238
Buckingham and Carnatic Mills strikes, 34

Carpenter, Mary, 126
caste as an educational identity, 34–36
Central Hindu School, Varanasi, 74
certified schools, 11, 18, 121, 126–27, 132–35, 137–38, 140–44, 146–51, 153–54, 156, 158–61, 167, 171–72, 175, 231, 235, 240
Chettiar, M. Singaravelu, 66–67
Chettiar, V. Chakkarai, 41, 115
Chetty, G. Narayanaswamy, 119
Chetty, G. Rajamannar, 54
Chetty, M. Singaravelu, 117
Chetty, S. Venkatachalam, 106–07
chief presidency magistrate (CPM), 158, 160–61, 167–71, 176
Child Guidance Clinic, Bombay, 130–31
child labour, 5, 43, 59, 80, 111, 164, 215–16
Child Marriage Restraint Act (CMRA), 1929, 6, 181–82, 201–02, 204, 239
children as subalterns, 5–7
Children's Garden School, 7, 91–94, 96–97
Children's Hospitals, 107–10, 164, 184
Chingleput Reformatory, 126, 142–47, 168, 174
Chiranjivi, D. T., 94
classroom discipline, 90, 139, 148, 211

Cochrane Basin School, 117
compulsion, 25, 27–30, 37, 39, 42–43, 48, 56–59, 70, 117
institutionalised children, 69
compulsory education, 15, 20, 24–25, 28, 30, 35, 43, 80, 95, 100–01, 111, 115, 117, 134, 164, 211, 231, 234, 236, 240
emphasis to all children, 31–32
financial implications of providing, 38–42
compulsory education by Madras Municipal Corporation, 69–71, 234–35
aim of, 47
benefits of, 52
children as recipients of education, 53–56
debates chaired by annually elected president or mayor, 49
educated children by 1941, 49
Education Committee appeal to private for donations, 68
education for Muslims girl child, 66–69
implementation of, 56–60
introduced in 1924, 48–53
practical operation of, 48
schools for poor and depressed classes of society, 60–66
vocational courses establishment, 63
constitutional reform on children, 13–15
Constitution of India, 1950, 230
Coonoor Research Laboratories, 110, 119–120, 122

criminal tribes, 32, 128, 134, 150–51, 161

Dalits, 34, 41, 43, 49, 62, 113, 115, 233
  childhood, 116, 211, 216, 220–23
  education, 35–36, 61
  enrolment in school, 35
devadasis system of temple prostitution, 136, 162, 164, 180, 188, 191, 196–97, 200–01, 204
Devi, Akkamma, 216
director of public instruction (DPI), 30, 32, 38, 45, 87, 92, 101, 113, 143–44, 156, 165, 167
District Educational Councils (DEC), 25, 27, 37–39, 42, 44–45, 48–49
dyarchy, 14–15, 19, 107, 110, 116, 133, 154, 177, 181, 235

Education Act
  1920, 20, 25, 30, 38–71, 98–124
  1931, 114
educational communities, religion and development of, 32–34
Educational Survey of 1924, 35
Elementary Educational Survey Report, 1924, 31
Elementary Education Fund (EEF), 38, 40, 56–57, 113
English Education Act, 1902, 26–27, 32, 37

female education, 30–32, 49, 67, 83–84, 219–20
female teacher training colleges, 73, 79, 87–91, 96

Gandhian Harijan Welfare Committee, 222
Gandhi, Mahatma, 79, 95, 163
Geneva Declaration of the Rights of the Child, 1924 (Declaration of Geneva), 1–3, 12, 16, 51, 80, 107, 130, 158, 163–64, 196
godfathers, 19, 60, 70, 241
grandparents, 17, 108, 135, 199, 224, 227, 229
grant-in-aid funding, 35
Gray Commission on Panchamas, 35–36
Great Depression, 22
Guneskaran, K. A., 235
gurukala system, 92
guru-sishya tradition, 226

Hartog Commission on Education (1929), 31
health of schoolchild, 122–24
  all-India Jolly Report on medical inspection, 1941, 103
  feeding children, 117–18
  focus on poor and hungry child, 114–17
  and intellectual development, link between, 98
  interventions in, 98, 100
  medical inspection of schoolchildren, 100–02
  and modern science, 99
  nutrition for children, 118–22
  paediatric medicine and malnutrition, formulation of response for, 107–11

responsibility for health of children, 102–07

Ibrahim, K. Muhammed, 68
Imperial Education Conference, London, 1923, 78
Indian Criminal Law Amendment Act, 1924, 183
Indian Jails Committee (IJC), 1919–20, 125–26, 128–29, 132, 134, 172
Indian Majority Act, 1875, 188
Indian National Congress Party, 22, 49, 52, 237
Indian Statutory Commission, 74
infant education, 76
Iyer, B. V. Narasimha, 33
Iyer, E. L., 42
Iyer, T. R. Ramachandra, 27

Jesudasan, Albert, 68
Joshi Committee, 7, 10, 20, 184, 234, 236
journals
  Amar Chitra Katha, 86
  Educational India, 7, 11, 72–73, 75–77, 84, 86, 94–95
  Indian Journal of Social Work, 130
  Indian Ladies Review, 83
  Schoolmaster, 75
Justice Party, 22, 49–50, 54–55, 67, 101, 116, 237
  used democratisation of educational provision, 34
juvenile
  beggars, 140, 155, 160
  court, 20, 128, 131–32, 143, 155, 160, 166–73, 176, 178, 198, 237, 240

crime, 138–41, 177
delinquency, 80, 114, 126, 130, 151
institutions, 131
justice reforms, 56
justice system, 104, 112, 123, 125–27, 130, 141, 150–51, 153–55, 164, 174–75, 181, 203, 235–36, 241
penology, 127–29, 143, 150

Kalam, A. P. J., 208, 213, 217, 226, 235
Kesayan, C., 214
Khan, Abdul Hameed, 59, 116
Kindergarten movement, 75
Krishnasastri, C. B., 75
Krishnayya, G. S., 78, 86

Labour Department, 35–36, 45, 61
Lady Willingdon Training College, 73, 79, 87–89, 94, 96, 191–92
language politics, 22, 55
Laxman, R. K., 213, 224–25
League of Nations' Advisory Commission for the Protection and Welfare of Children and Young People, 12–13, 51, 130
Lindsey, Ben B., and Wainwright Evans,
  The Revolt of Modern Youth, 193–94

Macphail, E. M., 32
Madras Children Act (MCA), 1920, 15, 20, 125, 127, 132–37, 139–44, 150–51, 153, 155–57, 159, 161, 167, 169, 171, 174–77, 183, 191

associates in voluntary sector, 163–66
content of schooling, 144–47
probation and auxiliary services, 172–75
school and body, 147–50
Madras Children's Aid Society (MCAS), 7, 10, 94, 135, 158–63, 237
boys club, 175–76
Girl Guides company, 89, 147
Madras Corporation Child Welfare Scheme, 158
Madras Discharged Prisoners Aid Society (DPAS), 164, 166, 168, 173, 175
Madras Elementary Education Act, 1920, 15, 24, 26–29, 36, 44–45, 47
Madras Hindu Religious Endowments Act, 1929, 183
Madras Legislative Council (MLC), 6, 14, 25, 30, 33–34, 41, 44, 123, 132, 182–83
Madras Nurses Association, 120–21
Madras Presidency, 2, 15, 24, 47, 59, 98
castes differences, 22–23
children imagined within identity politics of, 25
education responsibility for, 36–38
and female education, 30–32
middle classes, emergence of, 21
public instruction figures, 31
religious communities, 23
Self-Respect movement, 22
Theosophy movement, 21

Madras Society for the Protection of Children (MSPC), 10, 133, 141–42, 155–57, 161, 164, 166, 177–78
Madras Suppression of Immoral Traffic Act, 1930, 159, 164, 176, 183, 194, 197
Madras Vigilance Association, 162
Manshardt, Clifford, 131
Delinquent Child in India, 130
Mayo, Katherine
Mother India, 9, 181
medical inspection of schoolchildren, 11, 98, 100–03, 106–07, 121, 231
Menon, Gopala, 120
menstruation, 184, 224
midday meals scheme, 20, 36, 59, 91, 99, 111–15, 117–20, 221, 239
missionaries, 12, 32–33, 75, 87, 92, 146, 239
Mohanty, Jagannath, 223, 226
Montague–Chelmsford Reforms, 1921, 27
moral education, 44, 52, 77, 81–82, 146–49, 213, 226
Mudaliar, T. R. Kothandarama, 57
Muslim Educational Association, 33
Muslim League, 49
Muslims, 23
education, 29, 61, 66, 217–18, 240
educational backwardness of, 32–33
girls, 21, 30, 33–34, 48, 66–69,

Naidu, Bakthavathsulu, 63
Naidu, K. Sreeramulu, 60
Naidu, M. Sundaram, 60
Naidu, T. Varadarajulu, 26, 49–50
Narayan, R. K., 213–14, 224

Natesan, C., 50, 61
Nehru, Rameshwari, 182
New Education Fellowship, 13, 75, 84
Niamatullah, Syed, 119
nutrition for children, 11, 99, 112, 118–23, 186, 201–02, 231, 239

Object Lessons, 75, 213
organisations
    Madras Children's Aid Society, 141, 158–79,
    Madras Muslim Ladies Association, 33
    Madras Society for the Protection of Children, 141, 155–59, 161, 164, 166, 177
    Poor Schools Society, 35
    Save the Children, 12
    Social Service League, 35
    Theosophical Society, 12, 15, 164, 178
    Women's Indian Association (WIA), 31, 121, 157–59, 187
Other Backward Caste Commission, 1971, 221

paediatrics, 11, 98, 122
    a distinctive medical discipline, 231
    medicine, 107–10
Panchanadeswar, S. N., 94
parental authority/decisions on education, 42–44, 54, 70, 161, 223–24
Patro, A. P., 38
Paul, C. Swamikannu, 13, 75
physical education, 118, 144, 212
Piaget, Jean, 78

pial or *tinnai* (village or veranda school), 74, 211–12, 219, 224
Pillai, T. S. Nataraja, 55
Pillai, V. G. Vasudeva (champion of the Depressed Classes), 59
play, 86, 90, 92–93, 144, 148, 192, 196, 209, 211, 218–19, 227
    cooperative, 81
    as a medium of education, 8, 11, 81
probation system, 129, 137, 140, 153, 155, 160–61, 172–77, 235
progressive education/pedagogy in Madras Presidency, 72–74, 95–97
    activity based learning, 76–78
    gendered child, 83–84
    Indian educators and home, 84–86
    and new education, 74–76
    and normal child, 80–83
    pedagogy as science, 78–80
    and traditional education, 74–76
    training of teachers, 86–91
    working out in local school, 91–95
Project Method, 75
prostitution, 17, 85, 136, 139, 162, 180, 183–85, 188, 200, 232
Provincial Labour Party, 41
puberty, 11, 184–85, 199, 202, 239

Rajagopalan, N., 52, 54, 115
Rajah, M. C., 27, 34
Rajalakshmi, S., 92
Ramakrishna Mission, 94
Ramasami, Periyar E. V., 197
Rao, N. Subba, 43
rape, 182, 184–85, 188
Rau, M. Rama Bai Madhave, 185

Reddi, Muthulakshmi, 13, 107–09,
    163–65, 178, 185, 190, 196–98, 210,
    219, 239
Reformatory Schools Act, 1897, 126,
    132, 142
Religious Endowments Act, 1929,
    188
resistance in the classroom, 214–15,
    220–23, 233
rice diets, 120–21
Round Table Conferences 1930–32, 62

Sankaran, N., 63
Sarma, M. S. Srinivasa, 78, 81–82, 85
Sarvadhikary, Sir Devadasi Prasad,
    196
Sastri, T. R. Venkataram, 94
Sastry, D. Nityananda, 75
Sattanathan, A. N., 235
Satthianadhan, K., 76, 83
Satyamurti, 54–55, 116
Satyanarayana, K., 206
self-government practice, 99, 236
Self-Respect movement, 15, 22, 55,
    62, 114, 116, 197, 202
Seshachalam, M., 75
sexual behaviour of child, 180
    local reformulations of global ideas,
        193–98
    state role in policing sexuality,
        198–202
sexual maturity, 180–204
Sharma, Ellen, 91–95
Sharma, V. N., 91, 93–95
Singh, Saint Nihal
    Plea for an Indian Juvenile Court,
    129

Slater, S. H., 36
Society for the Protection of Children
    in Western India, 129
Srinivasan, Rettamalai, 222
Stanford, Hume, 13, 157, 159–60, 164,
    168–70, 178
St Christopher's College, 7, 73,
    87–90, 96
Stree Seva Mandir, 94
Stri Dharma, 161, 163–64, 176
Subbamma, M., 235
Subbarayan, P., 113
Suppression of Immoral Traffic Act,
    1928, 159, 164, 176, 183
surrogate parents, 92
Swaminathan, Ammu, 53, 114
Swaminathan, S., 52

Tagore, Rabindranath, 75
    Shantiniketan, 80
Taittiriya Upanishad, 81
Tata Institute of Social Sciences,
    Bombay, 130
textbooks, 52–53, 62, 232
Theosophy movement, 21
toys and play method, 8, 89–90,
    93, 148
trafficking, 59, 162, 185, 189, 191,
    196–97, 204
    anti-trafficking campaign and
        measures, 195, 203, 238
    of girls, 108, 180, 183
    of women and children, 12, 183,
        236

uncles, 3, 18–19, 60, 179, 203, 225,
    229, 240–41

United Nations Convention on the Rights of the Child (UNCRC) 1989, 3–5
universal citizenship, 16–17, 52, 84
untouchability, 219–20
  as an educational problem, 34
  See also Dalits

Venkatarangaiya, M., 75
Viramma, 210, 215, 220, 224, 228,

Women's Indian Association (WIA), 31, 121, 157–59, 187

Yati, Nitya Chaitanya, 214, 225, 227
Yerrayya, Gullipalli, 233